HOW I BECAME THE KIND OF WRITER I BECAME
AN EXPERIMENT IN AUTOETHNOGRAPHY

LIFESPAN WRITING RESEARCH
Series Editors: Ryan J. Dippre and Talinn Phillips

The Lifespan Writing Research series publishes single- and multi-author empirical and theoretical approaches to studying writing through the lifespan that inform and/or challenge established lifespan writing frameworks. The series encourages a wide range of theoretical, methodological, and philosophical perspectives, and particularly inter- and multi-disciplinary perspectives. It also supports cohesive and integrated edited collections that explore particular issues in lifespan writing research from a range of perspectives, as well as those that recount, explore, or critique the recent and emerging history of lifespan writing research.

The WAC Clearinghouse and University Press of Colorado are collaborating so that these books will be widely available through free digital distribution and low-cost print editions. The publishers and the series editors are committed to the principle that knowledge should freely circulate and have embraced the use of technology to support open access to scholarly work.

HOW I BECAME THE KIND OF WRITER I BECAME

AN EXPERIMENT IN AUTOETHNOGRAPHY

Charles Bazerman

The WAC Clearinghouse
wac.colostate.edu
Fort Collins, Colorado

University Press of Colorado
upcolorado.com
Denver, Colorado

The WAC Clearinghouse, Fort Collins, Colorado 80523

University Press of Colorado, Denver, Colorado 80203

© 2023 by Charles Bazerman. This work is released under a Creative Commons Attribution-NonCommercial-NoDerivatives 4.0 International license.

ISBN 978-1-64215-188-6 (PDF) | 978-1-64215-189-3 (ePub) | 978-1-64642-499-3 (pbk.)

DOI 10.37514/LWR-B.2023.1886

Library of Congress Cataloging-in-Publication Data

Names: Bazerman, Charles, author.
Title: How I became the kind of writer I became : an experiment in autoethnography / Charles Bazerman.
Description: Fort Collins, Colorado : The WAC Clearinghouse ; Denver, Colorado : University Press of Colorado, [2023] | Series: Lifespan writing research / series editors, Ryan J. Dippre and Talinn Phillips | Includes bibliographical references.
Identifiers: LCCN 2023037878 (print) | LCCN 2023037879 (ebook) | ISBN 9781646424993 (pbk.) | ISBN 9781642151886 (pdf) | ISBN 9781642151893 (ePub)
Subjects: LCSH: Bazerman, Charles—Authorship. | Authorship—Study and teaching. | Ethnology—Biographical methods. | Ethnology—Methodology. | English language—Rhetoric—Study and teaching.
Classification: LCC PN181 .B36 2023 (print) | LCC PN181 (ebook) | DDC 808.0092 [B]—dc23/eng/20230908
LC record available at https://lccn.loc.gov/2023037878
LC ebook record available at https://lccn.loc.gov/2023037879

Copyeditor: Caitlin Kahihikolo
Designer: Mike Palmquist
Cover Art: Photo used with permission of Charles Bazerman.
Series Editors: Ryan J. Dippre and Talinn Phillips

The WAC Clearinghouse supports teachers of writing across the disciplines. Hosted by Colorado State University, it brings together scholarly journals and book series as well as resources for teachers who use writing in their courses. This book is available in digital formats for free download at wac.colostate.edu.

Founded in 1965, the University Press of Colorado is a nonprofit cooperative publishing enterprise supported, in part, by Adams State University, Colorado State University, Fort Lewis College, Metropolitan State University of Denver, University of Alaska Fairbanks, University of Colorado, University of Denver, University of Northern Colorado, University of Wyoming, Utah State University, and Western Colorado University. For more information, visit upcolorado.com.

Land Acknowledgment. The Colorado State University Land Acknowledgment can be found at https://landacknowledgment.colostate.edu.

Contents

Acknowledgments vii

Introduction 3

Part One. Writing From Where I Was

Chapter 1. Contexts for This Writer's Journey 17

Chapter 2. Starting Down a Path: Earliest Dispositions, Interactions, and Education 23

Chapter 3. Writing in Secondary School: Learning to Confront the World through Writing 29

Chapter 4. Family Troubles and Academic Identity 37

Chapter 5. Political Awareness and Political Passions 45

Part Two. Writing to Find Myself

Chapter 6. Telluride House: Are We Home Yet? 53

Chapter 7. First-Year Composition: Setting Terms for College Writing 57

Chapter 8. Writing in Non-Literature Courses 63

Chapter 9. Writing in Literature Courses Through the Third Year: Learning Close Textual Analysis 69

Chapter 10. University Crises and the Search for Meaning: Where Do I Belong? 79

Chapter 11. Dramatic Literature, Dramatic Performance, and the Drama of Life: Casting About for Meanings 87

Chapter 12. Playing Out the Vision: Other Writing About Literature in the Senior Year 97

Chapter 13. Graduate School, Take One: Imagination and Discipline 105

Part Three. Finding Writing as a Way to Be

Chapter 14. Into the World: The Social Value of Writing 113

Chapter 15. Finishing Graduate School 119

Chapter 16. Teacher of College Writing: A Meaningful Commitment 123

Chapter 17. First Steps in Academic Publishing: Bringing My Writing into the Published World 129

Part Four. Learning the Writing Scholar Trade

Chapter 18. Becoming a Writing Researcher: The Classroom as Design Inquiry 139

Chapter 19. Science Studies as Writing Studies 151

Chapter 20. Studying the Changing Genres of Science and Figuring Out How to Write about It 163

Chapter 21. Following Rhetorical Innovators: Why Were They Writing That Way? 177

Chapter 22. Edison: How to Write About Complex Multi-Dimensional Social Projects 185

Chapter 23. Becoming a Writing Theorist: Keeping Abstractions Tied to the Ground 191

Chapter 24. Elaborating the Theory: Finding a Point to Stand On 199

Part Five. Participating in a Field and Its Future

Chapter 25. Editing as Writing and Developing Writing: Understanding What Others are Doing in Their Writing 209

Chapter 26. Administrative Writing: Making Genres, Actions, and Topoi Work in Institutions 219

Chapter 27. The Production and Circulation of Environmental Knowledge: Can Historical Scholarship on Writing Effect Social Change? 229

Chapter 28. Data Gathering and Methodology in Writing: Fact Production and Use 237

Chapter 29. Writing and Thinking: Psychiatry, Psychology, and Consciousness 245

Chapter 30. Writing Across the Lifespan 259

Chapter 31. Learning to Write Across Borders 265

Chapter 32. Looking Backward and Writing Forward 269

References 277

Charles Bazerman Publications, Interviews, and Edited Book Series 281

Acknowledgments

This lifetime of writing has been made possible by an unending number of people at every stage of life, some of whom are recognized in these pages, many of whom escape my memory, and many others whom I am not even aware of. But for the last fifty years, my constant companion in writing has been my partner Shirley Geok-lin Lim. Though we rarely review or comment on each other's manuscripts, we share a world of books, writers, teachers of writing, students of writing, writing chatter, and constant writing itself. Without her my life of writing would not have found its space and soil in which to thrive.

This book itself is the direct result of repeated prods by Pearl Pang, a participant in the 2015 Dartmouth Summer Seminar and the 2016 Dartmouth Summer Institute. Despite my continual demurrals, she repeatedly reminded me I had a story to tell. At the time, I was engaged with the lifespan writing development group (see Chapter 30), and they also pushed my reflections further and got me to think more systematically about the many things that go into the development of a writer. Then a group of younger scholars in the Writing through the Lifespan Collaboration, led by Ryan Dippre and Talinn Phillips, kept me thinking about how writers get to be the way they are. When Ryan and Talinn decided to initiate this book series and invited me, I knew where the manuscript I was working on belonged. I appreciate their careful editorial support.

HOW I BECAME THE KIND OF WRITER I BECAME
AN EXPERIMENT IN AUTOETHNOGRAPHY

Vita brevis, ars longa, occasio praeceps, experimentum periculosum, iudicium difficile

Life is short, art is long, situations fleeting, experience treacherous, judgment difficult

– Hippocrates, Aphorisms, Aphorism 1

Photo courtesy of Charles Bazerman

Introduction

I have spent most of my life writing, teaching about writing, talking about writing. If evening comes and I feel I have not done my share of these during the day, I feel a bit empty, as though the day had been wasted. Not everyone feels this way, nor should they. People have other obsessions and other sources of meaning in life. But increasingly most people do need to do some writing to carry out whatever is important in their lives. We all have different paths into writing and goals to accomplish through our writing.

Our lives lead us to write different things, drawing on different experiences and resources. Those differences create different trajectories of writing development. Even those who do similar kinds of writing within relatively static social or organizational worlds write different things creating unique communications, drawing on their different pasts, presents, and projected futures.

After 77 years of constant plugging away at writing, constantly solving the problems that each new writing task poses, I am still only successful with some kinds of writing. Others I may do passably, but I am a rank amateur at others, and there are many, many others that I couldn't even imagine where to begin. Moreover, I am not even aware of an infinity of kinds of writing, some of which may not even yet be born.

So we are all different writers, we all have become different writers within the lives we lead, drawing on the literate experiences and resources that come our way in order to accomplish what we want, should, or need to do. Each of our stories is particular. This book is my experiment in saying what I can from my perspective about my development as a writer. Through this narrative I hope to open up questions about lifespan development of writing and how writing emerges within the conditions, relations, and needs of life. In its uniqueness, as every writer's story is, my story presents no norm or ideal. It is just one story of one person who has spent a lot of time at writing. We need many such stories from many kinds of writers, reflecting on what opportunities, needs, experiences, and resources came their way and how they iteratively solved the problem of what to write and how to write it, as they saw it. Then perhaps we can start to see if there is any larger coherence or commonality in these stories. If there are such commonalities they are likely to be found in the shaping parameters and underlying processes rather than in the particulars of the sort I narrate here.

What Kind of Book is This? For Whom?

In one sense the answer is simple: It is the story of how I became the writer I am now. And the audiences are writers and writing teachers who are curious about such things in order to reflect on their own writing and that of their students. This book is a bit like the literacy autobiographies we writing teachers ask our students to do, having them reflect on their writing experiences, beliefs, and values, to prepare them for their next stage of growth and to let us know their orientations, attitudes, and resources. This writing autobiography, however, covers a long trajectory (about seventy-five years since I first could grasp a crayon) and has been inflected by all the teaching, theories, and research I have engaged with along the way. Further, the reflection is not so much to prepare me for future writing, though I hope I do a bit more. I see this more as an experiment in how one can construct a story of a lifespan development of writing to contribute to writing studies' inquiry into writing development—using personal documents, memory, introspection, and self-examination. As I have elsewhere been speculating about the meaning and possibilities of investigating the lifespan development of writing, I thought I might test out the ideas on myself and see what the results are. I hope this narrative can help identify some of the elements that might bear on writing development.

What Do I Understand an Autoethnography to Be and Why I Use It Here?

I do not intend this to be a memoir, an autobiography, a confession, a story of struggle, nor other genre to recount an interesting life. I exclude most of the interesting events and places of the kind that make John Swales' life story so intriguing (Swales, 2013). While my relationships, emotions, and life experiences are part of the story of my writing growth, they are not the central focus, as they are in Eli Goldblatt's literacy autobiography (Goldblatt, 2012). Nor do I attempt a social commentary through my life, as has been done so effectively by writing scholars like Mike Rose (Rose, 1989) or Victor Villanueva (Villanueva, 1993). I simply want to say everything I can about the experiences and conditions that shaped me as a writer and what I learned through addressing writing tasks throughout my life. I bring in other events and relationships as I see them bearing on my writing, and I try to draw the net as broadly as I can around this theme so as to open up questions and data that future scholars of writing development may want to explore, as I see writing development as multidimensional and heterogeneous.

Nonetheless, some parts of my life I do not currently understand as consequential for my writing development, and so I do not discuss them here. For example, though I do discuss some parts of personal relationships that I see as relevant to my writing development, I do not discuss my adolescent clumsiness in dating, nor do I discuss aspects of personal relationships beyond what I can see as relevant for my writing development. Much of the work of a writer is technical, wrestling with words to bring meaning into being, so the story I have to tell is largely technical, though situated within my life conditions and challenges as I describe here.

Ethnography as I understand it is a phenomenological enterprise, reconstructing the view from the inside of what people are perceiving, thinking, and doing. It reveals the meanings they attribute to the social and material worlds and the logic of the consequent actions that take. Ethnography seeks the privileged information of consciousness and semi-consciousness about sense-making which only the individual subject has direct access to. Ethnography, however, is usually reconstructed by someone other than the subject—using various techniques of observing, questioning, interviewing, participating in life events, interpreting, and the like to get at the state of mind of the subject, which is then narrativized for the reader. But in this autoethnography I am directly presenting how writing looked to me at various moments, and what I did and thought I was doing when writing. Through memory and examination of collected texts, I try to reconstruct what I experienced, how I saw each task, what I worked on and what problems I was solving. As someone who has immersed himself in writing studies, however, I also have many analytic tools and concepts I have since come to understand, which offer an added interpretive layer to the story. This gives me a double vision situated in the past and situated in the present looking backward.

This simultaneously personal and yet professionalized view gets as close to the personal experiences as retrospect will allow, although it also is in danger of self-justifications, personal myth, and biases that might come from any introspection or retrospection. To provide some objectivity for all this self-dealing I attempt to adopt a clinical perspective, at times almost comically so, while still feeling the presence of lived memory. But this double consciousness is also part of who I have become as a writer, feeling the press of meaning but reflective about the how that meaning can be realized, knowing I only having the thin line of words to bring my meanings into the world. Writing I see as a kind of sincere performance, but performance nonetheless. When I started to take voice lessons at age 55, my music teachers told me that singers have warm hearts but cool minds, as they perform with split consciousness, feeling from the inside and simultaneously thinking about sound production, diction, phrasing, and how they appear to the audience. This lesson came easily to me as I had long before learned this as a writer. As a young man I was greatly moved by Wallace Stevens' poem "The Snow Man" that begins "One must have a mind of winter" and ends

> For the listener, who listens in the snow,
>
> And, nothing himself, beholds
>
> Nothing that is not there and the nothing that is.

In retelling my development as a writer from both the remembered inside and the analytical outside, I feel like a doctor who tests a medicine on him or herself, to see what happens. If the experiment works and produces some useful or interesting accounts, it may suggest some lines for future lifespan research to explore. But, of course, it may release the repressed id and narcissism of my inner being—the Mr. Hyde hidden within the respectable Dr. Jekyll. The writer I know best is myself, but it is also the writer about whom I have the most self-protecting myths. Such stories tend to make a hero of oneself, facing challenges and overcoming them. I am further tempted into this bias because a key mechanism I propose for development, and around which I tell this story, is learning through problem perception and problem-solving. Since I am usually writing about writing (practice, teaching, research, or theory), the intellectual problem-solving feeds back directly into development of my practice as a writer. Or at least I would like to think. How much this story of situated problem-solving discovery and self-making is delusory, a satisfying fiction so I can think well of myself, I leave for others to sort out.

What Kind of Story Do I Tell?

The narrative and the associated details in this book present writing developing through solving the problems posed by the sequence of writing tasks encountered in life, as understood through the perceptions, motives, and meaning making of the writer. Two people sitting next to each other in the same classroom or business enterprise, addressing the same institutional writing demand, may not only understand the same task differently, but also will bring different histories, resources, and perspectives to the task, will define the task differently, and will feel the need to solve different problems to complete the task. The problem solving and learning while completing the task coalesce in the text produced, but also may result in a changed perception of the world and the writer's rhetorical situation within it, further transforming the writing. I proposed this mechanism in Bazerman (2009c), following Vygotsky's views on development (see Vygotsky, 1978, 1986). This pattern of changing understanding of one's world and one's role as a writer seems to appear in a number of writers I have studied (see chapters 21 and 29). I have since attempted to gather some evidence for this mechanism. (e.g., Bazerman, Simon, Ewing & Pieng, 2013e). and it also seems to be consistent with some of the causes Pennebaker has proposed for the efficaciousness of trauma writing (Pennebaker & Chung, 2007).

A related Vygotskian idea central to the narrative is that of leading activity. Vygotsky introduced the idea of leading activity in considering how children in play experiment with ways of being in the world beyond their current ways of thinking and being, thereby engaging in their zones of proximal development (Vygotsky, 1967, 1978). Other psychologists have elaborated the concept with respect to childhood development (e.g., Zaporozhetz, 1997), and a few have applied it to adults (such as Stetsenko & Arievitz, 2004). I see the idea of leading activity as particularly relevant to writers. A writer is recurrently and persistently engaged in writing the next thing, understanding the situation and possibilities, looking for meanings and ideas to be expressed, identifying the resources appropriate to the task and audience, and solving the problems posed by bringing the text into being and achieving its final form. The writer places themself inside a problem-solving moment, doing the best job they are capable of, playing with possibilities within the semi-private reflective space of mental rehearsal and drafting. Each new piece of writing potentially poses new kinds of problems which may even give rise to considerations the writer never seriously addressed before. Thus as writers develop, they recurrently engage with leading activities, by which they bootstrap their understanding of what they are doing and of what their situation and goals are.

I am selective in the texts and moments of writing I discuss, based on which tasks I now perceive as most challenging and formative to my writing development, and thus reveal most sharply the leading activities I was working on at the time. In the earliest chapters, moreover, I have only a few artifacts and memories to be discussed. When I get to discussing high school and college, however, I have more to work with and give granular attention to. My high school and college years I also see as broadening my repertoire at the technical level of sentence, organization, stance, and intertextual choices even as I work through major life issues in the writing. But even then, some texts and memories get greater attention than others, depending on the learning I now attribute to them. As I move into my adult and professional life, I discuss less at the granular level as my problem-solving attention focused more on abstract social and intellectual issues. In addressing research or teaching concerns, I am learning new ways of writing. These new approaches to writing may require some new choices at the text production level, to be resolved locally, but tend not to be as transformative for my development. I selectively focus on those texts that I saw as most challenging and consequential for development. Since most of the texts I discuss from my later life are published and are mostly available, they also don't need to be described in as much detail as those texts from my schooling years. At the end of this volume is a list of my published work.

So the enterprise of this book is deeply phenomenological, as it considers development from the inside of the writer, making sense and making choices while addressing new challenges and coming to new kinds of solutions. The data come from the inside looking out in order to bring new texts into the world, thereby changing what I am able to express to others and myself. In doing so, I change my capabilities and understanding as a writer.

In considering relevant contexts in which development occurs, I lean heavily on the socioeconomic analysis of writers in their historical moment, inspired by the work of Deborah Brandt (2001), as such factors formed the conditions of my learning most evidently in my early years. In later chapters socioeconomic factors turn up in the structure of academic work, in the changing conditions of universities and my employment opportunities, and the evolving academic domains I engaged with.

My earliest experiences of writing were about learning writing as a form of play, expression, and communication, which our society encourages in children (discussed in the opening chapters). Writing in my adolescence and early adulthood became directed toward understanding my place in the world and making life choices, associated with making sense of trauma and personal formation. Yet this personal sense-making occurred largely within academic tasks, often associated with liberal education (most of Parts 1 and 2). Once I found my professional calling the leading activities directing my development concerned the needs of others and finding ways to reach them (Part 3). Then as I became a researcher, I focused on the activities and forms of professional writing, pursuing inquiry and gathering evidence methodically, and arguing persuasively for what I found. The later chapters accordingly take on a more cognitive and activity systems orientation, looking beyond details of text to the social worlds and functions the texts were being created for (Parts 4 and 5). Throughout there are strong connections between my writing development and my personal, social, and intellectual development.

A Secondary Motive, but Other Motives to Be Disappointed

Beyond the impulse to see what I could reveal about my development as a writer, I have become aware of a secondary motive that may be of interest to some writers. Given some of the idiosyncratic paths I have taken, I like to think I have learned a few less common things about writing, which I would like to share with others to help them along their own particular paths and to add to the common store of resources. Of course, some of the things I have learned are quite common—I am not the first to pass through the now well-known discoveries of emergent literacy or to successfully complete curricula resembling that of my 1950s New York suburbs. Nor am I the first to learn lessons most department chairs learn in carrying out their responsibility to their colleagues and their institutions. Yet I believe we each learn these lessons in our own ways, making our own sense of them, drawing on all we have experienced within the complex mix of our lives.

This sharing motive is largely consistent with unpacking the conditions influencing my writing development and my motivated response to those situations, so it shouldn't conflict with my primary purpose of telling as complete a story as I could of this one writer's development. Indeed, as our approach to writing grows as part of our changing understanding of what writing can do in the world, that understanding frames the problems we solve in writing. Thus, unpacking how I have come to study and understand writing is also part of the story of my development as a writer.

Since writing is an invention, actually a historically continuing series of inventions, what we can learn to do is endless and infinitely varied. While the basic inventions of written scripts have gotten the most attention, that is just the beginning of the story that sets the stage for all the interesting things we have learned to do with writing since and will continue to learn to do in the changing conditions, technologies, and needs of the future. We have a lot to learn in seeing each other's tricks of the trade which we have learned in our different paths. As I will discuss in the pages below, I have learned much from mentors who have helped me on my way, and some writers long gone that I have studied, both in their practice and their understanding of what writing does. In my account, I honor by name mentors that have had a substantial positive effect on my development as a writer, but I largely (though not totally) leave nameless those I found less helpful in my path, even as I do discuss the effects of my encounters with them.

In general, however, I have left out all the colorful anecdotes and personalities that may make the arcane autobiographies of academics a bit more amusing. I report the most boring parts, though those boring bits are a large part of a life spent mostly at a desk, in coffee shops, or in archives, scribbling away or staring into space. Writers tend to be nerds, at least once they settle down to their crafts—often belying the exotic personalities they may project to their audiences. Practice, practice, practice. Every day engaged in the minutiae of what to write, gathering materials to write about, designing projects and texts, crafting words and sentences, communicating with editors, but always at work, moving projects forward. This narrative of what was going through my head and fingers onto my keyboard would make a very boring movie. While some readers may be interested in me as a person and while of course this book will present some biographical details, they may be disappointed in all the things I leave out, like places I have visited, people I have met, emotions and relations that have moved me deeply. In others of my writings, I have given somewhat more personal accounts of my experiences, (e.g., Bazerman, 1998i, 2006b, 2011f) and I have given a number of interviews (see listing in the bibliographic appendix).

Another group of readers may also be disappointed. Since my writer's journey has taken me through important transitions in the field of writing studies and my own writing has participated in those transitions, this account may provide some details relevant to the story of the growth of the field in the last fifty years. However, the narrative here is neither centrally nor coherently an account of the growth of the field or of what I perceive as my contribution to the field. Nor do I offer here a sense of the trajectory of where the field might be going. Because writing now is so central to so much of modern life, the interests of writing studies have been highly inflected by externalities, from the government changing curricular policies and funding priorities, to the structure of the workplaces where our students would be employed, to changing national and international economies, to changing technology and communicative platforms, to cultural movements and equity concerns, to changes in the climate and ensuing international crises. The forces that will change the direction of writing research in the future are thus hard to foresee, as this entails predictions about the future of our society. The story of the development of the field I present here is only a backdrop or a set of conditions within which I address writing problems in order to contribute effectively to the field in those changing conditions, and it is told only through how things appeared to me at the time and thus how it inflected my writing development. The last few chapters of this book do lay out unfinished research agendas I have recently been trying to move forward and some of the writing problems I addressed in trying to see how the issues could be studied. I do hope others might find these issues of interest and will pursue them, but this is a hope and not a prediction. Readers interested in the history or future of the field might find more directly what they are looking for in the reference works I have edited (such as 2008b) or my accounts of my research programs (such as 2008d and 2017c) or my guesses at futurology (such as 2016d and 2017d). Yet these are based only on what I am coming to see and hope others will see. I have no idea of what others are coming to see that will change the course of the field.

So I reiterate, this is most properly an experimental phenomenological inquiry into what can be said about writing development, from my insider's position about my particular path of development, distinctive from others' paths of development. Some experienced and reflective writers may be drawn down their own hallways of memories to be reminded of their own paths, but they will see their paths, I hope, as much as through contrasts and differences as through similarities, and even those similarities are likely to be only resonances. While there may be some seeds of generalities in this story, we are all different writers and write different things. Those who are viewed as most accomplished are most distinctive, and their paths become increasingly distinctive as they develop what we call their voice: the distinctive things they say and the way they go about saying them. This autobiographical narrative, if it is successful, will not be a final word on development, but rather needs to stand alongside many different accounts of many different writers before we see what commonalities might underlie the pervasive distinctiveness and variability.

The Methods of This Account

This writing autoethnography will rely heavily on the collection of texts that I have retained throughout my life. Starting with the last year or so of high school I kept almost all my school assignments and college papers, as well as much of my personal and creative writing. Since entering professional life I have a full file of publications, kept both for sake of ego and job considerations. These publications are listed in an appendix, but only some are discussed, indicated in the asterisked chapter references at the end of some of the entries. I selected the ones to discuss in large part because I remember them as posing the largest writing problems and thus being the sites for my greatest developments. Each, nonetheless, is indicative of the kinds of writing I was doing in other works at the time and thus can be seen to stand in for a larger group of texts. Also, the issues I focus on are those that appeared most salient as I examined the texts and remembered writing them, and thus indicate leading activities for me at the time. No doubt there were other aspects that have gotten lost in my selective memory and attention, which at other moments might make other texts and episodes salient for the narrative. Thus while I can vouch for what I positively attend to in this account, I can only (quixotically) hope I did not omit much important.

In a fit of garage cleaning a few years ago, I got rid of many drafts, but I still have all the major products. From recent years I have whatever computer files remain readable. Much of what I report in the following chapters depends on systematic reading and analysis of this extensive corpus. While others reading through this corpus using different analytical methods would likely come up with different, and quite likely, more objective, consistent and replicable conclusions, I can offer a different and more personal perspective that draws on my memory of the process of writing, my perception of the situation it arose in, my purposes at the time, the problems I was trying to solve, and the role the text took in my life and trajectory.

Organizing and examining these files, I remembered many other earlier or more incidental pieces of writing, some of which enter into the narrative, allowing me to discuss my early years of schooling as well as writing in some other parts of my life. Memory also serves another and more pervasive function. Artifacts from the past, especially those we worked on, can bring us back to the place and time we worked on them—a common interview technique. As I reexamined my pieces of writing I was flooded with memories of the time and context of many of them. Even more I remembered the feelings, thoughts, and moods engaged in writing many of them—this sense memory was often quite visceral. From early childhood I had a strong recall, and over the years I have engaged in a number of activities that helped build the capacity for revery, memory, recall of events, and accompanying moods and thoughts. Memory turned out to be a rich resource to locate what was on my mind as I wrote. Of course, many details and readily made choices will have dropped from my memory, but what was most on my mind, the leading activity, remains vivid in my memory and manifest in the resulting text.

At the same time as the collection of texts served as prods to memory, they also exist outside of myself and can be examined as objects in themselves. I try to do so with the eye of someone who has taught and commented on writing for over fifty years and who has been a reviewer for journals for at least forty years. I have examined the archives of my writing for purpose, structure, audience, and style. On some of the papers from my school years, teacher comments also provide additional perspectives on how they saw the papers and in bringing back memories of how I reacted to their response.

While there are limits to this phenomenological mode of analysis, I am the only one who has access to my remembered dynamics of problem-solving, attention, and growth. My presentation resides at this odd cusp of the personal and the textual, of remembered process and resulting project, trying to reconstruct what I saw then, yet also looking at the text from my current perspective.

Introspection and personal memory have many well-known limitations, including a constant re-narration of our past through the lens of our present, a present that wants to find a logic in our past, and wants to maintain a positive story about who we are and how we have faced the adversities of life. Further, both the original experience and our later re-narrations are from the inside looking out, not seeing how we look to others, nor seeing the objects of our creation as they appear in the world. We want to see our writing as we imagine it to be, as instantiating the meanings we intend (or even exceeding our intentions), rather than how we and our products look to others and what meanings and evaluations they might attribute to them. On the other hand, only we have any clue into what we were thinking and what we were trying to accomplish as we were writing. We write from the inside out, no matter how many external resources we may draw on, represent, and deploy in our writing. In composing fresh statements we re-orchestrate all we draw on and re-present it in sending it back out to others. If we think of writing as not just the texts we are producing, but the processes we are engaged in, we are the only deep source of crucial data. Further, if our research interest is in how we grow and develop through our writing experiences, then what we carry from prior problem-solving to our next encounters with writing, is precisely where the action is.

The notes and drafts of this book were produced and revised during the pandemic in 2020–2022, which afforded me time to travel through my memories and reveries, prompted by the texts of each period of my life. I went through that history sequentially as does this book, for some weeks dwelling on each period, viscerally reliving the past, while still maintaining the second eye of the writing teacher and researcher who has a more distant take on what he sees in the texts and in the younger person being remembered.

Another layer in the story is in a reconstruction of the times and locations I experienced. My memory of the neighborhoods, social groups, institutions, political and economic events has been enriched by historical sources and other internet resources, even from Google Maps and street views of buildings I lived or worked in.

So the recollections and narrative here have a multiple vision: the remembered experience and the persistent aura of past states of being; the critical lens of a teacher who has commented on papers over the years and experienced many different writers at different moments in their trajectories of development; the emotional distance and personal understanding that comes through time; the secondary reports and artifacts that place events in their locales; an understanding of multiple cases and findings uncovered by research; and the theoretical frameworks built from the experiences, findings, and collected research of others.

The retrospective vision I now have on my writing experiences at this point in life is of course informed by all the literature in writing studies I have read; all the discussions and seminars I have had with colleagues; all the practice, research, and theory courses I have taught; and all the positions I have taken in my own writing. Readers familiar with writing studies will no doubt see in the narrative the impact of studies on process, genre, activity systems, transfer, writing as discovery and epistemic, writing as identity-forming, socio-cultural studies, institutional and academic writing, economic class, as well as more traditional studies of argument, metaphor, imagination, literary form, and historical studies of creative writers. But I will leave these for the most part implicit, as they are embedded in my experience and knowledge of the time and my vision now looking back on the texts. People knowledgeable in the field should also be able to see the stance I am taking at different moments and I have given an extensive account of the theories and findings that have informed my vision of writing in my two volumes on literate action (Bazerman, 2013c, 2013d). But here I want to keep this study truly ethnographic in the sense of being phenomenological—how things looked to me then and how they look now.

The narrative here will be basically chronological, and will fall into several sections that correspond to periods in my life, typically marked by changes in life conditions. Chapters, nonetheless, may overlap as I follow multiple threads of early conditions and challenges of later professional life. Some chapters will hint forward to later consequences, and others will harken back to previous events. The story will be ragged not only by the messiness of chronology, but because life itself is filled with accidents and randomness, at the whim of forces and events beyond our ability to make sense of them. But I will try at least to show how they seem to have affected my writing and what I wrote within those conditions, given who I was, where I was located, and how I was motivated. I will talk a lot about luck, because despite challenges, I was offered enough resources and opportunities to find my way. With just a few differences things could have been much worse, and not just my writing would have suffered, but fortunately I could work my way through challenges to successes.

In the universe of writers' stories, I hope this might take a particular place. Our society tends to glorify people who have achieved literary fame and look to their stories for clues to the secrets of writing. But most of the writing most people do is of different sorts, and we also need accounts of the writing lives of scholars, lawyers, doctors, business people, union organizers, office clerks, and all the many others who make the textual world we live in, the built symbolic environment.

Even for literary writers our knowledge of their development is much less than we might hope for. The hundreds of *Paris Review* interviews have gone furthest in asking about how poets, novelists, screenwriters and memoirists write, and how they got to be the writers they are. But even here in these interrogations of prominent literary figures, the stories are limited. Writers tend to be shy about how they actually think and work. Perhaps the acts of creation are hard to recall or analyze outside the heat of engagement, perhaps so much happens beyond the reach of conscious awareness or monitoring, or perhaps they fear the constraining power of awareness that might infect their creative zone. Or perhaps they want to maintain a mystique. For whatever reasons, we rarely get detailed insight into the nerdy daily work that takes up most of writers' lives—there seems to be little interesting to tell there, but that is indeed where the real development of writers happens, as they work at the mine face of bringing meaningful texts out from the obduracy of experience, research, and language.

A Note on Being Homo Scribens

All those of you reading this book are those strange semiotic creatures called humans. Our capacity to communicate through human invented symbols emerged at the conjunction of a number of biologically evolved capacities and impulses—including high degrees of social orientation, extended childhoods under the watch and guidance of adults, specific brain capacities developed for other functions, a suite of features supporting joint gaze and attention, and a consequent capacity to evaluate the knowledge, attention, and states of mind of others—leading to complex and flexible collaboration. Some of these features are shared with other animals, but some are either unique or more highly developed in humans (Tomasello, 2019).

In particular, a number of animals (as well as some plants) have various means of attending to each other and more particularly communicating states of being, attention, and action with each other. Such means, fitting with the evolved biological capacities of each form of life, extend each individual's awareness beyond its own sensory information of the ambient world and internal neurological processing of that information, to gain from the experience of others and potentially collaborate with them in joint endeavors. But this communication also comes at a cost of diminished information and complexity of processing, as the interindividual channels are reduced and simpler than internal neural processing.

Human language relies on humans' evolved biological capacities and tendencies, and humans specifically invented languages to fit in conjunction with those capacities and tendencies. While the capacity for language may be a surprising wonder, it is not a surprise that language fits humans and humans fit language—no more surprising than a hammer fits the human hand and relies on the leveraged strength of our arms. We made hammers to be so. Human languages, nonetheless, are more complex, creative and evolving than communicative means of other creatures, allowing us high degrees of joint attention, action, knowledge, calculation, and coordination built through these diminished channels of communication. That is, while human language supports extensive communication and formations of complex social coordination beyond the skin barrier, it is in some ways reduced from the richness of the internal sensation of each individual. Yet language also reduces some of the loneliness and limitations we experience within our purely private sensations.

On top of all these capacities that support human language, about five thousand years ago (a short time within human history, and a minuscule one in biological evolution) some humans invented written language, which has rapidly evolved and spread widely, transforming the nature of human life and our means of social organization, culture, and accumulating knowledge. My particular pathway in learning to write is predicated on all these strange capacities as well as the five thousand years of inventions and uses of written language which have created the resources and conditions within which I have developed as a writer to meet challenges of the literate life. Indeed, much of education is to make available and intelligible these extensive resources from across five millennia and the planet's cultures. In the chapters to follow, I will specify some of the more immediate conditions that helped define the particular resources familiar to me and the pathways of development open to me, but it is hard to overstate how odd the whole human enterprise of writing is and how odd that I find myself one of those so enabled creatures.

As I have come to teach this unusual but very useful art, it has made me wonder what it is, how we learn to do it, and what kind of creatures we become as we learn to do it. As I have come to understand better what is this thing we do, I hope I have learned to do it better. That, I think, is the plot of this book.

Part One. Writing From Where I Was

Figure 1.1. Upwardly mobile and hopeful immigrants—My parents' wedding. Photo courtesy of Charles Bazerman.

Chapter 1. Contexts for This Writer's Journey

Each writer develops in a time and place, pursuing perceived opportunities, resources and possibilities. I was born in Brooklyn, New York City on June 30, 1945, at the leading edge of the U.S. baby boom, midway between VE day (May 8) and VJ Day (August 15). I have lived my whole life in the post–World War II United States, apart from periods up to a year teaching abroad. My parents came to Brooklyn from Eastern Europe as children with their Yiddish-speaking parents, with their fathers finding working-class employment. My parents were upwardly mobile, succeeding in assimilating their children into mainstream white middle-class. I lived my life until age 45 largely in and around New York City and after that in California[1], employed as a teacher and professor, and as an adult I can be seen as part of bi-coastal professional culture. In my lifetime I have largely enjoyed unmarked white privilege.

My first language was English, during a period when it became the dominant language globally, in business and finance, diplomacy, entertainment, and (most relevantly for my life) science and the academy. What the linguistic future holds is hard to tell, but in the near term the hold of global English is not weakening. Because of my nuclear family's social mobility and separation from cohesive immigrant communities, I had little need to learn in any depth either my cultural or religious heritage languages, Yiddish or Hebrew. These linguistic accidents allowed me to advance in the educational and academic publication worlds without ever having to become seriously bi-lingual. Although people who grow up multi-lingual have cognitive and linguistic advantages, I have had the benefit of learning and working in a language and dialect that I have used daily since infancy.

"Melting Pot" New York City

Some familiar history is worth remembering in defining my literacy opportunities. New York City had been a multi-cultural, multi-racial center of immigration since its founding. Since the middle of the nineteenth century, it had been viewed as the quintessential melting pot, fostering educational and other programs aimed at Americanization of diverse groups. When I was growing up that meant learning an official version of U.S. history, values, and institutions, as well as white Protestant culture. Other identities and cultures were treated as private,

---

1. Around the age of one my family spent a few months in Mansfield, Ohio where my father managed a bar and grill. And from age 45–48 I spent six months a year commuting from California to Georgia where I taught at Georgia Tech.

familial, or community concerns, and other immigrant affiliations as secondary to the U.S. identity. As the US rose to international prominence and prosperity New York became its largest city and a financial, intellectual, and artistic center. It also became a place of political ferment and leftist sentiment during the Great Depression. After WWII it was poised for even greater prosperity, becoming a laboratory for the rise of suburbia and car culture. It also had three major league baseball teams, which were key parts of civic identity and competition when I was a child.

Since the late nineteenth century free public education had become increasingly present in American life. Following WWII, high school graduation was becoming the norm and national higher education (and academic employment) expanded, so that the majority of people now have at least some higher education. My academic career began as this expansion was starting to flatten in the early 1970s, but I did benefit from it. In recent decades, however, state funding of public universities has decreased. Budget pressures leading to increased use of contingent labor and over-production of Ph.D.'s have meant that tenured positions have been becoming harder to obtain and are associated with an increasing expectation of publication. The particular employment opportunities in U.S. higher education are part of the larger history of the university since medieval times, its disciplinary research-oriented restructuring since the late eighteenth century, and the particular version developing within the US which has made professorships more common, dispersing disciplinary power among more players.

During the post war period while I went to school, public education was informed by state administrative regulation and funding, with standardized curricula and expectations. In New York State common state exams were required at the secondary level, but there were no nationalized standards and testing, as were later to dominate American education. Further, the New York State Regents exams of the time created space for individual performance and schools rewarded accomplishments apart from the Regents exams. What standardization that occurred was mostly the result of commercially produced large-sales textbooks, which fostered a vision of middle-class suburban and small-town American life. On the other hand, teacher education and classroom practices were influenced by a progressive Deweyian, student-centered philosophy.

Child of Eastern European Jewish Immigrants

My parents, as Jewish immigrant children living in Brooklyn, benefited from public education as their families gained economic security in the new country. Both my parents became English-speaking in schools, and I developed an Americanized school dialect English, which served me well in my academic career. I never learned more than a few Yiddish words. My mother's family remained in the marginal working class and culturally within the immigrant community, as her parents spoke only Yiddish and her father worked as a sweatshop tailor. My uncle Moishe, whom we saw only rarely, was a cab driver; I believe my mother had an additional sister, whom I may have met once. Our weekly visits to my mother's parents' Williamsburg tenement were accompanied by frequent arguing between my mother and grandmother in a language I could not understand. My mother completed high school and was briefly enrolled in Brooklyn College. My father's family made more socioeconomic headway with his father opening a bakery and his many brothers gaining some success in business, attaining comfortable middle-class lives. My father continued with higher public education, getting a business degree at City College on New York, graduating magna cum laude, second in his class.

As with many New York Jewish immigrants coming of age in the thirties, my parents supported socialist causes. In fact, they met at a Young Communist League picnic. My father in college organized a fair to raise funds for the Lincoln Brigade, for which he was almost expelled, as he told it. My mother at times expressed nostalgia for the picket lines and sense of belonging in her youthful activism. While my parents didn't discuss politics much with me, my mother exposed me to the theater and museums of New York City. She also introduced me to some left-wing folk music, though she rarely discussed the messages in the lyrics with me.

During the war my father and his brothers were engaged in the essential petroleum industry, so they were all exempt from the military. As I was growing up, therefore, military culture and war stories were far from my life—only present on TV through reruns of wartime propaganda films, and comedies about the military experience.[2] After the war my father became a salesman in construction materials and then owner of a small storm window manufacturing business. My father's friends were also in business, and would often discuss business deals, sales, the character of other people they met in business, and the like. My father would take me into work when I was between about eight and twelve, where I would play with adding machines or do small tasks to earn a few dollars. I also accompanied him on some sales trips and trade shows. At his factory I noticed class and racial differences and felt some class anxiety about my future, as I saw the workers on the shop floor were mostly Puerto Rican, while my father's partners and other front office workers were Italian, Jewish, or other European origin. Shortly after my parents' divorce when I was thirteen, he lost his money in an ill-timed attempt to become a stock broker, and finances were tight for both my parents. He died of a heart attack during my second year in college.

Assimilating in the Post WWII Suburbs

When I was five in 1950, we moved from a Jewish neighborhood in Brooklyn to one of the early post-WWII Long Island suburbs, Forest City, next to Levittown,

---

2. A further discussion of my family's and my politics and the relation to my career as a writing teacher appears in Bazerman, 2011f.

the first large postwar suburb. The neighborhood was middle-class, totally white, and largely Christian. Even as my parents entered the middle class and moved to the suburbs, they remained Democrats and supported progressive causes. While they were aware of the racial and class inequities of the fifties, they were pleased to have reached the other side of the class divide. I experienced little discrimination (though I once did get in a fight when another six-year-old called me a Christ-killer). With time we were joined by other assimilated Jews. Institutional antisemitic preferences, if they did influence opportunities, did not become visible or important to me. Over my career as I moved into the academy as a student and professor, secular Jews had become an integral part of the intellectual community in the New York area and did not experience the penalties for being marked as "other."

My father was one of the founders of a reform congregation in the suburbs, called iconically the Suburban Temple (later renamed Temple B'nai Torah). He raised funds for Israel (I remember seeing an award he had gotten for his efforts from Abba Eban, the Israeli ambassador to the US and UN). I attended Sunday school, gained a smattering of Hebrew, and was fed an idealistic view of Israel with the holocaust rarely mentioned. Although the memories of the war and the experience of European Jews must have weighed heavily on the minds of my parents, their families, and their friends, I did not gain any sense of the trauma until I was a college student. It took me a long time to realize what the adults must have been talking about when they sent us kids out of the room. In the life I was leading, however, Jewish identity meant little, and I stopped attending synagogue and Sunday School immediately after my Bar Mitzvah, which I went through to satisfy my parents. For the rest of my teenage years I had some attachment to Yiddish culture, such as the Yiddish theaters on Second Avenue and Jewish delis, but my identification was attenuated.

The one thing that I was certain of, though, was that I was not Christian, although surrounded by a Christian culture. Even in the earliest grades I felt extremely uncomfortable as Christmas approached and we were expected to sing sacred Christmas carols. Awareness that I was passing in a culture that had little to do with my family's history dawned on me in college when I started to confront the Anglophilia that went with becoming an English major. Why was I studying this literature, this Anglo Saxon or even European culture, when my ancestors had little to do with those traditions, which were hostile to them? Further, they came to the US after living for generations in Eastern Europe, where their families were considered outsiders and were the object of periodic pogroms. My families were not Anglo-Saxon, had never been to the Caucasus mountains, were not Christian. We were not even very pale skinned.

As a suburban child in a white middle class neighborhood with good schools, I enjoyed both the positive privileges of mainstream life and the even greater privileges of not being marked as different, however I might have felt different inside. My political memory started only in the Eisenhower years, when I was at first happy with the status quo. At the margins, however, I became aware of J. Edgar Hoover, Joseph McCarthy, and the House Un-American Activities Committee. I learned to be cautious so as not to risk my future by being stigmatized by right-wing bullies. Nuclear testing and the cold war also began impinging on my consciousness when I was still in elementary school, and of course the discovery and administration of the polio vaccine was an early memory. At home we subscribed to highly-regarded and progressive local newspaper at that time, *Newsday*, and for a brief period when I was eleven or so I had a newspaper delivery route. By Junior High School I started reading the paper cover to cover every day and became engaged in the issues around me.

My public schooling started in the rapidly expanding Levittown school district. When I entered fourth grade, we moved a few blocks to a more progressive and well-organized Bellmore school district. In my years at the Sawmill River Elementary School, however, I saw only one black student. He was placed in a remedial program and did not interact with the larger group of students. He lived in an older, ramshackle-appearing house on one of the few wooded parcels just down the block and across the street from the school. I later found out that his family, the Jordan's, had lived there as freed slaves since before the Civil War and at one time owned almost all the land on which the school and modern suburbs had been developed. I also later discovered that the forbiddingly fenced-off land a bit further down the road, which we called an "Indian cemetery" and now known as Oakfield Cemetery, was actually the cemetery of the black families who had been living there for a century and a half. Even earlier the Meroke Indians and other Algonquian tribes had lived in the area, though they did not use that burial ground. Some of the indigenous people, however, had intermarried with the black families. The memory of those thriving non-white communities had been almost entirely erased by the suburban growth I had benefitted from.

After Sputnik was launched in 1957, I gained from public programs supporting science education, which I will discuss later. Supported by governmental and private scholarships I was able to enter an Ivy League school, Cornell, which with its state agriculture, industrial and labor relations, and hotel schools and rural atmosphere was more informal and egalitarian than other Ivies of the time. Education scholars have much more to say about the history of U.S. schooling and higher education, and the role of private elite universities, but here I will only mention these things to mark my location.

So I started life in a protected, moderately privileged environment; that is to say, treated with decency and respect while offered opportunities to develop my interests and talents. This kind of privilege is different from the kind of privilege one gets from wealthy parents or legacy entrance to elite institutions and jobs. I was not owed anything or handed anything freely, but neither were unwarranted obstacles placed in my way in a society that offered government sponsored meritocratic pathways, at least for those not excluded or marginalized. As a child this privilege allowed me find my own way through school and engagement with the world. I shook off the ethnic affiliation demands made on me, and I was protected from the historical traumas of my immigrant ancestors and relatives who were not so fortunate as to immigrate. What happened within my family, however, was another story, a story of disaffiliation and alienation, pushing me to new commitments, largely through education.

Chapter 2. Starting Down a Path: Earliest Dispositions, Interactions, and Education

Although we are in the metonymic habit of thinking of writers as minds, those minds reside and grow in bodies. Writers start within the bodies, genes, and neurology of their birth and the dynamisms of biological growth, which then interact with what the infant comes to discover in their world. So I start my personal story with some clinical details.

The Body That Reads and Writes

I do not know what cluster of genetic accidents, early physical and nutritional experiences, and early caregiver interactions went into forming my dispositions nor to those characteristics that fostered school success. As far as I know, I was born healthy with no major atypicality, though I wore glasses for as long as I remember, and had only a partially successful surgery for a turnout in my eyes (exotropic strabismus) when I was 12. I never did develop full binocular vision because of the discoordination in my eyes; this didn't impact much seeing the flat page, which I favored over the three-dimensional world. It may also have contributed to my sorry history in sports, which gave me more time with books.

I had similar physical endowments of those who invented writing and for whom writing was invented: eyesight with sufficient acuity (with glasses) to discern letters of standard size, hearing in the normal range (facilitating initial language learning and especially useful for alphabetic and other phonological based systems), standard vocal means of producing sounds (again facilitating language learning and preparing learning phonological correspondences), arms that could hold documents at anticipated distances, digits that facilitated use of standard inscription devices, etc. I also had sufficient cognitive capacities for processing written language and composing messages, though these capacities involved cultural retraining of capacities evolved for purposes that pre-existed the invention of literacy. I also had the biologically evolved orientation toward sociality and awareness of the intentions and attentions of others. These established the potential for imputing shared meaning in the oral and visual signs of others, creating a sense of collective intentionality—necessary for engaging in the ostensive practices of forming collective meanings through writing (see Tomasello, 2019). It is easy to overlook these evolutionary underpinnings of writing, but they are implicit in our practices and create substantial barriers to literacy for those who have difficulties in any of them.

At times I have wondered as well whether other less typical cognitive, affective, biologically dispositional, and neural endowments may have given me advantage over others for literacy success. At this point in our knowledge, however, it is too easy to make such attributions (offering genetic explanations for aptitudes that manifest years after birth) and too hard to disambiguate any such effects from post-partum cultural learning. Until such time as we know concretely what such favoring genetic predispositions are, if any, it is best to avoid such attributions, especially for teachers or any others who might have proleptic influence on the development of others.

Further, if I had been born within the first 97% or more of human history before the invention of literacy, writing would not have been available to learn, let alone as a primary lifetime vocation. Any biological advantages I may have had for literacy would have been of no particular value. Biological evolution, therefore, would be unlikely to have selected for any disposition toward writing and literacy; rather, cultural history has repurposed for literacy and writing capacities that were evolved for other purposes. Further the factors that made for success in the relations, institutions, and practices that formed in the wake of literacies (whether journalism, legal drafting, financial evaluation, novel writing, or the production of scientific articles) again would depend on cultural learning for the retraining and repurposing of our biological endowments.

Early Years of Family Life

My mother remembered me as an active, happy baby, not prone to crying or disobedience. She told me that she was ill during my first year and she had to be hospitalized for kidney and liver operations. She was weak thereafter and later had repeated operations. When she was ill, she could not feed me. She said she left cereal on the table for me to feed myself; when I was finished, I would place the inverted bowl over my head. I am not quite sure whether my comic compliance indicates an early habit of amusing others, a sense of needing to take care of myself, a disposition to figuring out things, or a lack of expectation of reliable guidance or support of others—or some combination. But I can recognize all of these in my adult self, and all impulses appearing my writing.

My father was distant, did little childcare, and did not teach me sports; most of my memories of him were around his business and his business friends. He was, nonetheless, very attached to his large extended family of brothers and sisters whom we would visit regularly. His parents had died before I was born. While he approved of my early school success, I think he wanted a more practical career for me and was not particularly supportive of my heading towards an intellectual life as a teenager. Later in my life, after his death, when I had achieved financial security and had shown some success in organizational administration, I had for the first time the feeling he might have been proud of me.

Early photos show I had no weight difficulties until I started schooling, but weight emerged in the earliest grades as a major problem; I remember weighing two hundred pounds before I was five feet tall. I was placed on a strict diet in junior high school when I was twelve to look good for my Bar Mitzvah. I was given amphetamines for several months which increased my irritability. I have since then constantly struggled with diet and weight, not always successfully. Fortunately, though, that was my last encounter with uppers stronger than coffee.

While I was active (playing active kids' games and riding my bicycle to meet friends or shop for my stamp collection in a city five miles away), I was klutzy and never good at athletics. I was the oldest player in the minor leagues of our local Little League baseball, never making it to a regular team. My attempts to play were accompanied by constant anxiety and shame at my regular failures. Nonetheless, I was a baseball-history and statistics nerd for a time, subscribing to *Baseball Digest* and reading all the available baseball biographies. While not making too much of this for my writing, it suggests I had problems as a child in proprioception—awareness and control of bodily position and movement, magnified by anxiety arising from failures. I used my cognitive and perceptual resources more successfully for internal intellectual activities and school success. It also suggests that I had difficulties in fulfilling the gendered expectations of young boys in the highly gendered world of fifties suburbs.

Figure 2.1. A reluctant Bar Mitzvah Boy. Photo courtesy of Charles Bazerman.

My family did provide a good literacy environment. The earliest picture of me is as a toddler amused by a comic book in my lap. Before I was able to read, my brother (five years my senior) read to me. As I started reading, my parents would buy me many of the inexpensive Little Golden Books. My mother would regularly take me when I was seven or eight to the community library and then a few years later to cultural institutions and theaters in New York City. The book shelves in our house had books from my father's college years, current popular novels (some steamy and risqué which I discovered as I approached puberty), *Reader's Digest Condensed Books*, and business self-help books. We had subscriptions to *Time Magazine* and Readers' Digest as well as the local newspaper. Surprisingly, though, given my parents' youthful politics and continuing progressive leanings, I remember no political and few historical books. This may have been part of a McCarthy era cleansing of our shelves. When Mad Magazine began publishing in 1952, however, it provided me a particularly formative critical window on the world, and I remained a loyal reader well into junior high school.

Early School Literacy

My memories of writing in the earliest grades (in Wisdom Lane Elementary School for Kindergarten through Grade 3, 1950–1954) are mostly sporadic and punitive, though I did enjoy the activity, sociality, and achievement in the early grades. In second grade I had problems making well shaped cursive letters and my mother was called in to a teacher conference to set up extra homework exercises for me in forming letters. In addition to the torture of the endless classroom workbook pages tracing Palmer method shapes, every night I was supposed to make endless circles and loops. I also was constantly enjoined to be guided by the ruled paper lines. Talkative and otherwise naughty in class, I had to write endless pages of "I will not talk in class." I remember a cramped hand, while building endurance to pain. The task did keep me busy and out of mischief for the time it took me to complete, but did not actually improve my behavior or automatization of handwriting that my teacher may have hoped for—though it primed me for Kafka's story "In the Penal Colony" and Bart Simpson's weekly penance on the chalkboard. These handwriting exercises left me with mild aversiveness and a "hell with you" attitude toward handwriting neatness—until I had positive incentives to make my writing intelligible to others.

My earliest report cards noted that I was talkative and highly verbal, but not always easily understood, as my words seemed to fall over each other. Throughout life, in fact, I have had impulses to talk a lot and I have often been hard to understand. I frequently called out in class and interrupted others. As an adolescent I wondered why ordinary talk of people around me seemed so wandering and unfocused. As I started to read play scripts, I wondered why conversations couldn't be as efficient and pointed; dialog tightness became an ideal that I consciously followed. Consequently, I came to see myself as more a writer than a speaker, as more bookish than gregarious, and expecting less from spoken interaction, which I found problematic and frequently misunderstood. As I became older, I became more strategic and reflective in speaking with others, learning to keep remarks simple, reaching out to what I imagined was familiar to my interlocutors, not talking more than necessary, and using indirection and questioning to build areas of common understanding. As I monitored my talk more carefully, I became more selective in what I said, and I came to talk more slowly with long pauses, staging step-wise sequences of statements. This pattern, however, means that I frequently do not get to complete my thoughts and need to return the discussion to prior moments to make my previously composed point.

Several of my early report cards also noted that I acted impulsively, in frustration or anger. Similarly, early report cards indicated I did not always take directions from others. These seemed to be harbingers of knowing my own mind and feeling impelled to follow my own head, even if it did not agree with others' views. I needed to be convinced of the others' rationale if I were to follow them. While this reliance on my own view has continued, I have learned to respect the views of others, and look for the value in perspectives that others are offering.

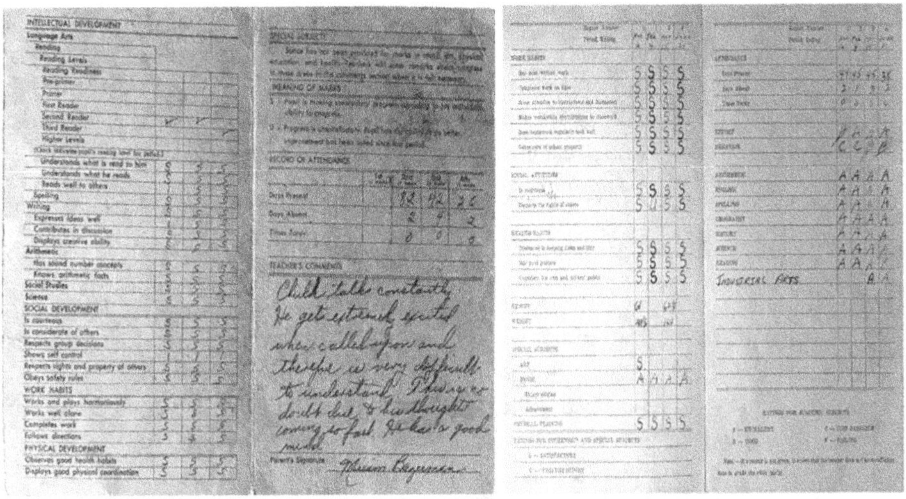

Figure 2.2. Second and sixth grade report cards identifying me as "difficult to understand," lacking self-control, and poorly behaved. Photo courtesy of Charles Bazerman.

The first time I remember having fun with writing was in fourth grade (in Sawmill River Elementary School, for grades 4–6, 1954–1957). Much of the writing was reporting dull information from dull textbooks. While this seemed a stultifying task (I still can visualize pages from the ancient history text that even then seemed itself ancient), it planted the seeds of intertextual skills, being able to report with accuracy on what I had read, and then to recall it. As for many academically oriented students, these practices continued to ramify in assignments throughout school, and became a basis for my own inquiries. Ultimately it can be seen as a source of my later studies of intertextuality in academic and professional writing—but more of that later.

The highlight of writing in fourth grade was the weekly spelling exercises. Each week we had to incorporate each of the words of our spelling list into a sentence. To escape the tedium, I set myself the challenge of using as many of the words in a single sentence as I could. This decreased the physical task of handwriting, but even more it inspired my problem-solving and competitive spirit. My syntactic cleverness and meaning complexity grew. I expanded from two or three vocabulary words in a sentence, to incorporating the whole week's list into a single sentence by the end of the year. Such early syntactic play helped give me the means to form complex relations among ideas. Only later in my twenties did I work on simplifying my writing, to make the meanings more transparent to readers.

My fifth-grade teacher, Mrs. Glickstein, provided us a much wider array of creative writing activities mixed in with the reports and spelling lists. I do not remember her class in detail, but I do remember it felt more fun and welcoming, and a place I did not have to struggle against or find tolerable niches of satisfaction. I have a vague memory of writing stories and poems in her class. I was also the class librarian. In sixth grade I again found myself contending with work I found tedious and unchallenging (My report card for this year shows some B's and C's for effort and behavior, while all my academic grades were A). I often finished early and was allowed to read extensively and visit the small school library, where I read through the entire Landmarks book series with its triumphalist, individualist ideology that gave inspiring stories of the great adventurers who made America.

Learning I had a Light to Follow, but with Doubts

By this time, I started to be aware and proud of being one of the top students, and I hung out with friends, all male, who were also higher achieving students. Since none of us were athletic or engaged in other typically "manly" activities, we felt separate from highly masculinized cultures, though no doubt we benefited from our teachers treating us as potential professionals. At sixth grade graduation I was recognized as the top all-around student. During the ceremony, however, as the awards for excellence in various subjects were being given, I must have been becoming visibly upset, as I remember my father from the audience (where he had the program with all the awardees listed) giving me a hand sign that all would be ok. So by this time I must have had an expectation of success with some self-confidence, but still looking for external validation of my internal self-evaluation.

In my life, as I continued to go further down my idiosyncratic path driven by my perceptions of what was right, my choices were not always accepted, recognized, or rewarded by those around me. I began to doubt my vision, but I had no choice but to follow my lights. Often enough I left traditional paths of success as I moved through majors in college, and then heterodox positions in literary studies, ultimately to leave the field for teaching literacy and writing. Then I began advocating research in this practice field, and pursuing sociological inquiry when what research that existed was linguistic and cognitive. At each point in my life I looked hard for corroborating evidence that I was not deluded or crazy, and I sought the support of those who might appreciate the directions I was taking. Sometimes that corroboration came from a very far distance, and sometimes I was deeply disappointed by those whom I hoped for more from. But these experiences only hardened me to keep following my lights, not be too bothered by those who didn't get me, but to cherish those who did. This tension between confidence and doubt also drove me to become knowledgeable about any theory and findings from any discipline I thought might bear on issues, to make my arguments as well reasoned as I could, and to be obsessive in gathering relevant evidence. I wanted to make sure I wasn't missing anything potentially relevant and I wanted to show others what I saw. These were good dispositions for a writer and scholar to develop, so as to share one's truth and vision with force, clarity, and evidence. Only later in my career, however, when my work started gaining recognition did this anxiety begin to fade, as I saw others were finding sense in the paths I was taking. But I still feel I must keep explaining myself. I am afraid even this book won't be the end of it.

Chapter 3. Writing in Secondary School: Learning to Confront the World through Writing

My suburban school district had two structural policies that framed my secondary education. First, grades 7–9 were in a mid-sized junior high school (Jerusalem Avenue Junior High School, 1957–1960) and 10–12 in a larger high school (W. C. Mepham High School, 1960–1963). Second, all students were placed in one of three tracks: advanced, academic, and vocational. Placed in advanced throughout, I shared my schedule with the same small group of students for six years, except for gym, shop (for boys, matched with home economics for girls), and languages (required only for advanced students, but having some others). In a sense I was part of small schools embedded within larger, enjoying the benefits (in friendships, resources, attention, and self-esteem) and costs (in social relations, social attitudes, and bullying). The advanced program required regular and increasingly challenging writing throughout the six years, which gave me the chance to move beyond plodding modes of organization and to experiment with more creative alternatives. When I reached beyond the anticipated responses, the creativity and idiosyncrasy of my writing experiments were often indulged.

The advanced English classes from seventh grade onward offered literary analysis and creative writing assignments, exploring personal and social issues along with the literary. In seventh grade I was baffled by my first literary critical assignment that required knowledge of the history of literary movements, which neither I nor anyone else in the class had—but the submission written by my brother, then a senior in high school, earned high praise from my teacher. The other assignments, however, were more transparent and I soon caught on to what was expected. (My father also insisted on writing my bar mitzvah speech that year—but that was a different story, as I was completing this rite of passage only under duress, he held a political leadership position in the congregation, while my parents were in the process of separating.)

In social studies we had a thoughtful sequence of writing assignments coordinated across the years to explore our immediate, contemporary worlds as well as the richness of history, philosophy, and political movements. These, initially in seventh grade, sent us to encyclopedia articles (which I copied verbatim) to report on the lives of major historical figures. The next year we were directed to a wider range of reference books, magazines, and interviews to report on countries and careers, when I started to learn how to rephrase and integrate sources. By tenth grade we were doing annotated bibliographies and discussions of historical documents; in the eleventh and twelfth grades we were assigned critical studies of historical events and their consequences. These assignments helped us formulate

30 Chapter 3

our own visions of the world, extending beyond the normalized, monologic views presented in our textbooks.

Roots of Contentiousness

I was given license to explore different ways of representing my ideas. While some teachers tried to rein me in to conventionality, others would indulge me in transgressive experiments (as long as I met basic standards of correctness and accuracy). I remember in eighth grade social studies being shown a classic film from the nineteen-thirties on the Johnstown flood, with a poetic narration consisting of overflowing Whitmanesque lines—I myself was reading Whitman at the time. I have in my files one paper from my English class at this time where I examine the contradictions and paradoxes in Whitman's poetic juxtapositions of the concrete and earthly with the sublime and idealistic in his word choice, styles, and perspectives. Though the phrasing in the five-page hand-written paper is a bit stilted, it is syntactically complex (I seemed especially to like conjoining clauses by semi-colons). The analysis is attentive to poetic line phrasing, lexis, and style. So when asked on a mid-term exam to write about the effect of the Johnstown flood, I spontaneously fell into tumbling, additive lines imitating the flood and the film narration. As far as I remember, I was not marked down for this strange response on an exam for which we were primed (as on all such exams) to write five-paragraph essays.

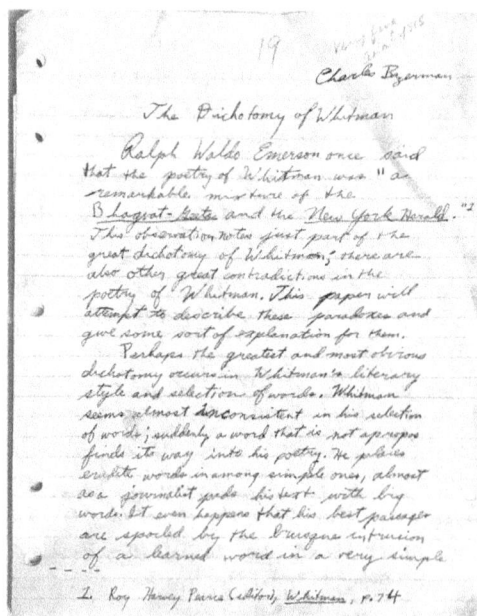

Figure 3.1. Opening page of the earliest paper I have, from Eighth-Grade English. Photo courtesy of Charles Bazerman.

Even our science classes asked us to explore topics in papers on our own, extending our knowledge as far as we were motivated. I remember in eighth grade earth science scouring popular accounts of astronomy to report on theories of the origin of the solar system, and in tenth grade biology reading articles in *Scientific American* to report on the new discoveries of interferon. After having to do frequent lab reports on dissections of formaldehyde-reeking creatures, we had to design, carry out, and report on an experiment with a lab partner. I remember a thoughtlessly cruel experiment feeding a pregnant mouse with hormones, obtained from my lab partner's pharmacist father. In other science classes, however, I remember only cookbook lab reports demonstrating principles from our textbooks, but at least we had to write them up fully, not relying on worksheets.

Teacher recognition reinforced my self-image and extended my social role as a smart student, even though I was also viewed by teachers as somewhat uncontrollable, digressive, and contentious. My report cards frequently paired academic grades of 98 or 100 with attitude grades of D or F. I found this amusing, and I joked that I guess they thought I wasn't working hard enough—though I knew it was because I called out in class, argued with teachers, expressed opinions controversial for the time and place, and was otherwise troublesome. No doubt some of my hostility and emotionality had to do with family troubles, but I was coming to see myself as an iconoclast, original, critical—highly successful but not giving into the system with all its restrictions. In retrospect I was fortunate in my schooling and particularly my writing education, especially for the time—both in the amount and range of writing experience and in the tolerance, sometimes even encouragement, for transgression.

While I was member of a number of intellectual, nerdy clubs like the international relations club, the one that most involved reading and writing was the debate club. With my debate partner and best friend Jesse, I would discuss late into the night the best way to phrase our positions or counter opposite views. I was not a member of the school newspaper, though some of my friends were, nor the literary magazine or yearbook, whose members were from circles I didn't travel in. I was a member of band (though never very good at trumpet), the chess club, and the math team (at which I was very good). I was to return to both music and chess later in life when I was already professionally committed to writing and made explicit connections between how what I learned about chess and music applied to the writing and teaching of writing. I imagine that these earlier activities formed part of my skills, consciousness, and orientations that fed into my ongoing development as a writer. Music taught me about discipline, attention to both written notes and production, organization, and the need for skills to build expression—as well as an appreciation for the rhythms of the line and the temporal unfolding of a crafted experience. Chess and math expanded my ability to calculate mentally, as well as to trust abduction and follow through on the implications of ideas. (In Chapter 16 I elaborate on how learning other arts affected how I came to teach writing.)

Taking Strong Contrarian Stands

While almost all my papers from elementary school through junior high school (except for the Whitman paper) seemed to have vanished, I did find in my files a paper from tenth grade, another from eleventh grade, and a larger group from my senior year. Now with the eye of a teacher I see them as clumsy productions of an opinionated adolescent. Cringing at their undeveloped and naïve views, I still recognize my ideas and writing skills developing. In the following description and analyses of my texts in this and following chapters, I will try to remove myself from pride and terror of ownership to describe the actual devices, organization, language, use of evidence, stances, strategies that I seemed to be learning and deploying and developing across the years.

Here are a few observations of my surviving high school papers in chronological order.

A tenth grade ten-page social studies term paper on "The Origin of Man, Science, and Religion" was highly opinionated and contentious, as the teacher noted. I opened with even-handed summaries of the contesting views, with two pages of Biblical narrative and quotation with no critical or even sarcastic comment followed by two pages of Darwin's theories and evidence, with no evaluation except a comment on the strength of evidence. However, the next three-page section recounting how religious leaders responded to Darwin, took on a more decided evaluative stance, as I presented the histories of rejection, suppression, insult, and other bad behavior of the anti-Darwinians, with over half this section devoted to the Tennessee "monkey laws" and the Scopes trial. By the time I got to William Jennings Bryan's arguments at the trial I began with counter-arguments and moved to contemptuous dismissal. I was equally selective and contentious in seeing Bryan's failed case echoed in evangelists of my time (circa 1960). While towards the end I presented without comment some arguments to reconcile Darwin and religion, I didn't grant them much credibility, quoting Bertrand Russell at length and ending with a peroration that says the future of religion, if it is to have one, would need to be free from superstition and supernaturalism. Not a ringing endorsement, but sixty years of hindsight suggest it was hardly a good prediction about the withering of supernaturalism. In terms of writing, the paper was pervaded in both structure and style by my experience in the debate club—beginning with a seemingly evenhanded statement of both sides, but clearly giving the better case to my favored side, moving through increasingly judgmental dismissal of opponents, then conceding some space to a middle position, only to reject that, leaving as little space as possible to the other side. The paper, following what I learned in debate, relied on some research and represented a number of points of view. I used paraphrase and quotation to assert my own stance, such as by setting up the Biblical point of view first in its most literalist form to cast it as absurd, and then ending the main argument with an extended quotation from Russell, who stands as my favored authority. For that same teacher I wrote an analysis and defense of *The Communist Manifesto*.

The teacher I remember being kind in commenting on it, but cautioning me to be careful about presenting those views too publicly (it was 1961).

From eleventh grade I have a seven-page English paper on the symbolism of J.D. Salinger. This plodding symbol-hunting typical of a high school student did, nonetheless, mark some further advance in my organizing and developing academic arguments. I started off, as I had with Whitman, observing the heterogeneity and contrasts of the many symbols, but here I tried to reconcile them in some synthetic relationship, looking across three of Salinger's books. Examining the books in serial order (and serially within each plot) I identified particular incidents or objects as symbolic, and iconic for the meaning of each of the texts. In my penultimate paragraph I noted that eight of the twelve items I discussed as symbolic refer to the sickness or phoniness of society. While hardly a unique observation nor unexpected from a teenager, it does indicate that as a writer I am identifying a uniform theme in separate items.

By my senior year, after the transformative Telluride summer experience (described in the next chapter), my writing became more organized through reasoned arguments and more tightly elaborated evidence, as suggested in the five papers I have from the spring of my senior year, three shorter and two longer. Four of them were from elective literature courses and the last from my regular English class, even though it was on a more historical and philosophical topic, perhaps to prepare us for the anticipated college research paper.

Four literary papers (three short and one long) from an elective on tragedy all examined themes as they played out in the plots of classic texts. One considered the possibilities of individual freedom within the determinism of the gods in Sophocles' *Oedipus Rex*, Aeschylus's *Agamemnon*, and Euripides' *Bacchae*. Another similarly pondered whether Othello was truly tragic or just evoking pathos in being duped by Iago's treachery. Events and quotations from the story supported my contentions, that unfolded in a more or less reasoned sequence, relying on plot sequence. The last short paper, on Brecht's *A Man's a Man*, argued that the play eliminated the grounds of character identity necessary for tragedy. Again, my analysis followed the plot sequence to examine events, and character identity trajectories, especially interpreting the enigmatic statements of the lead character. I also started to experiment with paradox, contradiction, and turns of phrase to pull together less straightforward conclusions, drawing inspiration and modeling from my then favorite author, Brecht. Brecht's social criticism of the corrupt power, capitalist predation, desperate poverty, and struggle for survival in post WWI Germany spoke to my growing political consciousness (see also chapter 5).

I continued with my passion for Brecht in the final longer paper for the course on tragedy, now explicitly arguing that Brecht intentionally sought anti-tragedy. I started with a two-page discussion of Brecht's theory of epic theater and his distancing effect which he explicitly set against Aristotelian catharsis which he argued dissipated the will to action by purging emotions vicariously. Brecht sought objectivity and action in life. I then followed this stance through the characters' struggles in *The Threepenny Opera* and particularly its songs, which directly addressed the audience with pessimistic, cynical lessons about the world's evils and the difficulties of survival. After a rapid repetition of my discussion of the destruction of identity in *A Man's a Man*, I offered a two-page analysis of *Mother Courage*'s self-destructive strategies of survival, which bring her further misfortune, even as she manages to endure when no other character does. The last two pages consider the more complicated case of the *Life of Galileo*, where the reputed hero of discovery is portrayed as cheating, flattering, and recanting out of fear, even as he recognizes his weakness. Morality (and thus the possibility of tragedy), collapses in the face of survival and a sumptuous meal. This paper again developed a sequential argument, but moved through different steps of reasoning within each play, looking at different kinds of evidence in each. All the analyses, however, fit within a theoretical frame I established in the opening pages.

Arguing against the premises of authors or societies was to continue throughout my college and even graduate career, and could be seen in my pattern as a scholar in seeking to move beyond current beliefs and paradigms to explore alternatives. This contrarian and exploratory disposition, as I have suggested, was grounded in personal, family-formed identity needs and desires transposed into academic identities. I built this alterity of stance through sequences of writing projects—inspired, sustained, and modeled by those authors in whom I found this disposition, whether humorists and satirists like Twain (or earlier the writers for *Mad Magazine*) or social critics, like Brecht. In high school and ever since I have enjoyed parodies. At that time Dwight MacDonald's anthology of parodies was one of my most treasured books, along with a collection of Brecht's plays. I can even see a direct line between these and my later attachment to visionary scholars in both sciences and social sciences. These authors taught me to dream big and wander far from conventional beliefs.

Finally, I wrote a twelve-page paper on German nationalism, surprisingly in my required twelfth-year English course. I do not remember the assignment, but the teacher I do remember was trying to prepare us for what she thought would be the expectation of university courses. My analysis rather ambitiously traced German political and philosophic history from Napoleonic times until World War II to consider both the impetus for unification and the rise of romantic nationalism. I drew on cultural artifacts, prominent academic histories of the time, and German sources (which I had access to at the Columbia library [see next chapter] and which I would read through my then almost six years of study of German). But I was not able to exercise historiographical critical evaluation, as I saw all sources as equivalent, whether in English or German and whether written prior to WWI, in the 1930s, or post-WWII. I did not recognize contradictions that could have clued me into the variety of views; I took all historical documents as authoritative and equivalent, such as the anti-Napoleonic sentiment in a popular folk song, and a 1936 German source that praised Napoleon's legacy of united, centralized state and bureaucratic rationality. Yet I was able to form a sequential argument moving from the reasoning and multiple forms of evidence within each paragraph, leading to the complex argument of the next. I did not follow a simple serial sequence, a five-paragraph structure, or a preset debate structure. Within a largely chronological structure I tied shifting circumstances and ideologies to discussion of thinkers of the time, with conclusions that reflected back on the prior pieces of the argument. This seems in retrospect to be an early step in developing a more organic reasoning structure, building a logic based on the selected materials. It followed the structure of the literary essays I had done comparing themes in several works, but took it a step forward in considering a larger socio-historic ideological trajectory. This paper also adopted a deeper use of sources than my Darwin paper of two years before, and was able to adopt a more objective analytic stance. Although I clearly was not a fan of German nationalism (less than 20 years after World War II ended), I nonetheless attempted to understand it on its own terms, as much as I could understand it as a high school student. I also find the paper's dispassionate tone a testament to how much I was insulated from the reality of the holocaust.

Coda

Overall, my six years of secondary education offered many opportunities to explore writing across all the subjects, with freedom to develop my ideas, arguments, and stances towards all the materials and information I was encountering. I enthusiastically took up these invitations to learn about the world and make sense of it in my own way. Some teachers gave me the space to try different modes and organization of expression, though I do remember run-ins with a couple of others who tried to rein me in to more conventional views of morality, politics, and ways of writing. Although I was more than ready to move beyond that world, in retrospect, I see how some teachers and some clever curricular sequencing prepared me to address my future. By that point I clearly saw writing as a way to make a sense of and make a mark on the world.

Figure 3.2. W. C. Mepham High School, Bellmore, NY. Photo via Google Street Maps.

Chapter 4. Family Troubles and Academic Identity

While I was finding academic success and a welcoming home in school, my actual home life was more troubled. Throughout my childhood and preteen years, until the time of my parent's divorce, my father was more absorbed in his business and his leadership in the synagogue than our family. My few memories of him have to do with him on some business trips when I was between nine and twelve, and driving with him to his factory on Saturdays for me to earn a few dollars preparing storm door hardware assembly kits. From watching him at work I learned a bit about business files, orders, logistics, sales, and the anxieties of small businesspeople always on the edge. I also witnessed the hard, corner-cutting business world in his office or on a sales trip, and heard about it when I listened in to his talk with friends and business associates. I promised myself I would have no part of that world when I grew up.

I also rejected what I saw at the temple he helped found. I went to Sunday school as my parents required through my Bar Mitzvah, gaining a smattering of Hebrew, a vision of traditional values, and taste of the communal pressure to maintain the people and support an idealized Israel. Since I had been so protected from stories of the holocaust, I did not understand how these communal pressures reflected the anxieties and traumas of just a decade before. All this seemed to have little to do with my daily life and the life of the school where I spent my week and made my friends. I quit attending Sunday school and religious services immediately after my Bar Mitzvah. My parents' divorce shortly after made my separation from the temple easy. I had become increasingly alienated from what I saw as hypocrisy between the lives led by my family and their friends and the values I saw being piously preached, attempting to enlist me in a tribe which had very little to do with the society I was growing up into. I did, nonetheless, take some of the more ethical elements from that world and some biblical phrases and rhythms pop up even now in my writing.

My mother tried to live out her frustrated academic and cultural ambitions through me. Though she saw herself as an excellent high school student and maintained a strong attachment to one of her high school English teachers, she had dropped out of Brooklyn College in her first year, for reasons I never learned. Despite some nostalgia for left-wing activism of the thirties, she was emotionally committed to cultural and economic mobility, and ostentatiously displayed middle brow symbols of European culture. These tendencies were not uncommon for those of her assimilating generation, but she seemed to exhibit a more extreme version than those around her or the parents of my friends, as her sense of worth and identity seemed to hang almost entirely on her display of signs of material success and awkwardly expressed cultivation.

I benefited, nonetheless, from her taking me to libraries, theaters, and museums, as well as supporting my music lessons and my book and record purchases. While she supported my academic achievements, she also wanted to claim for herself what I felt were my accomplishments, not giving me recognition for what I felt I had done. She used to claim me as "her" child, as opposed to my brother who was "my father's." So for her own needs, she had a high valuation of me, but to have any sense of myself, I needed to distance myself from her. As part of that same paradox of her needing my accomplishments, she sought opportunities for me, which introduced me to worlds that allowed me to form identities and affiliations far from the family.

More troubling was her deteriorating mental condition. My earliest memory of noticing her difficulties was a joke I repeatedly told myself when I was about seven: "I once had a mummy, but she got all wrapped up in herself." Throughout my school years her psychological condition became progressively worse, with increasing rapidity in the years just before and after her divorce. From around my age eight until thirteen when they divorced, I remember constant arguing and hostility between her and my father. For a fifth-grade assignment I wrote a play about travelers in a small airport waiting room being fogbound; they became increasingly irritated with each other as they were stuck there together. It doesn't take a lot of Freud to see the mood of the life I was living and the desire to travel on.

My mother's rants about my father's failings grew to include paranoid FBI plots, murderous dentists, and unknown forces guiding her to expose conspiratorial misdeeds and corruption. Her accounts of the interactions with my father were so far from what I had observed, her narrated plots were so delusional, and her rages were so unpredictable and frequent, that I soon gave them no credibility, though I regularly tried to read her thoughts to console her and to avoid triggering landmines. After a while I stopped trying to reason with her. The divorce was shortly after my brother's leaving for college, so I was left alone with my mother for almost five years to figure out how to navigate around her, not rile her up unnecessarily, and keep the rage and occasional violence from being directed at me—though I often failed at all of these. This experience evoked a deep sense of the cruelty of the world, which somehow I needed to atone for, cure, or maybe just remove myself from.

School as Home

As I distanced myself from her delusionary world, I pursued the opportunities she opened doors to, as in how I came to be part of the Columbia Science Honors program—a special program for scientifically talented secondary students in New York City and suburbs, created in 1958 just after the launch of Sputnik. My mother read about this new program in our suburban newspaper and immediately thought I belonged in it, although I was only in the seventh grade. At that time my school district was not nominating students for it, but after she persisted, the school nominated me for the testing program. I got in (and participated from eighth grade through completing high school), joined in following years by a few of my high school classmates. This program affirmed to me my specialness and I came to see this as my own, apart from my family; it was also a chance to spend one day a week in New York City away from the suburbs and my mother.

Fortunately, I was doing very well in school. I found it a predictable and sometimes fun place with friends and enough interesting teachers to counterbalance the others. With the lack of rationality, emotional support, stability, or even calm at home, I found school and other academic experiences increasingly important for my sense of affiliation, identity, and social contribution. Throughout high school I anticipated a career in physics. My intellectual life and commitment to the academic world became ever stronger as a counterweight, an escape, a stable world built on reason and evidence. I came to see myself as living through ethical relationships established by writing and the search for scientific knowledge. I felt myself more communicative, revelatory, honest, meaningful as a writer than the anxious, often sullen, angry, aggressive face to face person. I thought of myself as a writer rather than talker. Only with my quirky intellectual friends did I experience more tolerance for my stammering style, my thoughtful hesitations, my complex, digressive constructions, and my obscure jokes. My personal presence however was not appreciated by other parts of high school culture and I was frequently the butt of taunts and bullying. Self-deprecating humor became a protective shell, even as I gained a reputation for obnoxiousness. Whether this reputation was a response to my behavior, a reaction to my academic achievement and self-confidence, a targeting of me for my weight, weakness, and lack of athletic skill, or residual antisemitic discrimination, I do not know, but it did lead me to further self-deprecation and shyness except in circumstances where I felt confident of acceptance. This reputation as obnoxious also remained a puzzle for me as I attempted to improve my social presence in college.

My emerging intellectual left, social-reformist, academically-oriented identity, wrapped in a cynical, critical, self-deprecating, comic style, was channeled into scientific ambition in the post-Sputnik era. I was inspired by the ideologies of pure science exploring the far limits of the universe and the innermost secrets of the atom. I only later understood how this idea of pure research served to insulate post-war science from the entanglement with nuclear weapons development, ever-present in news of nuclear tests, and the cold war arms race, even as research remained robustly funded by government programs. I read biographies of the leading scientists and stories of great discoveries, in which I saw models for what I could accomplish. These stories appealed to my sense of elite possibilities and special talents. The Columbia Science Honors program, in particular, gave me the opportunity to meet every week with the top students in the New York metropolitan area and to be taught by Ivy League university faculty. Sometimes the material went over my head, and some books I brandished more for their prestige than something I could make sense of, but we were learning things way beyond what was available in high school, we participated in meaningful research projects, and sometimes we heard stellar talks from leading figures. I remember, for example, a talk from James Watson about his recent work on DNA.

I was a bit of a hick all my years there as many of the students were from magnet science high schools like Bronx Science and Stuyvesant or from elite schools in the more prosperous suburbs. I was from a good high school, but in an economically modest area without the resources they had. Yet I felt that I fit in, and could even excel (the rumor was that one year I got the highest score of all the students on the entry exam). It was affirming to be among the elect and among students who shared my sense of humor, attitudes, and interests. While I didn't write papers as part of the Columbia program, I read advanced science textbooks, learned to appreciate data and reasoning, formed expectations of theoretical coherence and analytic precision, and enjoyed the production of knowledge—dispositions that were to inform my writing in the university and as I became a researcher. I dreamed of discovering elegant theories that would make visible and explain unanticipated phenomena in the world. I brought some of this knowledge back to my high school classes and took on the identity of a budding physicist among my friends. I also tried to keep a low profile among the many others in the school who were not so academically inclined.

On my weekly Saturday trips to Manhattan, I explored bookstores and international newsstands and attended concerts, operas, and plays. I also had access to the Columbia University library, which put my high school research papers several notches above those of my classmates, though giving me some puzzling texts to deal with. My weekly adventures fed all sides of my growing intellectual and cultural life, and often I would not return home until the last train on the Long Island Rail Road, walking home the three miles from the train station in the early morning hours. In retrospect, I realize how little supervision my mother had over me in those years, or even attempted, except when she needed me to substitute for her vanishing social life by going out to dinner or movies. I increasingly resisted these outings that invariably turned unpleasant. She in turn became increasingly enraged and even violent when I would not cooperate.

During the summers, from about the age of eight onwards, I was sent away to summer camps. The first six years of sports, activity, and scouting camps were mostly painful and unpleasant, given my incompetence in sports and my weight which made me the butt of bullying. But when I was fourteen my mother identified an arts camp filled with budding musicians, dancers, actors, and artists that finally fit my tastes and her cultural ambitions. I suspect the camp owner/director spotted my personal dilemma and my mother's financial straits living off the remains of the divorce settlement, and accordingly provided a fee discount. I spent three happy summers there among kids equally cynical, snarky, and arrogantly self-possessed as I was. Though I was less artistically talented and less trained than my campmates and I was not from a family in the arts as most of them were, I was accepted as an intellectual with cultural ambitions. I got to do some acting, take a few music lessons, and even participated in a few dance classes. As well there were creative writing classes and discussions of the arts. My friends and I would wander off campus to the small progressive bookstore in the nearby village. This was my first taste of living among a crowd of people I liked and who appreciated me—and it was built around expression and production. After one of these summers, I took up letter-writing with a young woman with whom I practiced my wise-guy faux-Twain, Brecht narration of high school life.

My humanistic and scientific interests collided when, toward the end of my junior year in high school, I was selected for two special programs for top students in the nation at a time when such programs were rare. One was to participate in scientific research at the General Electric Laboratories in Schenectady, New York and the other was to be part of a six-week political theory seminar run by the Telluride Association at Cornell University that same summer. I felt intensely special being selected for both and had quite a dilemma to pick between the two, feeling I was at a juncture in my life. Surprisingly and fatefully, I chose Telluride to read the founding documents of American democracy and think about the nature of our political system. What I told myself then was that since I was headed for a life in physics, this would be the last opportunity to immerse myself in other domains of knowledge.

My application to the Telluride Summer Program required several essays that articulated my thoughts and interests, as well as included some of my earlier papers. I don't have a copy of what I wrote, and I don't remember exactly how I answered, but from what I came to know of the application process and evaluation, my answers must have forced me to be more explicit about what I was learning and how it affected my understanding of the world, my place and projects in it, and the meanings and values I held personally.

During the seminar I wrote a paper on the potential psychological impact of thermonuclear war and the challenges it would present for rebuilding a political order in a post-apocalyptic world. I scoured the Cornell library for whatever I could glean from historical, psychological, and sociological studies of disaster and traumatic events, but in 1962 I was able to find little beyond some post-hurricane evaluations and historical accounts of the wake of the Black Death; there wasn't even much post-apocalyptic, dystopic science fiction beyond Orwell and Huxley. I was shocked to find out so little was known or thought through beyond rosy predictions from a military perspective suggesting we could survive easily and move on—such as Herman Kahn's *Thinking About the Unthinkable*, which had come out earlier that year. From this I learned that even the most informed adults didn't know or hadn't studied what you might think they ought to have; this contrasted with the impression I had gotten from science, that although the boundaries of what we could know were always being pushed, it was based on a coherent, codified and well-grounded knowledge laid out in foundational texts that articulated well with each other. I have since found out that knowledge is not as comprehensive as it appears to be, even in the hard sciences. Work is selective and follows researchers' interests and opportunities, whether intellectual, economic, ideological, or political. What people haven't found a reason or way to study has not been studied. Further, what is difficult to study has been limited by the ideologies and assumptions people have held, the approaches available, and the methodologies of epistemic communities that would warrant the evidential credibility of what people claimed. This complexity of human knowledge creation leaves great spaces to explore and many phenomena as yet unseen to be made visible.

My seminar paper I would now characterize as a typical undergraduate critical and analytical synthesis from sources. For me it was the most ambitious paper I had written to that point; I had to develop ways of characterizing several bodies of literature and criteria for evaluating them, revealing the limitations and biases of their approaches. I then considered the policy and political implications of the absences and offered critical conclusions with recommendations for needed knowledge. While the work was based on sources, I had to carry out the synthetic, analytical, critical, and deliberative components on my own, without benefit of authority. While some of these skills might now be covered in undergraduate teaching of writing, at that time I had not gotten instruction in any of this, nor did any of the undergraduate writing textbooks of the time include much beyond basic bibliographic instruction. Later, when I started to develop my own pedagogy leading to the *Informed Writer* and *Involved*, I attempted to address just these skills.

Forming an Intellectual Identity through Writing

In this chapter the story of my writing has shifted gears. Before this chapter, the story was about the context I came from, the dispositions and emotional needs I brought to and developed within schooling, and what I learned as I addressed the tasks and challenges schooling offered. The story was about the forming of an academic orientation that led to school success and increasingly fortunate opportunities in enjoying institutional sponsorship. As I participated in these new forms of emotional and intellectual engagement, I increasingly left behind my earlier personal struggles in order to participate with high motivation in elite academic institutions, inflected by values, needs, and puzzles arising from my early troubled family life. Here the story shifts to one of intellectual development, underpinned and motivated by my evolving understanding of values and what was worth accomplishing.

Now with my academic, proto-professorial identity and ambitions taking shape, I returned for my final year of high school contemplating the world I felt I really belonged to and which provided a home for people like me (whatever that was). Writing wide-ranging speculative papers based on reading professional research and thinking now was centrally important to my sense of being. While I felt even more out of place in the limited world of high school and what I took to be the narrow vision of most of my classes, I took the opportunity of my assignments to write lengthy treatises on Brechtian anti-tragedy and the rise of German nationalism—as I discussed in the previous chapter. I also remember some rambling papers, now lost, where I wondered about philosophy of life and values, and speculated over where I was headed.

During this year I fell in with some other music-loving, political, college-bound people in the next town, and participated in some local civil rights demonstrations. At the end of the summer, I went to the 1963 Civil Rights March on Washington and then headed off to college. My mother moved to an apartment in New York City to live off the proceeds of the sale of the house, as she had exhausted the money from the divorce settlement (including the money that had been designated for my education), and was only minimally and sporadically employable. When I could not find a plausible alternatives or employment elsewhere, I stayed in her apartment, but psychologically and socially I was moving into the world I wanted to belong to.

Chapter 5. Political Awareness and Political Passions

My political life was evolving alongside the transitions of my personal and academic lives, and would ultimately come to underlay the values of my professional life, and thus my writing within the profession. Accordingly, my political awareness deserves a parallel account within the development of my writing (for another account of my growing political awareness see Bazerman, 2011f).

Suburban Disillusionment

While I have a few visual memories of pre-school life in a small Brooklyn walkup apartment on the Olmstead designed Eastern Parkway, my memories of the social and political climate began when we moved in 1950 to an early suburb—Forest City in Wantagh, Long Island. I remember being comfortable in our small ranch house (and five years later in another larger house a few blocks away in a different school district). Within the growing middle class of the post war prosperity, I was immersed in the early television of cartoons, Howdy Doody, and WWII movie reruns. But news of the right-wing manipulation of anti-communism by Joseph McCarthy and the House Unamerican Affairs Committee started to seep into the margins of my consciousness. Even more present were stories of nuclear testing and fallout threats, amplified by the duck and cover drills we practiced regularly in schools. All the while, through my early school years I soaked up the triumphalist, individualist, exceptionalist ideology of the inspirational making of America.

By the time I entered junior high school in 1957, I started to become more consciously critical, opposing nuclear testing and making minor acts of resistance, such as sticking anti-nuclear testing cartoons from SANE (National Committee for a Sane Nuclear Policy) to the walls whenever we were led out for bomb drills. My political education was magnified by my closest friendship from seventh grade until near the end of high school with Jesse Smith. While my parents had moved from thirties communism to fifties suburban business life, Jesse's father remained a working-class radical and union leader, even as his job as a school shop teacher supported life in a middle-class suburb. Jesse aspired to be a journalist, in the mold of Jack London, and introduced me to the work of Upton Sinclair, Richard Wright, John Dos Passos (in his earlier left incarnation), and radical novelists of the early twentieth century. We read *Brave New World* and *1984* together. He introduced me to *Catcher in the Rye*, and together with other friends discovered *Catch 22* when it was first published in 1961. We were partners on the debate team, spending hours arguing over rhetorical choices for our presentations and evaluating the various sources and their persuasive power.

Together we listened to Leadbelly and other early blues (which even my coolest eighth grade English teacher suggested was too unpolished and raw—again confirming my edgy radical credibility). Early in our friendship Jesse's parents took us to see the legendary off-Broadway production of Brecht and Weill's *Threepenny Opera* with Lotte Lenya, a major milestone in my left education. Afterward I played the cast recording endlessly, and then a recording from the 1931 German movie, which I finally saw when I was in college. Recently when I resaw the movie, I felt echoes of the emotional power it had for me when I was younger, arousing an intense cynical, despairing anger, yet gleeful in its critical opposition. I remained a Brecht fan through my undergraduate years—reading everything I could get my hands on, seeing every play production in New York, and collecting every recording available. Brecht gave a harder, more activist edge to my earlier, milder Mark Twain irony.

My papers for English classes became a search for social justice, as I wrote on Lorraine Hansberry's *Raisin in the Sun* and Langston Hughes' poetry. When I was required to write on nineteenth-century novels like *The Scarlet Letter* or *Jane Eyre*, I submitted critiques of Victorian morality. These latter called forth moralistic responses from my teacher—much to my delight in being part of a nonconventional vanguard. My research papers began weighing the implications of religious resistance to science, the *Communist Manifesto*, or the psychological effects of nuclear war.

Throughout my adolescence as I became aware of the diversity and vibrancy and resources of New York City in the late fifties and early sixties, I became dissatisfied with the conventionality, narrowness of thought, and limited resources in the suburbs. I first experienced the more eye-opening aspects of city life through the theater and museums. Hal Holbrook's reenactment *Mark Twain Tonight* was an early revelation. My eyes were further opened as I haunted the environs of Columbia and then the whole city on my weekly Saturday trips. In the magazine and book stores in Manhattan I found left wing magazines and bought my first copies of *The Nation*. I couldn't wait to leave the suburbs.

This budding critical awareness led me to question the military role of physics in the cold war atomic era. I began to puzzle over the ideological justifications of "pure research" that tried to insulate scientific complicity. This questioning was to continue in my search for values and meaning and my need for a socially useful career during my college years, and my disillusionment with the studies made available to me, even as I succeeded in them.

The Weight of the Vietnam War Draft

This search for a meaningful life was heightened by the problem of how to respond to the military draft. As I was finishing high school, U.S. involvement in Vietnam was expanding and the threat of being sent to war loomed over all young men. When JFK started to escalate the war in 1961, I was already suspicious of cold-war rhetoric and actions. As the war expanded, I wondered about my country's justification for engaging us in war, and I wanted to have no part of it. When the Johnson administration released its notorious February 1965 white paper giving its rationale for engagement in Vietnam, I remember discussing it with my classmates and dismissing it as a flimsy rehash of old lies already discredited in the press.

I had several physical exams for the draft and avoiding service became a major life theme as I went through college and graduate school. I neither wanted to be killed nor to put myself in a position of self-preservation to kill others for a cause I did not believe in. Yet I could not make any decisions about my life without considering whether it would make me liable for the draft. This anxiety about our futures and our potential complicity hung over most young college men of my generation, though we made different choices about it. A few embraced it. A few felt obligated. But most clung on to their 2-S student deferments, and then when that ran out sought alternatives. While some of us in the protected academic world were sensitive to the class and race divides that sent others to die instead of us, we did not see that sacrificing ourselves would do much to change the inequities, and the most we felt we could do was oppose the war at home.

Understanding Class, Race, Regional, and Gender Divides

My awareness of the nexus of race, class, and privilege crept into my middle-class life, at first through noticing the divides in my town and my father's business and then reading and writing about literature and history in junior high and high school. By the end of high school, I was on local labor picket lines taking up causes of Black workers, and participating in civil rights marches. While I was at Cornell, the campus was also starting to become more racially integrated, as was Telluride, particularly through the work of the Executive Secretary Bea McLeod, who actively sought out diverse candidates for the summer programs and then house membership. Yet, I have to say I barely began to understand the depth of the racial and class issues in the US until I started inner-city teaching, and even then I saw only the consequences and not the underlying structures, practices, and attitudes that have made racism such an obdurate problem. It is still something I am attempting to understand in myself and the world around me. Over my career, however, teaching in New York, Atlanta, and California has provided me with lots of experiences to think about and learn from. Not only has my vision expanded, but so many of my culturally received assumptions about literacy, audiences, and what was worth communicating have been challenged as I started to ask myself what was really necessary, fundamental, and equitable.

My understanding of the political world, reinforcing my personal identity struggles, drove my searches for meaning, my critical and argumentative attitudes, my choices of models and topics, and ultimately my commitment to literacy education and writing research that would contest traditional literary notions of literacy. Later when the opportunity emerged to support writing in Asia and then Latin America, I saw offering my support as a matter of social justice. Yet I tried not to overstep my position as an outsider—supporting local developments and decision-making, fostering regional ownership and perspectives, and trying to avoid neocolonialist tendencies.

My awareness of feminism was somewhat slower in coming. When I was in high school there were as many academically successful young women as men, so I never doubted women's talents and roles; as a non-athletic young man interested in the arts and intellectual matters, I felt alienated from the masculine culture I was surrounded by. The entire gender politics of dating confused me and I never was very good at it, but it seemed to me a problem of finding and appealing to young women who would share my interests. I did not yet understand how gender roles at the time limited the number of women who could express interests and modes of self-presentation that would make it possible for me to connect with them. Nor did I reflect on the low number of women in the science programs I participated in. By college I was already moving into a world of humanities where I was surrounded by bright and talented young women. So this just seemed the way things were, and people's interests fell along gendered lines.

Then when I began teaching of writing I found that the women were at least as talented as the men, and what I taught was equally applicable to both, so I found no differentiation in my teaching, though in trying to understand the motivations and resistances of individuals I did find some gender-related issues. Overall, however, I came to perceive writing as a means of acting with equality, engaged at social distance and with even potential sex and gender anonymity. All modes of writing seemed available to all people, at least in the educational settings where I taught.

As I came to study writing in the world, however, I saw that some genres, styles, and social actions were available only to those in certain social roles, and those social roles were unevenly distributed. I saw the best way I could intervene was to support the development of all people, including both women and minorities, so they could demonstrate their capacity to enact more roles. Only in my own workplace in the university did I have more direct means to influence equitable hiring and promotion practices.

When my personal friendships with women deepened, however, I become more conscious of the way sex and gender had been tied to victimization and domination, and had led to limiting roles for everyone. I also began to understand how sex and gender intersected with race, class, and other social positions. These are issues that I of course learned a lot about through my partner of a half-century, Shirley Geok-lin Lim.

The impact of feminism more directly on my scholarship I see as further muted. I appreciate the work of the many scholars who have recovered the work of pioneering women rhetoricians and have examined the consequences of the teaching of writing being a highly feminized profession, but that has not been my work. My studies of historical and social arrangements of writing have been looking at practices pervasively dominated by men, but in a way that was unmarked, so my historical work has been narrowed by gender because the history was narrowed. I foregrounded gender in my historical studies only when the role of women was changing. Those social roles, however, were still often gendered, as in the domestic consumerism and urban home aesthetics of the later nineteenth-century that influenced the marketing strategy of the Edison companies. As domains of writing and writing roles opened to women, my studies included all those who worked in those fields. In my studies of contemporary practices and classrooms, the study populations reflected the diversity of the writers in the school and workplace.

I had specifically chosen to enter teaching of writing for the very reasons some people historically had considered it as women's work and given it low status, in that it was practical and devoted to the development of young people. Accordingly, I have experienced many of issues associated with feminism simply as part of the struggles of the field to gain support and recognition. Practices of collaboration, listening, respecting silence and difference, which some people associate with feminism entered into my world through multiple sources. Attentiveness to others and understanding the importance of ethical personal relationships had been growing within me from high school days and then through undergraduate philosophical readings to be made effectively operational during my later therapy based on Sullivan's interpersonal psychiatry and progressive social scientists of his period, which also opened my thinking about collaboration. Even later I was to find such ideas in Joseph Priestley's low church views about collaboration and attentiveness to others (see chapter 21). Ideas fostered by feminism certainly influenced me, but I didn't see or experience them as particularly having to do with gender. They were in my mind just about being human with each other.

Discrimination, differentiation, and inequality, whether through race, class, gender, or other projected markers are constructed over generations at the macro-structural level, at the meso-level of conscious choices and decisions, and the micro-level of interactions. I have done my best to try to recognize these and act equitably personally on all these levels. Professionally and through my writing, moreover, I have tried to understand the ways writing wields power and makes things work—and then through my teaching to make that power of writing more widely available. I have, however, largely left it to others to examine how these structures of power with their uses of writing have come to discriminate as they have. That is one of the reasons, among many others, that we need stories of many different kinds of writers.

Part Two. Writing to Find Myself

Figure 6.1. An intense young man. Photo courtesy of Charles Bazerman.

Chapter 6. Telluride House: Are We Home Yet?

Over my high school years my experience and intellectual engagement expanded outwardly as my ego inflated inwardly. Then Telluride invited me to a four-year room-and-board scholarship in their residence at Cornell (and Cornell accepted me with some tuition support, supplementing state-sponsored scholarships), where I imagined I would have exciting thoughts among those with whom I felt I belonged. My undergraduate years, liberating as they were, turned out to be a painful transition as I worked through personal issues and confronted a challenging environment—in both good and bad senses. I will elaborate some of the painfulness and difficulties in Chapter 10. Here I will discuss the largely positive parts of the experience, particularly as they influenced my writing development, though the relevance may only emerge in later chapters.

Cornell, from its founding just after the Civil War, mixed a private arts and sciences college with a public land grant agriculture school, later expanded to include state sponsored schools of hotel administration and industrial and labor relations. This mix and the "centrally isolated" rural setting created a more informal atmosphere than in the other Ivy League schools. It was over two hundred miles from the major cities in each direction, located between two gorges on the slopes leading down to the picturesque Lake Cayuga. The campus and region offered much natural beauty which I was able to enjoy daily walking to class and on outings. It also had many faculty who were or would be quite prominent in their professions. Even some of my TAs were eventually to become well-known. At the time, the campus wore its traditions, neo-gothic architecture, and academic excellence lightly, offering young people a place to find themselves and develop their talents. Although it was clearly a bastion of privilege, during my time when some other Ivies maintained quotas it had a reputation for admitting many academically achieving Jews from the New York metropolitan area.

Telluride House was founded in 1910 by L.L. Nunn, an electrical power industrialist from the Western US, to provide liberal intellectual development for his company's engineers. It served as an instrument of cultural and influence mobility in his time, though initially only for a restricted group, racially, ethnically, and gendered. Nunn also founded Deep Springs College a few years later. Telluride House every year admitted a couple of students from that 2-year institution for them to finish their degrees at Cornell. Character and leadership, along with intellectual excellence, have been themes of both institutions; the goal was to produce young men who would enter the upper reaches of society and power. The house soon began to recruit more widely beyond engineers from Nunn's companies, and eventually was comprised mostly of undergraduate and graduate students from arts and sciences. During the mid-sixties there were few engineers or even scientists in the House. And it had been a while since any house member had come from Nunn's companies. Just before I entered Cornell the house began to include women, whose numbers gradually increased during my time. There was some racial diversity (which was to improve just as I was leaving). The majority of students, however, had come from professional or academic families. The summer program for high school juniors, however, had been more intentionally inclusive for a few years, and summer programs were starting to take place on HBCU campuses.

Initially the selection for the house and other scholarships that allowed me to attend Cornell confirmed my self-concept as entering an intellectual elite. In many respects over the next four years, the house provided a community of thoughtful, interesting people. The house included around thirty undergraduate and graduate students. Roommates were paired across generations. My freshman year my roommate for the fall term left little impression on me (though he was later to become a notorious architect of the second Iraq War), but my spring roommate Gabor Brogyanyi, a comparative literature graduate student, became a kindly older brother to me as he would talk to me about life and help me sort through some of my confused emotions. He also demystified many of the expectations of literary reading and essay writing, which prepared me for much of the writing described in the following chapters. He would talk me through my nascent ideas for papers and by questioning would help me address the expectations of writing assignments. I remember many times when he would make transparent poems I had found impenetrable. I have a vivid memory of him demonstrating with his cupped hands the precise imagery of water cascading down the tiered bowls of a fountain. Other older undergraduate and graduate members of the house provided me useful guidance and feedback on writing assignments. The influence of others, however, was more troubling, posing problems and choices that led me to define myself in resistance and opposition, as I will discuss in chapter 10.

The house also hosted faculty guests of some note for short- and longer-term stays, and many of the speakers who came to campus were invited for receptions. Among ourselves we had seminars and weekly public speeches. Over meals, late-night snacks in the kitchen, or long walks, we had endless discussions about ideas and issues that came up in our courses, our readings, and our musings. We pondered our own directions, choices, and goals. Further, the house was self-governing in conjunction with an association of upper division students and recent alums, so we had weekly business meetings, administrative committees, committees examining our endowment portfolio, and evaluation of applications for summer programs. I learned a sense of civic responsibility—as well as the politics of deliberative persuasion among a group of analytically sharp and academically successful people. I also learned details of non-academic practicalities from stock portfolio evaluation to purchasing kitchen equipment. One of my iconic memories capturing the heterogeneity of the Cornell Telluride experience was when I interviewed a professor of kitchen design at the Hotel School to become briefed on the options for a new commercial meat slicer for the house kitchen. My newly gained knowledge made for an authoritative recommendation, adopted after some overly clever debate at the house meeting.

The summer program application process required us every year during the winter intersession to read hundreds of applications of academically successful high school juniors nationally, so I developed an eye for those who were original, smart, and motivated in ways that might lead them to unique contributions to society. The most damning (and often repeated) thing we could say about an application was that it was "competent but dull." Each year we also needed to write our own applications for the continuation of our fellowship in the house and admittance to the governing association. These applications required us to reflect on our goals and experiences, as well as to what we valued in the reading we were doing and the projects we engaged in for our classes and the community. Consequently, we were recurrently reflective about our values, our choices, and our experiences. This habit of reflection has stayed with me in my professional choices, even when it had personal costs. I always felt I needed to be able to give a good account, a coherent account, of what I was doing, why, and what the moral and ethical grounds were for those choices. This is a very specific kind of integrity—in the forming and monitoring of a reasoned life project.

Figure 6.2. Cornell Branch Telluride Association. Photo from Cornell University Division of Rare and Manuscript Collections: Lucien L. Nunn papers.

Chapter 7. First-Year Composition: Setting Terms for College Writing

A Preface on My College Writing

I have an almost complete file of my undergraduate college papers including a number with teacher comments. In the next few chapters I will examine them chronologically and by subject, as I experienced them, starting with first year writing, which most directly and explicitly set the terms for college writing. This is not the first time I have looked through them, as my original impulse to save them was to keep track of my thinking. But now I see them through the eyes of a writing teacher to notice the learning of style, structure, text forms and functions, and processes of writing. Of course, the writing problems I was working on were related to the content and elaboration of ideas that I was thinking about; that is, the writing development was driven by the impulse to give shape to my emerging thinking. In the chapters to follow I will try to show that dynamic interaction of growing writing and thought. I also will focus on what Vygotsky called leading activity (1967, 1978)—that is the more explicit problems of both thought and expression I was consciously trying to solve, and thus what I was most overtly working on. The novel problems posed by the papers and the solutions are evident in the texts and how later texts differ from early ones, but as I examine the papers, I also recover my remembered state of mind—what I was worrying about, what I felt puzzled by, what I was pleased to accomplish, and other emotions.

I also was aware at the time (and still am in my current work) that realizations often follow in the wake of writing; it may take weeks and months, and even years, following writing a paper to recognize consciously the fuller ideas I was gesturing at and the force of their implications. I also have recognized how the ideas and practices I was realizing in one location might be applicable elsewhere. These leading activities, the problems I was solving, and the ideas I was working on frequently led me to new places where things started to look different and where new lines of inquiring, thinking, and acting opened up. In the chapters that follow I will tell the stories of a number of such incidents. We might consider these as instances of threshold concepts, both personal and academic (Meyer & Land, 2003).

In writing these papers I was working on many skills and strategies that would be embedded in my later work and issues that would remain thematic, so they will get a lot more attention than you might think undergraduate papers deserve. Nonetheless, to me they reveal much about my trajectory as a writer and my growing understanding of writing, and I will try to indicate that in the next several chapters. If still the discussion seems tedious and self-indulgent, my apologies.

Inviting and Accepting Experimentation

As I have reviewed my college papers it has become clearer to me how important the first-year writing course was in preparing me for later growth and setting trajectories od my development. My instructor for both fall and winter semesters, Jean Blackall (later to become a professor), provided an accepting atmosphere which recognized my prior unconventional writing and encouraged further experimentation. She also provided me with important tools to address the challenges and opportunities of my further courses. The teacher's assignments and relations to the class worked well for me, and I responded positively to her sympathetic reading of my work. Indeed, I wound up with a crush on her, though thirty-five years later when I met her again, she did not remember who I was, to my chagrin.

I always felt that she valued what I wrote, both in the quality of writing and in the message—that she took my writing seriously as a realization of my thought. This of course is now generally seen as good practice in the teaching of writing, but this communicative trust was extremely important for me. I had experienced this acceptance to a lesser degree in a number of my teachers in high school and in some of my other teachers in college—but never previously as intensely as with this teacher. The dismissal of my writing and thoughts by some other teachers hardened me and decreased my desire to write for or communicate with them. Learning to write is a growth towards the other, connecting to the reader, forging a communicative strength and richness. While at times a contentious relationship with others fostered an elaboration of arguments as long as I felt (or at least hoped) that my ideas would be heard and pondered, if I found my views being dismissed, discounted, or ignored my communicative energies shut down. Chill winds stopped growth. This need for engagement is now well recognized, but it cannot be emphasized enough. It is part of why success breeds success, to the benefit of some but not others who do not enjoy the sense of being heard.

Part of the permissiveness and experimentality of the course was the result of my not yet identifying as a potential literature major, still anticipating a career in physics. There were three tracks of first year writing course—the general one for most students, directed towards basic skills, correctness, and conventional forms. At the upper end was a course for potential literature majors who entered with high literacy scores on the standardized tests. As I learned from friends, this course was devoted to preparing students for more professionalized literary criticism and writing about texts from the literary canon. My course was for students who scored well by standard literacy measures, but were headed to other majors. The course was challenging, but not restricted to pre-professional forms, stances, and styles. We were introduced to a range of twentieth century fiction, poetry, and essays and were asked to consider issues of text organization and stylistic variation while pondering large social questions. The two-semester course organized around the theme of "Experience and Form," had us constantly writing—starting with one-page papers due every class meeting three times a week, then later weekly papers of about five hundred words each, with a longer paper at the end of the first term (mine was around 2500 words). The second term was organized around longer biweekly papers, again in relation to assigned books.

Attentiveness to Meaning, Structure, and Style

In looking over the first term papers some themes stand out. As would be typical in my literary courses throughout my undergraduate years, there was an emphasis on close reading, careful attention to symbols and meaning, and explication of texts—all in the new critical mode, popular in the middle sixties when I was a student. Both my sentences and teacher comments noticed paradoxical contrasts and oppositions in the texts. As the year went on, I used more and more paradoxical formulations of my own, especially to contrast the novel thing found in the text with the expected or conventional. Over the years since, I have had to break myself of the habit of using such contrasts when they weren't necessary, to go directly to the thing I wanted to say without noting how it was distinctive from something else. On the other hand, typicality and unexpected contrastive hybridity have been thematic in my theoretical interests throughout the years. In sentence style, the teacher especially recognized balanced sentence constructions along with pithy, witty summation sentences. I accordingly paid attention to sentence rhythms and learned to punctuate my long, complex sentences with short, pointed resting points.

The instructor emphasized making meanings explicit and clear, as in comments as "I don't see what you are getting at in your idea of . . . " or "Explain why. . . . " She also asked for grounding my observations in textual evidence. As the term went on, my claims became more elaborated and evidenced. Our assignments and class discussions asked us to look for coherence in the texts we read. The instructor repeatedly asked "What holds this text together? What makes it a single piece of writing?" Our own writing was also expected to be coherent, but we were encouraged to seek creative solutions to coherence. The instructor's comments throughout the year recognized a variety of idiosyncratic forms of organization I used. She even noted that in a second reading of one of my papers she saw why I had taken what initially seemed to her a sudden leap—but now saw I was preparing to show a change in attitude and direction.

I took her flexible idea of unity as an invitation to follow an organic structure of intellectual discovery in my papers. This matched well with my practice at that time of writing a single draft, often from sketch notes. I did much improvisatory work inside my head, putting the mentally-prepared parts together as I wrote out the text. I experienced argument as a kind of discovery as I worked through ideas and details. I would repeatedly reread my partial draft and move forward. In the papers in this course, I often belabored points as I tried to discover what it was I wanted to say. Only in later years when I began to revise consistently was I able cut out the exploratory phrasing that led me to a final clean formulation. This is still something that I consciously monitor in my revision.

Some Assignments

A number of the assignments asked for imitation of authors' styles or procedures. After we discussed the heterogeneity in Eliot's "Wasteland," we were asked to collect ideas in a poet's notebook and then in a following assignment to use those separate entries as the basis for our own poem. My notebook was, following Eliot, a collection of obscure cultural references and jingly-jangly verses of self-doubt and romantic confusion. As we started to look at some stories by Hemingway and D. H. Lawrence, we were asked to write a personal narrative that would open up a larger theme. I turned my experience registering for the draft into an ironic contemplation on how institutions gave us unformed, shy, identityless young people official identities and places in society. I stole my theme and stance from Brecht's play *A Man's a Man*. Then we were asked to write a Hemingway story in the style of Lawrence, and the next week a Lawrence narrative in the style of Hemingway. This pair of exercises gave me the chance to explore the interaction of sentence complexity, stance distance, and empathetic evaluation. After reading some essays of James Baldwin we were asked to write about something we felt deeply, which gave me the opportunity to assert my views on morality, thereby building a more assertive voice. After reading Joyce's *Dubliners* (and writing an analysis of one of the stories) we were asked to write an epiphany of our own, embedded in a narrative. I wound up telling of a (highly fictionalized) moment when the bravado of my high school crowd evaporated as we headed off to college, leaving me with a sense that I was alone.

All these assignments playing with imitation on multiple levels—in style, stance, voice, purpose, and form—gave me license to pursue idiosyncratic modes of answering more conventional assignments. In a second term assignment to analyze Faulkner's sentences, for example, I wrote the entire 1000-word essay in a single sentence (embedding an equally long quote of a Faulkner sentence). I learned a lot about text organization, sentence style, sentence rhythm, cohesion, and wit as the term went on. Though in retrospect my attempts look labored, the work of a self-possessed freshman, at the time I remember often being quite pleased with my playful efforts. At least I was learning.

Only a few of the papers I remember as dull and conventional, but in looking at those papers I remember as uninspired I now I see I was working out ideas important to me. One of the more painful papers was the fall final paper on essays by Joseph Wood Krutch, a writer I found terminally boring. Nonetheless, as a then science student, I used that paper to question whether science was the necessarily better path. My arguments against Krutch now look to be vague and sloppy invocations of intuition to suggest limits of rational inquiry; nonetheless, I was coming to recognize the role of imagination, abduction, and human intelligence in science—seeing science as created through human inquiry and agency. I used, of course, many sentences of contrast, opposition, paradox, and negation along the way—building my sense of rhythm and syntactic surprise. I also kept working on logics of organization, moving from one idea to the next determined by a reasoning path rather than a preset outline.

This search for meaning in science was clearly on my mind, as it appeared in a number of other papers throughout the first term. Although the literary analyses of the second term didn't create as direct a place for my ponderings on the meaning of life as the first term assignments, such thoughts crept in as I considered the values and moral dilemmas of characters. I began my paper on *Lord Jim*, for example, with the quote from the character Stein ". . . How to be. Ach! How to be." This problem of finding life meaning continued through my undergraduate life. It also became the ostensible reason I gave for my switch from the sciences to the humanities in the middle of my sophomore year, though a number of personal and academic situations contributed to the decision.

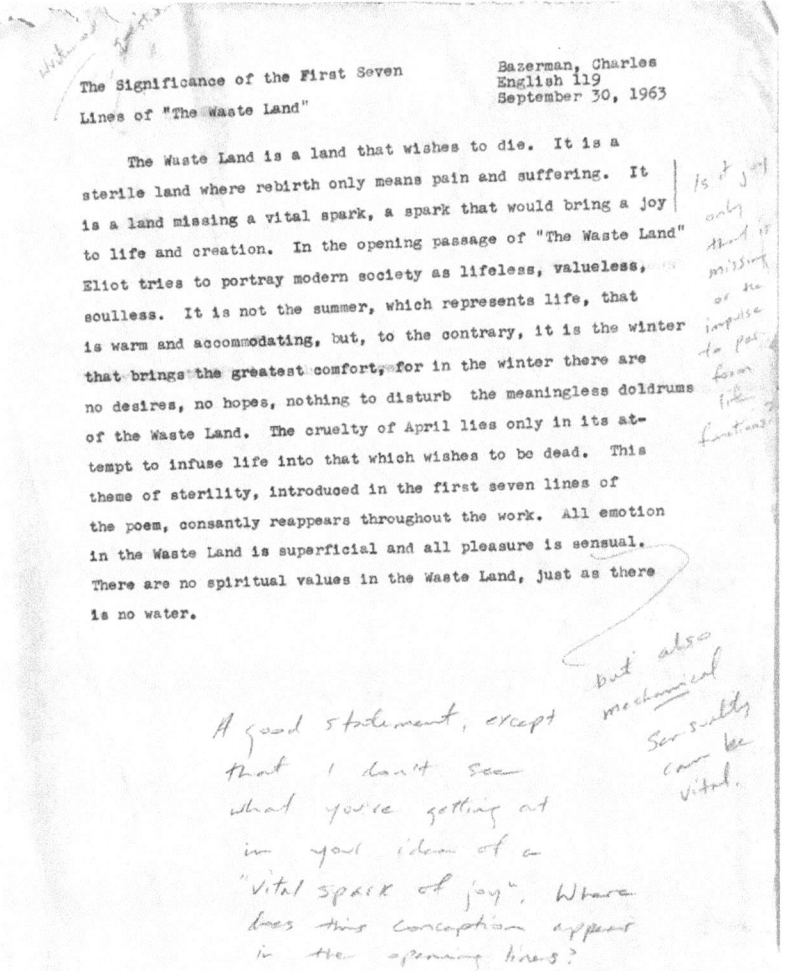

Figure 7.1. My first assignment in first-year composition. Courtesy of Charles Bazerman.

Chapter 8. Writing in Non-Literature Courses

As I fulfilled general education requirements and considered majors in my first years of college, I took courses in a variety of disciplines. The writing demands of non-literary courses I experienced varied, from the minimal to major writing challenges. But all required us to submit our reasoning and knowledge in disciplinary written form for evaluation, whether as problem sets, on exams, or in lengthy papers. In the contrast of the kinds of written work I needed to submit in different fields I became aware of how different and particular the thinking, ideas, theories, and practices of the fields were, and I also wondered how the reasoning of one might contribute to another, even far removed on the disciplinary spectrum.

Reasoning in Science and Mathematics

My basic physics and math courses had little writing beyond required problem sets, exams made mostly of such problems, and cookbook demonstration labs. I do not have any record of these, but I do remember needing to understand the reasoning behind the equations and procedures we were asked to apply to specific problems. As the coursework became more advanced it became less obvious which procedures and equations to apply, what values to place in the equations, what sequence of theories and equations would get us to a complex solution, and what reasoning steps would constitute a valid proof of a proposition. I had few problems in the selection of words, but application of concepts and precision of execution in proceeding down reasoning paths became essential to coming to accurate solutions. Conceptualizing what was essential within the problem facts and determining what variables and processes were at play in relation to each other pushed me to see problems having theoretical shape and coherence. While pieces fell in place readily for me in the earlier courses, in my most advanced courses, I could make crisp sense of only some of the puzzles offered, and I often didn't have confidence in my proposed solutions, nor could I determine what went wrong in those I couldn't solve. This bothered me, as I no longer felt I was understanding how the pieces of theory fit together and applied. The logic of some proofs in number theory (offered as the honors alternative to advanced calculus), in particular, remained obscure to me, because I was not familiar enough with the theory to see the logical entailments. This search to find theoretical coherence in the synthesis of disparate theories drove me later as I tried to understand what writing was, in its many dimensions.

In the social sciences writing, however, reasoning was expressed in more traditional academic essay form. In the large introductory lectures I attended in sociology, diplomatic history, and economics, however, writing was often limited to brief exam essays which I do not have copies of, nor much specific memory of. I do remember, however, that half of each exam usually required reproducing material from textbooks and lectures, so preparation would have involved mostly reading, note taking, and key information identification. These are useful skills, learned by most college students, but they did not push the bounds of my writing potentials beyond increasing a storehouse of useful academic phrases.

Reconstructing Intentions and Thoughts of Historical Actors

Other courses, however, posed greater writing challenges. In medieval history in my sophomore year, I wrote one 10-page term paper in the fall and another in the spring. Both were chosen from a list of potential questions circulated by the professor. The fall paper was an examination of Pope Gregory VI's letters to determine his sincerity in his acceptance of Henry IV's penitence. I remember hours puzzling over the grey-bound volume of his letters to find themes in his many actions and attempts to unify control and practices in the church. I connected his more contemplative letters with the transactional ones. In developing my analysis, I was learning to find order and coherence in a substantial corpus of documents, to establish criteria for analysis, and to synthesize my findings in a persuasive narrative. I organized the analysis sequentially, with transitional statements and focusing topic sentences. The first paragraph set up the historical dilemma faced by Pope Gregory and the importance for examining the letters. The second paragraph identified the evidence and the method for the examination of sincerity. The next four paragraphs elaborated the historical dilemma, adding excerpts from the letters presenting his perspective on the challenge he faced. The closing paragraph offered further quotations revealing his dilemma and confession of being humbled by the events. The few comments from the professor suggested I lacked some important contextual historical knowledge, but otherwise met the expectations of the assignment.

The spring paper was also an analysis of a substantial corpus, considering the humanism of the Goliardic poems, and interpreting them in relation to the Renaissance. I began by comparing definitions of humanism, but then rejected the definitional quest. At the conclusion of the initial paragraph, instead, I turned to how the Goliardic lyrics of the 12th century represented something new and compared them with quattrocento Italian lyrics. In the second paragraph, I excluded questions of the history of poetic form because I relied on translations and did not know enough about the emergence of rhymed metric poetry to replace Latin quality. Then I discuss who the Goliards were and the spirit they represented (though the professor corrected some of my less-informed assumptions). In the following paragraphs I recounted the themes and attitudes in the poems, supported by long quotations indicating tropes of sin, sensuality, drink, virility, and nature as lust. I compared them to the earlier Scotus who is more pious and then to the quattrocento, pointing out the Goliards were more conventionalized in poetic form, cruder in sensuality and emotions, and not attuned to spiritual issues. I concluded that the Goliards had a beginning awareness of humanism, but only a beginning. My paper was reasonably structured, but shallow in its readings and analysis.

Analyzing Governmental Structures, Motives, and Ideas

I have a larger group of papers from several Government courses, as I was considering that as a major. The first term first-year course on American Government asked for three papers. The first three-pager evaluated the seniority rule in Congress, the second four-pager examined the tension between the President's responsibility and authority, and the last of the same length weighed the benefits and weaknesses of the U.S. two-party system. All required me to summarize and synthesize various course readings and supplemental materials we sought on our own, select relevant themes and details, and build a coherent argument, adopting an objective yet evaluative stance while referring to some historical examples. All three submissions met with the general approval of the teaching assistant, so apparently, I was appropriately practicing and expanding skills for this kind of source-based argument, developing a reflective evaluative frame, and maintaining an academic voice, a bit different from the more personal voice and overt personal concerns in my English class. I did, however, remain baffled by the instructor's comment repeated on all the papers that he wished I had gone further and made some stronger conclusions. In retrospect, I think he was asking for some affirmative proposals for reforming the seniority system, the U.S. presidency, and the two-party system, probably based on his experience as a British citizen, though I am not quite sure how I could have done that as an eighteen-year-old who had not yet traveled nor even studied comparative foreign governments (that was for the spring term). It was not explicitly stated, however, that solving institutional problems was part of the assignments, and his comments about going further did not point me in any direction I then understood.

In the spring first year course on European systems, I only have one four-page paper in my files, and I believe the course relied more on exams. My paper was a response to the question of whether national socialism was a temporary aberration in German political history. I extended my high school paper on German nationalism, to discuss the history of governmental weakness prior to the formation of the German state, the progressive impulses behind unification, and then the social and economic disruptions following World War I. I drew on a range of philosophic and historical materials to sketch a large picture. Again, the same teaching assistant liked it but asked for stronger conclusions; again, at that point I didn't seem to have a clue as to what this instructor meant by stronger conclusions and how to get them. Even now with more than a half-century of academic experience, I can only guess.

I took two more political science courses and another on political philosophy. A political science course in the spring of my second year was on Congressional processes. I did two similar papers examining how interests drove legislation that regulated industries, which was a central theme of the course and was the focus of a book the professor was working on, as I later discovered. One, on hearings concerning the regulation of food coloring used for dying oranges, I do not have a copy of because the professor kept it for his own project without asking for my permission; he also did not provide any feedback beyond a middling grade. Another, which I do have a copy of, examined the legislative history of a bill affecting the trout history. The first three pages were an introduction to regulatory legislation and the relation to industrial interests, followed by a history of legislation creating and regulating the FDA. This was then followed by six pages of the legislative history of the bill affecting the trout industry. This history involved the reading of the transcripts of committee and subcommittee hearings to see how members of Congress from affected regions expressed the concerns of their constituent industries. Both parts were factual narratives told in an objective reportorial voice, except for a couple of evaluative phrases and what I thought at the time were clever ironies, such as in my title "Does Trout Regulation belong in the Pork Barrel?" I have only a carbon paper copy of this with no teacher comments.

The instructor's response to another paper in political philosophy from the fall of my second year also was obscure, providing no useful guidance. The professor, Alan Bloom, assigned us to explain Rousseau's account of the origins of human self-awareness and acts of will in the *Second Discourse (On the Origin and Basis of Inequality Among Men)*. I remember spending many days reading, re-reading, and puzzling over the set text and related texts of Rousseau and commentators. I developed what I thought captured Rousseau's hypothetical story of the formation of consciousness, though I confessed remaining puzzled by two passages. In my essay I discussed my difficulties with those passages at length. Along the way I tried to analyze what seemed to be elements of self-awareness, consciousness, and action—not easy topics to me then, nor even now, as I continue to read the proposals of neuroscientists, philosophers, anthropologists, psychologists, and others on the topic. I concluded with a final paragraph suggesting that Rousseau held either one of two views that to me seemed equally unlikely, so I confessed my lack of understanding, particularly of the two passages I discussed at length. Bloom's comments mostly note that I have gotten Rousseau wrong. No doubt I did, but I still can't see what the professor was pointing me towards, nor did he engage with the passages I confessed confusions over in order to give me some direction. His response taught me that meeting what I thought were the expectations of the assignment did not always serve me well, no matter how much work I invested in the task, if it did not match the values of the reader. I remember auditing a seminar the following term from this same professor (because he was very highly regarded by my peers and was a faculty guest living at Telluride—a story I will elaborate in chapter 10), but as an auditor I did not write a paper. From these and related interactions, I learned there were worlds that I could not make myself understood within, nor engage in fruitful dialog with, no matter how much I attempted to meet the formal expectations and practices, because my texts would not be seen as fitting or making sense within the views that circulated within that world.

I had a more affirming response in a third-year course on urban planning, just before I took a term away from the university. I turned the topic of the term paper (though I do not remember the prompt) into a contemplation on values and morality in science and government, far removed from what I remember as a rather technical course on such things as water and sewage infrastructure in relation to city expansion. I pondered such things as fact-value distinctions, technocratic approaches to decision making, cost-benefit analysis, systems analysis, the atomic bomb and the Vietnam war (this was written in January 1966 as the war escalated), ending with the need for moral reasoning in government. I was tying disparate materials into a reflection on my values. In looking now at the profile of the professor who was to become one of the leading theorists of progressive urban planning, I can see why he responded positively to the idealism and search for value in the paper even though I didn't really respond to any of the technical content of the course.

This paper reinforced for me that I could write in ways that seemed to exceed the situation and prompt if I could tap into the deeper values and concerns of the audience. Even from junior high school, I have found transgressive and boundary-bending ways of writing beyond what the situation called for, and often enough I was rewarded (though sometimes not). This transgressive reframing of writing tasks may seem to be in tension with my interest in genre, which was to become one of my theoretical and research obsessions—but I think to the contrary, I was becoming aware of boundaries and expectations as part of experimenting how to move across them to bring my interests and concerns into an acceptable space. Learning to say unconventional things in unconventional ways required a growing rhetorical, technical, and stylistic awareness of the expected as well as an evaluation of the risks and the courage needed to put pressure on those expectations.

At that point I was gathering credits for a government major, hoping I would be able to pursue a principled life in that sphere. This paper marked my final disaffection with the enterprise. Political science at that time seemed to me a cynical enterprise to provide technical means to support power and advantage. Whether or not I was misguided, I was pulling away from engaging in those discourses. It was after this course that I took a term off, to train for the Peace Corps, which I saw as the only way to take time out from the university in a way that conformed with my ideals at the time without also being drafted. The decision to leave was in retrospect complex, driven not only by my search for personal meaning and my disillusionment with the academic disciplines I was experiencing, but also by the recent death of my father and a need to pull further away from the needs and demands of my mother. All this was compounded by the complexities of living in Telluride House. In Chapter 10 I will attempt to make sense of these crises and how they bore on my orientation to writing.

Chapter 9. Writing in Literature Courses Through the Third Year: Learning Close Textual Analysis

Even as I pursued potential science and social science majors, I pursued possibilities in literature, taking courses leading toward majors in both English and German. In both potential majors I was supported and mentored by friends and housemates, although I had mixed experiences with instructors. In all these courses I was learning the skills of close reading and how to present my interpretations. In learning to reconstruct the meaning of texts according to standards of literary disciplines, however, I was also learning to see my personal concerns as reflected in the texts I explicated. Additionally, I started to sort out what I thought of the values, ideas, and stances of the works. Expressing what I thought about those values did not always go well, as I discovered that my professors themselves often saw their own values expressed in the texts they taught and wanted us to appreciate.

Apprenticeship in English Literature

Following my positive experience in first year writing, I enrolled in the second-year, two-term course in English literary criticism for potential English majors. There I found, however, less tolerance for my heterodox stance and opinions, nonconventional style, and organic organization. The emphasis was on professionalization into critical practices, primarily in the new critical mode of the time. There was a nominal awareness of historical and social context as we worked our way chronologically through the two volume *Norton Anthology of English Literature* (not including American, which at that time was still a curricular afterthought). Each of our tri-weekly assigned papers of around 1500 words (5–8 typed double-spaced pages) focused on close reading. I have been mentioning paper length here and elsewhere because for myself and my friends length identified the amount of challenge in locating content and elaborating arguments. Length was also a typical requirement of the priompt. Other than length, the prompts were all general, simply requiring that we do an interpretation or explication of one of the identified texts.

My first paper of the first term examined moral awareness in Chaucer's "Clerk's Tale" about Patient Griselda. The paragraphs were structured around an unfolding argument, on the character of the clerk, the genre of his tale as *exemplum* with its moral idealization, the social demands of her situation, and Griselda's virtues and self-awareness as the tale unfolds. I offered detailed evidence through quotations, word choice, and actions as modeled in class discussions. I then ended with an evaluation of her character and that of the clerk who narrates the tale, in order to analyze Chaucer's narrative intention and stance. The professor did not comment on the substance of the argument, but asked me to tighten my language, maintain appropriate register and diction, and create lexical cohesion (though he did not use these linguistic terms).

The next paper on *Hamlet* again evaluated a character's words and actions to reveal the stance of the work itself. The text moved through a series of logically organized paragraphs with even more evidence from the words and quotations from the work than in the previous one. I seem to have been able now to meet the instructor's expectations of the formality of language, though he still noted a few corrections of this sort. My sentences and sequences continued to rely on oppositions, contradictions, and paradoxes. In accordance with the topic and my evolving style, I attempted witty, epigrammatic formulations, particularly at the opening and closing of the argument. This paper begins "Hamlet's wit mirrors his awareness, but dulls his ability to act in an aware manner." And it ends "Hamlet is a considered wit, but a rash actor." Now I see this argument as static and predetermined, or at least pre-announced, ending where I began. This was actually a principle repeated often in my classes, that a good way to end a paper was to reprise a beginning. As I found that advice leading to boring writing, I was to modify this principle to reprise initial themes but seeing them in a fresh perspective that the journey of the paper has revealed. This modified advice is something I still tell my students.

The third paper was a close reading of Donne's poem "The Funeral," unpacking the poem's conceits and contradictory logic. I discussed line by line the tone, stance, imagery, and prosody to highlight the frustrated struggles of the narrator to come up with a compelling vision, but ultimately collapsing in comic self-mockery. My sentences are cumbersome, with frequent contrasts, exclusions, and reversals within the syntax ("Not this . . . but that"). Some sentences reach for epigrammatic and rhythmic conclusiveness.

The final paper of the fall term was on Congreve's *Way of the World*, laying out the code and rules of insincerity. The paper proceeds through the contrast of characters upon which the play itself is structured. An opening paragraph reviews the overall pattern I will demonstrate. The next paragraph examines the shallow concept of wit exemplified by the character Witwoud that contrasts with Dryden's definition of true wit. The following paragraph examines the statements and moods of another character who exemplifies this lower form of wit. Then I examine the more polished wit of Mirabell as exemplifying Dryden's view. Finally, I show how even the most sincere character uses the veneer of wit to hide her true love. The sentences are fairly tight and forward-moving, with no repetition or circling back, and some have a sense of rhythm and aphorism, especially in the closing lines.

From the second term, I have four papers of the same length and all addressing close analysis of a text. But my paper on the Wordsworth's "The Leech-Gatherer" adopts a perspective at odds with the viewpoint of the poem. I used Lewis

Carroll's parody "You are Old Father William" in *Through the Looking Glass* to establish an alternative critical stance. I remember having a lot of fun with this paper and learning a lot, being highly engaged in what I thought was a meaningful argument—perhaps one of the most meaningful of the term. However, while I identified paradox and contradiction internal within the artistic work (highly appreciated in the new critical world of the class), stepping outside the assumptions of the text was not well received. Although the teacher appreciated the fire of my critique, he wanted me to stick closely to the poem itself and take it on its own terms. In trying to articulate my own sense of the limits of the poem, rather than immersing myself in appreciation of the poem itself, I was distancing myself from what I came to view as the ideologies that supported some literary tastes. Perhaps a couple of decades later when ideological critique was more the expectation, the paper would have gone over better.

My next paper for my second-year English major survey, was on Keats' "Ode on a Nightingale," which I found more sympathetic. My analysis was based on a contrary motion within the text, and thus more appreciated by the professor. Fahnestock and Secor later (1991) note that paradox or contraries was one of the major tropes in literary studies. In this case the contrary was in the upward flight of the nightingale and the downward pull of the poet into numbness and forgetfulness. I did bring in an alternative view more cautiously in a footnote, only to reject it, saying a well-known critic missed the point of the poem. The instructor commented I should have made this critique more explicitly in the text—suggesting to me that one could cite a critique, but only if it was being rejected as not understanding the spirit of the poem, as I would then reveal in my analysis. I could criticize a critic, but I should not criticize a primary text or its author, as I had just learned in the previous paper. As Myers later found (1989), this taste for negative citation and contestation is not generally followed outside literary studies, and I later needed to learn more tact as I engaged interdisciplinary studies.

The next assignment on a readily understood essay did not require subtle analysis, only a distilling of the text's perspective and an evaluation of its application in life. After summarizing Ruskin's Christian idealist views on the flaws of laissez fair capitalism, I considered how in some ways his reformist principles had been realized in the US but through the wielding of economic and political power in the progressive, New Deal, and Civil Rights eras and not through Ruskin's ideals of justice. I used contraries and paradoxes as organizing principles while returning to some of the big historical pictures I had taken on in prior years.

However, I had not yet learned my lesson about rejecting the premises of the works I was commenting on. In my last paper for this course, I rejected the values of Browning's romantic escapism in the portrait of "Fra Lippo Lippi." My argument here is not so far from my critique of Wordsworth's "Leech Gatherer," finding in word choice, imagery, and projected character the construction of an unreal ideal that served the longings of the poet rather than providing insight into the actual characters represented. The ink on the teacher's comments has faded so I cannot tell if the professor wanted to guide me back into an appreciation of Browning.

That same spring of second year I took a course on Chaucer. The only paper I have is a take-home mid-term exam. Possibly there was a similar take home final, but it was not returned to me. The short four-page essay examines the "Knight's Tale" and the character of the knight, tying both to chivalric themes, the seriousness of the prose, and conventional Boethian dullness of thought. Although my essay was seen as interesting by the instructor, he also felt the lack of something more that would show a deeper appreciation—though no clues were offered as to what that would be.

The following fall, before leaving for the Peace Corps, I took two more courses taught by English professors. One was a comparative literature course on contemporary drama with a professor who influenced me greatly, and with whom I took a number of classes after my return. I will discuss my writing for all his courses in Chapter 11. Another was a course on selected Shakespeare plays. I barely remember the course, though I remember my fascination with the dramatic structure of the plays. I have no papers in my files and I don't remember writing any; likely only exams were given, which were not returned.

Aestheticism in German Literature

While I was exploring an English major, I also was considering one in German literature, building on my years of secondary school German. The German literature courses provided me a different critical angle, which I found even more troubling in its assumptions, conventionality, and aestheticism. My first year I took a two-term survey of German literature. We were assigned one ten-page paper each term. Full of ambition in the fall I wrote mine in German, on Gretchen's four songs in *Urfaust*. I was one of the few students unwise enough to take up the option of writing in German. I invested much effort into this and was especially proud of accomplishing such a lengthy paper in the language. My essay was in form similar to what I was writing in my English classes at the time—description and then commentary on each of the songs, looking at various elements and relating them to the unfolding events as well as the feelings and character of the heroines. I considered the songs serially and then made concluding comments about what the songs tell us about the heroine. As in English I had a taste for sentences with contraries, but the prose in German was more ponderous with few of the crafted, rhythmic phrases I was starting to use in my English prose. I also had a series of typos which may reflect my lack of familiarity with German as well as my carelessness. The teacher's extensive comments (27 numbered notes at the end and other marginalia) are in the majority about German lexical choice, grammatical form, and other aspects of my German, including pointing out some howlers (which really are quite funny). He also pointed to a few places where my interpretation of the text was inaccurate because of my mistakes with key terms. The comments related to the substance of my commentary were fewer, but pointed back to my lack of subtlety with German making my interpretation naïve. For years all I remembered was his final comment that the German was not well developed and the piece seemed like the work of a small child—and then he gave me the lowest grade by far I have ever received on a piece of writing—70. I never attempted to write a paper in German again (or any language other than English).

In the spring I wrote in English on Brecht's *Galileo,* considering Galileo's recantation. This thematic analysis allowed me to explore the value of science for human life, which was very much on my mind at the time. I compared the actions, views, and passions of Galileo to that of other characters, in response to the power and authority of the Church. I saw his passion for science equal to his other more fleshly passions, which he protects in the recantation. I go through the earlier actions of the play rapidly and devote the latter half of the paper to the recantation, and his realization of science as only meaningful in relation to the life of society. This is contrasted with the attitudes of a monk who is afraid science will destroy faith and Galileo's protégé Andrea who sees science in its mechanistic wonders. I recall this play was written in the wake of WWII (and my paper in the midst of the cold war). It is a competent thematic analysis of character actions and thoughts, largely considered chronologically. The sentences and paragraph organization are, however, pedestrian and blunt, with little wit, irony, or sense of textual nuance.

During my second year in the fall, I took a course on Goethe's early poetry and fiction, and in the spring a course on twentieth century German poetry and drama. The professor for the fall course was a prominent Goethe scholar, attached to the poet's values and ideals. Over the term, however, I began to reject those values as unbearably aesthetic and idealized. We had short 2–3 page papers every 3 weeks and a take home exam essay of similar length. The first paper was an explication of the poem "Lilli's Park." My introduction presented the overall theme of the analysis and characterization of the poem; following paragraphs offered details of language, imagery, events, and attitudes examined sequentially; the paper ended where the poem ends with a characterization of the meaning of the final action, placed within Goethe's biography. The teacher's comments mostly pointed to places where he wanted a more elevated style and greater care in diction. In one instance he offered a more precise understanding of a German word, and in two places he makes interpretive points that suggested I should be more appreciative of the poet's stance.

The second paper, a reading of the poem "Zueignung," was structured similarly to the first and carries out a similar task. Here the instructor wanted me to follow up more explicitly on comparisons and details. But the biggest complaint was about my "structure" which apparently had to do with the paragraphing rather than the sequence or logic of the argument. In this paper I was experimenting with shorter paragraphs, separating each action, but he wanted me to combine paragraphs to about three times their length to reflect larger clusters, so the body would consist of four paragraphs. The third paper on "Harzreise im Winter" follows the same organization and still has short paragraphs, though he no longer comments on them. But here I seemed to have found a way to make the kinds of points he liked with the level of diction he found acceptable. He even marked a number of my statements as good. I remember though not being excited by these papers and finding them burdensome, and rather ponderous.

The fourth paper on *Die Leiden des jungen Werthers*, however, appreciated the novel's ironic attitude to the affectation, egoism, and aestheticism of the *Sturm und Drang* self-representation of the protagonist. Noting such things as Werther arguing against revision in the novel that Goethe has himself revised and that the stylized and self-dramatized suicide turns ugly despite all the aesthetic planning, I concluded that Werther is not as sentimental as critics claim but is more ironically crafted. The paper's organization moves through selected moments and ironies. The professor took issue with some of my comments and found a higher justification for the ironies I noted. He also found some of my diction too common, and even said one of my phrases was not English, though I now find the phrasing perfectly normal, though not elevated. The instructor himself was Oxbridge British and seemed to be holding my diction to his dialect. He also asked me to remove references to the poet's self to explain the irony although I was discussing reflective subjectivity. The instructor, however, did like my evaluating the novel as subtle and ironic.

The fifth paper was on Schiller's critique of Goethe's play *Egmont*. Structurally this paper was much like the previous ones in this class and in preceding literature classes, except that here the assignment asked me to consider a third-party critique to set up the issue for critical examination. This may have given me the idea of how to structure my English paper on Wordsworth at the beginning of the next term (discussed earlier in this chapter). From the professor's comments I suspect that he wanted me to agree with and elaborate Schiller's point of view. The underlying issue seemed to be whether the play was a personal story of character complexity or an idealistic story of political heroism (Schiller's position). I chose the former and saw the last scene (which Schiller liked) as an artifice which pulled attention away from the character's complexity. From the marginal comments it appears the professor saw this last scene as a transfiguration. Although he liked my noting a transformation in the final scene, he did not appreciate my lack of appreciation of that transformation. However, I did not see anything that warranted or foreshadowed this reversal of everything the play had done to that point, and the professor didn't point me to any. I did use a more consistent formal diction, long paragraphs, and many details which the professor accepted—though he clearly also wanted something more. His comments treated the paper as though I was working on a puzzle I had not quite solved, though I was quite definite in my judgment. While the play fits into the Napoleonic idealism of the period, I wasn't buying it.

This rejection was part of my recurrent pattern of having a hard time in accepting some of the values and ideologies preferred by instructors. My appreciation for literature I was coming to learn was based on whether I could also be drawn into the ideological world of the text being considered. I was coming to see more and more how the literary preferences and evaluations of critics and teachers were tied to the texts they studied, in which they were finding their satisfying visions of life. More practically, I realized I should only write about authors and texts that touched me. I later extended this to the study of non-literary texts and authors, as I found much sympathetic in the rhetorical and intellectual growth of Joseph Priestley, Adam Smith, Thomas Edison, and in the development of the writing of various disciplines. Even when I did not always agree with the writers, I could see what they were doing and I learned from them. Similarly, my uptake of theoretical and methodological orientations largely depended on what made sense to me and what was useful. Coordinately, I was learning to deal delicately with readers' ideologies and not rile them unnecessarily. Part of my learning to write was learning how to position myself intertextually—not only to draw on supporting sources, but to place myself among those who inhabit a universe that makes sense to me and I can communicate with. My task became to draw readers into my universe by finding the connecting points, rather than knocking other positions down. Eventually I became more careful in sidestepping minefields for readers and choosing positive claims I could substantiate. I also focused on empirical strategies that made visible instances or cases that could not be denied.

But I had not learned such tact by the end of this course, and I ran full tilt into the windmill in my take-home final exam which asked me to consider Goethe's representation of the poet *Torquato Tasso* as a misfit in society. This paper was written shortly after my father's death, and the instructor gave me permission to submit it late as a take home. At this time I was personally attempting to address what I was coming to consider my own self-pity and overdramatization, accompanied by a sense of alienation. So I had little patience for what I saw as the poet's self-indulgent whining about being an outsider while insisting on being a poet free from social responsibilities. The structure of the paper was similar to previous ones, setting up the problem in the opening sentences, then elaborating through details of character, events, and diction. I contrasted the play's dichotomous representation of two kinds of poet—one as a civic hero speaking to civic values and the other driven by personal needs to express—which is what Tasso elects, leading him to dwell on his personal suffering which he sees as unbearable. He distrusts those around him and makes selfish demands. I rather sided with the citizen role and responsibility which Tasso rejected. The professor's main comment was "I think you have too utilitarian a view of poetry to understand this play fully." Perhaps. At least I had the wisdom or personal distaste not to take the professor's follow-up course on Goethe's later works, as I did not see the point to carry on the fight further, particularly since the professor held all the cards.

In response to the teacher's marginal annotations calling into question my interpretations I wrote my own marginal counter-annotations, with a long argumentative note, though these were not shared with him. I couldn't be sympathetic with the poet's choice to be a self-expressive alienated outsider, no matter how I perceived my own history and perspectives as being different from others. This articulation of my emerging values here and in other papers (for example, the previous year's paper on Brecht's *Galileo*) can be seen as a precursor of my attraction to teaching as well as the rhetorical motives that drove my writing as a professional.

In the spring of my second year, nonetheless, I continued with another German course on 20th century poetry, predominantly Rilke. The first assignment I have in my files is an original sonnet, assigned so we could how understand how difficult it was to write one. I took as a challenge to overdo the constraints at the same time as covertly demonstrating my pique and contempt for the assignment. I wrote a pun-, anger- and insult-filled Joycean diatribe, in metric and stanzaic form, drawing on central conceits of eyesight and battle. The teacher seemed to enjoy it and either deliberately ignored or missed the insults in the title (Alphabitchyouary #2), and even more the acrostic insult of his name on the second letter of each line. Anyway, I had malicious fun in intricately designing this over a week, sharing it among my friends, learning a lot about rhythm, puns, emotional stance, tightness of phrasing, and discovery through fulfillment of form. So I guess in a way I fulfilled the intent of the assignment through my pique.

I appreciated the intricacy, rhythm/prosody, and formal tightness in Rilke's poetry. My first regular paper was an explication of Sonnet to Orpheus I, 15 on the experience of tasting an orange. I remember being methodical in preparing the analysis, making multiple carbon copies of the poem, and annotating each with a different element—prosody, imagery, experiential content, assonance and rhyme, etc. In overall form the paper was like the explications I had been doing in a number of classes, though a bit longer (6 pages) and more tightly written. I paid detailed attention to prosody and punctuation, trying to convey a sense of the dance of the poem that went along with the synesthetic and multisensual experience described, starting with an overview and then walking through the poem. According to instructions, the paper was preceded by an attached text of the poem. Then I repeated each line or cluster of lines before discussing each. After finishing this detailed commentary, my final comment related the last word of the poem providing closure to the command of the opening word (wartet. . . . füllt). I was getting pretty good at this kind of writing, especially when I found delight in the text analyzed and could whole-heartedly represent the experience.

My final paper for this course was a bit longer, 8 pages, but still in the same vein, demonstrating the thematic similarity of Keats' "Ode on a Grecian Urn" and Rilke's sonnet "Archäischer Torso Apollos," realized in the poetic technique of each. I opened with an overview of the shared theme of the two poems, but I added an additional paragraph offering historical evidence that Rilke probably had at most passing knowledge of the Keats poem. The third paragraph returns to the comparison, showing the similarity of the climactic conclusions, and pointing back to the several paths by which they got there. This launches over three pages of analysis of the unfolding of the Keats poem followed by about three pages of analysis of the Rilke poem, with a final page elaborating the similarity of the life-changing experiences of the urn and the statue mirrored in the perfection and power of the poems. I clearly was into intricacy and crafted aesthetic objects at this point, although I still had problems with the self-absorption and alienation of the aestheticized poet. I was influenced by new critical appreciation of paradoxes and intricacies to seek an intricate and witty kind of writing. The professor, as others had, asked for an unspecified more, but seemed happy with what he got. This was my first use of an extended comparative structure, which I was to use again in later papers.

These last two papers highlighted for me a pursuit of aesthetic perfection that would overwhelm the readers. The shimmering perfection would be both a pleasure in itself and would transform one through the intensity of experience. "Archäischer Torso Apollos" final words "du musst dein leben ändern" became a recurring motto for me. This pursuit embodied in the two Rilke and one Keats poems became embodied in my own growing ambitions as a writer. When I was to become a researcher in graduate school that was to be transformed into my goal of writing truth-poems, works of scholarship that through evidence would present readers with undeniable realities that they would need to accommodate into whatever ideological views they were committed to. As Nabokov said in his autobiography *Speak Memory*, in a phrase that would also become a motto for me: "Things once seen that cannot be unseen."

Chapter 10. University Crises and the Search for Meaning: Where Do I Belong?

When institutional forms asked me about my ethnic identity several decades ago, I started answering "academic," first as a joke, but with increasing conviction over time. The academic world is the one that I affiliate with, that has people I enjoy being around, that is the place where I feel at home. Whenever I have felt rootless in my travels, a visit to a local university campus would give me a sense of belonging. Even today, I prefer to travel not as a tourist or a leisured vacationer, but to be attached to an academic community—teaching, giving talks, or just hanging out at the snack bar. So when I reached the university as a student, it felt like finally I had found my home, finally leaving the houses and people I had grown up with, who had already been leaving my life. But this new academic home was also filled with troubles, turmoil, mood swings, and suicidal thoughts.

Family Troubles

After my parents' divorce I had only a bit of contact with my father, and even less after he moved to Chicago and remarried. He did not seem particularly supportive of my academic interests nor my attending an Ivy League school—he had graduated the public City College with a business degree, and looked towards more practical success. Years later, long after his death, after I had achieved economic comfort and was a successful department administrator, I had a feeling he would have approved. I did visit him and his second wife in Chicago briefly the summer of 1963, but because he was hospitalized with a heart attack, I spent most of the trip at the home of a college friend in that city. My father died a year and a half later at age 48. I flew out for his funeral, missing the final exams in the middle of my sophomore year. My professors kindly allowed me to skip or postpone final exams and papers. My emotions at the funeral and after were muted as he had not played much of a role in my life for many years, and certainly not since my parents' divorce when I was 13. I felt guilt for not feeling more, and sought father figures in the ensuing years, mostly among academic mentors.

My mother remained a haunting and unpleasant presence in my life, despite my trying to distance myself from her. That distancing process itself was a struggle that went on many years until her death in 1974 at age 58 and even beyond. During my college years I remained in contact with her and stayed in her apartment when I had no alternative. Although she had spent on herself my education funds, I still relied on occasional small checks from her. Following phone calls with her when she would repeat my father's alleged misdeeds and other conspiratorial theories, I would be deeply distressed about the world's cruelty and have suicidal thoughts or desires to retreat to a monastery. As I tried to express to some of my housemates my struggles and my intense dislike of my mother, none seemed to be sympathetic and I was accused by some as being overly dramatic and self-pitying. Only when I was to enter into therapy a few years later did I begin to gain some peace with this estrangement.

I still occasionally met with my brother until his death in 2003 at age 63, but the experience became increasingly unpleasant as he seemed to enjoy baiting me for my interests, my politics, even my savings. Since he was four and a half years older than me, his experience of the household was very different than mine and he had his own struggles.

Lost in the Academy

While these family pains weighed on me, particularly as an undergraduate, I never doubted that the academic world was the right place for me. I achieved enough appreciation and reward from some within the academic world to feel that here were at least some people like me. While I often enough ran into people who were conventional and narrow, I also was able to find people of fresh, unconventional, articulate views that helped expand my own vision and with whom I connected. This sense of academic belonging started during my high school experience in the Columbia Science Honors Program, and was confirmed by my years at Telluride House at Cornell. But life at Telluride also was troubling, ultimately leaving me again feeling the outsider, confused and rejected in my sense of difference, even though it was hard to imagine a future outside the academy. By the time of graduate school, I was very much at loose ends, which only became resolved when I started inner city teaching. In this chapter I want to recapture the state of turmoil in my undergraduate years and how that influenced my trajectory of writing development.

I have in previous chapters discussed my evaluations and unhappiness with physics, political science, and German literature. I have presented these as largely intellectual issues of articulating and assessing my personal values and seeing how they matched with the values I saw embedded in those fields. But that search for values started in my sense of displacement from my family—and the resulting need to find my own meanings and purposes in my life and life projects— accompanied with the need to find mentors and surrogate parents. That sense of alienation and rejection was also in the cultural and political air as the intellectual and countercultural malaise of the fifties moved into the radical politics of the sixties (one of my high school friends later commented the only thing that made him proud of the high school we went to was to discover Lenny Bruce had gone there twenty years before). That personal and societal alienation may also have increased the resistant style of my writing—deeply unsettled and unhappy, but often filtered through irony and parody.

This personal emotional stress played out during my college years among my friends at Telluride House. While I invested my greatest hope and greatest identification in this special place, I found the environment complex, troubling, and painful. Everyone in the house was idiosyncratic and quirky, as talented students tended to be, each seeking their own path. At first my own quest and troubles were accepted as a matter of course in such a quirky community. We were in constant dialog over our intellectual quests and fundamental values as well as the latest ideas we were getting from our courses and readings. Telluride was making early efforts to diversify, though still largely in token numbers. Women started to be resident in the house during my time there. Our affiliation with Deep Springs also brought some rural students from western states. Nonetheless, the house still was preponderately eastern, urban, and male, disproportionately from professional families. Yet for me it was a much more diverse and exciting environment than I had experienced in my suburban high school.

The house also gave special access to the campus resources. Many of the speakers brought to campus would be invited to receptions and dinners, and stayed in our guest rooms, so we got to hear more from them and could engage in dialog late at night and over breakfast. We lost the awe of being in their presence, and would ask challenging questions and engage in arguments—even with Nobelists. Of course, we often imagined we had gotten the better of them and told anecdotes to each other about our own purported cleverness, though we did appreciate when they had great comebacks to cut us down to size.

Madame Frances Perkins, the Secretary of Labor under Franklin Roosevelt and the first woman cabinet member, spent her final years in the house prior to her passing in May 1965. She was an inspiration to all of us. Another multi-year faculty guest during this same period, however, was much more problematic for me, though many of my fellow students found him a life-changing mentor. Alan Bloom's presence and his association with the political philosopher Leo Strauss became a defining feature of the house. His mentees came to dominate the leadership of the house and their views pervaded all the institutional and daily evaluation processes. Over the ensuing decades a number of them were to become part of the neo-con brain-trust influencing U.S. government policy. That cult commitment (as I soon came to see it) became a large problem for my existence in the house. Some of my close friends with already solidly formed identities in the arts and humanities could keep their distance from the Bloom coterie, viewing them as an interesting curiosity. But in my quest for values, identity, and community, I was torn between wanting to be accepted by the Bloom cult and following my own lights. I was not persuaded by what seemed to me to be unintelligible assumptions and an arrogant sense that they knew better than others how others should be governed. While questions they raised about the nature of governance, its relation to the way of life, and our responsibility as citizens were deeply engaging to me, I could not follow down their Straussian paths and their search for hidden wisdom of ancient philosophers. I was in fact quite baffled by how such apparently smart people could accept such doctrines, except perhaps that it fed the sense of personal superiority we all hung onto.

Over time they became disappointed with me and I with them. My personal emotional struggles became a further reason for me to be categorized as an unreliable outsider—a viewpoint fostered by Bloom for his own reasons, perhaps to create greater cohesion within his coterie. This rejection by Bloom was particularly painful, as I sought his approval even in my difference, as I quixotically hoped he would value my independence of thought. The result was that I was not elected to house leadership roles, and then I was rejected from association membership at the end of the second year (the usual point at which it was granted). Then unusually, they continued my house scholarship, along with another friend deemed not yet ready for association membership. As far as I know this was the first time people had been continued in the house without being granted membership after two years. I took the rejection emotionally very hard. I cried inconsolably for several days. I continued to live in the house the next fall, because of financial need as well as no other sense of social identity, but I became more of an outsider. I then left for Peace Corps training in the spring term, escaping a difficult situation while I continued to deal with my father's death, estrangement from my family, and disillusionment in my majors.

Hiatus and Return

The structured life of Peace Corps training gave me some equanimity. The press of constant language lessons and preparation for community work asked for little writing and left me little time or energy to pursue much of my own. But the program I was assigned to, to lead a YMCA in Venezuela, did not match my interests or even basic competence, and I realized I belonged back at the university. Nonetheless, the break did me good and allowed me to return somewhat cleansed of my most troubled perspectives. So before placement in Venezuela, I returned to Cornell and applied once again for Telluride membership and scholarship. Again I was rejected for association membership while still being awarded room and board scholarship. This was even more unusual than the previous time. But by this time I was hardened to it, and knew the scholarship and the friendships I maintained meant that I simply had to deal with what I perceived as an overall unwelcoming environment.

The three annual applications I submitted for renewal of the fellowship (and which I have copies of) track my unsettled emotional condition and search for values and identity over my college years. The questions each year asked me to reflect on my education, career objectives, community activities, practical work, readings, philosophic view, and the purpose of the association. In all the applications my diction was informal and personal, and the organization loose and associative as I tried to explain myself.

The application at the end of my first year was self-absorbed in my confusions, disillusionment with science, and need to find meaning. My voice was critical, but also self-abnegating, doubting my high school and work experience, and dubious about what I was learning at the university, although I relied on papers I had written for courses to articulate the important realizations I had come to.

Figure 10.1. A young seeker. Courtesy of Charles Bazerman.

After my second year I expressed my desire to take a year off from college, but recognized the constraint of the draft. My personal and life philosophy essays discussed my confusion about the directions of my life, including rejection of physics. I questioned the discipline's objectifying perspective and the focus far from daily life. I expressed a desire to explore the world and follow my "romantic" impulse, to find out how life might be different elsewhere. I have a brief discussion of my participation in the drama club but dismiss its importance, calling it just fun. My work the previous summer as a counselor in a camp for inner city children I saw as more meaningful, revealing the damage poverty had on the children. Trying to understand the children was the first seed of what was to become a calling a few years later. I do mention a non-classroom text—Harrington's *The Other America*. But my essay on my reading was a literature paper on Restoration comedy. This was the first application which was rejected for association membership, to my deep dismay.

I completed the third application just after returning from Peace Corps training. Two papers from my course on dramatic literature discussed in the next chapter were the center of my application. I introduced these papers as part of my formulating a new attitude of acceptance towards life, explaining how they helped me frame new perspectives which I kept thinking about during my time away from school, and how it took me months to understand the implications of what I had realized through writing these papers. My essay on practical work experience discussed working with underprivileged children—as a camp counselor, as a Head Start assistant teacher, and during my Peace Corps training. From these experiences I learned that local needs, local perceptions, and local control were crucial and that mutual understanding, cultural relativity, and individual experiences and perspectives presented challenges to collaboration. Coming in with good intentions was quixotic and you needed to work with what people wanted. Although I did not recognize it at the time, this was setting up attitudes, values, and perspectives that would lead me to teaching and to the orientations I would have toward student development, local control, and phenomenological diversity. It was also distancing myself further from the budding philosopher-kings in the house who thought they knew what was best for large categories of others.

These three applications were written simply, with little attempt at crafted wit, but by the third I had clear standpoint and voice telling a coherent story from a coherent standpoint rather than from the self-abnegating, doubt-filled, and confused stance with broken sentences and broken narrative in the earlier ones. Interestingly though, in the third, I talked at one point of myself in third person, to describe my meanderings—literally putting myself in perspective and giving an account of this character.

In my last year at the house, my personal journey took another turn (discussed at the end of the next chapter) which allowed me to live in the house while distancing myself from the culture and values that pervaded it. Yet, for years, the house would recurrently appear in my dreams every time I had an intense intellectual experience. As painful as my years at Telluride were, they were a kind of refiner's fire that elicited more coherent reasoning, detailed precision, and higher standards of ethical and civic engagement. Those years fostered a seriousness of purpose and desire to contribute, driving professional commitments and writing to follow.

Personal Struggles, Building Reflective Strength, and Professional Voice

Why are these personal struggles relevant to understanding my writing development? First, after years of growing complexity in my writing which I continued working on in some academic work, I was developing a simple, direct voice that could tell a coherent narrative about my feelings and values. I was to mobilize this style increasingly throughout my career—to communicate with students, in my textbooks, and administrative documents. I was also in a few years to use this voice during a period of writing poetry and fiction narratives, which in turn prepared me for some historical and other qualitative narratives, as well as autobiographical reflections and attempts to make my theory as transparent as I could.

In dealing with these challenges, I also developed a habit of narrating and reflecting on what I was doing and where I was going. I was starting to articulate to myself and others a coherent story about who I was, what I valued, and the kinds of actions that made sense to me. This was to guide me in my later choices and projects no matter how arcane they may have seemed to others. Later, as my pedagogy and research developed, I was to write a string of texts that attempted to explain the coherence and meaning in my work, integrating the relation among my research, my experience, and my teaching. I kept trying to explain to others the relation I found in the parts of my work, which in part would lead me to the kinds of theorizing I discuss in Chapter 23.

I was also building strength and confidence in expressing what I saw despite how others might evaluate what I wrote. I became willing to assert what evidence, reason, and compassion showed me. I stopped looking for authoritative wisdom but became willing to accept whatever extended my vision and showed me light through the murkiness of difficult times. I would like to think during these times I began to open myself up to an awareness of others, their perspectives, their needs, and their struggles. This too has guided my writing in the subjects I take on, and in the stance I take towards the people I discuss and the people I communicate with. Perhaps you will see these themes reverberating through the other chapters of this book, where I attribute like developments to other experiences and causes, but I believe they rest on the personal struggles that lay beneath them all. For several years these lines from Wordsworth kept running through my mind: "A deep distress hath humanized my soul" (Elegiac Stanzas Suggested by a Picture of Peele Castle in a Storm, Painted by Sir George Beaumont, 1807).

When I first approached writing this chapter, I thought it would be a trauma narrative, to explain the confusions and stresses I felt and how that was connected to my writing in college. But now I see it as a narrative of writing my way out of the trauma into a positive trajectory for my later writing life. It helped me make sense of my experience and allowed me to face the future. In doing so, my writing gained a simplicity and focus that made possible more complex projects. These years crystallized a commitment to writing as a way of life. The next chapter, which covers academic work just before and after my hiatus makes a bit more visible how the academic analytic transformations went hand in hand with this more personal formulation of consciousness.

Chapter 11. Dramatic Literature, Dramatic Performance, and the Drama of Life: Casting About for Meanings

I had frequented New York theater from early adolescence, with a special attachment to musical comedy, Gilbert and Sullivan's sly operettas, and then Brecht's plays of social critique. As an adolescent, I had my first taste of (bad) acting when I went to an arts camp. During my first year at Cornell, I had small roles in campus productions. These earlier experiences intersected with my writing in a series of courses taught by a newly-minted professor Scott McMillin. He asked us to think of play scripts as only preliminary sketches for actual stage performances within specific sociohistorical moments, witnessed by audiences located in time and place. I was excited by his perspectives more than what I had found in other literature courses, where meaning began and ended with the text. McMillin expanded my ways of looking at drama, at all writing, at all art, and all life, even as he kept careful scholarly focus on the works themselves. At least for me. As for him, I doubt he thought of himself as a writing teacher or a life coach or philosophic mentor; he only talked about the theater, specific plays, specific productions, and how they could be most fully understood.

As I now reread his comments on my papers, I see ideas that would only become familiar in literature departments in following decades, but he never was explicit about his theoretical sources, nor did I ever hear his views on anything beyond the analysis of the works under study (even when I read his later critical works). Yet absorbing his perspectives and writing from them in his class reverberated throughout my understanding of the world and a quest for a meaningful life. I see in my papers for the three undergraduate courses I took with him ideas and analytic perspectives that gave a legitimacy, focus, and systematic method to the ill-formed ideological criticisms I was making in other courses, rejecting the stances of particular literary works. The perspectives nurtured by this professor continued to reverberate throughout the remainder of my schooling and my professional life as I moved from the study of literature to literacy and its teaching.

The World's a Play

In the fall of my third year, on the recommendation of a friend, I took Professor McMillin's course on comparative contemporary drama, from Ibsen and Chekhov through Brecht and Pirandello. The first paper (about 1500 words) was an analysis of a single character, in the context of the unfolding of the play. My analysis of Madame Ranevskaya in Chekhov's *The Cherry Orchard* focuses on a single scene as iconic. I think I had adapted the idea of an iconic moment from a previous course on Chaucer, where the professor had lectured on the icon or emblem as a prominent device in "The Knight's Tale." In this paper on *The Cherry Orchard* I did not explicitly use the term iconic, but I distinctly remember thinking about using the device to focus on one scene as emblematic of the whole work. I used the explication techniques I had learned in close reading of poems, but here I placed the words within the unfolding dramatic actions and dialogue located within the social context of the play's production. I also looked at the psychological motives behind the lines, standard practice in acting. In my final evaluation of the character, I identified with Ranevskaya's acceptance of human weakness and her consequent modesty and gentleness. Professor McMillin, however, in his comments asked me to pursue the analysis of the key speeches in greater detail, which I was to do in the final paper of the term.

The second paper (about 1000 words) again looked at specific scenes, but focusing on secondary characters rather than the protagonists in Shaw's *Major Barbara* and Brecht's *Good Woman of Szechuan*. The paper compared the working-class characters in both plays to investigate the revolutionary stances of the two authors as embodied in dramatic structure. This was a bit more sophisticated dramaturgical approach. I first discussed Shaw's proletarians, suffering but self-aware, leading their best lives under the circumstances, and then turned to Brecht's paupers, who have less class consciousness and more veniality. I end with two long paragraphs comparing the political programs posed by each author, and the play form—semi-realistic comedy vs. epic theater invoking alienation and audience critical reflection. McMillin's comments directed me towards reconsidering my naive invocation of "basics" as separate from form; now I would say he was trying to get me to confront essentialism and recognize that what we view as material is experienced ideologically through systems of meaning. At the time, I was not ready to fully understand what he was driving at, though my final paper for the term does take some further steps in this direction.

The final assignment was to construct a four-play repertory season and provide a rationale. The paper I wrote (around 2500 words) was deeply personally meaningful at the time and for a long time after. In retrospect I see it as the start of a set of positive commitments, beginning with my entering Peace Corps training the next term and ultimately to the teaching of writing and understanding how writing transforms the world. I still find this paper moving and eloquent of my state of mind. I remember the process of writing this paper as almost in a trance. I became exhausted after writing each part, falling asleep in the middle of the day, waking only for meals and writing another paragraph or two, then immediately falling back into sleep for more hours, then dragging myself up, writing a bit more, then falling back into sleep. This went on for several days, as though I were in a deep and exhausting meditation, floating in and out of a dream, but a dream so drugged I had no memory except the impulse to take the next step of the journey. This was the kind of experience vatic priests must have had when they felt the words come from elsewhere but channeled through them, knocking them down, knocking them out. Reading and writing until exhaustion is something that has in fact been part of my process, often falling asleep over my typewriter or over my books in the library and then upon waking, having a sense of what to write next—but never again to this extreme.

I do not know how much the tight sentences and moral vision were a product of the psychological crisis that had been building—as I broke from my dysfunctional family, as I questioned my personality and identity, as I looked for acceptance and meaning in the world and my actions. But I could see that this also was a product of my intellectual journey, bringing together pieces from my earlier papers into a more integrated vision. Perhaps my emotional and intellectual journeys were the same thing. That is, I had been using writing to figure out the world, my place in it, my values, my relations to others—what was important and how I felt about things. In doing so I was forming a new identity and way of being in the world, one that became more coherent at this moment and that became worked out in the following years as I formed new relationships, new responses to others, new interactions, and new goals. I remember thinking around this time, particularly around this paper, that it took time—even months or years to understand what I had written and what it meant in life. I awoke from the dream with a new direction and new sense of self.

Twenty years later James Pennebaker was to start the research that led him to understand the powerful effect of trauma writing, which he was eventually to attribute in part to allowing the writer to confront distressing events by building a coherent story one could live with (e.g., Pennebaker & Chung, 2007). Around 2000 when a graduate student introduced me to Pennebaker's work establishing that trauma writing could even improve our immune system, blood counts, health outcomes, and other biological markers, I recognized from my experiences the implication that writing could reach down into the core organization of ourselves and anxiety systems, and thus could influence the way we perceived and responded to the world around us. This paper for an undergraduate course brought together a deep and comprehensive story about the world and my life which I had been struggling with since high school. It crystallized an important reorganization in my life.

The paper designing the four-play repertory season started with a thematic overview as with other papers, but this introduction stretched across four long paragraphs (almost three pages). Not until the fourth paragraph did I get to the core point, that these plays raised the fundamental question of the forms of life in which we found ourselves or chose to live. This form of life guided our relations, and our understanding how to be and how to respond to others' being. The first three paragraphs built on the syntactic pattern of paradox, contradiction, negation—not this, but that—that had pervaded much of my earlier writing. Here, however, I was arguing with my own earlier approaches to drama, which had attempted to extract meanings or build a critical, alienated point of view, or even assert a superior moral framework. By the third paragraph I was transitioning to how I came to a deeper experience of each of the four plays that were in this repertory, even though I had previously approached them in one of the ways I now rejected. In the fourth paragraph I landed on my new perspective, which I then elaborated in the remainder of the paper through discussion of each of the plays—Beckett's *Waiting for Godot*, Pirandello's *Six Characters in Search of an Author*, Brecht's *Mother Courage*, and Chekhov's *The Cherry Orchard*. I considered the dilemmas, stances, situations, and actions of the characters in relation to the frames provided by the playwrights and in the consequent relations established with the audiences. The discussion, register, and style were almost philosophical, in the manner of Kierkegaard and similar authors I was reading at the time. The structures of the plays were analyzed to reveal the set of assumptions that framed the actions and how these assumptions directed the meanings to be found by the characters, or which they refused as they came to understand the worlds they were caught in. A number of my sentences reached towards terse, rhythmic assertiveness, set against longer, slower moving discursive passages. The paper ended with a paradoxical instability between the tolerant resigned acceptance of Chekhov's Madame Ranevskaya who appreciates the declining world as it is, recognizing the sad fateful delusions of the other characters, and Brecht's assertive rejection in *Mother Courage* of the illusory world the characters cannot see beyond: "We live, then, in hope of a revolution, but despairing it will ever come."

McMillin's few comments were appreciative, suggesting a few places I could have confronted the paradoxes even more strongly. His final comment was: "A+ Right. You are if you think you are. I am." At the moment, and even now, this support was powerfully meaningful to me. At that time, it was a sign that I was absorbing his perspective and that he recognized it, and in so doing he understood and approved of my journey. Now I see his comments as a reminder of his profound acceptance, understanding, and influence for me. After I withdrew my enrollment for the spring semester, passing through New York City on my way to Peace Corps training, I attended the latest avant-garde hit *Marat/Sade*. I wrote a long letter to Professor McMillin, following up on the paper, pondering the ironic vision of life in this play—but never mailed it.

Returning to McMillin's World

After returning to Cornell from Peace Corps training, I talked a lot about the perspective I was gaining, and by that, I think I meant something like the stance I had developed in the previously discussed paper. That final year I took two more courses from this professor who was providing me the supportive space and ideas to work through my new vision—in the fall a survey of British drama, and in the spring a specialized course on Elizabethan revenge tragedy. My first paper in the fall was on the opening of Marlowe's *Dr. Faustus* (about 2000 words), raising the same issue that I had pursued in my longer paper the previous fall—of a character caught in or escaping from the imposed dramatic world. I underspecified the concept of ritual, although that was the central concept of the paper and had to do with the question of position within structure or form. That failure was commented on by the professor, though he agreed with the gist. This paper begins by noting the negations of the play's prologue, in contrast to the more typical prologue that set the scene. Rather than defining a context, it is denying a context. I note Faustus' declassee birth, and his lack of institutional rise, leaving him an outsider. I follow his sequence of thoughts and rejections of the opening scene as he discards the books of his disciplines, ending with philosophy and medicine. He does not finish sentences he reads as he cannot engage with the facts of his mortal existence. He turns to magic. I then make some brief, hand-waving comparisons with the ending, but do not examine it in detail, nor any of the moments between the middle and the end. McMillin's comments indicate that my lack of attention to the end limited my understanding of the play and Marlowe's presentation of Faustus. Coordinately he pointed to my ill-defined use of the terms "ritual position" and "external structures" which I rely on in my argument. He notes "you seem to be using these terms out of some private concern, and you need to give them full public meaning." Here as elsewhere his comments identify and challenge me on core issues to gain theoretical clarity. He, as always, was directly on target—and in ways even more than he could know, as that year, despite my religious skepticism I was experimenting with observing Jewish Law under the guidance of a young orthodox rabbi who was also a graduate student in philosophy. Even this adventure in religious practice, directed by the structures of Halakah, can be seen as influenced by ideas about the organizing force of forms to give motive, as I will explain at the end of this chapter.

The next paper on Beaumont and Fletcher's transgressively comic *The Knight of Burning Pestle* started out as a reflection on conventionality and the need to accept and understand the conventionality of the theater and the particular form of theater being watched—the private elite theater, in contrast to the more public, multi-class Globe. After two pages I applied this reflection to consider how the elite audience of *The Knight of Burning Pestle* would have viewed the conventions of the play and the attitudes towards the working-class characters who disrupt the play within a play, *The London Merchant*. The play within the play is vapid, not even living up to expectations of romantic comedy, having nitwits as characters, and thus would be viewed by the audience more as a burlesque than even a parody, while making fun of the middle-class morality enacted. I examine the stolid citizen and wife (placed among the audience) who view the play as bad because they do not understand the conventions of romantic love nor do they understand the difference between actors and their roles. They view their apprentice Ralph who is acting as the knight as an actual knight, in real danger, so they yell out with a warning at a melodramatic moment. While my analysis delights in the madness of the conflicting and collapsing conventions, the actual audience didn't enjoy it, which I explain as the discomfort of how the play positions them, recognizing their class positions and disdain for others. The teacher comments how the opening pages of the paper were a bit routine as I attempted to respond to his previous request for greater conceptual clarity, but I did succeed in being explicit and clear in my analytical ideas. Once I got into the analysis of the play, the characters, and the position of the audience, he commented that "it's hard to imagine how anything more valid and interesting could be said about the play." In addition to the pride and confidence this comment gave me, it also reconfirmed that I was absorbing his way of looking at things and forming arguments.

The final paper (about 3000 words) was again a four-play repertoire with a rationale. I focus on the prologues and endings of all the plays, following the analytical strategy I had tried with *Doctor Faustus*, but focusing on the relation formed with the audience. Prologues I considered as bringing the audience from their daily lives into the world the playwright was creating. The endings sent them back out again into their social worlds with directions about how they should remember the play and how it might relate to their post-theater lives. I chose plays from four different periods—Jonson's *Epicoene*, Sheridan's *The Country Wife*, Wycherly's *Way of the World*, and Shaw's *Man and Superman*. Each established a different presence for the author and different ways for the audience to interact with the play's events and characters. Jonson, I claimed, teases the audience about the relation of the play to life, but then says it is to be taken only as a fictional entertainment. I argued Sheridan suggests societal roles are as theatrical as on the stage, and ends with a scourging of the males in the audience, casting Restoration life as much as a game of upmanship as the theater. Wycherly takes that stance a step further in seeing life and theater as artifice. I end with the observation that modern realistic theater, in a way is freed for greater fictiveness and removal from the everyday world of the audience, even as it removes theatrical prologues and epilogues that mediate the relation to life. The connection to the world is through the ideas or perspective of the author, which Shaw elaborates in non-theatrical print commentaries.

In reading this paper now I am not convinced of all the parts of the argument and I see it forced in some of its interpretations, especially by an attempt to construct a neat historical sequence. The professor's comments indicate he also was not convinced by some of my interpretations and patterns, though he thought the topic was a good one and some of the observations were on target. The paper also had more than the usual number of typos and syntactic slippages, and even stylistically cumbersome sentences—which the careful reading by the professor caught. All this indicates this paper was not fully worked out—whether this was because of time pressures with other papers due, because I was still working the ideas out, the ideas were just unworkable, or I was just sloppy, I don't know. But from the point of view of my constructing a diachronic argument of genre and the relations of author, readers and content, this paper at least represents an early attempt at the kind of historical argument about changing authorial stance and relations to audience I was to use later in my career.

From my final course with McMillin on Elizabethan revenge tragedies, I have only a midterm paper in my files. I vaguely remember it was a practice at that time to excuse graduating seniors from final papers, but perhaps I wrote one and never collected the comments. The 3000-word paper on Webster's *The White Devil* took the opening word "banished" as defining the experience of the world. As I had done previously, I considered how the audience was brought into the world of the play—in this case by the single opening word "Banished." This word becomes thematic in the displacement and ambiguity in the characters, the lack of a central character, the fluidity of settings and scenes, the evaporation of a moral center, and the audience experience of conflicting impulses, uncomfortable voyeurism, and repulsion against shallow and reprehensible characters. Yet the persistent attraction of lust and voyeurism keeps the audience engaged, as it engulfs and destroys all the other relations.

The paper was structured around the opening scene, which it analyzed in some detail. I then considered disruptive displacement later in the play. Much of the paper is a theoretical expansion and explanation of how displacement creates an uncomfortably ambiguous experience of lust and voyeurism. I ended with the one character, Vittoria, who cuts through all the displacement by denying the pervasive troubling tensions, providing an amoral center and clarity: "Ha, Whore, what is that?" McMillin in his extensive comments throughout the paper liked where my analysis was going and the insights I offered about the play, but he persistently pushed for greater conceptual clarity and precision, more detailed analysis at key moments to elaborate ideas, further rationale for some assumptions, and more attention to Jacobean conventions. So while he liked my paper, as elsewhere he kept pushing me to develop my ideas further, while providing guidance as to where that development might go.

Transitions in My Writing and My Self

This experience with McMillin marks another juncture in my journey as a writer. In my primary and secondary school years, I learned to play with language, discovered how to explore my feelings and values, and developed viewpoints. I learned to use some standard forms, work with sources and evidence, make judgments, and build basic arguments. These are the typical things we as writing teachers hope for in writing education. In my first years as an undergraduate, I then learned the preferred academic genres of the time, particularly literary explication, fulfilling the genres' expectations, and exploring their expressive potential. I learned to elaborate arguments and pursue them in greater objectivity and public persuasiveness with detailed analysis and evidence. My writing became longer and more intellectually sophisticated, able to incorporate varied kinds and structures of arguments with their differing entailments for their elaboration. As I learned to project my emotional and personal needs into academic questions and goals, I was able to build an academic voice and identity that distanced me from the troubles of my family. But I also ran into some roadblocks as I did not always feel in sympathy with my studies and I had no coherent standpoint from which

I could argue. Rather I bristled in ad hoc resistance to those texts and teachers that didn't make sense to me, or didn't fit with what I was perceiving and how I was developing. I did not yet have a compelling vision of the relation between the represented world of texts (whether in science or art) and the experienced world by which I could gain some coherence of understanding.

McMillin's courses in drama and his rigorous challenges to my nascent observations, however, started to give me an intellectual orientation I could live with, a way of understanding life as drama, given meaning by the frames that organized our relations, activities, and values. Within those frames we had possibilities of understanding and action that could transform our relations and emotions, and even transform the frames themselves. Yet this understanding did not yet provide me the concrete means of forming social relationships and enacting daily life that would grant life satisfactions. Coping with family and peer traumas left me increasingly anomic, even as it had forced me to question my values, relationships, and place in life. This reevaluation started to crystallize under McMillin's tutelage, but personally I was still adrift. The structured life of Peace Corps training had provided some stability and relieved some daily anxiety, but when I found I did not fit the program I was in, I again did not know quite what to do other than return to school and Telluride, under the cloud of both the draft and financial exigencies. But in the house, which had been the center of my social world and identity, I had been rejected and I felt again the outsider. I was looking for something that would provide me community and structure that I could connect with.

Seeking a Life Order

So, despite my explicit and continuing secular atheism and distance from religious identity (though maintaining some cultural affinity), I was tempted by the argument that one could never understand belief from the outside and that only by following Jewish law and living an observant life, could one come to understand religious commitment and emotions. During my senior year I first found my way to the soft-core campus Hillel, to which I reacted with the same distaste I had to my family's congregation as an early adolescent. But I soon connected with a more intellectually stimulating orthodox rabbi who was a doctoral student in philosophy. In addition to my regular coursework I began studying Hebrew again, was brought into the first stage of Talmudic study, and began to observe as much of the religious laws as I could comprehend and manage. And I spent Shabbos regularly with the rabbi's family.

This new way of life had the additional advantage of creating an identity of difference in the house, allowing me to avoid the communal meals and eat kosher TV dinners in my room. I found a way to have the financial support of the house, maintain a few friendships I still had, but yet remove myself from being a "member" of the house and needing to find validation within the intellectual world of the house. I was able to restructure the conditions and relations of my life without radically adjusting the material conditions of going to college or disrupting my scholarship arrangements. This religious excursion was a kind of odd consequence of the views I had been developing with McMillin, though I would hardly blame him for this. It was my clumsy attempt to put into practice the idea of having an order or structure that would provide life meanings.

I remained skeptical about the underlying faith that would justify this way of life, though I was desperate to discover transcendence. I was particularly moved by the fervent appeal in the liturgy to "god of my fathers," hoping to find a sense of tribal connection through the urgency of the thrice-daily prayer. I read a bit in mysticism and even visited and danced all night with Chassidim (whom I associated with my Eastern European forbears), and liked the idea of it, even if I never could understand it or feel it. I made a pilgrimage to the rabbi of my rabbi and visited other sites of religious study in the more rational tradition he came from. I was carried forward by the emotional well-being offered by my young rabbi and his family, feeling the warmth of the family celebrations. Yet I never felt any stirrings of belief and faith, never overcame skepticism, nor connected to the generations of fathers and their god. Within a day of leaving campus after graduation I left it all behind. I awoke as from a dream, realizing it was not a life that made sense in the world I lived in, and I was not moved enough to join a sequestered world of the faithful. After a day of tumbled thoughts and images as I walked around New York City, I stopped at a street cart to buy a non-kosher hot dog. The first bite marked the end of the year-long experiment.

One practical, but odd consequence of this religious chapter for my writing life was my choice of graduate school, affecting the programs and mentoring faculty I would encounter. I had applied to several graduate programs in literature (again because of the draft I felt there were few other options) and received some fellowship offers. I chose Brandeis over another more prestigious university, in part because I felt the atmosphere and expectations of the other colder and removed from my interests, but also because Brandeis had much more appetizing kosher food options, which was still important to me when I had to make the choice, but meant nothing to me by the time I got there. I still think it was a lucky choice, for reasons I will elaborate in later chapters. Such are some accidents of life that also influence writing development.

Another consequence of the year's sojourn into orthodoxy was that it added a bit to my scriptural and Talmudic knowledge and interpretive procedures (though my Hebrew never got very far). Shards of Jewish knowledge and scriptural prosody have crept into my writing from time to time. I also started to appreciate a bit more the phenomenology of different historically emerged religions, as forms of consciousness and belief were integrated with forms of life, relationships, and community—all associated with particular emotions, values, and affiliations. This phenomenological conjunction would enter into my understanding of writing and activity systems and the relationship of perceptions, meanings, and ideology with those forms of activity. And, of course, in Judaism as much as any religion, these phenomenological conjunctions found their grounding in the study and adherence to sacred texts. As I later came to understand, literacy was infrastructural for complex societies.

Even as I came to appreciate these different ways of life, while rejecting them as mine, I no longer felt the need to identify as an atheist. Atheism seemed to exist in a dialectic of opposition in which I was no longer caught. Religion and belief were no longer a question to which I needed an assertive answer. I lived in this world. This also meant, however, that I needed to understand human sociality and community in realistic ways without any of the supernatural explanations for the good that others might invoke.

This sojourn and its end also taught me that I had better ways to live out the insights and elaboration of ideas about structure and life than simply trying to impose something on myself or latch onto other people's structures. I once again was off to pursue my own path.

Chapter 12. Playing Out the Vision: Other Writing About Literature in the Senior Year

While I was working through the insights gained from my studies with Scott McMillin and exploring orthodox Judaism, I continued to complete the requirements for an English major. Given I had taken such an array of courses for different majors previously, and also took a term off for Peace Corps training, during my last year I took mostly literature course in order to fulfill graduation requirements. I now had enough direction, context, and motivation to enter into my studies energetically, and I was able to graduate within the top 5% of my class despite my wanderings in the middle years. During this final year, I continued to grow as a writer through the extensive assignments in my courses and in interaction with the literature I was writing about, but I was mostly drawing on the insights gleaned from McMillin and my religious adventure rather than gaining much from other instructors who at best were serving as competent guides through the texts I read for their courses. Some other instructors served more as foils to react against.

Shakespeare's Orders and Disorders

To amass the credits for graduation (as well as to quickly leave my mother's apartment) upon leaving the Peace Corps I almost immediately went back to Cornell, rented a room in a shared apartment for the summer, took up a short-term job, and enrolled in summer school. Hoping to continue my engagement with drama, I took a course on Shakespeare's history plays. Drawing on the ideas from the previous drama course, I found Shakespeare particularly interesting in the way he had structured his plays similarly across tragedies, Greenwood comedies, and the late romances. The professor, however, I found dull, and he gave no guidance or direction for the two assigned papers.

I wrote two linked papers on the three *Henry VI* plays and *Richard III* as growing out of and contrasting with those earlier plays of the cycle. The argument stretched across both lengthy papers, and I clearly identified the first paper as a preliminary part of an argument which would not be completed until the second. I began the first with a discussion of two dichotomous readings of *Richard III* which had dominated criticism, one a traditionalist view that the play's end marked the conquering of evil to reestablish royal order, and the other a nihilist modern view, valorizing Richard's disruptive amorality. I suggested that both were true, which my reading of the full cycle would show. In the first paper I focused on the patterned search for order in the Henry plays, expressed in ritualistic repetition and rhythms, and in the second I elaborated the amoral disruptiveness of Richard, rising to power through transgression against those seeking conventional order. His violent action was undergirded by his awareness of appearances, dissembling, and a witty tongue that turned the words of the conventional against themselves. I then traced his decline and deterioration as he became a victim to the reassertion of order at the end of the play. From my early adolescence, I loved this play, identifying with the disruptive transgressiveness of Richard, so I was predisposed to take the modernist, nihilist reading of the play. What was new for me was positioning this within the demands for order and understanding the self-destructiveness of Richard's actions leading to loss of control and power, leaving him weak and isolated.

The papers were related as two chronological, but overlapping stories—the first of the imposition of ritual order and the second of disruptive amorality. My analysis flashed forward and backward to signal themes or recoup earlier orders. I returned to reinterpret earlier scenes in light of the new dimensions the later argument has added. So the two papers together formed a whole, with different rhythms and foci in different sections to unpack the differences among the different parts of the cycle. The paper's prose has balanced sentences, paradoxical turns, rhythmed syntax and careful observations, as I had learned were expected of literature majors. The professor of this course made a few comments (such as disagreeing over the intent of a critic I cite), but there is nothing that led me to look further into my argument or think through ideas or even sentences where he suggested that I straighten out intentionally stressed syntax.

A Void

The fall of the senior year I took a thematic criticism course on the void, a specialty of the professor, who was then working on a book on the theme. He lectured with no discussion as far as I remember, though the room was only modestly sized. We were given no particular prompts nor assigned texts nor any other limitation, and we were told only to submit any combination of papers totaling 25 pages. I was not much motivated or excited by his lectures and was hard pressed to find something to write about. The unfocused assignment tacitly invited submitting work we had prepared for any other course—which is what I did for 15 of the 25 pages. While the ethics of this were questionable, he didn't proscribe this double submission nor did he seem to care—and I was far from the only one in this class taking this option. One new paper I did write described the comic anti-masque figures in a series of Ben Jonson's masques, showing how these figures of disorder increasingly took over the presentations. This paper, almost a retelling of a series of jokes, pursued a curiosity about some masques I became aware of in McMillin's survey of British drama, and was organized much as the sequential interpretation of plays in a repertoire as McMillin had assigned. The last paper was something I pulled out of the air at the last minute to make up the last few required pages, an analysis of the principles, ideology, and class attitudes revealed in one of Bacon's minor essays on architecture, which I then connected to themes in some of his better-known essays. This used the icon device I had used previously, in seeing the larger themes in the smaller object. As well, ideological analysis was something that I took from McMillin's courses.

In this class, however, the professor's comments were brief and perfunctory, suggesting that he didn't read the papers very carefully, sometimes missing the point entirely and at other times indicating he was not expert in the period of the literature discussed, although he did not restrict the assignment to any literary period or region. His grade on each was coupled with the number of pages each paper contributed to meeting the required total. One thing I did learn from this experience was that not all literary scholars and critics shared the same knowledge, nor did they have the same perspectives or evaluative criteria, as this professor's brief comments on one of the papers did not recognize some historical facts I had relied on, and which were highlighted in the other course. A deeper version of this realization was that I was writing papers for specific professors within the intellectual worlds being built within their courses, and readers from outside that space would not share the same orientation, response, or even knowledge of basic facts.

Writing Without Stress

That fall I also took a comparative literature course on Greek classics in translation. Every week we needed to write a short paper (usually 500–800 words) on the week's assigned readings. We would then would read our papers aloud in class. The assignments were narrowly aimed to familiarize us with background historical scholarship and classical literary theory such as from Aristotle or later in the term to comment on the plays and poems we read. The professor, a senior classicist, said little in class or in response to our papers, though he did provide some written feedback, particularly on helping me understand Aristotle's *Poetics* at the beginning of the course. We then had to submit all the papers in a portfolio at the end of the course. I remember being disappointed that he was not delivering the brilliance we expected from our professors, but he did put the responsibility on us, letting the readings transmit the content to us. This course, nonetheless, convinced me I could write papers on demand without turmoil. I often wrote the papers hastily, making only a few handwritten proofreading corrections at the last minute. The paragraphing was not thought through and was often lengthy, but I could churn the papers out and was proud of it. In retrospect it also made me listen to myself reading aloud my own writing to my classmates—and to listen to my peers and see what they were up to. In some ways this pedagogy was in line with some later recommendations from the composition world, and it certainly was a change of pace from the one-way lecture pedagogy that dominated most of my classes.

The first assignment for this course that was more than reading notes was an essay on Odysseus's amorality (at least by modern standards), noting through a series of incidents his lack of concern for life of others, and the egoism of his actions. The essay is in the form of an argument over values, and bears some relation to my earlier essays rejecting perspectives of other authors. But here the professor only comments "well-observed," taking a scholarly distance from the values and viewpoint of the text. An essay comparing Aristotle's, Theophrastus', and Platon's characters, considers the limits and situational appropriateness of stereotypic representations; there was no comment here nor for most of the rest of the term, not even noting misspellings. My essay on the *Illiad* considered the preciseness of the small stories and personal squabbles within the diffuseness of the large story and currents in the conflict. The essay on Hesiod's *Works and Days* examined his pervasive presence and ethos as a teacher, and his admonishment of his flagging student-audience and his delinquent brother. The paper on the anonymous Homeric hymns considered the anthropomorphism of the gods, their motivating passions, and their intermingling among mortals. Consideration of one of Pindar's Olympian odes looked at how he placed himself and the Olympic contenders in human and divine hierarchies. The paper on the *Oresteia* trilogy evaluated the impact of the audience's foreknowledge and the dramatic display of bodies on the *ekkyklema* (a piece of theatrical machinery rolled onto stage) at the climax of the first two plays. I argued that the dread that pervades all three plays sets up the civic resolution of the third, where the dread extended beyond the fate of the characters to the fate of the city. The next paper compared the *Elektra* plays by Aeschylus, Sophocles, and Euripides, considering the situation, staging and motives and themes surrounding the murder scene in each. The paper on *Oedipus* examined how his initial political identity is overcome by his personal story and psychological transformation, which led me to consider how the state was seen as an extension of the king. Here (as in a number of papers that summer and fall) I contemplated the egotism and hubris of the characters, something that I had been working to put to rest in myself. In the final paper on Euripides' *The Bacchae*, I commented on the madness of the play, the comic absurdity of the stage events, and the delusional isolation of the characters, each in their own mental world. This set up a discussion of the central mad divide between Dionysus and Pentheus—finding the tragedy in the inability of the gods and man to talk to each other—leading to heightening conflict in their madness. The influence of McMillin is evident and manifold in all the papers on Greek drama.

Trying to Comprehend Milton's Grand Vision

The papers for the final course that term on Milton showed a care and intensity that I did not give the classics course. The first five-page paper on the opening lines of Lycidas presented the poem as a search for order. The larger theme and the trajectory of the whole poem were sympathetically laid out in the opening two paragraphs, and then I returned to the opening to walk through a line-by-line explication, focusing on the poet's distress in the compelled picking of berries and dolorous description of an action out of order, too early, unripe. King's death is withheld to line 8, when it too is described as a disruption of nature. I ended with the start of a new broader cycle of expanding disintegration in line 10. This paper reflects the skills I had developed in structuring a close reading, looking at many details, and using openings as a way of creating the world and problematic of the work revealed in multiple dimensions—theme, prosody, imagery, action, and structural movement. The teacher commented on two statements and corrected a couple of comments, but mostly thought it was "artfully done."

The next five-page paper on Comus did not go so well. The theme I pursued was shallower as I walked through the poem pedestrianly, showing that every time Comus offered a delight it was undercut. I remember not being sympathetic to the poem, but I was also aware the professor was deeply committed to Milton's world view. I found it hard to say much interesting on the masque without getting into the kind of conflict that occurred in the Goethe course. I remember avoiding saying anything inflammatory, but also avoiding saying much of any interest. The professor in return said little to me; he objected to some of my more unusual word choices, noticing some vagueness in my pronoun references, and remarked on my typewriter's dirty typeface. His comments on my linguistic and device hygiene reinforced my growing awareness that teachers' evaluated student interest, sophistication, intelligence, and general worthiness for mentoring attention through the written work the students submitted. Giving students the tools to overcome the negative stereotypes that kept reinscribing these educational inequities was to become a major theme of my teaching once I found myself on the other side of the desk. My commitment to supporting writing in the disciplines was in large part to help students find acceptance and positive attention from teachers who would support only those students they saw as "promising" and judged were capable of learning to talk their talk.

At the time, however, I did learn my lessons about neatness and about making a deeply structural argument on the next paper—the major one for the term on *Paradise Lost*. In its 8 pages the prose is taut, well structured, with lots of forward energy in the telling and complex reasoning as it moved paragraph to paragraph. In the opening paragraph I directly identified a structural narrative problem at the start of Book 11: how does one justify and carry out the two final books of expulsion when the story of the fall already seems resolved? The next two paragraphs outline the solution of connecting abstract good and evil to the complex world we live in, and the fourth paragraph specifically lays out the structural solution, of prospectively presenting the history of humans, creating the power of the journey forward, encapsulated in the closing lines of the poem. This structure elaborates the loneliness and suffering ahead, but also the hope. Book 11 presents despair and Book 12 hope, destruction, and resurrection. In the middle of the paper's third page, I began examining the details of the narrative seriatim, casting

Adam as the lonely just man moving through history. I was clearly identifying with Adam's dilemma as I felt laden with doubt and despair in a sinful world, while looking for an ancestral home and seeking faith and hope during my year of religious quest. The professor really liked it, and in his comments raised some questions in relation to Milton's theology. He now clearly gauged me as capable of considering such questions.

My final short 2-page paper on *Samson Agonistes* compared Milton's self-controlled, articulate, intellectually distant Samson with the sensual, violent, inarticulate, impulsive Samson of the Bible. Milton's and Samson's development of inner light changes the emotional actions reported in *Judges*. The paper has a simple two-part comparative structure. The teacher liked the analysis, and made little comment.

Some Final Essays

In the spring term for a course on Anglo-Saxon poetry, I wrote on the *Anglo-Saxon Exodus* poem, presenting a rationale for the interpellation of the stories of Noah's and Abraham's covenants within the deliverance from Egypt, in contrast to the standard interpretation at the time that treated the insertion as accidental, though since then the standard interpretation has come to align with my undergraduate intuition. My argument was structural, placing the events within the larger theme of covenant and Moses' laws, including insertions during the march across the Red Sea of histories of past floods, the sacrifice of Isaac, and other genealogical and historical events connecting god's deliverance at the Red Sea with other affirmations of the covenant and moments of divine protection. This is a trope related to my analysis of Book 11 of *Paradise Lost* placing an historical vision at crucial transition moments within a divine relationship, and is tinged with my then current concerns with Hebrew history and Talmudic law. My analysis is detailed, contrasting what would be expected with what actually appears. My prose is concise and energetic, carrying the argument forward, but the spelling is sloppy. The professor calls the argument rushed and slapdash and lacking knowledge of milieu— but he considers the novelty of the idea promising, suggesting a fresh perspective on the poem. I should also note that here as in several other papers throughout my undergraduate years I included small ironic, self-abnegating comments, abashed by the idiosyncrasy of my perspectives. Here it was reflected in the title of my paper "A Misreading of the Anglo-Saxon 'Exodus.'" Since at least adolescence I had developed self-deprecating humor to defuse my sense of seeing things differently than others. It has always been, and continues to be, difficult to speak and write in a full-throated way, though I have tried to expunge markers of self-abnegation or apologies for that difference in my writing. I have also come to learn that my ironies are often missed in both speech and writing, so I have learned avoid them or to mark them much more clearly when I do use them.

The one last undergraduate paper I have was for an unusual music appreciation course devoted entirely to Bach's *B Minor Mass*. The professor, the prominent composer Karel Husa, thought the best way to introduce non-music students to a deeper understanding of music was to dig deeply into a single great work. Each week we worked through a section of the mass, looking at how the elements of music contributed to the power of the music. Since my musical training was more limited than most students in the class, the course proved a challenge, but it was exciting. I did not have, however, a large set of musical analytic tools to address the assignment for the major paper, to comment in depth on one segment, so I drew on what I had been learning in dramatic literature. I examined the one movement that represented anything like a dramatic scene—the Sanctus depicting the chorus of angels praising God—comparing it to a more overtly dramatic work by Bach, the *St. Matthew Passion*, in particular to the opening chorus of the Passion where the distressed crowd is witnessing Christ's journey to the crucifixion. Both presented the response of a crowd to a divine event, but the tense emotionality of the crowd witnessing the events leading to crucifixion contrasted with the timeless awe of the Sanctus. This contrast highlighted the way the mass creates a liturgical experience of absorption into timeless divine connection. I follow this idea through contrasts of dramatic structure, sequence of events, musical structure, musical emotions, text choices with repetitions and disruptions, chorale exchanges, relation of the chorale words to orchestral sound, counterpoint and harmonies, and total emotional experience. Even though I was examining musical issues, the analysis used detailed musical evidence in much the same way I had been using details of dialogue, setting, and action in my literature papers. Other parts of the paper read very like the theoretical parts of the papers I had been writing for the drama courses. I remember having spent a lot of time and thought on this paper and consulted regularly with my music major friend, who was amused by my attempt to compare such different works using an approach from drama. He repeatedly commented, "well I guess this proves you can compare anything to anything." The professor, however, liked the paper, calling it "very well done," and gave only a few notes about historical and cultural context.

Having Completed My Undergraduate Apprenticeship as an Academic Writer

So by the end of my undergraduate years, I was fairly skilled at writing detailed literary analyses while locating them in larger theoretical themes about structures and experiences of works. As well, I was developing a budding sense of how to consider historical, cultural, and ideological issues in relation to the meaning and experience of the works. I also had some sense of the implications and underlying logic of genres, and was able to move my writing appropriately across different kinds of literary and other artistic objects. When motivated, I also wrote rhythmic, pointed prose, while articulating more complex ideas with some clarity and precision. I was able to write papers that made original points and gained approval by the professors. As a writer I seem to have accomplished what my liberal arts education aimed for me to accomplish, giving me the necessary space, challenge, reward, and confidence.

While I remember spending some time with yellow legal pads, sketching out some of ideas and phrases for more complex papers, I don't have any evidence of drafts, nor memory of revisions. The kinds of passing syntactic and spelling tangles along with typos indicate I was not a consistent proofreader. In fact, I remember being averse to rereading my papers in the short time between their completion and their submission. Only later, after they were returned could I face them again. Nonetheless writing each of the papers and the conclusions from them were memorable and meaningful, as I experienced them then and I look back on them now.

The writing throughout my college career, though almost all on academic topics working within the purposes and expectations of disciplinary courses, also served important personal functions as they helped me think through the issues and problems that troubled me personally. My writing allowed me to form an understanding of the world I was living in and to develop values and stances to guide me as I went forward. Sometimes the personal meaning was overt and thematized, but more often it was embedded within the critical task and subject matter of the assignment. Not only did the assignments allow me to puzzle through my view of life and my commitments, each assignment increased my intellectual, representational, and evaluative sophistication. The papers I wrote were part of my journey as a writer and my journey through life, much in the way they were for the four students described by Anne Herrington and Marcia Curtis in *Persons in Process* (Herrington & Curtis, 2000).

Upon graduation I had no clear idea of what the next chapter in my life would look like. I felt deeply unsettled, but my writing as an undergraduate had formed a way of looking at things that would crystallize in the coming years. As I finished undergraduate life, the times and the draft seemed to have given me little alternative except to continue in graduate school, though not with much of a sense of direction or vocation. I looked forward to something new, but I still felt unease about where I would fit in and what community I belonged to. I was adrift again, though headed for Brandeis, having made my choice on the basis of kosher food which now had no particular meaning for me. Though I did not realize it then, I was on a path that would eventually provide the meaning and purpose that I sought.

Chapter 13. Graduate School, Take One: Imagination and Discipline

The summer after graduation I returned to my mother's apartment (now in Manhattan). Within 24 hours I recognized that my experience of religious orthodoxy brought me no closer to belief and was not a way of life I wanted to maintain. Feeling at loose ends and wanting to get away, I drove to the Adirondacks to hike. In one of the towns I passed through I saw a last-minute job posting for a summer camp counselor job, which I signed up for. In midseason, however, I became impatient to get on with my new life in graduate school, left, drove to Boston, and found an apartment in Cambridge. I soon starting hanging out for the year with some grad students in a co-op house around the corner. When classes started, I would go to Brandeis a few days a week, but with several seminars meeting in professors' Harvard Square apartments, my life centered in Cambridge.

Exploring Romantic Imagination

For the remainder of the summer, I read Romantic poets and Coleridge's theory of imagination and metaphor. I wrote poetry. I got interested in arts of contemplation and meditation, which continued over the years in different forms and would be incorporated in my writing processes. I previously had at times high degrees of focus and concentration extending over days, which the psychologist Csikszentmihalyi was later to call flow (1990), but I wanted to be able to invoke that state more regularly, as well as to understand where it came from and what it might mean. I welcomed associative reasoning and abductive leaps, to be filled in and confirmed later.

A related personal psychological development was a growing ability to recall prior emotional and attitudinal states. As long as I can remember I had a strong visual memory, especially for texts, as I could recall exactly where, and on which page of which book I had read something and often could visualize the page. I could also recognize and find my way through places I had been to only once, and I could readily create mental maps. I could visually recall places I had been, and what transpired, including my emotional and attitudinal position in that setting. This then was expanded as I found myself engrossed in texts, by others and myself, and the worlds they created. When I entered psychotherapy a couple of years later, recall of specific interactions was central to discussions with the therapist. For this therapy, I also began writing dream journals to improve dream recall (see chapter 15 below and Bazerman 2001a for fuller accounts of this therapy). At the same time, I briefly studied acting, where accessing emotional and physical memory was central to the method acting technique. Much later when I started studying singing as I have been doing now for twenty years, I regularly used method acting techniques to guide my interpretation with the result that singing invoked and replayed moments, emotions, relationships, and actions in my life. In the intervening years, every time I had to read a text aloud, and particularly every time I delivered a paper or lecture, I kept in mind the acting dictum not to utter a single word until I could picture and feel the meaning. All of this is to say that I have kept working on building the relationship among the world I experienced, my inner world, and what I expressed outwardly. This nexus of outside, inside, and expression has become an essential component of my writing process, allowing me to locate what I have to communicate and how to project it out into the world.

When the fall term started at Brandeis, I found its graduate program in English and American Literature very much in the mold of other graduate programs of the time. My fellow graduate students were from varied backgrounds, much more than the undergraduates at the school, and the program had a decidedly secular, non-sectarian cast. The program had a strong faculty, focused on canonical literary texts and organized around historical periods—though it did grant more attention to contemporary American literature than was common at the time. Its smaller size and informality, however, offered flexibility to accommodate less conventional students, which was to my liking.

The metaphor-laden, associative-meaning mood that had absorbed me that summer pervaded my approach to my course-work. For a first term course on literary theory, I wrote an extremely associative paper, leaping across centuries among ideas, authors, and theological structures that had been floating around my mind in the preceding years. At the time of writing this paper I had been lost in reading Thomas Mann's *Dr. Faustus*, where the imaginative force of a demonically-inspired musical composer is recounted through the shuffling voice of a scholarly narrator. The voice of my own paper adopted this doubled perspective, as the professor and poet Howard Nemerov noted. He seemed sympathetic and amused by the paper, but pushed me towards more clarity, explicitness, and audience awareness. I used a similar associative, abductive path in a paper for a more narrowly focused course on bibliographic method, to transform an assigned comparison of the first and second editions of DeQuincy's *Confessions of an English Opium Eater* into a speculation on DeQuincey's motives and state of mind. The more conventional professor of this course thought I lacked point. I also turned a related technical assignment to evaluate the process of creating a bibliography into a comic poem in heroic couplets, dripping with self-deprecating irony and attempted literary wit. I undermined the assignment as I manipulated facts to make better jokes and more tortured rhymes, as the professor noted. Only in a paper on Wordsworth's *Prelude* for a course in the Romantics did my ponderings on consciousness and meaning come together as I examined how the poet, in implicit contrast to *Paradise Lost*, created an Epic of the Self, offering a theology of the artist's imagination. While as an undergraduate I learned to explicate canonical texts in detail, now I seemed freed to consider those created worlds more globally, comparing theologies, visions, and ways of thinking, trying to identify my own truths. Only at times did I bother to give the details of works or the evidence that justified my confidence in my judgments.

In this mood, it was not surprising that in the spring term I was attracted to Lawrence Sterne and imitated his digressive style at the organizational, syntactic, and typographical level, switching voices and stances from moment to moment. In my extended paper on a minor satirical pamphlet, *A Political Romance*, I started out in a more descriptive and sober voice to set out the historical facts but soon turned to Sterne's rhetorical, satirical, and comic strategies, showing them as precursors of the tricks he was to use in *Tristram Shandy*. At the point I entered that analysis, I shifted my voice to use all the Shandean devices that I had described in my exposition, indicating a self-diminishing authorial presence. The professor (the same one who did not appreciate my digressive essay on DeQuincey), however, thought I was only making jokes and missed the analysis. An earlier oral presentation for the same course, on an Alexander Pope satire, was more straightforward and expository, with lots of historical detail and examination of the text aims—and was much better received.

To make light of the literary criticism I was engaging in, I started writing literary criticism in the form of limericks. One of my favorites I wrote then was:

> There was a young poet named Donne,
> Who was inordinately fond of the sun.
> > He courted his mistress,
> > And brought her to distress,
> By claiming she, and Donne, and the sun, were all one.

My oral presentation for a Shakespeare course, constrained by the expectations of the task, was a more conventional exposition of the history of stage conditions, with some critical comments on the impact of devices and stage organization. I also have notes for another oral presentation of *Love's Labors Lost*, which walks through the play, describing the structure and thematic devices. Both these are handwritten on yellow legal pads, which I favored at the time, using some three by five cards for initial notes. If the papers were to be submitted and not just read, I would type them directly on corrasable typing paper (a transient and now vanished technology of the final years of the typewriter era) or spirit masters (also now a vanished technology) to make copies for seminar distribution. I am not sure of the amount of revision, but my typing indicates some continued sloppiness, and my style had residual casualness, as noted by some instructors. When my papers had heightened styles, like the literary theory or the Sterne papers, I had lots of visible prosodic tricks. Elsewhere the syntax was flattened, but with good control in longer sentences, using serial lists, contrasts, and parentheticals.

J.V. Cunningham's Discipline

In the spring of my first year, I took a seminar on American poetry with the poet and critic J.V. Cunningham, who was to become my dissertation advisor. His detailed historical scholarship reined in his criticism, and form constrained his poetry. The book of his collected poems, in fact, was entitled *The Exclusions of a Rhyme*. If student presentations did not meet his standards, he would simply ignore them, as not worth commenting on, simply muttering "next." I lived in dread of that dismissal. His discipline was a major corrective to my recent immersion in Romantic poetic theory, harnessing my imagination to evidence, public defensibility, and clear statement. My papers for him were responsive to his perceived sparseness and demand for evidence. My paper on E. A. Robinson's "Isaac and Archibald" was a close analysis of prosody, syntax, narrative technique, voice, and structure to reveal Robinson's intentional poetic choices. When we came to Emily Dickinson, he commented in class that half-rhymes were to her equivalent to full in her hymn meters. I was at first dubious about this, particularly as I was using half and tortured rhymes intentionally for comic purposes, so for my presentation I analyzed all the rhymes in the full collected edition of her works. After a week of counting rhymes, I had to admit Cunningham was correct, but this did lead me to some comments on the role of rhyme in hymn meters, and Dickinson's awareness of the difference in a few cases when full rhymes had particular effect. Afterwards, having immersed myself in her rhymes and rhythms, I amused myself with a parody of her poems.

The last paper for this seminar attempted to impose a philosophic plot outline on the several disjunct segments of Wallace Stevens' "The Man with a Blue Guitar." I offered brief paraphrases of the philosophic positions on the potential of art in each of the sections, showing how they formed a sequential reasoning path. Cunningham remained skeptical of the overall assumption of an argumentative order, as well as the presumed relation to the famous Picasso painting, but he did engage with my argument and made some approving comments on some of the interpretive paraphrases (and some not). I found here and elsewhere his blunt questioning of what he considered flights of fancy and his reliance on facts refreshing, and I remember I thought he was the first one who ever accurately cut through my BS. I took seriously what he said and needed to live up to his standards. I no longer could follow my inner obsessions. My writing style simplified and struggled towards conciseness.

His mode as well changed my poetry from overly complex to more pointed. I joined a reading group of students gathered around him to study prosodic theory and analysis. On Cunningham's recommendation I read Puttenham's 1589 *The Arte of English Poesie*, treating it as a practical textbook, coming up with my own examples for each of the tropes and devices Puttenham discussed. Cunningham's spirit helped me maintain focus on literary studies during the next two years teaching elementary school in Brooklyn. When I returned, he agreed to advise my dissertation.

The last task for the spring was a single text M.A. exam, which we were to prepare for during the term and then write over several hours under controlled conditions. My year the text was Shakespeare's sonnets. In addition to studying the poems intensively, I read all of the extensive criticism I could find. I developed very decided views, largely around the importance of form and convention (aligned with the continuing influence of McMillin and the new influence of Cunningham). I saw much of the criticism as presentist and fanciful, and I saw even the most powerful and most famous sonnets in the sequence as the apotheoses of the conventions of his time, rather than a rejection or transcendence. So when the question was phrased in terms of transcendence of the form, I took exception, and after arguing with the question, I discussed the value of a few of the poems usually dismissed as merely conventional. I then showed how some of the more famous sonnets built on those same conventions rather than transcending them. I don't have a copy of my exam or of the comments, but remember well the process and the reviewers saying I spent too much time arguing with the question, but that I had some good things to say after that. So once again I got in a bit of trouble by not buying into assumptions I could not accept, but at least I was able to give a positive account of my heterodox views. I received my M.A.

Farewell to Grad School, for a While

Over this year in graduate school, I became increasingly unhappy with literary studies and criticism, as I saw as them alternatively dry and unflavorful or filled with unanchored speculative fancies. Even more, devoting myself to literary studies seemed to subordinate myself to the work of others, who were treated as in a class apart from us mere mortals. Why would I devote myself to the study of someone else's imagination, and not my own production? And what benefit would it serve anyone to have another study of canonical works of canonical authors who already had endless commentaries? I was still something of a lost soul, though now having more of the craft of writing to hold onto, as a way of being. I felt that if I was to stay in the field it would be as a writer elaborating my own world.

As the academic year was drawing to a close, the military draft once again pressed in as deferments for graduate students were removed for the following year. I was opposed to the Vietnam War as a purposeless destruction of a people. I also felt, however, that if I were drafted and placed on the front lines I would be put in a position where I would have to shoot others to protect myself. I feared this more than I feared for my own life—or at least this is what I thought and said at the time.

Given my unhappiness with grad school, I was not heartbroken at having to leave, but I needed to find an alternative. I knew I did not fit the qualifications for a conscientious objector. I made a brief trip to Canada to explore the possibilities of leaving, but during the whole trip I was enraged at the thought of war-hawks making me give up my country so that I could not absorb the possibilities of life in Canada. Finally, I found a program that would provide me an emergency credential for inner city teaching in New York along with a draft deferment. I went for it. It was incredible good luck, much more than I could have imagined, despite all the challenges those next two years would present.

Part Three. Finding Writing as a Way to Be

Figure 14.1. P.S. 93K, 31 New York Avenue, Bedford Stuyvesant, Brooklyn. Photo taken from a vintage postcard.

Chapter 14. Into the World: The Social Value of Writing

In late August 1968, after a nominal and uninformative 6-week training for an emergency teaching credential, before the start of classes, I went out to Chicago to visit my college friend, drawn by word of an anti-war protest going to be staged outside the Democratic Convention. Not knowing what to expect, on the first night of the Convention Marty and I cautiously watched on TV and saw another friend being teargassed. On the second night, enraged, we joined the demonstrations and chanted "the whole world is watching." Although a march through the city did not have an official parade permit, Dick Gregory told us from the stage there was nothing wrong with him inviting the thousands of us to visit his home. We joyfully began to walk until we ran into military vehicles, barbed wire, and tear gas. Filled with adrenalin we ran towards them until we could no longer. Every night for the remainder of the convention week I was on the streets, pushed by anger. This brought home to me that we were living through history, which was made by our actions as individuals and groups. I also realized this was a media event, on both sides, to display our alternate resolves and to project our points of view. The show of it became absolutely clear to me, when a couple of us retreated to a local cafeteria to recover. Some nearby tables were inhabited by the same police that had just confronted us. We all just quietly nursed our coffee now that we were off-camera and off-stage.

So visibly seeing that history unfolded through our actions, but our actions had to leave their mark, motivated me to make a transformative difference as a teacher, changing what I found oppressive, stultifying, and discriminatory about schools. I needed to do more than just hide out from the draft. Actually, teaching transformed me much more than I transformed teaching. Earlier experiences primed me, but two years teaching early grades in Bedford-Stuyvesant, Brooklyn crystallized new ways of writing, acting, and relating to others. I learned to communicate with students, found ways to develop their literacies, wrote collaboratively with them, and created elementary school materials through daily writing. During those same years I did my own creative writing, took some acting lessons, appeared in a couple of off-off-Broadway productions, formed new kinds of friendships, entered therapy, and changed my orientation toward the world—finding satisfaction not in the search for meaning, but in need-fulfilling relationships. My new commitments mobilized all I had learned and focused my energies to supporting other people's needs. I began to know why I wanted to write and to help others to learn to write.

P.S. 93K: Communicating with Young People

I was assigned to PS 93K in the heart of Bedford-Stuyvesant in Brooklyn, and I rented a studio apartment in Clinton Heights, a block from a Middle Eastern neighborhood with fresh pita bakeries and cheap restaurants. I was ready to set out on an adult life. But the sixties kept happening. The first day of instruction in the fall was met with the Ocean Hill-Brownsville strike over community control of schools. New York City, as an experiment, had decentralized the assignment of principals and teachers to community boards in the largely black Ocean Hill-Brownsville district, resulting in the displacement of many union teachers. The neighboring Bedford-Stuyvesant district including PS 93K also experienced the strike which lasted almost two months. I sided with the community and was one of three teachers who "liberated the school" by using massive bolt cutters on the locked chains at the front gate. For the first few days I held a semblance of classes for the lowest grades, and then taught fourth grade for the duration of the strike. When it was over, the community took control of the school through death threats to the principal, and then appointed their own.[3]

While I had the support of the community, I did not enjoy the support of the returning teachers. I was assigned a third-grade class, with the students the other teachers wanted to get out of their classrooms. I had little mentoring, virtually no supplies (one ream of decomposing yellow paper), and a few ancient textbooks. I created materials every day by getting up far too early, composing stories and math exercises directly on spirit masters. I then went to the school before anyone else, entering the basement school supply room with an illicit key to run off copies of the day's materials, using paper I had purchased on my own. I frequented my local used bookstore where I would buy children's books for pennies each by the box (thank you, bookman Sam!) to create a class library. The classroom did have an overhead projector but I had to buy my own acetates. I haunted school materials stores and took kids on field trips through New York City by twos and threes every Saturday. It was the sixties. As a bow to conventionality, I did wear ties, but they were a mile wide and psychedelic. I tied back my shoulder length hair in a pony tail.

I was impressed by Sylvia Ashton Warner's *Teacher* (1963), Herbert Kohl's *36 Children* (1967), and James Herndon's *The Way it 'Spozed to Be* (1968)—all of which drew on children's experiences. In my own neighborhood I met some cartoonists working on the pilot for *Sesame Street*, then also in the works. I did some trial scripts for them but wasn't brought in, yet that too gave me ideas for an approach. The *Bank Street Readers*, the first urban focused graded reading series, appeared in 1965, but they were not available in my school—or at least not for my class. Still, the critique of white suburban readers was in the air, which led me to make my own version on daily spirit masters. My undergraduate confidence in being able to produce writing on demand, and my literary analysis of structure and community situations helped me create stories about a boy and a girl living in the same neighborhood as my students and engaging in the same daily

---

3. Maurice Carroll, Parents Bar Principal from School in Brooklyn. *New York Times*, November 20, 1968, p. 32

experiences of cooking, shopping, family, neighborhood problems, and getting into trouble with big kids. I drew on what kids told me and what I saw of the world that surrounded them.

I also led the class in collaborative story and script writing, based on TV shows and movies they were familiar with as well as their everyday lives—people on their block, how to fix cars, how to fish. We then used these as regular reading activities. At first we created short pieces of a few sentences, but eventually we wrote a five page play based on a then popular TV cartoon show *Crusader Rabbit*. Composing and producing it took us several weeks. Events and lines were initially quite random as children excitedly yelled out ideas, and I remember the chaos of trying to bring some coherence and closure to the plots. The transcribed versions showed signs of that chaos, but all managed to somehow to get to "The End." Bringing some semblance of order to these chaotic collaborative composing sessions taught me how to organize discussions as a teacher, provide productive responses to student writing, and move creativity forward. These experiences with young children first taught me how to tap into the perspectives and interests of authors, giving them their space, while providing guidance that would allow them to express their thinking more fully and to open up higher levels of thinking. Working with unruly eight-year-olds prepared me well to later lead faculty meetings and to pull together editorial projects. One thing I learned was that general directives to the whole group were usually futile, and I needed to address people individually and specifically: Dari, please be quiet. Joseph please be quiet. . . . Professor Jones, please organize the committee. Bill, could I see that draft by January 15.

I also learned to be more clearly communicative. To write on the chalk board and on overheads legibly I became self-conscious about handwriting, and I developed legible block printing. I adopted simple sentence structure and narrative sequencing for my classroom materials and newsletters to parents. In my tasks and instructions, I attempted to remove anything that would distract students from the learning and practice at hand. I eliminated anything that might stand between students and the targeted learning.

The first year of teaching was stressful and exhausting given the situation, the size of classes, and lack of materials, leaving me little energy for creative work beyond the classroom. I did keep a small journal, especially documenting my excursions through the city with students. In my files are only a handful of attempts at poems during this year, but these also became simpler in syntax and narrative. When I had any energy left, I continued to read through the literary canon and translated the lengthy Middle English "Pearl Poem" as I was particularly fascinated by its unusual stanzaic form. In this way I was able to stay in touch with my grad student identity, despite my unhappiness the previous year. It was hard to imagine myself as anything other than an academic, even though I was finding there was more to life.

The school year finally ended and I had summer off with a very little bit of money (my annual pay was just under $7,000 and I spent a lot of that on books and materials for the class). Through the intervention of the community which supported me because I had supported them in the strike, I also had a job for the next year, despite attempts by the returned teachers to have me removed. So in the summer of '69, in the spirit of the times, I decided to discover America, and drove my convertible across country. I passed through farming communities across the Midwest enjoying local family restaurants, though I got strange looks and cold shoulders as the hippy outsider. Several times pickup trucks with gun racks trailed me to the county line. I also enjoyed the great national parks across the North and into Canada. I was overwhelmed by the grandeur of the Rockies, and realized how small we humans were. I shared the mind-enhancers offered by my hitchhikers. I got out to San Francisco just in time to see the moon landing televised on the ceiling of the Fillmore West during a Joe Cocker and Country Joe and the Fish concert. "Far out, man. Like really far out." The movie *Easy Rider* was released just two days before I left, but I only saw it when I got back home. Though my trip was not nearly so dramatic as the movie, there was enough for me to identify with and feel part of the times that were a-changin'. I didn't do a lot of writing on the trip, but did come back with a greater opening to risk and even less attachment to conventionality.

That fall I was part of a team, teaching first grade students identified as having emotional difficulties. The small class gave me lots of opportunity for individual interaction with troubled and demanding students, though I had no professional knowledge of psychology to make sense of what was going on with them. Since the materials and curricula were well established (though I was hardly enamored with them) and responsibility was shared among the team, there was little work to take home and I had more energy and leisure to devote to my personal relationships and other activities. I started writing poems more regularly, in a more direct, personal style. I wrote a few short stories and opening chapters of novels, though never getting further. I read at open mic nights at bars and poetry circles. I began drama classes and by the end of the year was in a couple of productions at a progressive theatre in Brooklyn Heights. Among the many things I learned from acting was transposing my own memories and experience into the meaning I was communicating and drawing strength and inspiration from my fellow actors in unfolding situations. I also became aware of my physical presence, location on stage, and what I would look like from the audience's perspective. All of these intersected with what I was simultaneously learning from therapy. They also were ultimately applicable to writing.

Interpersonal Psychotherapy; Communicating with Adults

The second fall of my teaching I fell in with a group of people who were in psychotherapy following the interpersonal principles of Harry Stack Sullivan. I formally entered therapy with Tony Gabriele when my girlfriend at the time, tiring of my novice self-analysis, complained "I'm not your shrink." While the therapy was directed towards improving my interactions and communications in daily face-to-face relations, I believe it had deep impact on my writing, as I was coming to understand writing relationships as an extension of face-to-face relationships, only being played out on a more distant stage.

A core element of the therapy was learning to recognize anxiety while continuing to pursue important needs and activities without digression or distraction, despite the anxiety. Writing, of course, is fraught with anxiety, and also open to digression, distraction, or even avoidance. This learning to recognize anxiety while continuing to act helped give stronger direction to my writing and helped me deal with the avoidance and procrastination that plague even the most skilled of writers, particularly when the task is emotionally challenging. Understanding how anxiety could distract and disrupt spontaneous impulses also helped me locate the things that I really wanted to say and write rather than those words that would protect me from anxious feelings.

Second, I came to understand more clearly that personal interaction was aimed at collaboration and mutual need satisfaction rather than protecting self-esteem or impression management. I came to understand my writing as communicative, aimed at successful participation in activities. This gave me different criteria for setting my goals, elaborating my meanings, and revising my writing. I came to look for different satisfactions from my writing—in getting things done, in being effective, in making the situation work.

Third, I learned to recall, recount, and analyze in detail how interactions unfolded and how they were disrupted by anxious behaviors. In my weekly sessions I was asked to report on how interactions evolved second by second, and how my interactions would have looked if I were observing from a corner of the room. Even more difficult, I was asked to observe what I did without controlling or consciously directing spontaneous behavior. This ultimately led to changed spontaneous behavior, as I came to perceive situations differently and to be less distracted by anxiety into counter-productive behavior. I began to understand how interactions evolved, with each response, no matter how minute, influencing what happened next. In my writing this attuned me to how each word in a text affected the reader to engage or disengage with what followed—and to build meaning and response temporally.

Further, as part of the self-discovery process, I wrote more about myself and my emotions—through autobiography, dream journals, dream poems, expressive poems. My dreams were vivid and plentiful. Writing was bursting forth from me, even as I was also occupied with teaching, acting, friendships, and relationships. I have more drafts, notebooks, and files from that one year than ever before. Some of my poetry and a short story from the period were published in small journals. That productive energy continued afterward, though to be invested in my professional work.

Self in Society

Finally, I was introduced to interdisciplinary social theory about how individuals developed within social worlds. I read Sullivan's books and discovered his connection with an interdisciplinary group of scholars of his time, such as Margaret Mead, Ruth Benedict, Edward Sapir, Gregory Bateson, W. I. Thomas, and Harold Lasswell.[4] This started me thinking socially. This was a time of much mental rearrangement on my part as I faced new situations, became more participatory in more collaborative relationships, and learned more about the people around me and how they interacted. These experiences were more mind-bending than any of the chemical enhancements which I soon left behind.

The theory world I started to become familiar with also helped crystallize a rationale behind the values I had been developing. As I came to understand the deeply social nature of human life and needs, and the impulses toward sociality embedded in our biological and cultural evolution, I no longer wondered about the loss of divine warrant for ethical social behavior, the desire to do good for others, and the satisfactions of cooperation for human betterment, local and global. My questions about a meaningful life were put to rest and purely secular answers were more than satisfactory to give my life direction.

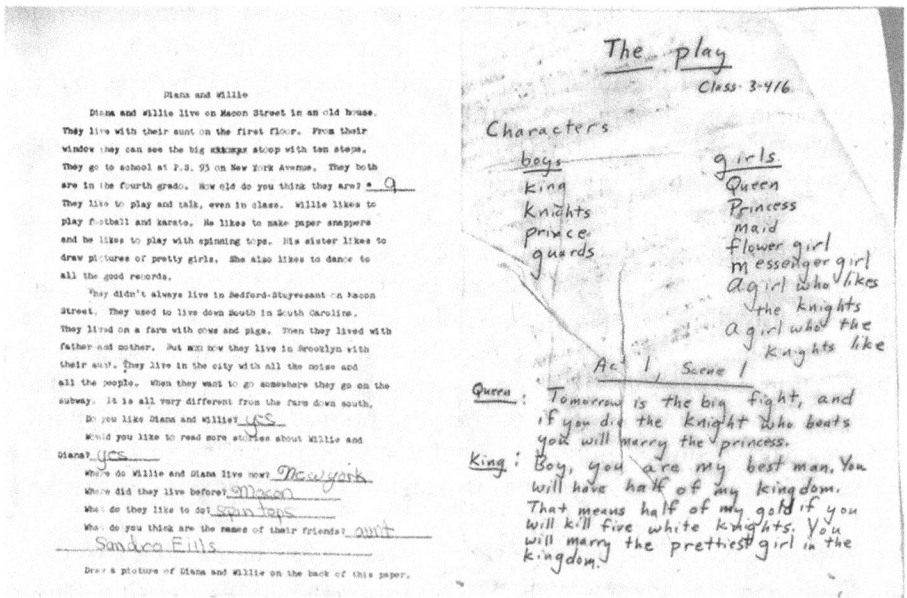

Figure 14.2. Writing in third grade. Photo courtesy of Charles Bazerman.

---

4. I was later to put together my understanding of Sullivan's work and that of his group in a study of his journal *Psychiatry* (see Bazerman 2005f). In another pair of studies I explored the connection between his work and that of Vygotsky (see Bazerman 2001a, 2001d)

Chapter 15. Finishing Graduate School

The two years teaching elementary school were transformative, but I was drawn back to university life, the student role, and the particular writing expectations of academic inquiry. Despite the community protecting my job for two years, I was not renewed—whether for failure as a teacher, or unconventionality, or other transgression I am still not sure. I am also unsure whether my finally gaining a 4F draft status was the result of letters from my therapist and an anti-war medical doctor who identified stress-related ulcers or a sullen dramatic performance at my army medical intended to confirm my therapist's diagnosis. In any event, for the first time I could make life choices free of the draft. I contemplated several options. I did not feel ready or networked enough to make a go of being a writer or actor. I was tempted to continue in elementary education, but I only saw constant struggle against bureaucratic constraints and debilitating conditions of work that would undermine whatever pleasure I could get from connecting with the students. Although I now see that opportunities then existed which would have made elementary teaching possible, I did not see them at the time. Maybe more significantly, I had from an early age never imagined myself as anything other than working within the academic world, though I was often uncertain and confused about which part of that world I would fit into. My imagination of futures was impoverished. Although I was not excited about returning to grad school which had been so dispiriting before, it was familiar, and it was easy to reactivate my matriculation. I figured I would sort things out afterwards.

During my two years away from Brandeis, there was a fortunate change in graduate requirements. The M.A. previously had required only a year of courses and a major text exam, while the Ph.D. had required more coursework and comprehensive exams, followed by dissertation. While I was away, however, under the pressure of a student strike, all the coursework and comprehensive exams were moved to the M.A., and the Ph.D. required only a dissertation. Any work beyond that was to be negotiated with the advisor. Having already received my masters, I needed only to be accepted by an advisor for my dissertation. The no-nonsense Cunningham found my reading list during my hiatus sufficient knowledge of the field for me to go directly to a dissertation. After rooting around the library for a bit I came up with a proposal that pursued a question that had interested me since I was in junior high school: why people wrote books. A microfilm edition of all the books in *A Short-Title Catalogue of Books Printed in England, Scotland and Ireland, and of English Books Printed Abroad 1475–1640* had recently been released. This collection let me escape the blinders of canonical literature to see the full range of what people were writing. I narrowed the focus to 1603, which had double the books of the surrounding years, because of the death of Queen Elizabeth I and ascension of King James I. I focused on books specifically related to those events. The works were of now canonical authors, such as Ben Jonson and the lesser-known Michael Drayton, as well as authors now no longer recognized or even remembered. The authors represented all classes, and almost all the works were poetic, in eulogy of the deceased queen or celebration of the new king, wending his way from Scotland down to London. All the poems were occasional, a class of poetry that was little studied and little respected but which I found fascinating because they were connected to historical and social events.

One of my first tasks was to understand occasional poetry, about which there was little theory in 1970. When I examined the poetic theory during the Renaissance, I found it barely a explicit category, though there were many examples of poems we would now consider occasional. Using the theory of that time, I identified a variety of terms that were relevant to the kinds of poems I was finding, and examined the implications of those terms for occasional verse. From these terms I constructed a definition. My thirteen-page working paper elaborated each of the terms in the definition from theory and their application to the poems. My advisor suggested this was a way station to understanding, helping me understand what I was looking at and how it differed from my prior expectations of poetry. I did not, however, use any of this definition explicitly in my dissertation, which was a description and catalogue of verse, and a description of the events they fit into. The catalog and description were organized around styles, formal characteristics, and function within the events of the royal transition. These features turned out to correspond to genre, sorted out according to the social class of poet. In the end this social analysis seemed more powerful to understand what I was seeing than the fulfillment of an abstract definition.

This project was novel for me in many respects. First, I was writing about non-canonical literary texts. This meant the focus was not to show appreciation or evaluation of the text. It also took the focus away from interpretation; that is, treating the text as difficult to understand, making the critic's task one of exposing non-obvious meanings or effects. Rather these texts' meanings were readily accessible, even with the historical distance of three and a half centuries.

While I had worked with corpora or collections of texts before, I had organized the analyses along interpretive tasks, considering repertoires of plays or poetic collections. I even took an interpretive stance in considering the letters of a Pope or the transcripts of Congressional hearings. But here the task was more to describe the nature and character of these texts, to place these texts in the society, literary culture, and historical events of the time, explaining what motivated each of these texts and how they functioned in their specific moments. I also noted how styles and genres were inflected by social class and event. I was beginning to work out a sociological, activity-oriented, genre-based analysis which was to guide much of my later work when I turned to consider non-literary works, in different social spheres.

In a sense the novelty of the methods of analyzing this corpus came from taking occasional verse seriously, rather than as a reduced or lower form of poetry, not worthy of literary attention. Taking occasionality seriously posed the problem of what was the occasion—which then led to the question of what was happening historically, who were the participants in their social positions and roles, and what the poet was trying to accomplish in the circumstances with the available and expected forms of communication. I was led, step by step, to learn new ways of dealing with, describing, and organizing the material in the corpus. The theory to come from this orientation was not well developed or explicitly articulated in the dissertation. Rather the implications appeared in the close-to-the ground description and organization of the over 100 texts, from which I quoted extensively, with full texts of some of the more interesting poems that had not been republished in over 360 years. I was still trying to harness this study to the literary task of recovering worthy texts with an extensive historical contextualization.

Cunningham was a deep and demanding influence on me. He was a person of few words and one gained his respect by saying only the few, necessary things. I was most proud when he said that he thought my dissertation should have ended with "Q.E.D." (*Quod erat demonstrandum*—which was to be demonstrated), the traditional end of a math proof. I thought of my dissertation as a kind of truth poem, deserving of the same care with language and aiming at the same intensity of communication and immediacy expected in poetry. Here, however, everything had to be grounded in evidence, and to expand our understanding of realities. This idea of "truth poem" was to become a mantra of mine in years to follow.

I wrote some poems during this time on the experience of writing a dissertation and my relationship to Cunningham. I include a few lines of one here because they reflect his influence on my writing and scholarship.

> I move to what I fear,
>
> My outer limit of confusion.
>
> Beyond the glassy sphere
>
> Of my self, for invitation
>
> A teacher breathes, hard and tired,
>
> A ghost of knowledge transposed.
>
> By his breath, the glass is shattered.
>
> What I know is recomposed.

In this experience I see a foreshadowing of how I was later to come to understand Vygotsky's Zone of Proximal Development, a period of puzzling supported and guided by someone with fuller understanding, culminating in a moment of development when inchoate parts reorganize into a new coherence (see Vygotsky, 1978 and Bazerman, 2009c).

I managed to finish the dissertation in one year, so my contact with graduate training was limited. I used to joke that I wasn't in grad school long enough to be ruined by it. Even more, during the fall term I still lived in Brooklyn, driving up to Waltham one day a week to consult with Cunningham and sit in on his seminar. In the spring, when I was finishing typing up the dissertation on my deteriorating portable typewriter, I moved to Waltham where I met another of his advisees who became my life partner. Shirley Geok-lin Lim, at that time an international student from Malaysia, is also a writer—of poetry, fiction, and academic work. We do have somewhat different views of writing and even perceptions of the influence of our shared advisor on us, yet we understand the practical needs and moods of writers and have been able to organize our lives around this. Through her work and her academic and writing networks in Asia (Malaysia, Singapore, then Nepal and Hong Kong) I expanded my view of writing and writing education beyond the borders of the US These experiences opened me to the value of other international experiences as over the years I also made connections with the teaching of writing and writing studies in Europe and Latin America.

Figure 15.1. James V. Cunningham. Photo by Thomas Victor

Chapter 16. Teacher of College Writing: A Meaningful Commitment

The year I finished my doctorate, the academic job market collapsed for the first time since the post-WWII expansion of universities. My hundred letters of inquiry turned up nothing. With no money and no prospect in sight, I signed up for the summer to be on a team writing a textbook series for K-12 English. Assigned to write workbooks for kindergarten and first grade, I began developing materials and activities following what I had learned about the need to be understandable and focused on the lessons at hand, eliminating opportunities for distraction or digression, while still engaging students' experiences and imaginations. I studied children's nursery rhymes to see how they mixed rhythms with phonetics for memorable instruction. I soon ran into conflict, however, with a supervisor who had traditional expectations of classrooms, and I found my imagination blocked by her directions, so I left. The series, as it happened, never was published.

As the fall term approached, I pieced together a couple of last-minute contingent positions in New York metropolitan area colleges, teaching basic writing and first-year composition. A term later, one of them turned into a full-time tenurable position at Baruch College, City University of New York, where I spent the next two decades, teaching in the same building where my father got his business degree in the 1930s, when it was the downtown branch of City College. As a child he had taken me to see the plaque in the entrance where he was recognized for graduating Summa cum Laude, but the plaque was gone by the time I worked there. My position was specifically supported by the SEEK program (Search for Education, Elevation, and Knowledge) for students from traditionally underrepresented groups, initiated at the time of open-admissions in 1970, just a year before my arrival. This was exactly the kind of work that I was excited to participate in. Although political conflicts over open-admissions erupted at the city, university, campus, and department levels, I was able to keep my head down and work to support our new students with similarly motivated colleagues across the 18 CUNY campuses.

We were soon to form a system-wide organization, the CUNY Association of Writing Supervisors (CAWS), under the leadership of Bob Lyons from Queens College and Harvey Wiener of LaGuardia Community College, sponsored by Mina Shaughnessy, who by that time had a system-wide administrative position. I was not, in fact, a writing supervisor, as at Baruch we had no distinct writing program, just many sections of required courses administered through the department chair, who was mostly interested in scheduling and staffing. Our departmental Composition Committee had no powers other than to make proposals for departmental deliberation. I was the most active member of the committee, and soon chair, and then the sole member. By default, I became our representative to CAWS because no one else from my campus was interested in serving. For the first two years of the organization, I volunteered as secretary because I recognized that creating the record created the official history, and even more framed current commitments and actions. I organized the minutes around action items we had agreed on. I took an active role in meetings to craft language that would be acceptable to all parties and would fit the conditions of the different campuses. I excluded the detailed discussions from the minutes in order to allow us to air all views without having the differences become enshrined in official history. Later, from 1978–80 I served as co-chair of CAWS. Eventually, Baruch did get a writing program director, but by that time I had made too many enemies in fighting for the program. We hired from the outside, and that person took over Baruch's representation at CAWS.

Initially, I was not invested in research or publishing, as my graduate experience had not excited me about literary scholarship, though I did need to get publications for tenure. And I had no awareness of the potential for scholarship in the teaching of writing, which was in fact limited at the time. My total professional commitment was to the teaching of writing to underrepresented students and helping them succeed at the university. My energies went into understanding what students needed to learn, preparing materials for my classes, and commenting on their work. I imagined the students as the older cousins of the children I was recently teaching in Brooklyn, but who had managed to survive a punishing school system to gain a high school diploma. In my years at Baruch most of my teaching was split between developmental writing courses for less well-prepared students and the required two-term, first year writing sequence.

I first attended to the obvious problems students presented in their writing—grammar and syntax in the developmental courses, and coherence and elaboration in the required courses. I soon recognized, however, underlying problems in engagement, stance, sense of language, and motivation. I came to see the core challenge was to help students discover writing as a vehicle for meaning and thinking rather than a target for correction and stigmatization. I wanted to learn more about students, their processes, and their prior experiences in schooling. I needed to observe my students and listen to what other teachers were saying about them. I compared notes with teachers with whom I shared a large bull pen office, and then at CAWS we discussed practical issues such as proficiency exams and shared teaching objectives. We organized local conferences, seminars, and reading groups. These were my most engaging early professional experiences.

Learning From Other Arts

To decompress in my spare time, I returned to avocations from my earlier years, initially chess, which I had played in junior high school, and then squash, which I played at college. With my competitive personality I enjoyed improving. Since I worked in Manhattan, it was convenient to join clubs with people far more accomplished than I was, take lessons with internationally ranked professionals, and play in novice leagues—spending my little discretionary income on these luxuries. This was a repeated pattern throughout my life as I took up hobbies with a passion—joining groups of the more experienced, reading books on the topic, and taking lessons. From each avocational adventure I learned skills and orientations which I could apply to writing. I also observed the ways teachers of these different arts transmitted their skills and practices, which gave me new ways to think about the teaching of writing. So although I never moved beyond basic amateur in any of these, I observed how the more skilled performed, and I learned a lot from them.

Figure 16.1. Downtown City College where my father graduated around 1937, second in the class, later redesignated Baruch College where I worked 1971–1990. Photo by Lester Ali.

From immersing myself in chess I thought about how to balance strategy with tactics, connecting details with the big picture in order to choose the strongest move. Large intentions needed to be built on small decisions. Even good plans could collapse without accurate execution. A principle taught to beginners is that the order and timing of moves were crucial; two good moves could be disastrous if done in reverse. At the same time, good plans needed to attend to the opponent's plans. Interesting games were a collaborative art. I learned the value of building positions and then at the right moment of converting one kind of strength into another—an advantage in space, for example could then improve position and coordination of pieces, which would later support dynamic conflicts and ultimately material gain. Each of those moments of conversion changed the character of the game and center of action. The game also gave me more practice in listening to my inner voice—at the end of rational assessment of the moves, you still needed to let the pieces speak to you to make the final choice. The game continued to build my concentration and ability to call on it on demand—as well as to play with focus despite uncertainty and anxiety.

All of these were lessons I remember consciously applying to writing. I also applied some of the techniques of chess teaching to the teaching of writing, such as highlighting the commitments made in opening moves (or essay openings), and pushing students to have sharp but accurate follow-through on those commitments, paying close attention to order and timing of statements. I came to believe that every move in writing was taking a risk, making a bet on what would work—and that you had no other option than go with your best sense of what your best bet was. You needed to put yourself on the line.

I didn't get as far in squash, but I learned the importance of habituation through practice, and muscle memory—pointing out the good shot and recognizing how that felt rather than being overconcerned with the bad shots. Strategically I learned how important it was to recognize where your center was (which for squash was a physical location at the intersection of lines on the court floor, a bodily balance, and a concentrated attention) and how to keep returning to it.

In individual instruction in these and other activities, I came to appreciate the power of the instructor's one-on-one attention to the novice's practice. This reconfirmed my own sense of the value of working individually with students, giving close attention to how they worked and what they were trying to do. Whenever possible I have scheduled individual consultation with students about work in progress. I have also engaged in extended dialogs in the classroom with individual students over their emerging projects so other students could observe and think about how the issues we discuss might apply to their own work. For such reasons I have come to believe that working as a tutor in a writing center is one of the best apprenticeships for becoming a writing teacher, revealing the individuality and complexity of student thinking.

Three decades later, as I began voice lessons, I started to think of public dialog with students about their work as similar to master classes, where the more experienced musician coaches the novice to a higher level of performance while others would observe the process. Learning to perform music made me more aware of the long slow process of mastery and the importance of nurturing goal setting by teachers—just challenging enough, but not beyond the current scope of the student. I also saw the teacher's role in building confidence to perform the piece with comfort and then to perform in public. These are good lessons to think about with writing.

From music lessons I also thought a lot about the relation between expressiveness and technical skill, which depends on the role of practice, scales and other exercises to work on precision, clarity, beauty of tone, and proper production. Yet every lesson and every practice session need to include practicing repertoire, playing real music—enjoying not just the technical improvement of the sound, but experiencing the expressive beauty and play of the music. Playing music, joining with others, and performing are all essential to keep the learner motivated and engaged, making all the scales and exercises worthwhile. In the teaching of writing, we seem to separate the technical from the expressive, the work from the pleasure, rather than keeping them in balance, feeding each other.

Locating the music hidden in the inked notes on the written score is also an important lesson for literacy, as transcribed notes are incomplete indicators of the composer's sense of the music which the performer must then reconstruct. To play is to interpret, to animate the music. In the same way writing is to give clues about our intended meaning and the force we hope to inspire in the readers, who must perform the words as an engaging meaning, making the words come alive for themselves. This does not mean that readers, any more than musicians, should follow their unfettered fancy. Music teaches us the more deeply we enter the written notes, the more we discover the resources, nuances, and beauties placed there by the composer. The process of learning a piece is a path of discovery at the intersection of what the composer offers and what the performer brings technically and emotionally, in the same way as actors animate the playwright's script. Writers also need to make their words performable by their readers and in that performance make the writers' meanings come alive. The writer has the task of engaging, inspiring the reader's resources, even while drawing the reader into the meanings one hopes to convey. But the readers then must take up their responsibility in creating meaning from the words.

Finally, music is a temporal experience, even though a score can be looked at synchronously as an architecture. It is performed and heard over time; to be interesting the piece must evolve over time, bringing the listener to new places, constantly reengaging the listener's ears, drawing on what came before to enrich and add to the experience. Writing also is temporal, usually read sequentially over time, with the reader building meaning and going to new places as the writer leads them. Even if the text is skimmed or read out of sequence to find specific pieces of anticipated information, that too is done over time and the writer must design the text to deliver rewards in a timely way to keep the reader engaged. The journey into the text moves forward, where even digressions need to be understood as advancing the journey. The conclusion, even if it reprises the beginning, must do it in an enriched and deepened way, revealing the discoveries of the journey, recognizing where you have come to.

At the same time the work is architectural and the reader gains by recognizing where they are on the constructed path through the work, even if only intuitively by noticing familiar markers or signposts. The better the audience or reader comes to know the text or the musical piece, the better they also come to know the architecture more explicitly and analytically, thereby providing a frame for the unfolding meaning, attuning them to a fuller experience. The writer as much as the composer can guide the reader into a greater synchronic sense of the whole that frames the temporal movement through the space.

These are the kinds of things I learn from studying arts other than writing. These other arts are never quite the same as writing with their particularities of pleasures, crafts, meanings, and play—but they also teach me about writing, and they represent important parts of how I became the writer and teacher I have become.

Chapter 17. First Steps in Academic Publishing: Bringing My Writing into the Published World

Despite my commitment to teaching writing, in order to gain tenure in my department I needed to publish on traditional literary topics. I delivered literary papers at my campus and regional conferences and managed to publish one article on Kurosawa's film adaptation of *Macbeth* (1977b). That paper relied on the trope of order and disorder I had been interested in since undergraduate years, but here realized in cinematic terms. Other than the challenge of analyzing filmic images and tempos, this was by now for me familiar turf. I also spent far too much time writing for literary critical collections that never appeared, though my individual chapters had been accepted by the editors. The main lesson I learned from these attempts was never to write for a collection unless I had solid assurances that the book would appear. One project that never reached publication because the collection collapsed, however, stretched me as a writer. My task was to place Nabokov's late novel *Lolita* within the development of his entire corpus, in particular showing how his fictional structure and authorial stance emerged in its mature form; I was later to return to such lifespan corpus analysis when I looked at the writings of Joseph Priestley, Adam Smith, and Thomas Edison—and then in recent years as I made lifespan development of writing and its relationship to consciousness formation a focal issue.

The one kind of literary writing I found most engaging and from which I learned the most was a series of eight book reviews for *The Nation* magazine (1972–1975). This made me think much more about the needs of the reader and the purpose of my evaluations. I had the good fortune of the editorship of Emile Capouya who was my colleague at Baruch as well as publisher of *The Nation*; he had a long and successful career as an editor at a number of progressive publishers including New Directions. He gave me wide latitude in selecting books to review and encouragement in developing my point of view—a welcome freedom from the pressures I had felt from undergraduate days to avoid criticizing works prized by the instructors, which usually meant the texts they assigned to write about. Now I was free to like what I liked and even more to dislike what I didn't. His editorial suggestions were mostly directed toward the pacing of my articles, to make my dense prose "breathe a bit," as he said. At one point we collaborated on a proposal for a textbook on critical reading, though we could not find a publisher. He taught me a lot, and publishing in the journal gave me confidence to express challenging views to wider audiences (though the magazine's readership was still a pretty rarified, educated, progressive group).

Writing about Writing

I was, however, more enthusiastic about sharing ideas about teaching writing among similarly interested colleagues. In addition to conference presentations, I wrote a few short minor pieces, some published, that expressed my early views on the teaching of writing. One early unpublished essay (which seems to have been written no later than 1973, my second year of teaching college writing) was a kind of credo. "Simple Writing" was a series of short epigrammatic, sometimes enigmatic sentences, appearing to be influenced by Cunningham and perhaps the later Wittgenstein and Nietzsche. All the statements were presented as skeptical, self-assured, and transgressive, with the rhythm and format of my recent poems, which I was still writing, but which soon ceased. I was trying to develop an authoritative professional voice that focused on student needs and dynamics in learning to realize their expressive intentions, finding their words from within. Although I still was caught in literary ideologies of expressivism, individuality, anti-specialization, and skepticism of expertise, some ideas explored issues that I would expand later as I gained experience and developed research. I, however, was not yet paying attention to larger social systems, nor understanding the classroom itself as a specialized communicative system.

In a short joint statement from CAWS on standardized testing which was published in *College Composition and Communication* (1976b), I started to learn to collaborate with colleagues and come to agreement on principles. I was also learning collaboration on other documents that circulated locally. Skills of coming to shared language that mediates differing viewpoints to create shared commitments are important for institutional agreement. Such skills of finding shared language turn out also to be important for singly-authored work, where one needs to craft findings and ideas in ways that will enlist readers of varying perspectives while still staying true to what one has found. Making strong statements while avoiding misunderstandings and distractions, being careful with terms that some may find volatile, avoiding non-essential quarrels and other potential landmines—all these require thought and developed skill, and are not always successful. At the same time, I began to learn how to recognize the limits of what was possible to get agreement on, how to limit claims to potential areas of agreement, and how to calibrate potential audiences in terms of where agreement is possible. This knowledge of the complex socio-ideological landscape one is speaking to is something that continues to grow with wider experiences and is one of the later developing areas of skill (see Beaufort, 1999).

Nonetheless, my initial statements on writing were fairly conventional within the writing community and my first major collaboration was a traditional classroom handbook, with a few specific innovations. I met my co-author Harvey Wiener through CAWS where he was one of the founding co-chairs and I was secretary. He invited me to join with him on a project he had already had a contract for: an *English Skills Handbook,* which combined principles for both reading and writing (1978b). That combination was one of the book's major innovations, contrasting with the traditional focus of handbooks only on writing. The other was to present principles in as direct and simple a way as possible for a basic writing student, minimizing technical language and avoiding barriers to understanding.

Combining reading and writing was Harvey's idea and the basis for the contract. He initially brought me on to write the writing skills component. I reviewed all the extant handbooks, identified the topics covered, and made the presentations and examples as easily understood as possible. However, in reviewing the handbooks, I found at that time very little on writing processes (which was just emerging as a research topic and pedagogic priority), so I added a section on this. Additionally, I added a brief chapter on essay examinations, a common form of writing students needed to address. For me working on this book was an introduction to the world of textbooks, and simplifying the formal suggestions of a handbook to be appropriate for a basic writing audience challenged me to adopt an even clearer style and careful selection of what was essential. The book also got me thinking about the relationship between reading and writing and the limitations of the then current ways of making that connection.

From a marketing point of view, combining reading and writing in a single book turned out to be not such a good idea, since courses in the two were largely separate at the time, and often taught in separate departments. Speaking as directly as possible to basic writing students, however, was much needed. So, we separated the two parts and went through many editions and versions of each half (a total of 27 books by the end). The last spin-off appeared in 2006, almost thirty years since the first book appeared. As this series of books continued to sell, I became attuned to how textbooks were used in classes and how teachers used these books for various purposes. I started to think of textbooks as creating activity structures fitting within the activity structures of classes. I continued to work on making the books speak more directly to students, although presses made publication decisions and teachers and committees made adoption decisions. I had to learn to wend my way through complicated audience structures, with numerous levels of choice makers and users. Failure at one level could then lead to failure at others. Sometimes I was more successful at this than others. Even if books were contracted, if editors and salespeople did not understand them, editing and marketing could distort projects and lead to unsellable books. If the committees and teachers could not imagine how the book would fit with appropriate courses, it would not be adopted. If the book didn't work with students, adopters would not renew and publishers would be disappointed—and most importantly students would not benefit. Consequently, I learned to pay attention to the reaction and reviews at each level, even if I did not always agree with the suggestions. Each complaint flagged a problem in reaching the audience, even if it didn't clearly diagnose or resolve the issue. Each complaint indicated something I still had to work on.

Figure 17.1. Some Textbooks

In revised editions of the *Writing Skills Handbook*, I reorganized and elaborated key parts to emphasize the process of composition and how to write about sources, moving beyond the traditional narrow focus on citation form. I included a section on the research paper, as I started to understand its role in teaching skills of writing about reading, through fostering closer reading, response, and evaluation, despite the obvious artifice of the assignment. Mina Shaughnessy in *Errors and Expectations* (1977) had made some brief, unelaborated comments on academic writing and use of sources. From my experience as a student, I saw academic writing as going beyond matters of form and convention to deeper issues of intellectual development and elaboration of thoughts. I began exploring what was to be the pedagogy of *The Informed Writer*, discussed in the next chapter.

The reading skills books went through even more editions and versions than the writing skills book, addressing different skill levels and different focuses, including reading textbooks and cross-cultural readings. I began to take shared responsibility for these books, developing my writing in two specific ways. First, I worked on selecting materials that would engage students and would practice the kinds of skills we were targeting. I had been doing this since I had started teaching, but here the challenges were higher and the audiences larger and more widespread. Harvey and I spent many hours looking at candidate selections, developing criteria, evaluating choices, considering the contribution of each selection to the whole ensemble of each collection, and sequencing readings. The second area of work was to construct study questions. While the questions were standard in format for previewing, skimming, content comprehension, inference, and evaluation, I soon realized these questions could be more than random: they could serve as sequential paths to a deeper reading and understanding of each selection. Framing sequences of questions to move the students beyond a superficial "correct" reading became my major challenge. This sequencing of questions helped make more explicit for me what was involved in more subtle and sophisticated reading of even apparently simple texts.

Learning About My Own Writing from Teaching

My teaching of writing started to influence my own writing practices. The first impact grew from what I had been learning while teaching early grades, about keeping my students' understanding, engagement, and practice activities in mind. In preparing materials for developmental students at the university, I became explicit and clear in what I presented and asked for; at the same time, I sought ways to engage students' feelings, experiences, and complexities of thinking as young adults in a rich urban world, whatever their level of achievement in academic literacies. As a student I had grown most rapidly in the presence of teachers who engaged my concerns and were receptive to the ideas I was trying to formulate. As a teacher, I needed to follow the students' perceptions, interests, and needs, and then to show how what we read and wrote about would help them pursue their compelling concerns.

The simplicity, focus, and explicitness of style for my teaching materials continued as writing goals while I engaged less familiar and more complex materials in my pedagogy, research, and theory. I tried to make difficult topics as clear and simple as I could, without distorting or over-simplifying the materials and issues at hand. When first working through my ideas I used the terms most meaningful for me, but then would revise what I finally came to in terms intelligible and meaningful for the intended audiences. This was a process Linda Flower was memorably to call transforming writer-based prose to reader-based prose (Flower, 1979).

As part of setting out a clearer path for my readers, I started to incorporate a practice I learned from textbook publishing: using subheadings and other text organizers to help the reader through the different sections and to make the logic of reasoning and exposition more visible. This had the added benefit of making the logic more explicit to myself, leading me recursively to elaborate some of the connections and transitions in my reasoning. These subheadings are now sometimes integrated into my planning, though sometimes I create them in revision, bringing out the logic and continuity of material I had been creating. This is related to another practice I now use and sometimes recommend to students of creating an outline when I am part way through a draft, to uncover the logic of the emergent reasoning.

Becoming Mindful About Process

As I was teaching in the early years of the process movement, I tried to incorporate more drafting and revision in my classes. This made me more conscious of my own processes, more planful, and more energetic in the emergence of my drafts and revision. Since my first year of college, although I had regularly reworked my creative writing, my writing of academic papers had largely been done in a single draft. While I may have done a lot of mental work beforehand, by the time I started to sketch out some brief notes and then type a draft, the writing was pretty much in final form, followed usually only by brief (and often inadequate) proofreading. Even if I had written out a draft by hand on yellow legal pads, I revised little as I typed it out, perhaps fiddling with a few words and phrases. I had actually been proud of how much work I was able to do in my head, thinking it a sign of how clever I was, but when I saw the effect of a process approach on my students' writing, it dawned on me that I might start practicing what I preached. This was a great revelation to me as I discovered my texts improved, and I could focus on different levels of the work at different moments, without having to worry about everything all at once. I didn't have to worry about keeping my syntax simple and correct when I was first articulating or connecting ideas, nor did I have to elaborate examples fully when I was feeling the forward press of my argument.

I noticed, however, that I was quite attached to my first formulations and found them hard to revise. They seemed to capture what was on my mind, and I felt great relief at finding a way to express my thoughts. In order to see the text fresh, I began to assign myself a main question or task to carry out with each revision, although when I noticed other things, I still jumped levels. These new procedures coordinated well with the standard advice at that time of setting aside the text for a day or two, or having someone else read it and give some feedback. Each of those could give me a fresh eye and identify issues for me to formulate as revision questions.

Having a focused task for each level of revision helped me also develop criteria for identifying spots that needed work and for having adequately addressed each trouble spot, whether it was to establish coherence and sequences of thought, to provide concrete examples, or to straighten out the rhythms, sentence organization, and forward motion of the text. When, after systematic examination, the revision had met the criteria for that level, I could move on to the next issue. Once I had answered all my questions and taken all the perspectives that occurred to me, I would have no more leverage on the text, nothing that would suggest further change. I then knew when I had finished revising (at least until I got comments back, which might have given me new issues and perspectives to work on).

This systematic revision also gave me greater confidence when I received questions about the difficulty of some of my writing. I would check that my sentences weren't too long or involuted, my vocabulary was not obscure, my text was organized with enough logic and transition markers, I gave sufficient examples to allow readers to identify what I am talking about, and so on. If all such issues passed muster, I could then surmise the difficulty came from the unfamiliarity of content or perspective, or objections readers may have that led them to resist going down the path I laid out, or some other intellectual differences.

This revision process, of course, was aided as I moved to word processing, with my first home computer in 1983—an early Kaypro II, which the manufacturers optimistically claimed was portable, but which had the look and weight of WWII military field equipment. It pretty much stayed on my desktop. For a while I still used legal pads for early drafts and sketches, but when I began a draft in earnest I moved to the computer. Now I use handwriting only occasionally for early notes and jottings, and I have closet shelves filled with aging stacks of stockpiled legal pads and boxes of crisp color-coded manila file folders (along with some sheets of unused carbon paper and corrasable bond). My son found it funny as an adolescent that he had inherited my pleasure in haunting the aisles of office supply stores.

Working with my students on time management and deadlines also made me more intentional in setting interim goals and deadlines, in order to let the work evolve and grow. I noticed that one of the biggest reasons for subpar work from students was that they left their assignments to the last minute. As I started to assign interim process tasks, they began working on their writing earlier and returning to it over an extended period. They had more time on task, time for ideas to cook, and time to address each part of the process. This stretching of the timeline improved the quality of writing greatly. Even such a basic thing as asking students to write a sentence or two with preliminary ideas about how they would address an assignment, and then revisiting their plans in later classes would give them the space and time to let the project evolve, apart from any feedback or discussion that might come from me or peers.

In my own writing I began planning the kinds of interim documents I would need and setting time lines for accomplishing stages of the work. I would then recognize that all these interim tasks meant that projects would take time to ripen. As an undergraduate I was somewhat predisposed to this, as I would keep up with readings and discussion throughout the term. I looked on with dismayed wonder as some of my classmates crammed all their reading into the closing week of the term, while I was able to review quickly what I had done and get a good rest before exams. I, nonetheless, was addicted to last-minute all-night writing of papers despite turning over ideas in my head and reading relevant texts for days or weeks. After teaching for a while, however, I had internalized more complex time management. I was able to work on multiple projects at the same time, each at different stages. I could let some lie fallow while others moved forward, and I could vary the level of work so as to not burn out my cognitive resources—perhaps in one day doing some deep early planning on one project, then proofreading on another, then taking notes and marking up analysis for another. So, each project could ripen, while all kept moving forward.

Further, as I became more explicit about how students needed to report on, analyze, respond to, synthesize and integrate their sources, I also became more aware and self-conscious about these activities myself, incorporating some of my own advice, particularly elaborating what the reader is to get from the quoted material and being explicit on my comment or analysis of it.

This interaction between my teaching and my own writing was to continue throughout my career, as my understanding of writing grew. I was soon to add research into this interaction, as teaching and writing presented puzzles for me to explore and insights to confirm and elaborate. The research fed back into my teaching and writing practice, as well as led to theoretical elaborations at all levels. Organizational experiences and international teaching then extended my opportunities to experience and observe more, further expanding the resources I was able to bring to teaching, writing, researching and theorizing.

Finally, teaching and writing textbooks led me to reflectively codify what I knew about writing, in order to share it. In those days I thought about this sharing as a socially radical project of making available what I had learned through my elite education to those who had not had those opportunities—"spilling the beans" as I thought about it then.

Part Four. Learning the Writing Scholar Trade

Figure 18.1. On a path. Photo courtesy of Charles Bazerman.

Chapter 18. Becoming a Writing Researcher: The Classroom as Design Inquiry

Starting out as a teacher of writing, I thought I understood what writing was and how to do it. I looked into myself and the experience of other writers to become more explicit about what we knew. I also learned about my students to be able to motivate them and find out what they needed to learn. But some colleagues prodded me to realize that we didn't yet understand some fundamental things about writing. This was the next transformative moment in my development as a writer, turning me into an investigator, which I first pursued by experimenting with the design of classroom activities and then by more systematic research. This moment arrived shortly before my tenure, which then freed me from economic and evaluative insecurity to pursue what I thought was really worth doing. I never wrote on literary subjects again, except briefly to place literary writing within a more comprehensive theoretical picture about all writing (Bazerman, 2003d).

Textbooks as Pedagogic Knowledge

Pairing reading and writing in the *English Skills Handbook* (1978b) made me question how we were using reading in our writing classes. As in many classrooms across the country, I had used anthologies to provide students material to comment on and examples to follow. I found, however, as had many other teachers, even when students read assignments for class, they often had difficulty understanding what the sequence of reasoning was, what points the authors were making, and how thoughts of people represented in the text fit into the author's perspective. In discussions, students could not remember ideas or details from the readings because they did not have a frame for making meaning from the separate details. I found that mapping out with students the argumentative structure of challenging readings could prompt more interesting discussions of their own ideas and experiences in relation to the articles. Yet they still had difficulties gaining such understanding on their own. I then asked them to paraphrase and summarize readings before the discussions in order to put the responsibility for gaining meaning from texts on them. These exercises helped them attend more carefully to what the texts said, helped them remember what they had read, and made their interpretations visible to me. As the readings became more complex and indirect, I found student difficulties in understanding to go far beyond the basic skills which Harvey and I dealt with in the handbooks. To help them connect with the readings I also asked them to write response journals and essays.

At Baruch, the second term mandatory writing class included a required research paper. While this requirement had been traditional, teachers wondered whether it was a meaningful task. It seemed ill-defined and artificial, not related to anything students would write in any of their courses or their careers afterward. Students, more often than not, did not produce very satisfactory work, often just incoherent cut and paste collections from sources only loosely related to their topic or to each other. I shared in these concerns, but I also saw academic writing required engaging with knowledge sources. I explored what activities and skills could make the research paper a more meaningful task, tied to student intellectual growth. While at that time textbook coverage of the research paper went little beyond citation form (Ken Macrorie's *Searching Writing* was not to appear until 1980), I began to explore how a better-defined library research task could engage students with inquiry topics that were meaningful for them, drawing on both their experience and what they found in sources. I found, as well, smaller interim assignments could help them find more meaning in the inquiry process.

What was the Writing Requirement for?

Recognizing how writing was a means for intellectual growth increased my curiosity about what students had to write for their other subjects. When I started teaching writing in the early 1970s there were many views about the purposes of writing instruction, which ranged from fostering grammatical correctness, to developing literary style, to job preparation, to self-discovery through personal writing, to psychotherapy. All of them were valid concerns for writing, as writing was capacious, complex, and varied, but the immediate question was what we should teach in first year writing. For the non-traditional students I was working with in an open admissions environment, the most pressing task was for them to write sufficiently well to pass courses and complete their degrees, first in general education and then in their chosen majors. It seemed obvious to me that this was the reason writing courses were required, and I took this as my mandate. Accordingly, I discussed with students the writing assignments they were getting in other courses, and found the instructions were often ill-defined and vague, sometimes just asking for a "term paper" with no other specification.

I decided to survey faculty at my university to see if they could give me a more precise answer as to what they wanted. Although that kind of survey is common now, at that time I had not heard of many. The first survey in 1975–1976 established that teachers assigned writing and took it seriously. They had policies that showed more concern for organization and thought than correctness. Another survey the following year found that over two thirds of the writing was directly about reading in the form of reviews of literature, responses to reading, book reviews, or critical analyses—while almost all the rest of the assignments indirectly relied on reading for original theses, reports, or exam writing. I wrote up the findings of the surveys in internal reports and presented them in regional composition conferences. These reports and presentations were my first experience arguing with quantitative evidence since I had written up cookbook labs in first-year college physics. I learned it took a lot of examining data to see where important trends lay and then to find the best tables and figures to highlight the findings. I had to overcome the first temptation to present the results narratively, where they would be hard to follow. While graphic display skills were then taught in undergraduate technical writing courses and social scientists early became familiar with them, to me with my humanities training, they were novel. Then I had the challenge of presenting these quantitative findings persuasively to humanities audiences.

These survey findings gave further impetus to my emerging writing about reading pedagogy. I experimented with assignments that would engage students in greater detail and depth with readings and develop their thinking in response. While composition journals had discussed readings as sources of content or springboards for thinking, the advocacy was general with few activities and procedures and little that would lead students to more careful reading. Similarly, textbooks offered little useful advice on creating a more dynamic and careful interaction with reading. Even anthologies of essays offered little beyond some content comprehension questions and general prompts for response. Only a few books like Ronald Primeau's *Writing in the Margin* (1976) started to address seriously how to build detailed response. For pedagogy to create more careful reading, I had to go back to Mortimer Adler's 1940 book, *How to Read a Book*, I. A. Richards' 1942 response, *How to Read a Page*, and Richard Altick's 1946 *Preface to Critical Reading*. Much earlier in the first decades of the century a number of books carried paraphrase and summary exercises, though without much in the way of instruction.

From the few hints in these books and several years of classroom experimentation, I developed a sequence of tasks combining the newly emergent process approach with these earlier methods of writing about reading. The sequence alternated response writing with writing tasks that attended closely to the meaning, structure, and argument of their readings. These led to essays of analysis, evaluation, and applying the ideas in readings to observations and experiences. From writing about a single text, assignments moved to synthesis of multiple sources and then developing arguments from that synthesis. This sequence gave focus and purpose to the research paper as a culmination of engagement with reading.

Learning to Write Innovative Textbooks

At that time, and still to some extent today, one of the most effective ways to share pedagogical ideas in composition was through a textbook. Houghton Mifflin supported the concept of the pedagogy I had been working on and offered me a contract. The first edition of *The Informed Writer* appeared with a 1981 copyright (Bazerman, 1981a). I also wrote a rationale for the pedagogy appearing in *College English* in 1980: "A Relationship Between Reading and Writing: The

Conversational Model" (Bazerman, 1980b). During the life of the book (the fifth and last edition appeared in 1995), the book was by far the better vehicle for sharing the pedagogy than the article. Total sales across all the editions was around 300,000 (not including the used book market), but the article was only sporadically cited until after 2005. Parts of the pedagogy soon started working their way into other textbooks without citation (as is common in textbooks) including the general idea of writing from sources and the synthesis essay being a significant and challenging intellectual task. The essay of synthesis also was to become a substantial focus of research, beginning with the work of Nancy Nelson Spivey (Spivey, 1984). As I initially hoped, working with the assignments in classrooms gave teachers a more persuasive experience of the pedagogy than a theoretical presentation, as they saw what students were capable of accomplishing with some guidance. For the students, the practices of writing about reading have now been naturalized into taken-for-granted academic activities.

Coming up with the sequence of chapters and activities was a challenge addressed over years, through repeated iterations in my classrooms, with the last few iterations being field testing of the manuscript. In writing and revising the book I found it a challenge to break down more complex and unfamiliar skills into simple explanations and instructions. I learned to rely on extended illustrations of student processes and analyses of their products to form major components of the chapters. I also had to solve the problem of selecting accessible, yet engaging and challenging materials that would help students experience the serious intellectual world of the university at the same time as they would recognize the relevance to their lives. Students entering college, I had learned in my teaching, were often motivated by feeling they were entering something very different from high school, a world of more serious inquiry and thought. Yet many students also needed to see how these new ideas were meaningful and not just "academic abstractions" in the worst sense. The book needed to excite students to engage in the hard but rewarding work of reading and writing they would be facing in the university. While the sequence of activities set up the backbone of the book, this rhetorical motive drove the energy of the chapters.

In the late 1970s, as I was writing the first edition of *The Informed Writer*, the WAC movement began growing. In subsequent editions I began to address disciplinary differences. I also started to think about different disciplines in terms of written language communities, as a metaphoric extension of the linguistic concept of spoken language communities, used to identify geographically localized dialect differences in pronunciation, lexical items, and grammatical features. I presented a paper with the title "Written Language Communities," at the 4C's in the spring of 1979, trying to make the concept of community apply, but I was already uneasy with it as not subtle or differentiated enough to characterize the multiple social positions and interpretive stances of the various individuals participating in disciplinary discussions. I drew on contrast cases to indicate the complexity and subtlety in traditions and the different roles different participants, readers and writers, might take. Drawing on the pedagogy I was developing, I tried to formulate how readers' interpretations, responses, and actions identified the consequences and thus the practical meaning of texts. Further, because writers design their texts anticipating audience response, their social orientation of writers went beyond a naturalized use of the dialect that they grew up in and accommodated toward.

In thinking through the complexity of the social interactions mediated by writing, I was soon to reject the term "communities" as not specific enough about the social relations and activities realized and organized through texts. I was trying to find a vocabulary to describe social interaction of writing and how texts form context for each other, reaching towards ideas of intertextuality, genre, and activity systems—but I wasn't yet there. At the same conference, however, I met Carolyn Miller and heard her first presentation on genre from her dissertation in progress. I found her characterization of genre and its mechanisms for formulation, emergence, and replication to be powerfully clear and precise. Further, she showed specific linkages between rhetorical and sociological theory, with some implications for cognition. This conjunction between sociology and rhetoric allowed me to bring together several tracks of my thinking at that time. Later I would fold this into a larger theory of activity.

The writing problem I was working with was finding the right conceptual term. An inexact term could lead to a lack of clarity and impede analysis, obscuring phenomena. It also required more words to talk around a phenomenon that was not yet grasped firmly[5]. But the right terms could bring the phenomena and repeated processes into focus, leading to further inquiries, evidence, and discoveries. This growing awareness of the value of correct terms drove my desire to develop formulations I could stand behind with precision. Although I started avoiding the term community except when I found it narrowly appropriate, I saw many other people using the term to recognize the sociality of writing. I did not, however, enter into a terminological argument at that time, because I was glad at least they were starting to take a social view of writing processes. Nonetheless, in my own work, I sought a more sociologically precise and complex set of terms to elaborate the social positioning of writing.

As I gained some clarity on the different roles and activities people took within disciplinary work, I saw that students in most undergraduate courses were not expected to write in the genres of professional publication, although they were often expected to read professional disciplinary texts that they would then write about in student genres. They would need to understand disciplinary texts, though not write them[6]. Further, I was finding that although most disciplines had

---

5. I found Yehuda Elkhana (1974) particularly clarifying on this problem as he recounts the conceptual difficulties incurred in 19th century physics by different terms used before energy and how this impeded discovery of the concept of conservation of energy.

6. Cheryl Geisler's work on students' authorial stances and purposes in a philosophy

distinctive names attached to departments, professional organizations, conferences and journals, yet multiple kinds of writing appeared within each, and that some writing in one discipline resembled writing in quite different disciplines. So while I was coming to appreciate the value of genre to understand readers' expectations, I was also seeing genre as not stable enough to dictate formal templates, nor did I see genres mapping crisply onto the boundaries of disciplines. Academic writing was a complicated landscape about which we did not know enough to make simple generalizations that would not be misleading to undergraduates. Even the traditional distinctions of humanities, social sciences, and hard sciences obscured the variety within and across the fields. So rather than following a simple taxonomy of disciplines or assuming that each discipline had a clear uniformity, I looked to the kind of evidence collected, displayed, and argued from in each text. A textual logic followed from whether fields used historical evidence, contemporary evidence from actual events, or evidence from designed/experimental events. If, alternatively, texts talked mostly about ideas theoretically, in relation to the ideas of other authors, they followed another logic. I presented this approach to evidentiary differences in disciplinary texts in the third edition of the *Informed Writer* appearing in 1989. Since I thought students would be more expected to read such disciplinary texts and perhaps write about them, but not to produce them, I focused on making sense of and discussing disciplinary texts. I added a subtitle to the book to indicate the engagement with disciplinary writing: *Using Sources in the Disciplines*. This question of production and use of evidence in different disciplines for me turned into an enduring and as yet not fully resolved research question, being implicit in many of my studies to follow, and more explicit in some recent ones (see Chapter 28).

In visiting campuses that were using *The Informed Writer*, I was shocked to see how the teachers' manual was used in TA training and standardized course syllabi. What I had written at my desk at home as some preliminary ideas to seed local creativity had turned into a set of requirements to be enacted by contingent employees. This drove home to me that consequences of writing existed in the uptake, over which I had little control. After the text left my desk, it belonged to the readers to understand and use as they would. As a writer, this increased my sense of responsibility for being as careful as I could in what I offered. This recognition ultimately would lead me to activity theory[7], which in turn led me to view classrooms as communicative activity systems within particular constraints and arrangements and using various tools, such as textbooks.

---

course was particularly provocative in helping me see this. She found that students approached texts in a course on ethics in practical ways to help them deal with issues in their lives instead of in the abstract puzzle solving way of the professional philosophers (Geisler, 1994).

7. I was greatly influenced by Yrjö Engestrom whose work I first became familiar with at a conference in 1992.

I followed up on these realizations in a 1989 anthology, *The Informed Reader*, which helped guide students into more in depth reading in the disciplines. The readings were organized around major issues from each disciplinary area that might be of potential interest to students—the literary canon (literary study), upward mobility (sociology and history), memory (psychology), productivity (business), greenhouse effect and climate change (earth sciences), nuclear power safety (physics and engineering), and artificial intelligence (interdisciplinary). From a perspective of more than three decades later, I am surprised how several topics remain of current importance.

This anthology also presented some issues of writing design. First, was the challenge of leading students from their non-expert positions into engaging with specialized disciplinary texts. The article clusters were organized to start with more general public statements, such as newspaper and magazine articles, setting up the importance of the issues and providing some basic terms and explanations. The selections then moved to more information heavy presentations such as from textbooks, then finally to core disciplinary articles. By the time students worked through the earlier readings they were prepared to understand the importance and content of more specialized texts.

A second challenge was to use the textbook apparatus to scaffold deeper engagement—in understanding, in critical engagement and application, and in a technical understanding of how the text was put together. I built on the strategies I had used in the more basic *Reading Skills Handbooks*, but went further in guiding students to deeper readings. Initial support came through headnotes and glosses, but deeper engagement was guided by the exercise activities. The exercises for each selection also introduced a specific rhetorical or stylistic issue which the students had to analyze through annotating the text, and then answering analytic questions using the evidence from the annotations. This analysis aimed to reveal in detail what writing choices were made and why. Finally, more general essay questions for each article and each section would allow students to consider the meaning and importance of the readings in relation to their own perceptions and interests. These sequenced classroom activities were designed to have students recognize the value of well-researched information, to be able to incorporate research grounded articles into their writing, and to give them the confidence to be able to read and respond to the disciplinary texts they would encounter in their other courses.

In 1997 I published another textbook, *Involved*, on similar principles, but incorporating my continuing research and theorizing. This book empowered students to analyze the activity systems within the classrooms they would encounter, so that their writing would successfully meet the learning intentions and expectations of the course. The book asked students to consider the logic of their classes and how the readings, activities, and lectures fit together, so they could analyze what their assignments needed to accomplish, what constraints and expectations would frame the evaluation of their assignments, what resources they had available, and ultimately how these tasks could satisfy their own interests and curiosities. The advice and activities asked students to develop their own perspectives, evaluations, and thoughts in response to course materials and their assigned tasks. The course ended with investigation in archives and field. The book also added guidance and activities to foster complexity of reasoning and problem solving, which would allow them to do higher quality work, revealing the value and rewards of serious inquiry into difficult problems.

Learning From Textbook Writing and Working with Textbook Publishers

The writing of textbooks had many consequences for my own development as a writer. I developed an authoritative and direct expository style. I sorted out what was important to discuss and what was digressive. I considered how to lead readers from a simple explanation of concepts and practices to more nuanced complex understanding. I learned how to realize concepts in examples and practical activities that would make concepts alive. I learned how to present related concepts systematically and progressively over chapters. I became more adept at using subheadings (a standard textbook practice) to guide the readers' understanding of the sequence of thoughts. Perhaps most, I advanced my sense of how to use my writing dialogically to prompt students' own productions and thoughts, by setting up situations, materials, and questions to pose puzzles for students to work through in their writing.

Working on textbooks also gave me a fuller sense of published, distributed writing as complexly collaborative. Textbooks are corporate, marketable, sellable products. A successful product, however, has to be something that teachers could use and would integrate with their own approaches and methods, supporting them in their classroom work. And then it would have to be successful with students in leading them to the kind of learning teachers valued. These ends were different than the typical academic work that sought to contribute to the knowledge of a field and possibly be intellectually or emotionally intriguing. Textbook editors (and their sales and reviewer networks) could identify projects that would meet classroom needs and could provide support to the textbook's development, but they could also be obstacles, especially if editors were switched part way through a project. Disagreements with editors who understood and believed in the book's concept could be quite productive. Disagreements with editors who did not believe in or understand the project could be harmful, leading to a tension, even incoherence, in the final book. Sometimes, however, even these tensions could lead to some creative invention to speak to editors' concerns, while maintaining the book's vision. A sales force that understood the book could locate places where the book would prosper, but the book could wither if the sales force could not see what the book could accomplish and could not present it appropriately to textbook committees and teachers.

Extensive reviewing could be helpful directly—even when it seemed misguided or based on misreading. Reviews forced me to ask how the text could have avoided the misunderstanding, or how I could have better supported the book's classroom usefulness. If one reader had these problems, others would also likely have them. Reviews also could identify who the book would appeal to: the book was not for everyone.

While my pedagogy emerged out of my specific teaching experiences and the discussions among colleagues within City University of New York, the opportunity to elaborate these ideas in textbooks and the interaction with other writing programs that supported further development was dependent on a nationally organized publishing industry, its economics and corporate structures, the structure of the textbook markets, and the strategies of the industry to address the markets. In some ways authors are like the front person in a band; you need a lot of people on stage, backstage, and in the business office all aligned to deliver something in the name of the lead singer. So learning to write textbooks also meant learning to produce content that fit within the larger structures, expectations, and needs of the industry, including marketing and sales.

When Harvey Wiener invited me to join him on the *English Skills Handbook* series, the books were already contracted with Houghton Mifflin, where the books stayed through most of their editions and versions. Because of the positive relationship formed with Houghton Mifflin, I stayed with them for my ensuing projects. At that time, it was a moderately-sized, privately-held, independent company, with a reputation for educational quality. The reputation of its educational division built upon the publisher's history of eminent books on literary and social issues, going back to the middle of the nineteenth century. It was one of a group of independent publishers that were known to share literary and academic values and were a recognized part of an educated national culture.

Even more fundamentally, in the United States, unlike in some other countries, there was no national curriculum, textbook policy, or governmental production. Primary and secondary purchases were typically made at the school or district level, though within state policy and parameters. Higher education was even less regulated with textbook decisions made largely by the individual instructor, or for large multi-section courses, by a department or departmental committee. Some disciplines such as chemistry are highly standardized in the expectations for their basic courses through professional organizations, following developments in the field. Writing courses are less regulated, but are often guided by traditional expectations. Departmental decisions were common for required writing courses, especially when there were large numbers of contingent or new instructors, or where there were campus pressures for common expectations and standards, as first year required courses were often seen as a service to the campus as a whole. Further, since these courses were often administered through English

Literature departments, literary values influenced what was seen as good writing to be encouraged. Accordingly, publishers were motivated to contract and produce books that appealed to broadly shared, traditional expectations, attractive for larger adoptions at bigger schools. As a result, the composition market tended to be conservative, although a book gained by having noticeable distinctiveness to make it more attractive than similar alternatives.

The three standard kinds of books used within writing courses had been stabilized as handbooks, rhetorics, and anthologies. Handbooks were basic references presenting standards and expectations for correctness, with minimal instruction or exercises. Rhetorics provided overt teaching material aimed at developing skills, through introducing writing concepts, providing examples, and offering activities. Anthologies provided readings for discussion, analysis, and models, whether organized around themes, text types or other principles. Some anthologies were literary, others expository, others focusing on civic, social, or personal issues. Because of the book resale market and students' practices of selling books when they were done with courses, publishers were motivated to produce new editions of successful books every few years in order to drive the older editions off the market. This then created the need for a certain amount of ostensible novelty, and perhaps some real innovation in response to what was learned from the use of the earlier editions, though not enough to turn off users of previous editions.

Books were produced for the most common patterns of courses. Required writing courses tended to be for one or two terms within the first year, with sometimes remedial courses for students identified as needing preliminary work. When there was a required two-term sequence, the second often included a required library research paper. This matched the curricular sequence at Baruch, so my teaching matched well with the structure of the market.

The English Skills Handbook fit a clear niche in this market, adopting the standard form of handbooks which set basic expectations, but addressed to the growing part of the market for developmental courses, through simpler, less technical explanations. Further it placed within that format reading instruction, often needed by developmental students, who were now being admitted under open admissions and similar programs. As developmental reading courses were most often distinct from writing courses, even taught in different departments, the books prospered better once split into separate writing and reading books.

On the other hand, some writing courses were taught by people with long experience and some degree of autonomy as semi-permanent lecturers or tenured faculty members. This then created within the market the potential for more original products, appealing to more sophisticated or evolving ideas of writing instruction. Anthologies, though fairly stable in formats, could express novelty in selections and organization. Rhetorics, however, had the most flexibility to offer new modes and topics of teaching. These niche opportunities increased as the field became professionalized and research and graduate degrees emerged, which happened during the life-cycle of my textbooks. Sometimes more trained and confident instructors also gained control of the committee decision making processes, creating possibilities of more novel books to gain larger adoptions.

The more novel pedagogies of *The Informed Writer* and *Involved* found this more creative space for innovation within rhetorics. Over five editions *The Informed Writer* evolved and created a new kind of approach to composition about writing with sources and writing for disciplines, with books by other authors consequently taking up its general approach. As well, aspects of the approach were integrated into books with more comprehensive approaches and some anthologies. The innovations of *Involved*, however, were not taken up and so it did not have a wide impact on teaching. By the time *Involved* appeared, as well, the publishing industry had changed. Textbook publishers were merging and being bought up, to be part of large corporate enterprises, publicly held and driven more by corporate culture with the need for strong quarterly earnings rather than being part of educational, academic culture. This created greater pressures for standardized products with larger markets and adoptions. More boutique innovative products were not marketed as vigorously.

Chapter 19. Science Studies as Writing Studies

Teaching academic writing and uses of intertextuality made me wonder how disciplines were organized and how individuals came to engage in academic writing. I was not at first aware of the field of sociology of science, nor had I taken any sociology courses since my first year of college. The interpersonal approach of my therapy, however, had primed me to think about sociality. When at a faculty party I started describing the way I was thinking about disciplines and disciplinary writing to a colleague from the Sociology Department, he suggested I needed to read some sociology of science. He also suggested that I contact Robert Merton, the founder of the field, who was just a subway ride uptown at Columbia University. Merton generously invited me to participate in the graduate seminar he shared with Harriet Zuckerman, starting in 1978. I continued to participate weekly for at least four years. Through the seminar I got to know a number of the rising and established scholars of the field. I also began attending science studies conferences, most regularly the Society for the Social Studies of Science.

Inventing the Analysis of Scientific Texts

At first, I had little idea what studies of scientific writing might look like. While some rhetorical theorists had argued that science might be considered rhetorically, little empirical study of scientific writing had been published. I have a notebook stretching through two years full of ideas trying to think through how I should proceed, what problems I should focus on, what texts I might study, and what modes of analysis I might use. It also contains notes about my presentations at seminars, meetings with other scholars, and responses to provocative readings.

I began by doing what I was most familiar with from my literary training: looking at texts from historical anthologies of exemplary scientific writing from the ancient world through the twentieth century. I started by taking informal notes on selections that looked interesting, without much of an idea what I was looking for. After looking at what I had noted on my first attempts, I developed coding sheets to record parallel observations on each example (including basic information such as length, primary claim, empirical materials, number and use of citations, subheadings, and organization) as well as more interpretive evaluations (such as source of problem addressed, representation of author and audience, representation of methods, and main argumentative strategy). I thought I was distancing myself from literary criticism and its assumptions because I was noticing different kinds of details than were most important in literary texts, yet

I was aware that I was still using my skills in noticing textual details, organization, themes, and stances. I eventually also incorporated analysis of genre, class, social and historical location, and social relations which I had developed in my dissertation. I also drew on what I had been learning in my teaching about how writers were referring to and discussing texts in their fields. Many of the questions and plans in that notebook I now see as continuing through the following decades, including the role of data and data production, the relationship of internal thought and expressed thought, the role of changing textual form and its relationship to structure of arguments, and the formation and communication of knowledge collectives, and the role and evolution of disciplinary literatures.

Since I would not know what a persuasive analysis of scientific texts would look like until I did some, I moved from note taking to writing a full paper and seeing what issues arose within it. I was anxious and uncertain while writing my first analytical presentation of scientific texts for Merton and Zuckerman's seminar because I had to solve many for-me novel problems. In order to highlight disciplinary contrasts, I picked examples from natural sciences, social sciences, and humanities. Since I had no principled way to identify typicality of writing in those fields, I chose highly cited articles for analysis—under the assumption that recognition indicated that the articles met the values and needs of their fields to become certifiable contributions, even though they inherently were not typical in their distinctive success. In order to organize the comparison, I initially drew on the traditional communication triangle that had many incarnations from Aristotle through James Kinneavy, all of which had some variation of the author, audience, and world/subject at the vertices. In my early drafts, however, I struggled with how to organize the discussion of the prior disciplinary literature, which was everywhere, but not well represented in the triangle. Each of the three vertices relied on the literature—as markers of authority and ethos, as shared knowledge of the field, and as establishing relations with the audience. As well the literature established criteria of judgment, methods of inquiry, and markers of argument legitimacy. When I presented an early version of the paper to Merton's seminar, he reasonably pointed out that I seemed to want to make the literature an additional vertex—which would of course allow interaction with the other vertices. When I turned the communication triangle into a triangular prism (at the time I inaccurately called it a pyramid), the problem dissolved, and I wound up using this triangular prism explicitly (and sometimes implicitly) as an analytic heuristic in my work for many years. This helped me see how fundamental the literature was in academic writing. When the term intertextuality came along a few years later, I began using it, though I had a few qualms about the baggage it brought. The term *intertextuality*, as used in literary studies, kept a distance from the other elements, whereas the triangular prism formulation highlighted how interactive the literature was with authorial identities and representation; audience knowledge, expectations, and criteria; and stance towards the phenomena in the world being discussed (see Bazerman, 2004c for a fuller discussion of the different uses of the term).

Figure 19.1. Robert King Merton

When I showed an early version of this presentation to Karin Knorr, an ethnographer of science, she pointed out to me that I was relying on a number of stereotyped, folk-belief assumptions about disciplines and their relation to each other. This was an important lesson, pushing me to greater precision in characterizations and questioning common sense ideas about social phenomena. I became more cautious and specific in my claims, and more careful about theoretical generalizations. I read more deeply into sociological theory and findings. As I started to draw on other disciplines within science studies, I tried also to respect the knowledge and perspective of each of the fields I was drawing on, at the same time as I pursued my own questions derived from writing studies. While I remained confident in my textual analysis of each of the three articles, in the published version (Bazerman, 1981b) I backed away from any claim of characteristic differences among fields. Rather I characterized the analyses of these articles only as individual spots in a complex landscape we did not yet have a more extensive and detailed understanding of.

This cautiousness also led me to be more intentional and careful in defining corpora and the generalizations to be drawn from them. I remember a comment from one of the other participants in Merton's seminar when asked about the limitations of his sample and analytic methods—he acknowledged the limitations and uncertainties of the empirical materials but then commented that his claims were modest and did not ask a lot from the data. I took this to mean there was not an absoluteness about what methods to use, but rather one should calibrate one's materials, methods, and claims to be adequate for each other. The amount of detail and precision available would affect the nature of what one could claim, and, inversely, the nature of the claim could determine the necessary evidence and precision needed to warrant it.

In Merton's seminar, as typical in sociology, research methods were examined and critiqued. Further, the role of replicable methods in the production of science, the limits of replicability, and the purpose of representation of methods in research articles were explicit topics within science studies. Accordingly, I became more aware of the importance of making methods explicit in a way that was not part of my training in literary studies nor was common within studies of rhetoric and composition. As I began publishing studies of scientific writing, I became as painstakingly explicit in laying out my methods as I could be, even when it involved creative, critical, or interpretive methods. From that time forward I made it a point of specifying methods, in the design of the study, identification of research site, formation of a corpus or other data collection, data representation, and mode of analysis. I also have worked where possible, to make the initial representation of the data distinct from its further analysis; in literary and rhetorical studies often these two steps are conflated and the audiences see the empirical material only through the critic's interpretive vision and critical conclusions.

One particular methodological principle I learned in Merton's seminar and have attempted to employ in my consequent studies has been the idea of the strategic research site. That is, particular research sites display the phenomenon of interest with unusual empirical prominence or clarity; in less favorable research sites, the phenomenon might also be at play, but may be entangled with harder-to-parse variables or may appear with smaller and less visible effects (Merton, 1987). For my first study, the choice of prominent articles from three different fields was strategic for displaying text differences and how those representations are presented for evaluation. It was not strategic for looking at typicality or systematic differences among the fields, which would require larger corpora with careful criteria of inclusion. Nor was it strategic for examining the processes of writing or the actual modes of investigation, which would require ethnographic examination of research and writing practices. I have also come to advocate an inverse of this idea of strategic research site: if I have access to certain materials and data, so what are they good for, what can they show me? At some point I transformed this realization into a question I repeat to students, that every bit of empirical data is evidence of something, but the question is "evidence of what?"

This kind of principle has guided me both to look for places to investigate specific research questions and to identify the potential use of materials or research opportunities that might fortuitously become available to me. This principle has helped me navigate between intention and luck, allowing me to build a coherent view of related concepts grounded in investigations while being flexible in recognizing and responding to opportunities (see also Bazerman, 2008d for a further discussion of method.)

When I shared a draft of this early paper with colleagues from literary and composition studies, they found my formulations complex, unfamiliar, and hard to understand. I first made typical excuses that the concepts were hard to understand because they stood at the intersection of disciplines and theories. But one reader commented that the conceptual complexity increased my responsibility as a writer to make the text as understandable as possible, explaining clearly the concepts from different theories and disciplines along with their relationship. Since I had been advocating this principle for a number of years, I was quickly shocked back to my better revision angels. I became more mindful of how to lead the readers into the ideas without dumping them suddenly into unclearly defined concepts and relationships. While I have been able to find some recognizable, concrete, and familiar ways to connect readers with my ideas, I have not, however, eliminated the strangeness or novelty of the ideas that made them hard to process. Insofar as contingencies, subordinations, relations and other complexities needed to be represented, I have tried to present them sequentially across paragraphs, well-marked by textual signposts. The more I did this, the more readers could follow me on the journey, seeing more of what I was trying to show, and the longer they would tolerate the length and difficulty of the journey. Also, individuals could select the parts they were interested in and prepared to accept and did not have to take the entire intertwined package. Over the years, however, as my conceptual world has become more elaborated, this problem may even have become worse. I, however, have accepted my responsibility as a writer to make the work as accessible as I can.

After all this feedback and the mandates for revision, and after multiple presentations, including at the meeting of the Society of the Social Studies of Science, in September 1979, the article was published as "What Written Knowledge Does: Three Examples of Academic Discourse" in the journal *Philosophy of the Social Sciences* in 1981. While over the years I have been gratified by the reception this article has received, I continue to wonder why this first attempt to sketch out an approach which I have been elaborating and refining for the next forty years still remains more highly cited than some more recent papers which I think are more sophisticated in method and theory, as well as conceptually clearer and easier to read. But I'll take it. This reminds me that readers have their own reasons and interests which determine how they will take up work. The best I can do is offer multiple entry points which can then lead readers more fully into what I view as a consistent research and theory program.

A Next Step into Interdisciplinarity

As I became more familiar with science studies, I felt the need to make sense of the implications of the field for scientific writing. This impulse fortuitously coincided with an invitation to contribute to a volume on scientific and technical writing. I proposed writing a review of literature of social studies of science from the perspective of writing: "Scientific Writing as a Social Activity" (Bazerman, 1983a). This essay synthesized the different perspectives I had become familiar with, both in how they saw the function of writing within social systems of science and more specifically about what they pointed to in the structure, goals, and processes of scientific writing. This synthesis required developing a critical perspective on work from other fields that made claims or assumptions about writing, particularly if the fields were not well immersed in language and writing studies.

In thinking through how I would respond to the invitation, I was starting to learn how to match my research and intellectual interests to the publication opportunities that came my way. Of course, this is something most publishing researchers learn to do, improving throughout one's career. For me, finding that match meant having a sense of the next steps in my own research along with a sense of the audiences, venues, and genres that might be appropriate contexts for those pieces of work. Sometimes when opportunities came along the parts would spontaneously click and I would realize, "oh, this would be exactly the place to move me forward on this part of the project." But sometimes it might take longer to think through what would touch the interests of these editors and their audiences, what kinds of evidences and theories and arguments might be powerful for them, and then how that argument might advance what I was trying to understand. Sometimes the pieces matched almost exactly and I could just propose something I was already working on. Sometimes the opportunity would suggest to me something I had not yet considered, but I would see as a valuable next step. At other times I would see a task that might take me temporarily away from my main line of work, but which would carry me forward in a plausible way that might ultimately be useful. At other times, however, anything I came up with for the opportunity would be too much of a digression from where I wanted to go; then I would give the opportunity a pass—especially since I was by then tenured and no longer felt compelled to take every publication opportunity that would have a quick payoff. In this case, I had not previously thought of doing such a review, but I soon realized how such a review would help me (and my colleagues in writing studies) make better sense of the sociology of science literature and think through the implications for writing. I even began thinking about the review article as the equivalent of writing a graduate comprehensive field exam in sociology of science, though my own doctoral requirements were long past.

Such a review was different than other syntheses of sociology of science as I was applying the work to a different field. Writing this review in fact helped me get my priorities in focus. As I became more engaged with other fields, I was finding it hard to stay focused on what this material showed me about writing and how it could contribute to writing studies. It was too easy to get caught up in the intriguing problems and research agendas in those other fields. I have recurrently had to pull back to remember what was of importance to writing and the teaching of writing. Ultimately, I was only a tourist or amateur in those other fields. Trained historians, philosophers, and sociologists would be better equipped and more appropriately focused to address historical, philosophical, or sociological questions. That was their work. But I could make sense of and use their products, and what they found might be of interest to colleagues in my field. Even when I felt that as a writing researcher I could contribute to sociological, philosophical, or historical issues, I found there were limits to how much I could engage with people in those fields and persuade them as my perspective, modes of analysis, and evidence were so different from what had become persuasive in their fields. At most, some of the empirical things I and other writing researchers found might gradually become visible in the other fields and gradually work into their view of their fields, but they would have to pursue the inquiries and findings in their own terms. So even as I continued to learn from those fields and translate their work into my own field, I found that there were limits as to how much I could bring my perspectives into the discussions of those other fields.

A Further Step into the Problem of Facticity

In early 1980, writing a review of Latour and Woolgar's recently published *Laboratory Life* helped me sort out further what criteria successful analysis of scientific writing should meet (Bazerman, 1980a). This book was groundbreaking in many ways and would have a large impact. I appreciated many of its perspectives and insights, and found its detailed ethnographic observations around writing production important contributions. But I also found that the authors were not always knowledgeable about the complexity of language or writing processes. The book made a number of questionable assumptions, inappropriate analyses, conceptual conflations, leaps of reasoning, and unwarranted conclusions, which I noted in the review. In particular, the book did not seem careful enough in thinking through the differences of spoken and written language. So while I shared much of the enthusiasm most readers had for the book in the way it showed the centrality of inscription and text production in science, I was one of the few reviewers that questioned some of the book's more radical conclusions based on what I viewed as flawed reasoning and analysis of language. From the point of view of my own development as a writer, this exercise helped me think through the kinds of precision in analytic method and reasoning I would need to make and the standards of argument I would need to meet in order to produce work that I would consider warranted. This review also made me cautious about producing work too colored by a predetermined philosophic stance that might distort selection and analysis of evidence and frames of interpretation.

Substantively, the review focused me on the nature and quality of fact production and fact accounts. Latour and Woolgar had talked about this process as one of forgetting, as data became inscribed and materiality was left behind. As phenomena are reduced to inscriptions, whether graphic, numeric, or verbal, much is lost of the vitality, materiality, complexity, and multidimensionality of the phenomena. Nonetheless, the inscribed aspects of the phenomena are carried forward and thus remembered, although this was not considered by Latour and Woolgar. The inscription choices are intentional and purposeful, focusing attention on the phenomena the researchers are interested in. The question then becomes as much about what is remembered as what is forgotten, why certain things are chosen to be remembered, how that remembering happens, and whether that selection does violence to the phenomena and research questions. These were issues that stayed with me and would be behind a number of my later inquiries (see Chapters 26 & 27).

A number of additional themes introduced in Merton's sociology seminar have continued in my writing. Many of them I have recognized and discussed in some of my later theoretical pieces, and many are implicit in my growth of sociological imagination[8]—that is, seeing phenomena as part of social processes rather than only individual choice. One major theme that stayed with me was citation and codification, that is, how later work evaluates, selects, builds upon, and organizes earlier work. Citation studies were prominent in Merton's world, elaborated by Eugene Garfield and early citation indexing (currently called the Web of Science). Some of Merton's students worked within Garfield's Institute for Scientific Information (ISI) and the seminar had a number of presentations from Garfield and his research team. This work fed my growing interest in the use of sources in academic writing, and how scientific literatures formed emergent networks of knowledge. The work of the ISI helped me think about each individual article being part of a dynamic quasi-stable communal process of knowledge production.

Increased awareness of the emergent and changing nature of disciplinary literatures also focused the purpose of my own writing and publications: to propose persuasive findings and ideas that would carry forward discussion, reorient future work, or enable others to address evolving problems. While persistence of my own claims over time might be affirming, moving the literature as a whole forward became more important to me. This at times might mean, for example, opening up new areas or approaches with claims or ideas that would be rapidly superseded but which nonetheless could suggest directions others might take.

During my time in this seminar the English translation of Ludwik Fleck's book from the early 1930s, *Genesis and Development of a Scientific Fact* (1979) appeared. Merton was one of the editors and we devoted several sessions to this work. This book introduced the idea of thought styles (which in my reading of the book appeared to be representational styles) within thought collectives. Fleck's approach connected individual cognition, sociocultural organization, activity, and representational form realized in texts. Further, Fleck argued that culturally shaped activity was passively constrained by material conditions. He added that scientific cultures actively maximized the passive constraints of material experience on human representations of knowledge. This way of thinking gave me a means to formulate epistemological implications of writing processes by

---

8. The term was introduced by C. Wright Mills, 1959.

connecting research methods, representational methods, and analytic methods in writing in different disciplines; namely, how methods actively worked to constrain claims though the passive demands of evidence of the world. This also led me to think more about the production and use of evidence in my own work and the work of my students, and how those practices intersected with the culture of the field of writing studies. I came to see epistemology as a practical matter, realized in all the practices leading to the ultimate piece of writing. Epistemology, consequently, could be a site for empirical research and not just an abstract philosophic matter.

Fleck's formulations also helped me resolve the tensions between the relativist and empiricist accounts of science and scientific texts. I found much to value in the relativist analyses of scientific texts as human constructions (after all, language and writing are produced by humans, using the human inventions of textual representation, to communicate with other humans). Nonetheless, I still saw value in the empiricist account that scientific representations helped us understand and live more successfully within our material worlds. Fleck's formulations along with Vygotsky's accounts of how we develop our thinking at the intersection of our spontaneous experiences, our disciplined learning, and our interested engagement in the material world helped me formulate positions in the debates during this period, known as the science wars. While my formulations did not get much hearing from people entrenched in the alternate positions, I believe they do quietly persist and define credible research programs, even as the more absolutist positions on either side have softened and lost their vitriol. My struggles with developing and articulating my position, nonetheless, did give me the framework from which to develop my theoretical position in Chapter 11 of *Shaping Written Knowledge*.

Learning to find a middle path in those divisive times further built my skills of synthesizing and integrating radically different perspectives—respecting all sides, avoiding landmines, and recasting or sublating opposing views into a more comprehensive framework. This of course is a standard dialectical process, enacted repeatedly within Vygotsky's writings, which provided me models of how to do it successfully. I have used this discursive strategy not only in moving past the empiricism and relativism divide, as I have tried in the years to integrate psychological, sociological, historical, rhetorical, linguistic, textual, curricular and practical production approaches to writing. This synthetic orientation also guided me as an editor and leader of collaborative enterprises as I tried to bring out the nature and value of each contributor's line of work at the same time as seeing its connections, boundaries, and consequences for different lines of work. In later years, for example, this helped guide me in creating reference books like the handbook and the reference guides that attempted some kind of order, coherence, and intersection among the different contributions. Even more it was evident in the kinds of syntheses I fostered within collaborations on the lifespan development of writing.

An Introduction to the Rhetorical Tradition, Carnegie Mellon Version

After the first year in Merton's seminar, in the summer of 1979, I also participated in an NEH summer seminar at Carnegie Mellon University led by Richard Young. This was my first systematic introduction to the classical rhetorical tradition and its more contemporary elaborations. At CUNY we had focused on basic writing and open admissions, with a strong emphasis on understanding students and their thinking, but at CMU the focus was on the nature of argument and the early process work, which was framed within the classical canon of invention. This seminar helped me be more attentive to the rhetorical tradition which was looming large in writing studies, and I would draw on it where I found appropriate. But I also found classical rhetoric limited in scope, with many of the concepts and problems closely tied to a limited set of genres within institutional and activity settings derived from classical models (see Bazerman, 1993c). A few of the concepts I was able to apply more broadly, such as *kairos*,[9] but I found that not all writing was best understood as argument nor were all the phenomena of interest to me capturable within rhetorical theory as then constituted. Drawing on an increasingly broad set of interdisciplinary concepts and approaches, I have had an uneasy relationship to rhetoric which some see as foundational for writing studies. Only as I was eventually able to redefine rhetorical theory to serve as an umbrella for my more interdisciplinary approach could I cast my work as rhetorical. I discuss this more extensively and explicitly in Chapter 24 and in my two books on *Literate Action* (Bazerman 2013c, 2013d).

My major paper for Richard Young's seminar examined the reflective narratives in the collection *Sociologists at Work* (Hammond, 1964) to understand how research processes were tied to text production, from the early stages of developing background knowledge and theories (largely through engagement with the literature) and problem definition, through research design and data collection, then analysis and writing up. That is, I characterized the entire research process as leading toward research publications. To parse the processes in the narratives I used the TOTE (Test-Operate-Test-Exit) model proposed in Miller, Galanter, and Pribram's 1960 book, *Plans and the Structure of Behavior*, which was one of the core texts in the CMU cognitive world. In my paper I analyzed how the sociological researchers framed their tasks and problems at each stage and by which criteria they felt they had resolved that level of work and proceeded to the next. This rough seminar paper was heavily weighted down with detailed presentation of the accounts in the volume. The analysis and conclusions were only partially cooked, and I never got to present the paper at the seminar nor received feedback from the other seminar participants or by the seminar leader.

---

9. But I also saw this as more complex and needing reinterpretation, see "Whose moment?" (appearing as a chapter in Bazerman, 1994b)

I did, however, present this work at Merton's seminar at Columbia, and got engaged feedback from participants who wondered about the normativity and limitations of the accounts I was using as data. This led me to greater cautiousness in interpreting and evaluating the accounts I might use as data and pushed me towards more intensive studies of distinct cases. As well, several people (including seminar co-leader Harriet Zuckerman) wondered about the assumptions I was making about how directed the research work was towards publication, which led me to greater caution about the teleological directiveness of the research process. Yet the project did get me thinking more about how the earlier parts of the research process were consequential for the publications that would emerge. This extended orientation to text composition or formulation stayed with me and worked its way into a number of my studies afterwards, from my critique of Latour and Woolgar's *Laboratory Life*, to my examination of how Compton came to design his study and record his data, to how Newton characterized his investigative processes in different kinds of documents, and ultimately to how students learned to collect and inscribe data in their projects (see Chapters 20, 21, 27, and 28, among others).

Merton, on his part, while wondering about the value of considering the entire research process from the perspective of text production, did see the importance of the published archive and asked me to look into Karl Popper's World Three, which is the material productions of human knowledge, such as books (Popper, 1972). Popper's consideration of knowledge as a production helped give some shape and robustness to my conceptualization of disciplinary literature and its operations in the material world.

Given the issues raised about this project which made the conclusions I drew questionable, I never revised the paper to submissible form. I was never able to find a good strategy to revise the material into something I could stand behind with confidence. Yet the project still marked a major moment in learning how I could investigate and understand writing more deeply and what criteria my writing would have to address to be credible.

Another Inflection Point

This period posed many new problems and explored nascent solutions that would set a trajectory for my further writing development. I was no longer using writing to figure out what it was I wanted to do; I was figuring out how to do it. I had found my mission in life in the teaching of writing and had identified basic pedagogic imperatives and strategies. Now I was forming approaches to research and ultimately theorizing—figuring out research questions and empirical methods to pursue them, locating interdisciplinary resources while learning to stay true to my motives and intellectual interests. I recognized that writing studies would benefit from a sociologically oriented research program to supplement the on-going cognitive psychological research program of process studies. I also started to gain the sociological and historical tools to understand how I could support the substantive research along with institutional presence and legitimacy of writing studies (see Chapters 26 and 27, among others).

This inflection point also changed the intertextual field I had been working within. The explicit scholarly literature on writing that I had attempted to contribute to was in a small, marginal corner of the humanities and consisted of only a few books and one journal, *College Composition and Communication*, that regularly published research along with the practice-based articles that dominated the few other journals and newsletters. The journal *Written Communication* did not appear until 1984. As I had discussed earlier, textbooks, by far, were the largest vehicle for sharing ideas about composition, and they were not seen as part of the scholarly literature. So keeping up with the literature and citing sources was not hard—the problem was paucity and not overabundance of resources. But now I was drawing on multiple well-established social science disciplines and specialties each with their journals, books, and intellectual traditions. I needed to learn to select from complex literatures, identify their relevance for my emergent project, and explain their relevance across disciplinary divides. While my own research and pedagogy were helping me to recognize and analyze the role of intertextuality in different disciplines, I had to deal with complex interdisciplinary intertextuality as a practical matter. Having developed ways to work with complex interdisciplinary intertextuality, I no longer felt bounded by the limits of the literature of writing studies, even as the number of journals, publishers, and books in the field increased. As I continued to see how writing was imbricated with so many other aspects of life, I seemed to have no choice but to keep trying to expand the intertextual spaces I found relevant to writing.

Although I was using the literary tools of my prior education, I felt I was inventing new ways of proceeding, to produce work of both practical value and academic credibility, situated in a new interdisciplinary space. This sense of trying to invent new ways of studying writing was to continue in the following years, as my research program in scientific genres started to gain momentum. The train wheels were starting to roll.

Chapter 20. Studying the Changing Genres of Science and Figuring Out How to Write about It

After my first few attempts at studying scientific writing, I started to get a sense of what kinds of projects I might pursue. One study seemed to lead to the next, along with new writing challenges for each. In the course of addressing these challenges I was inventing the kinds of articles I was writing.

During this next stage in my writing development the leading writing problems I addressed concerned contributing to the advancement of the disciplines I was engaged in. I thought about forming research questions, identifying relevant data and resources, representing and analyzing data, and forming arguments within knowledge fields. Some of the earlier leading problems in writing development were no longer in the front of my concerns: developing sentence and argument structure skills; sorting through troubled emotions; clarifying values, commitments, and affiliations; extending my imagination and deepening my reflective contemplation; and even being communicatively accessible to different audiences. I continued to work on these earlier learned components of writing, but mostly in the context of larger questions which presented bigger problems to solve.

Accordingly, my narrative from this point forward will focus less on writing development at the text manipulation, personal expressive, or audience communicative levels, and will focus on issues such as social organization of activity fields, knowledge organization, inquiry methods, organizational structures, and strategies of texts as interventions within communal knowledge-making. My analyses of my writing choices and writing learning from this point forward will focus more on underlying decisions leading to the positioning and construction of texts than on the final textual forms in which I present my findings and ideas. The fundamental questions directing the project would motivate and guide the work of bringing the text into the world.

The narrative from this point forward may also seem less attached to life issues and emotions and more attached to abstract questions of knowledge investigation and formulation. Yet my commitment to advancing knowledge and practices of writing and writing education had by this point become deeply personal, defining my sense of value and accomplishment. This work was carried out to advance a professional field, rather than resolve personal questions of identity and commitment. My own research and the professional discussions it contributed to also changed my understanding of writing and thus the kinds of questions, observations, and explanations I had about my own writing, making my professional contributions personally meaningful. I hope the narrative to follow may reverberate with the experiences of other writers who find personal value in contributing to disciplines, professions, or other specialized organized social activities. Each will have a different set of experiences and pathways, but each will also find the meaning and value of their writing development within the practices, interactions, and development of their fields.

A Process Study of Practical Scientific Reasoning

My incomplete study of *Sociologists at Work* convinced me that disciplinary writing processes varied and were tied to inquiry processes. My literary training suggested that drafts leading to published work could reveal the origins and evolution of ideas, along with the explicit concerns of the writer. As I reviewed literary studies for robust examples of how I might proceed, I unfortunately found most draft studies limited to noting the technical details of dating different drafts or focusing on specific themes, rather than trying to understand more comprehensively the emergence of texts. So methodologically, I seemed on my own.

At that time, I was living in New York City where a number of scientific societies were located. When I asked the archivist at the American Institute of Physics about possible files of drafts leading towards major articles, he pointed me toward a microfilm copy of Arthur Holly Compton's papers (the originals were at Washington University in St. Louis where Compton had worked). Within this collection the most complete set of notebooks and papers came from a less-known paper that followed up on his well-known empirical confirmation of quantum theory (through what is now known as the Compton Effect). I had initially naively thought that I would find the drafts of the major 1923 paper which could then be interpretable as a self-contained case. Although any historian of science would know that major discovery papers often appeared within a series of much less well-known papers, I was surprised to learn that texts were part of disciplinary discussions and did not stand alone. Sometimes it is not even clear at first which paper in a sequence would be later identified as the most significant.

Consequently, in order to analyze the lesser-known paper that had the most notebook and draft materials, I needed to place it within a larger history of Compton's research program, as adding a new kind of evidence within an ongoing discussion, using the recently invented bubble chamber. This device indirectly showed the presence and trajectories of particles through photographs of condensation tracks left by particle movements. This method created for Compton a series of problems in selecting, representing, evaluating, and analyzing the data. Compton's notebooks in particular revealed the principles of selection of which photographic plates to use, based on the clarity and distinctness of tracks. All this was prior to his actually producing the article draft. Then within his draft and revision he was attentive to how he represented the world of nature outside the text and how he characterized those representations. In the draft and revisions he controlled the representation of nature by postponing topics in order to insert preliminary information about the equipment that produced the data or about other logically prior data. He extended discussions to make the nature of the data clearer; he fine-tuned the precision of the language; and he controlled the level of specificity and precision appropriate to the argument being made. He repeatedly adjusted the epistemic level of the discussion (whether, for example, he is discussing photographic data of the tracks, the calculated energies and trajectories of particles, or hypothesized theoretical characterizations of the particles and their interactions). He also adjusted the representation of his actions and judgments, and his relationship to the audience. Through his drafting and revision practices, including the timing and use of the abstract, we can see him bringing the inscribed object into the social world of science while being careful to identify exactly how and in what form experience of the material world is brought into the discussion.

I organized this story as one of temporally unfolding constraints from his professional standards, the prior discussions in the literature, his material actions in the laboratory, the recorded data artifacts, and the persuasive expectations of his readers. At the same time these constraints provide him the opportunity to make warrantable arguments through credible empirical evidence to intervene in disciplinary discussions. I argued his actions showed how disciplinary contributions could be produced with adequately reliable representations of nature—or as the original title indicated: "The Writing of Scientific Non-Fiction: Contexts, Choices, and Constraints" (Bazerman, 1984b).[10]

When setting out to do this draft process study, I started out simply to inquire into the processes of a scientific writer, although I was aware of the epistemological problem of representation, as discussed in the previous chapter. Only as I engaged with the materials, however, did it become clear to me that Compton's notebooks and drafts provided evidence of him being attentive in a practical way to the difficulties of precise representation and how empirical experience should be brought into knowledge discussions. He was not an epistemologist, a philosopher, or a science studies scholar, but as a practical experimental scientist he showed how epistemological problems are managed and contingently resolved within the empirical and argumentative practices of his field.

Because I was examining the emergence of a particular paper resulting from the constraints and choices influencing his process, I included in this essay the published version of Compton's article, as I had for the three papers examined in "What Written Knowledge Does" (Bazerman, 1981b). I wanted to make the central data available to an audience that may not have been familiar with them. This grew out of my undergraduate new critical practice of reproducing short poems

---

10. Later, when I was to incorporate this article as a chapter in *Shaping Written Knowledge*, I was to change the title somewhat and elaborate the discussion to focus on the process of making reference: "Making Reference: Empirical Contexts, Choices, and Constraints in the Literary Creation of the Compton Effect."

that were then examined intently or quoting extensively from them. In my next studies, however, I was to examine larger corpora, so I needed to find new ways of making the larger collections of data available to the readers so they could then evaluate the validity of my analysis and argument.

The Compton study had heightened my awareness of how located each scientific text was in an historical process, both in its general practices of scientific writing and the particular discussion it was part of. This awareness led me to the next question of how scientific articles changed over time. Fleck's concepts of thought collectives and thought styles further reinforced my historical interest—particularly as Fleck's treatment of thought style was tied to changing representational styles which formed shared ways of seeing and characterizing phenomena, mediating between individual and collective thought. Finally, working in the library and archives of the American Institute of Physics I met regularly with its director, the historian Spenser Weart, who helped me think about how science and scientific communication developed historically.

Historical Studies of Corpora

The AIP library contained a full collection of the society journal *Physical Review* since its founding in 1893, as it grew from a minor regional journal into the world's leading venue for publication in physics. Over this period the journal had proliferated in its editions, frequency, and page count, to well over 150 times its original annual length by 1980. An examination of the journal could provide a window into how scientific writing had changed since the late nineteenth century. However, studying such a corpus created many problems. Because it was so massive, I first needed to identify a sample based on a coherent set of principles and procedures to make any detailed analysis possible. Then, over the period so much had changed in physics—its theories, experimental techniques and devices, even the phenomena examined, many of which were not even imaginable in 1893. Further, the size, organization, and specialization of American physics had changed radically from when it was a marginal backwater of a field then centrally located in Germany. Consequently, I couldn't attribute changes in style, organization or other features of texts simply to changes in ways of writing. In order to minimize confounding factors, I sought a subspecialty that was stable in its work, methods, and arguments. Optical spectroscopy appeared to be among the most stable because its core task remained analyzing the differing wavelengths of light from a source using a prism to identify the composition of the source. I eliminated, however, electron spectroscopy and spectroscopic examination of nuclear events, which opened new directions to the field. Even within optical spectroscopy, theory changed radically. It turned out, in fact, the changes in the writing were most driven by the centrality of newly emergent theories to frame studies and analyze results.

Even this subspecialty, however, offered too many texts to examine them all in detail, so I needed to establish further sampling principles and procedures. This was prior to digitization of archives, so even quantitative work had to proceed by hand counting. Because each of the forms of analysis I eventually carried out required a different level of work, I wound up creating three different selections from the full corpus. The recognition that I needed multiple levels of analysis and multiple selections for those different analyses was itself something I had to work out as I proceeded through the project. For the gross quantitative analysis of article length, I selected all the articles from 1893–1900, then all the articles from every fifth year through 1950, then only the first few issues from each fifth year through 1980. This increasing selectivity reflected the growing size of the journal and number of articles. For the second level of mixed qualitative and quantitative analysis of number of references, graphic features, organization and mode of argument, I focused only on optical spectroscopic articles appearing in 1893 (the first year), 1900, and every ten years after (if less than three appeared in the selected year, I included the next year; if more than six appeared in any year, I only used the first six in the earliest issues of the year)—for a total of 40 articles examined. Then, for detailed examination of syntax and vocabulary, I looked at all the optical spectroscopic selections from 1893–1895, 1920, 1950, and 1980. The time intervals and size of samples of the second and third corpora were influenced by qualitative judgments I made as I looked through the larger corpus based on the trajectory and rapidity of changes that appeared to be emerging. I wanted to be granular enough to capture change.

The quantitative results at all of the levels showed that there were noteworthy changes in length of articles, numbers of references, and sentence syntax, but the meaning of these quantitative results were baffling. Only qualitative analysis could make sense of these and other changes over time. From this I learned that quantitative measures could sometimes locate where there were phenomena worth investigating, but the meaning of the changes could only be teased out by qualitative analysis, which might also reveal the interaction of the several features counted. The article length, for example, had to do with the changing nature of the arguments as well as with the data compaction of theory, which was also revealed in the changing character of the graphic elements and the citation lists. The abstraction and aggregation of the theoretical orientation were counterbalanced by the complexity of theory needing explanation and application to the case. The increasing role of theory in structuring the argument also influenced the different sections and the appearance of unique section headings to highlight the reasoning path, even as generic headings for methods and findings increased (Bazerman, 1984a).

In the course of this study, I found that my understanding of physics was too limited to fully understand some of the more recent, theoretically organized articles, so I hired a graduate student in physics as a specialist informant to walk me through the articles to unpack the ideas and the rhetorical strategies. Since then, for briefer periods, I have often relied on unpaid specialist colleagues of various sorts to guide me through historical scholarship, intellectual property law, liability litigation, information science, and many other areas that my work touched on. I also found it useful for understanding disciplinary cultures and knowledge to present myself as uninformed and asking for guidance.

The study of *Physical Review* showed me that I could turn runs of journals sitting on library shelves into corpora for the study of historical changes in writing. Another lucky break soon led to my next corpus study. I was at the National University of Singapore for a few months in the summer of 1982, accompanying my partner who had a visiting research position. The library, it turned out, had a complete original run of the *Philosophical Transactions of the Royal Society*, the first scientific journal in English. I later found out this copy was acquired when the library was restored after the Second World War. The story goes that Derek de Solla Price was posted there and charged with keeping watch over the journal; he stacked the volumes of the journal by years against the walls of his rooms as the library building was being restored. That's how he claimed he discovered his hypothesis about the exponential increase of science. Since that bit of serendipity, the volumes had been rarely used as many of the centuries-old pages were still uncut when I examined them. The library did not have many restrictions on circulation, and cheap, no-questions-asked photocopying was readily available. In the years before digitization and internet access, this was an incredible opportunity for me to acquire an important corpus for later study. I was able to photocopy all the articles from volume 1, 5, 10, 15, 20, 25, 30, 35, 40, 50, 60, 70, 80, and 90; this gave me a good sample from the journal's founding in 1665 to 1800.

When I returned home, I tried to make sense of what I had. On the face of it, the journal contained a heterogenous collection of genres, especially during the early decades. The first volumes contained mostly letters to the editor, Henry Oldenburg, but the correspondence soon was directed to the society for their regular meetings. Then the journal offered reports of what happened at the meetings, and finally it presented free-standing articles. The journal was becoming over time a venue in itself, separated from more personal interactions or society meetings. The rapidity of change in the early years of the journal meant dividing the corpus by traditional genres would highlight discontinuity and lose the trajectory of the change.

From the very beginning, nonetheless, a number of articles claimed to report on experiments. We would not currently consider many things then called experiments to be experiments, so even the idea of experiment seemed changing and emergent. I formed my corpus of those articles that specifically used the term "experiment." Tracking what counted as an experimental report and how it was reported became the focus of the study.

I counted the number of articles and pages along with the percentage of the journal devoted to such articles. These numbers revealed that experiments were initially only a small subset of articles, but they became increasingly prominent over the next hundred thirty-five years I studied. Given the obvious changes in the articles, I also needed a qualitative analysis of what kinds of accounts were being called experimental. I first informally described the articles to see what they were trying to do, which led to a list of questions I then subjected all the articles to in my more formal analysis (specified in Bazerman, 1988a, Chapter 3, p. 64).

I could identify trajectories of change in the articles along several dimensions. Some articles led the change and others lagged behind. Over the entire period, experiments showed increasing degrees of intentionality and design. They also reported greater procedural detail under more controlled conditions. Witnessing the experiments became more accessible to wider audiences, ultimately through providing instructions for all readers to recreate the phenomena. Results were presented with increasing precision and quantification. Research was more associated with theoretical issues and focused questions, embedded in reasoning, and ultimately within argument. All these developments moved toward modern forms of the experimental article, but prominently missing was the modern use of literature and associated citation practices. This absence left open a question for later research.

As I wrote these studies of corpora of journals over time, I became aware that I was making a different kind of historical argument than was typical in the history of science, which tended to focus on individual actors, their ways of working and thinking, their series of discoveries, and their contacts with other scientists. A few historians also studied scientific organizations and the individuals who formed or influenced them. But I was arguing that the textual forms themselves were a kind of institution, influencing the character, ends, and reportability of scientific work along with creating networks of interchange, critique, and theory. I was making the case that the changing form of texts was in fact part of the history of science, creating infrastructure for contributions and interactions as much as the formation of societies and other institutions that created spaces for individual actors to carry out their work. The few historians who shortly thereafter did start to attend to scientific writing adopted a more traditional historical approach of focusing on local stories of individual actors (for example, Dear, 1991).

The Effect of Individual Historical Figures on Scientific Writing

In order to speak more directly to historians of science, I began to look into greater detail to the work of individuals and the institutions they created. Again, luck entered in here as a number of trips to Britain for conferences and talks allowed me to examine the archives of the Royal Society in London and the Newton archives at Cambridge University.

In examining the history and archives of the Royal Society along with the recently published correspondence of the first Secretary and first editor of the *Philosophic Transactions*, Hans Oldenburg, I found new roles emerging in relation to the exigencies of producing and evaluating articles for the new journal. With the emergent complexity of the roles and the kinds of problems perceived by the stakeholders, I started to see how people took on multiple roles which had conflicting obligations and pressures. The evaluation criteria for the journal, in turn, interacted with the changing form and contents of the articles. I looked to sociological theory about role, role conflicts, and conflict mediating devices in order to shed light on participants' actions. The parts started clicking in place when I connected role conflict theory with Merton's norms of science, namely communality, universalism, disinterestedness, and organized skepticism. These norms I saw as ways of juggling and resolving role conflicts by creating different stances, commitments, values, and identities for the scientists. These norms fostered greater dispassionateness in evaluating the work of others and allowed scientists to identify with a communal endeavor which buffered the inevitable bumps, bruises, and outright losses resulting from competitive advocacy for findings (Bazerman, 1987b).

Seeing how changing forms of writing evolved in response to role conflicts and changing norms pushed my writing to be able to explain coherently how multiple theories could come together in a complex mechanism of interlocking parts. Multiple pieces and theoretical accounts started to move around in my head and one thought led to another. Over several weeks of lightbulb moments, I had a continuing cascade of thoughts "oh that's why this occurred . . . oh that's how that fits . . . oh, all the parts are here." In its own way this was as extraordinary an experience as my somnambulistic undergraduate paper writing described in Chapter 11. But here I was wide awake, actually in a return visit to Singapore on a visiting professorship, and I remember many of these light bulbs going off as I was swimming daily in the apartment complex pool. As these pieces fit together, they each became more meaningful because they worked with each other and coincided with the historical facts I was putting together. I initially presented this work at the National University of Singapore and then published it as an article before including it as a chapter in *Shaping Written Knowledge* (Bazerman, 1988a).

As I was working on this second study of the early *Philosophical Transactions*, I continued to be intrigued by a series of articles surrounding Newton's optical theory in the earliest years of the journal, which didn't quite fit the evolving patterns I had been noting. This well-known controversy extended over two years in 16 published articles by Newton and his critics (with several more unpublished letters in Oldenburg's correspondence). Historians had studied this exchange as an intellectual disagreement, but they had not looked at from the perspective of rhetoric or writing, that is, how Newton carried out his side of the argument or how the differences of the situations and functions of the texts would have influenced his goals and strategies in each form, potentially explaining his rhetorical strategy that crystalized in the *Opticks*. As I started to look into the case, I became further intrigued to find that Newton had made several explicit statements about his argumentative strategy. Ultimately he rejected journal publication as not being conducive to the kind of extensive theoretical elaboration he needed for people to understand his claims. He found his conducive form of argument 30 years later in his book *Opticks*. I also found out his initial journal article and consequent response articles were not his first attempt to formulate a theory of light, which started in his undergraduate notebooks, continued in his lectures as Lucasian Professor at Cambridge (both fortunately published for the first time in scholarly critical editions shortly before I started this study), and several other unpublished manuscripts (Bazerman, 1988a, Chapter 5).

This study indicated both Newton's atypicality in his initial frustrations at the journal interchange and his rhetorical leadership in forging modes of argument in his book that would come to dominate a century later. By learning how to address the extensive historical research literature on Newton with a detailed study of his manuscripts as forms of writing, I was able to develop a way of talking about the way transformative scientists thought rhetorically about how to make their novel ideas visible and persuasive. In this way they changed not only science, but the way scientists wrote to formulate and argue for their science. I would later find this rhetorical leadership in other figures such as Joseph Priestley and Adam Smith.

Figure 20.1: Shaping Written Knowledge

Studies of Contemporary Practices

As I was looking into the history of scientific writing, I continued contemporary studies of how physicists read published scientific studies and how social sciences adopted and adapted scientific genres. Each of these contemporary studies taught me new methods of inquiry and new forms of presentation. In order to understand what readers got from articles and how they went about reading, I had to learn how to carry out interviews and *in situ* observations, triangulating between what a group of physicists told me about their reading practices and what I observed as they actually searched for articles, made decisions about the depth of reading they would engage in, and went about making sense of the articles they read for their own research purposes. These are techniques and writing challenges well known to qualitative, ethnographic social scientists, but for me they were new and made necessary by my interest in how people interacted with texts. My observations were particularly hybrid as I asked think-aloud questions of the physicists while they were interacting with the journal contents; I needed to correlate what was being said with my notes on what the subjects were looking at and the actual texts they were reading. In doing so I came to see how fundamentally their worlds, planning, and work were shaped by historically emerged structures of articles, publication procedures, publishers, and evaluation systems. Articles they read formed what they knew, how they thought, what they contributed to, and what was expected in their contributions. Their readings concretely realized the collective wisdom of the scientists who had come before and contemporaries with whom they interacted (Bazerman, 1985a).

There was a logic in the sequence of my research questions. As I learned how differentiated and emergent scientific writing was, I began to inquire into how embedded the emergent forms of writing were in social and publication arrangements, and how those forms and expectations emerged through the rhetorical, persuasive choices of individual writers, great and small. Genres, though recognizable through conventional forms, were dynamic sets of options forming and reforming within the goals and social organization of their fields. Each of these inquiries led me into different materials, along with different methods of collection and analysis to reveal patterns and processes. Insofar as the work was historical and archival, I needed to locate moments and archives where issues would be robustly evident, and then each study would suggest different forms of analysis. Some of the inquiries, however, would require stepping outside of the archives to gather evidence of contemporary practices of scientists.

One question that started to nag at me was how the social sciences began to write in what they considered scientific genres. As I started to see that scientific writing was historically changing and differentiated among and within disciplines, I wondered when, why, and how social scientific writing evolved from the natural sciences, and with what consequences for current practices. This ill-formed issue came into focus when I was invited to participate in a conference on *The Rhetoric of the Human Sciences,* with papers to be collected in a volume of the same name. When I discovered both Thomas Kuhn and Clifford Geertz would be participating in the conference, I felt even more pressured to find a coherent approach grounded in careful evidence. Textbooks about writing in the disciplines and the interdisciplinarity of my research had made me aware of the great influence the *Publication Manual of the American Psychological Association* (3rd ed., 1983) had throughout all the social sciences. The influence was most visible in citation practices expected at all levels from undergraduate papers through the published research articles in a number of disciplines. The APA publication manual, however, regulated many other areas from pronoun and verb choice, through text organization and use of subheadings, to experimental design and survey subject choices. In Kuhnian terms, it was paradigmatic in regulating the disciplinary matrix of psychology and other social sciences which adopted its standards. I quickly found that, of course, the APA manual had a history. That history was relatively short, little more than a half century (at that point), growing rapidly from a six-and-a-half-page article of advice to graduate students, passing through a number of forms on its way to a separately bound volume with 132 pages in its third edition in 1983 (and now in 2020 appearing in its seventh edition with 427 pages). I compared the contents of the various versions, the length devoted to each of the topics, and the regulatory directiveness of each recommendation. But that was only a part of the story.

Establishing a set of rules hardly means people were already following it or that they would uniformly follow it after the fact. Rules are usually made to control behavior because at least some people are doing otherwise. As a wise institutional mentor told me, "No one puts up 'don't walk on the grass' signs unless people are walking on the grass." I decided to compare the recommendations of evolving versions of the *Publication Manual* to the professional practices within psychological publications from the time of the field's separation from philosophy in the late nineteenth century through the earlier versions of the manual. It turns out that the writing in the psychological journals was more varied and more philosophically intensive than the narrow empiricist formats suggested in the manual, even among prominent behaviorists. The recommendations and then the compulsory rules were not enshrining already established, universally accepted practices of manuscript evaluation and publication decisions. They were, instead, conscious attempts by a small group of disciplinary leaders to impose a particular approach to research and to what would count as a contribution to psychology. This imposed approach embodied particular theories about psychology and psychological science, which further entailed beliefs about the appropriate roles and forms of reasoning available to psychologists, since psychologists themselves were psychological beings. The knowledge they would produce, accordingly, would only be considered reliable if they were guided by the epistemic principles of this version of psychology. So my study of the archival materials moved from comparative content analysis of the regulatory documents to close textual analysis of articles, embedded with an historical contextual analysis of the discipline, its journals, and the field leaders. These analyses then led to an ideological analysis of the intellectual program realized in the various editions of the regulatory manual. The study did not pass judgment on the theory, epistemology, or research practices of this view, but only pointed out the nexus that was intentionally advanced by key players as they came into control of the means of publication. Unsurprisingly, this approach to psychology remained contested, even as holders of alternate views had to accommodate to the publication rules and criteria. The contestation has in fact increased since my study, as the approaches in the field have proliferated and gained strength (while others have been pushed to the margin as not rigorously scientific), though the publication regulation has stayed in place to influence other social sciences. While the style (or parts of the style) may in fact be convenient to other fields for their own reasons, I hope my analysis brought to awareness some of the implications of that style (Bazerman, 1987a).

Creating Coherence out of Separate Studies

I initially saw the studies described in this and the previous chapter as separate, but after most were written and several published, I began to see how they fit together into a big picture, which would gain meaning and force if I brought them together. Conceiving a book posed the problem of how to sequence and frame the studies, and provide transitions among the parts. It also made me think about and commit to an overall argument and the evidence needed to support it. The result was *Shaping Written Knowledge: The Genre and Activity of the Experimental Article in Science* (Bazerman, 1988a).

Given my underlying practical motivation in the teaching of writing, I felt obligated to show how these arcane interdisciplinary studies could contribute to improved pedagogy. The first chapter argued why interdisciplinary and historical research was necessary to understand the complexity and specificity of academic writing in order to guide instruction and practice. The second chapter expanded on the value of detailed study of research writing through an adaptation of my initial study showing the radical difference among writing in different fields; this chapter would demonstrate to the readers the warrant for the consequent studies. Over three chapters, I then created a narrative of the emergence and changing form of experimental reports in journals during the 17th and 18th centuries in relation to the changing social arrangements. A next section of three chapters then spoke to 20th century uses and practices of scientific writing in physics, and a further section considered the uptake of scientific genres in the social sciences. The penultimate chapter of the book addressed theoretical issues arising from the studies, particularly concerning how writing mediated between our experience of nature and our organized, inscribed, published knowledge. The last chapter then returned to the practical implications for contemporary science writing and the teaching of academic writing. In this structure I see echoes of my college papers on the role of dramatic prologues and epilogues, bringing the audience from the street into the world of the drama, and then at the end returning them to their everyday lives, but somehow bearing the message of the performance.

As I was putting the finishing touches on *Shaping Written Knowledge*, I still had open questions about the emergence of scientific writing, leaving work for future studies. I already had more than enough material to write this one book and already had taken a number of risks. Rather than having studies focused by easily recognizable problems within a well-structured disciplinary literature, I increasingly found myself inventing new research questions and problems elaborating the theoretical picture I was constructing through the sequence of studies. I kept going further and further out on my own limb. I was making bets on the future that eventually enough people would get what I was doing and that over time the logic of those studies would become more apparent and relevant. This bet, however, pressured me to explain the connections I was making. As I reached towards different kinds of questions than were common in the field of teaching of writing and drew on literatures that were far outside the field, I was imposing on myself an obligation to introduce, explain, and show the relevance of these disciplines to my colleagues, in the hope that they could see why I was wandering so far afield. Perhaps they might also become engaged in some of these literatures. To some degree these were good bets, but even the best bets often lose, so that while some have pursued lines close to mine in some respects, other parts still hang out there, and the total intersection of questions and literatures that I pursued still appear to me to be idiosyncratic. So I still feel compelled to keep explaining myself, like the Ancient Mariner, bending the ears of polite, but impatient wedding guests.

Chapter 21. Following Rhetorical Innovators: Why Were They Writing That Way?

Shaping Written Knowledge revealed some outlines of change in scientific writing and had started to identify how individual choices influenced emergent textual patterns and social communicative systems. The book also gave evidence of how the emerging genres and systems influenced the behaviors of individuals, but variously in different fields and at different moments, filtered through individual perceptions. One prominent piece, however, remained missing: how and why the modern system of text reference and citation arose.

Additionally, through writing the book I had become intrigued with innovative individuals whose writing did not quite fit within the genre expectations of their time, yet who often influenced both the content of the science and the ways scientists would later come to write. Because forms of writing embodied ways of thinking and acting, the development of these innovators' understanding of writing could be revealing for the implicit assumptions of those who later followed their lead, as I had seen in the case of Newton. I came to think of these unusual scientific writers as strategic research sites because they could make visible tensions, processes, and dynamics that might later become hidden, submerged in taken-for-granted practices. Their innovations suggested a felt need to produce atypical texts arising from alternative visions of the possibilities of knowledge.

Finally, I wanted to begin specializing in a narrower domain of science, so I could follow the scientific developments along with the players, the social networks, and communicative systems in the field. As I surveyed the various fields of physics with which I was most familiar, electricity seemed a good bet. Electricity had a long history, explored since the ancient world and emerging as an increasingly important area from the eighteenth century until today. Yet initially only static charges and lightning were noted in nature and they were considered distinct phenomena, having little to do with each other. What we commonly recognize as electricity in the modern world is literally a generated phenomenon, visible through human agency by means of humanly constructed devices. Further, our knowledge of electricity grew in relation to human devices and applications. That knowledge in turn allowed us to produce more devices and more uses, and is the basis for the electronic revolution of recent decades. What we have come to know of electricity is because humans have made it, relying on our growing collection of representations through scientific publications, engineering designs, and financial systems. That is, we didn't come to know electricity until we could produce it and then come to know and report in our scientific publications what nature would actually do when we twisted its tail. We couldn't make nature do things it wouldn't do, but we could make it do many things that would not happen without our intervention.[11]

These three motives came together in my next project.

Joseph Priestley and Referencing the Literature

As I started to look into the history of electricity, I came across mention of Joseph Priestley's *History and Present State of Electricity*, first published in 1769. This book was the first work in English that resembled a review of prior research, though a few years earlier a shorter, less detailed list of previous work had appeared in German. Priestley's book seemed a rather odd work including, in addition to a discussion of prior findings and theories, a section on history of electrical machines and devices, a discussion of how to recruit neophytes into the field, a list of electrical parlor tricks and diversions, a series of open research questions, and narratives of Priestley's own experiments and inquiries. This apparent miscellany under one set of covers led me to wonder what he could have been thinking in putting such an odd-seeming collection together and what that might have to do with his comprehensive discussion of all the prior literature. In order to pursue the logic of this collection, I returned to a mode of inquiry I had adopted in my unpublished study of Nabokov (see Chapter 17) in interpreting a later work on the basis of the concerns developed in the corpus of earlier work.

Earlier in his career, Priestley had lectured on rhetoric and published a *Course of Lectures on Oratory and Criticism*, so I suspected he would be reflective and intentional about his writing. His lectures on oratory relied on an associationist psychology which included experience of the world as an essential component. It was no surprise, therefore, that he would put a lot of weight on increasing material experience and empirical inquiry. To understand his vision as a writer I found I needed to enter into his wide-ranging millenarian enlightenment vision revealed in his many books on many subjects.

The more I found out about Priestley— as a radical defender of liberty who migrated to the early United States, as a dissenting Protestant preacher, as an educator and head of a dissenting academy, as an historian who reputedly invented the timeline, and as author of many publications on many topics—the more curious I became about his ideas about writing. He saw that the improvement of life depended on our listening to the collective wisdom of mankind. He believed that scientists needed to aggregate and make sense of all the prior work including the material conditions under which the work was produced (thus the concern for electrical devices) in order to know where to take up and how to carry on the work. His attentiveness to prior literature and the historical emergence of

---

11. The imprecise attribution of twisting the tail of nature to Francis Bacon, nonetheless captures his gist (Merchant, 2006).

knowledge through communal practice, implicitly brought into science his social millenarian vision of improving the world through collective endeavor. He consequently recommended that science should be written as transparent discovery accounts, including all decisions, wrong turns, and failures—in order to make one's work and reasoning available to others who would continue investigations. The field also needed to recruit new investigators and educate them, as well as to gain the support of broader publics to be made aware of the phenomena, even if only through parlor tricks. By tracing through Priestley's expanding vision of the social world and the role of communication in it, I came to appreciate the sophisticated rhetorical thought expressed in his scientific work, far beyond what he had presented in his early lectures on oratory. This placing of his later work within his emerging thinking throughout his career also made more evident to me that a writer's rhetorical project, rhetorical understanding, and specific rhetorical designs developed within the writer's changing understanding of the world and society (Bazerman, 1991c).

Von Guericke's World

Priestley's decisions as a writer showed me that reconstructing innovative writers' developing perceptions of the social and material worlds they were writing in can provide a way to analyze the social and epistemological consequences for those who adopted their innovations. These stories of the development of writers' consciousness revealed how rhetoric was closely tied to evolving visions of the world. This is an issue I pursued in my next project on electricity examining a seventeenth-century German Catholic scientist.

All my studies to this point had been about writing within the main line of modern science, particularly within the British Protestant tradition. All the writers I had studied, no matter how idiosyncratic, spoke within and to this tradition. But I was curious what empirical investigation might look like and mean if it were pursued within a different tradition and a different form of consciousness. This curiosity led me to the electrical discoveries of Otto von Guericke, who is credited (within that mainline tradition) as having discovered electrical repulsion. But was that how he saw his work? He was working during almost the exact same years as the founding of the Royal Society and its journal, but he was part of the Continental Catholic intellectual tradition which had different assumptions, including that the divine still actively intervened in the world, so that the age of miracles was still with us. Von Guericke's purposes, his role as a knower, the genres in which he presented his discoveries, the social networks he distributed them in, the meaning and interpretation of what he found, and the social value of the discoveries differed greatly from those of his British contemporaries. As I documented in my study (Bazerman, 1993e), he as a *magus* was demonstrating his powerful knowledge of the inner secrets of the universe, establishing his authority as a political and social leader.

Thinking myself back into van Guericke's mental frame drew on my experiences in historical literary studies that had attuned me to other cultural worlds, as it was so different from the scientific world view I was familiar with. Dealing with von Guericke's Latin text was also a challenge until I discovered by tremendous luck the manuscript of an unpublished translation in an archive I had been using, the Burndy Library. As far as I know this was the only extant copy of the only translation. In this, as in some other studies, the archivists and librarians of collections I worked in were of tremendous help. Asking the right questions of the right persons to find out where to look at the right moment is a kind of hidden writing skill that I continue to work on. Then, once I had all the archival pieces in place, I had to narratively represent this unfamiliar ideological life world, just as I had learned to characterize the imaginative worlds of poets like Wordsworth and Milton.

Two Other Innovative Writers

My planned next step for a book on the textual emergence of electricity was going to be a chapter on Edison, who brought electricity into everyday life through material production. In the next chapter I will describe what happened to that project once I started to look into the Edison archives. In the meantime, other opportunities allowed me to continue examining questions of writing innovation.

A conference on the rhetoric of economics in 1991 gave me the opportunity to look at a contemporary of Priestley who had an equally broad intellectual scope. Ever since I had learned that Adam Smith, now viewed as the founder of scientific economics, had published a rhetoric early in his career I was curious about a potential connection with his *Wealth of Nations*. He was a puzzling figure to many because of the contrast between his *Theory of Moral Sentiments* and the seemingly antithetical *Wealth of Nations*, which was his next and final work. As I looked into all his writings across his whole career, however, I concluded he was engaged in a rhetorical project and vision that extended far beyond the economy or even moral philosophy. He was concerned with how social order was possible in a post-hierarchical, post-monarchical, post-religious world; he saw the problem largely as one of social communication.

Smith's *Theory of Moral Sentiments*, as with the theories of the other Scottish moralists, asked us to see ourselves as other might see us (as Robert Burns memorably put it), if they knew the situation as well as we did—and acted accordingly. He saw this refined self-knowledge, however, available only to those who had the education and leisure to do so. He understood, moreover, people were constrained by their interests and class experiences, as well as an impulse to admire those they considered more elevated than themselves—that is, the nobility, the wealthy, and the powerful. He also saw people driven by anxieties and uncertainties, seeking certitudes of unifying beliefs. Thus, his vision of human betterment called for means to coordinate among people of different interests, desires, perceptions, and ideologies. Seeing economic exchange as a common means to coordinate among others, he argued in *The Wealth of Nations* for government policies that would facilitate markets (while still constraining the rent holders or capitalists, whose interests did not coincide with society as a whole). Long before Smith had gotten to these two books at the end of his career, however, he had pondered the psychological and communicative bases of social order in his works on rhetoric, the history of science, the nature of invention to improve life, the role of philosophers as inventors, and jurisprudence to ameliorate relations among people.

As I entered more deeply into Smith's texts, starting with some of his earliest, which were as explicitly rhetorically reflective as Priestley's, I was even more challenged in laying out the parameters of his copious mind and his understanding of the communicative universe. I had to explain an unfolding coherence in his views, which he himself was concerned with, along with how he saw this coherence contributing to the betterment of society. To be explicit, Priestley Smith's changing views of society and the social order went hand-in hand with his changing views of how he could best intervene as a thinker and writer. These views were both explicitly elaborated in his texts and implicitly changed his views of the social world he was communicating in—thus transforming his rhetorical strategies to communicate with and contribute to that social world. His evolving understanding of the social world drove his rhetorical innovations. With both Priestley and Smith, I wound up telling a different kind of story than was typical: a phenomenological reconstruction of how the authors saw the societies they lived in, their roles in it, and how they framed their rhetorical projects to speak to that perceived social world (1993g).

Through writing about the unusual figures of Newton, Priestley, and Smith, I was developing a way of telling the story of their growth of consciousness that drove and shaped their writings. I also came to see writing innovation as a deep-seated response to perceived rhetorical problems, seeing communicative situations and tasks in new ways that called forth new communicative solutions. These solutions were grounded in the genres of their time, but they also transformed, hybridized, and re-created those genres to offer new knowledge, relations, and activities. As I reconstructed their evolving phenomenological, action, and writing universes, my own perceptions of the possibilities of writing expanded, although I did not buy into all their views nor did I accept their formal innovations as absolute. Yet I came to appreciate the wisdom in their quests and visions of the world, along with the logic of their rhetorical engagement with knowledge and their audiences. Recognizing how much their evolving rhetoric was grounded in and a response to their vision of what could be accomplished by the written word encouraged me to take further risks in my writing to follow what my evolving research and theory was telling me about how writing could act in the world.

Another opportunity to examine an unusual text came about when Jack Selzer organized a casebook of different analyses of a single unusual article by Stephen Jay Gould and Richard Lewontin that used ideas from the humanities, social sciences, and life sciences to challenge foundational assumptions of evolutionary biology. Selzer wanted the casebook to demonstrate what different kinds of rhetorical analyses could reveal about scientific texts. My contribution analyzed intertextuality, as Gould and Lewontin's article cited an historically deep, interdisciplinary range of sources. I examined all the works cited in the article I could obtain (38 of the 41—including all in English and German), and compared my reading of those texts with how Gould and Lewontin represented them. I also examined the full symposium in which this paper appeared as a challenge to the other papers. I then traced the controversies of the symposium back to some earlier publications in order to understand the rhetorical context of the controversy over the proper approach to evolution.

From the citations and the papers surrounding the article in the symposium, I could see how Gould and Lewontin constructed the literature for the article and how they positioned their argument within that literature. This was not a study of the development of the writer's rhetorical understanding and rhetorical strategies, but only a snapshot of one aspect of rhetorical strategy at one moment to carry the controversy forward, although the article had intertextual backward glances—we might say framed cameos of earlier literature placed in the background of the snapshot, including cameos of the authors' own prior works. I was well practiced in the kinds of textual analysis here, and my analysis largely followed the pattern of following the article sequentially with a focus on the feature of interest to me—in this case the articles cited—as I had initially learned in my undergraduate explications. Even the organizational novelty of breaking up the sequence with some interludes considering contextual issues goes back as well to what I had learned as an undergraduate. There was a lot of information to juggle and keep track of, but I had also done that in a number of my prior projects, and I had developed methods both of record keeping and of mental organization.

The double interpretation of the original articles and then how they were represented in the Gould and Lewontin article added a challenging wrinkle, as I had to form my understanding of these texts independent of Gould and Lewontin's presentation of them, even though I was a disciplinary outsider to the fields of most of the articles. I then used that independent reading to see how Gould and Lewontin were using the literature. While trying to understand technical articles presented some challenges (which required that I read further into those fields and the context of their work), the biggest challenge was getting access to some of the more obscure publications. The most striking thing I learned was the degree of flexibility writers had in constructing the intertext to set the stage for the current argument. While previously implicit in my writing-from-sources pedagogy and explicit in my study of Priestley, this study put in high relief the idea that the meaning of the previous literature was always being renegotiated as the knowledge of the field moved forward, offering new perspectives and posing new intellectual challenges. This study, moreover, raised the question of what might be the boundaries of accurate and ethical representations of prior work even as earlier work is always open to reinterpretation (Bazerman, 1993f).

Figure 21.1. *Innovative Writers from Early Science— Isaac Newton, Joseph Priestly, Adam Smith, Otto van Guericke.* Photos in the public domain.

The Influence of Location on Writing

I should note that I shifted institutional locations twice in the early 1990s, to the Georgia Institute of Technology in 1990 and then the University of California Santa Barbara in 1994, where I have remained. These moves were motivated by my wife's and my search for positions that would better support our work and held promise of more compatible programs. Dual career moves are often complicated, as ours was, but it had a happy ending. The main consequence for my writing was increased time for research and international travel. The new positions also increased expectations and rewards for publication, though by this point I hardly lacked for motivation. The other consequence was the intellectual influences and opportunities available at each campus. Georgia Tech supported some of my continuing interests in science and technology studies and introduced me to newer technologies and collaborative technology projects. At UCSB I found a strong interdisciplinary group in interactional sociology which taught me much about method and theory along with some other colleagues interested in the sociology of culture. Then when I was able to move my position from English to Education at the end of the 1990s, I found myself happily within an applied social science department closer to my academic interests, intellectual culture, and practical engagement with students and pedagogy.

Figure 21.2. University of California Santa Barbara, where I worked from 1994–2022. Daily Nexus file photo.

Chapter 22. Edison: How to Write About Complex Multi-Dimensional Social Projects

Before visiting the Edison Archives and National Historic Site in West Orange, New Jersey in the fall of 1989, I was still conceiving my then current project as a rhetorical history of electricity from the seventeenth through the nineteenth centuries, with Edison being the subject only of the final chapter. Within hours of my arriving at the place where Edison had established a laboratory in 1887, however, the book transformed into a study about the decade it took him to conceive, invent, and build a centralized system of power and light. As I barely dipped into the archives, a new vision fell in place. It was that simple, though it took me as long to finish the book as it took for Edison to build an electrical empire.

Mobilizing Writing in Multiple Documentary Systems

On that first morning, to warm up to the over 5 million pages of documents in the archives, I looked at the folder of letters Edison received in the days just after he had announced to reporters in September 1878 that he had solved the problem of incandescent lighting. He was already a newspaper celebrity for his phonographic and telegraphic inventions. In those letters I saw his importance to people as varied as investors and widows with limited funds to urban mayors to technologists and inventors. Each letter writer pinned hopes and anxieties onto this media celebrity. Although all the documents were personal letters, they each suggested different activity systems and systems of genres in which Edison had meaning and value. These letters appeared to me as entry ways into the many different kinds of documents in the archive. I confirmed this intuition by leafing through the finder volumes, which listed the contents of the various archival boxes. I immediately knew I had a book just from those archives, interpreting them as documentary systems covering at most ten years, until central power had been established and the Edison companies had been consolidated into General Edison, then General Electric. I put aside the earlier book plan, thinking I would get back to it, but I never did as the Edison project addressed my initial research interests and more. By the time I walked to the local diner for lunch, I began plotting a book outline with chapters corresponding to the different communicative systems and genres—and I spent the rest of the day sketching out the plan of work. The book plan would evolve a bit as I got deeper into the story, but essentially this first outline guided the work of a decade.

I can't say *The Languages of Edison's Light* (Bazerman, 1999c) wrote itself, as endless work was needed to examine the documents in detail; solve puzzles of who did what, when, and what their relation was; what genres and activity systems the documents were part of; how these systems and their genres emerged and evolved; and how Edison and his colleagues worked or innovated in each. I then had to create aggregating narratives and structuring ideas. The material was fascinatingly revealing about the complexity of genres as they arose historically and how they provided vehicles for Edison's symbolic actions. The investigation got me into places I never imagined I would have examined, like the histories of the patent office, stock markets, department stores, and urban domestic aesthetics. Issues of corruption in late 19th century journalism and the New York City construction licensing and inspection system soon were apparent. I came to appreciate how innovation and conventionality influenced each of the documents in the Edison papers and his communicative strategies at each moment.

There was much drudgery as I had to pile into documents day by day. This was made a bit easier when I received a small university grant to purchase a microfilm reader and a set of films. Yet the overall design was so clear from the beginning I pretty well knew what the next problem was to solve, what the next paragraph was to write, and what the next chapter was going to be. At some points I had to modify the plan by reorganizing material, adding relevant digressions, moving chapters around, and placing theoretical interludes into the historical narrative. But many chapters were similarly structured: the history of the systems at play; the organization of interactions and genres at Edison's moment; Edison's perception of his opportunities and strategies; what he and his colleagues wrote to fit the moment; and what consequences resulted. The book introduction framed the inquiry, but got down to historical narration rapidly. Most of the theory was withheld until the final chapter, so as to let the narrative tell its compelling story. So in some way the book did write itself—following the vision on that first morning. It just took ten years to do it, dragging me along the way.

Of course, I was prepared to see what I saw that first morning by how I previously had come to conceive of, organize, and present materials and articles; by the ideas and methods imbibed from other disciplines; by my previous studies and the theories developed from them; by the ways I had come to reconstruct the rhetorical thinking and development of innovative figures in sciences and social sciences. Edison, however, worked at the intersection of more socio-communitive systems than those I had previously worked with. These differences became part of the core problematic of the book: how large worldly projects required engagements with multiple kinds of documentary activity systems to create presence, meaning and value.

Rhetorical Puzzles

As the parts of the Edison project came into focus, I had to think through who I wanted to reach by the book. The earlier planned book about the rhetorical emergence of electricity had a narrower academic audience in writing studies and social studies of science, in order to show how knowledge emerged through documents produced within activity systems. I wanted to show how these documents were the result of creative actions of individuals, engaged with the material world yet speaking to their contemporary social words. That engagement would be symbolically represented in their texts and would constrain what could be accountably represented. Analysis of documents would also show how systems of genres and activities arose, and how they became playing fields for individual strategic writers. While the multiple disciplines that comprised social studies of science and writing studies each had their own framings of these problems, relevant literatures, forms of argument and warranting evidence, I had been working with these and attempting to bridge them in prior studies.

I still wanted to reach these specialized disciplinary audiences, but I saw the Edison book could reach other audiences beyond the academy to demonstrate the importance, pervasiveness, and situated complexity of writing. I saw the chance to reach readers of biographies of innovators, to show them Edison as a communicator as well as an inventor, opening them to think about other historical actors in their communicative dimension. The book might also reach current entrepreneurs and others engaged in carrying out large social projects to help them reflect on the rhetorical complexities of their own undertakings.

I had hopes for a compelling narrative with wider circulation. I wrote the introduction to have only enough theory to indicate the kind of story that would be told. From the opening chapter, I tried to engage the readers into the unfolding events and Edison's rhetorical position. Each chapter kept the story of the production of light and central power moving forward as I examined Edison's rhetorical strategy at each moment. I used historical flashbacks within chapters to situate the texts and activities in the chapters within the activity systems and Edison's experience with them. With most of the explicit theorizing in the final chapter, when theory was needed earlier, I used extended footnotes.

Structuring the Story

The first chapter encapsulated what I saw in the archives on the first day—the personal letters that came in response to Edison's announcement that he had solved the problem of incandescent light, that immediately got a lengthy story in the *New York Sun* on September 16, 1878. The interests in each of those letters came from one of several different activity systems: lecturers were looking for good materials to present in their public presentations; investors were looking for opportunities; widows were worried about their investments; patent managers were looking for business; small businessmen were looking for franchises or local representation; technologists were looking for jobs. All the letters were framed within a cultural narrative (fostered in the contemporary newspapers) of the heroic inventor who could deliver the fulfillment of their desires. I first published this material separately as an article in a technical writing journal with a bit more explicit theory (Bazerman, 1994c). In the book I presented this story as the opening moment of the complex narrative to follow, giving glimpses of the multiple communicative systems that would be elaborated in the rest of the book. This was easy to write because I was fleshing out a vision that had come that first day.

Another early publication opportunity for an electrical industry journal gave me a chance to put together how Edison had amassed such celebrity and public credibility that his suggestion of success would get such a big response. As this article was specifically for a non-academic audience, it gave me an opportunity to practice writing the material as a biographical narrative with almost no explicit theory. This material was to be much elaborated, reorganized and rewritten to become the second substantive chapter of the book. Again, this article was easy to write as the materials I was examining told a powerful story about the development of Edison as a communicator. He learned the power of new kinds of newspapers in a changing society first as a boy hawking newspapers on a commuter train, then as a brash telegraphic inventor, and ultimately as a celebrity inventor of the phonograph. Among other things, he learned how to give good interviews and play the reporters to advance his own interests. The article was entitled "The Publicity Wizard of Menlo Park" (Bazerman, 1993i).

Indeed, many of the chapters fell in place as I dug into the documents which told compelling stories. The structure of the chapters was largely narrative, with subheadings indicating the events and actions, or background. The sequence of chapters was chronological, although some chapters overlapped, as clusters of activity systems moved in parallel. The documents together made evident how documentary systems developed, how events unfolded, and how Edison and his colleagues operated intentionally and strategically in their particular historical, communicative environment. Their actions were often clever and rhetorically savvy within the practices of the time, even if we today would consider some scandalously corrupt and contrary to the modern iconic myth of Edison.

It was striking to see how the young Edison had learned the potential of communication and publicity and how he dealt with the press and governmental corruption of his time. He leaned on private trust networks to gain and maintain financial backing and then found ways to draw on the emerging potential of public equities. The strategies he and his agents developed for dealing with the patent filing system and patent litigation revealed the actual workings of the system behind the public face of intellectual property at his time and to some extent still in ours. It was also remarkable to see how he transformed the private inventor's notebook into a coordinating document in his newly-minted industrial laboratory at Menlo Park. Edison's attempt to gain presence in the technological press and legitimacy as a scientist uncovered some of the messy early history of U.S. technological and scientific institutions. In sum, the materials told me stories not only of Edison, but of the professional, financial, commercial, and public institutions of late nineteenth century United States. Even the rise of celebratory fairs, department stores, and gender ideologies became part of the story as Edison sought to place electric lighting in everyday life.

Much of the writing occurred just in the process of juggling and making sense of the materials, making connections among the many pieces I was finding, and then identifying other literatures I needed to read in order to gain enough understanding of the context—such as the history and theory of intellectual property, feminist history of nineteenth century urbanization and middle-class home life, organizational theory, and theories of charisma (to understand Edison's role in the organization of his many companies and their consolidation into General Edison and General Electric). It was exciting to see the great variety of communicative systems involved in bringing the electric light and central power into the world. Sometimes the work seemed liked drudgery, as I was just putting one foot in front of the other describing the materials and then whittling sprawling texts down into tight, but well-documented stories. Yet the inherent interest of what the material revealed kept me from feeling overwhelmed. I was learning a great deal about story telling as I brought the pieces together, as the final book did not have the labored carefulness and overburdening documentation of my earlier studies where I was learning how to be rigorous and systematic in presenting evidence.

Themes

In writing the chapters, I was identifying theoretical themes that would come together in the final chapter. I had worked through some ideas in smaller articles, conference papers, classroom discussions—anywhere I could bend someone's ear about material I found fascinating. Simultaneously, I was working on an integrated theory of writing, how it might be viewed from several angles and frames, trying to find the right form in which to put these ideas together, as I will discuss in the next chapters. So as not to burden the Edison book with the weight of an incomplete theory, however, I elaborated only those ideas that directly clarified the Edison story, leaving other ideas implicit in the way I told the story. The final chapter's theory only quickly sketched out an intersection between social studies, technology studies, and rhetorical discursive studies, drawing on these literatures and elaborating concepts that bridged them. My subheadings in this chapter foregrounded the essential concepts and were designed to serve as a map through them, with each section being approximately a page in length. It was an attempt to create the impression of a forest through making visible a few tall conceptual trees: Heterogeneous symbolic engineering; systems of document circulation; differentiated values; satisfactory representations in specific discursive systems; material accountability; the rhetoric of operations; persuasion as an influence on consequent actions; conditions of accomplishment; symbolic integration and the process of enlistment; representational resting points; interpretive variability; structurationism and social learning; the individual and society; electrification as revolutionary and conservative. Each of these sections explained and elaborated these concepts to make them more intelligible and to connect them with the detailed evidence in the book. Obviously, these terms were denser and more obscure than the straightforward narrative I had offered to this point. Anyone who found them too technical, abstract, or obscure could skip this chapter.

Although I was drawing on much the same materials available to the authors of other books about Edison's accomplishments, my background, interests, and theoretical questions led me to a different story. The other studies viewed Edison as primarily an inventor, secondarily as a person, and never as a writer. They treated the documents largely as evidence of his inventive thinking and his life. I instead approached Edison (aided by all his colleagues and agents) primarily as a communicator and writer. I viewed the documents as strategically produced texts for communicative purposes within specific social systems and circumstances. This different story was not readily absorbed into the conventional view of historians of technology nor supported by the many museums that celebrate the mythic, heroic Edison, but the story has had some uptake among technological entrepreneurs who are looking to find his secret sauce. The role the book will take in writing studies is still in process, though I see it as particularly relevant to lifespan development of writing as well as to writing for multi-dimensional social accomplishments.

Figure 22.1. The Languages of Edison's Light

Chapter 23. Becoming a Writing Theorist: Keeping Abstractions Tied to the Ground

Disillusionment With Big Ideas

In my education I was often tempted by big ideas, but over time I became disillusioned with theory and broad generalizations, as I saw many clever people coming to strange conclusions guided by entrancing ideas. In high school I enjoyed the confident assertiveness of physics, but I came to understand how one theory inevitably replaced another, how pervasive errors were, how different ideas spoke to different human concerns, and how knowledge enterprises were funded by political agendas. My resistance to the absoluteness of knowledge was heightened by my being surrounded in my college years by bright people who seemed so arrogantly sure of their ideas that they believed they knew what would be best for others. Many of them wound up being in the neo-con brain trust, making choices that could be considered war crimes and crimes against humanity. Happily, my own uncertainties and respect for the viewpoints of others led me to resist their certainties. I learned to appreciate particulars and differences, even while nostalgically desiring certainty and absoluteness.

After my college senior year experiment in suspended disbelief as I explored Jewish orthodoxy, I returned to distrusting big ideas and learned to dwell on facts, living the life in front of me, forming personal relationships, and professionally committing myself to helping individuals in their lives as they saw them. As discussed in Chapter 14, these motives came together when I lucked into teaching literacy. My therapy helped me focus on the life as it emerged and not any imagined or idealized world. Finding my satisfactions and meaning in working with the students in my classroom, I initially had little interest in pursuing research after finishing my Ph.D. In seeking tenure publications, I stayed close to detailed evidence, attending to the text structures and details. In my book reviews I was impatient with what I viewed as ideological arrogance while I appreciated sharp tongued social critics. When I gained tenure, I dropped all attempts to publish in literary studies or more general cultural venues.

Further, as I became familiar with the uses of theory in the humanities, I found conceptual looseness and vague approximation. Theories could spark interesting, powerful, and even admirable ideas in readers' minds, the kind of mental explosions associated with poetry since the Romantic era, but loose associativeness also made theoretical ideas slippery as they grew by accretion and displacement within each reader. Even more this slipperiness made ideas hard to prove or disprove as each reader would bring to bear their own experiences and examples—either through explicit memory or implicit feelings and perceptions. Even more troubling, the conceptual slipperiness of theories made it impossible to articulate them precisely with other ideas equally exciting, as each would build their own symbolic pantheons, potentially rife with internal contradictions, incomplete connections, or outright gaps. Even if one person could come to an understanding of terms they were satisfied with, it would hardly translate with any precision to the system of ideas of another. No useful common knowledge and understanding would emerge to support coordinated action in the world. Only internal individualistic worlds of continuing mental excitement were fostered.

Dragged Back into the Swamp of Ideas

My wholehearted commitment, however, grew in the teaching of writing and the impact it had on the lives of students. A few early pieces (published and unpublished) tried to articulate my student-centered orientation, but I needed research in order to understand students' writing needs and situations. This research eventually led to theorizing, even though I resisted it. I felt uneasy as I fell into a theorizing mood. I initially would only theorize when the ideas were necessary to understand the data I found, but I gradually ventured into ideas that grew out of the evidence. Over time, the wider applicability of these ideas to society became more evident, pushing me to frame them more broadly so others might find them useful in opening up their own views of writing. I, nonetheless, constantly felt the need to base the theories on evidence, to avoid unfounded generalities and judgments, and to be as precise as I could to support coherent syntheses with other work.

I could only overcome my unease by ensuring that my ideas were grounded in publicly shareable evidence—available in shared archives or made transparently accessible through carefully articulated methodology. Tying concepts to observable and documentable things could increase clarity in the meaning of the concept, and firmer distinctions could be made among differing concepts. As well, starting with a small number of well-articulated and evidenced concepts could provide a more solid grounding for a larger universe of related concepts that might count as a theory. Additionally, evidentiary transparency could connect with what other people had found through other perceptions and reasonings. That is, the experiences of others would be respected—they had seen what they had seen, even if a new theory might propose different terms to understand what had previously been seen. Nothing legitimately seen was unseen, just renamed and reexplained. Millennia of subtle observations about texts and personal and social processes associated with writing have given us a wealth of experience to build on. New ideas might understand those observations differently but that richness of experience and observation can only serve to make our new accounts more comprehensive and more closely tied to material realities, as I had learned from Joseph Priestley's broad attention to all observed phenomena associated with evolving concepts of electricity.

Replication of research through shared methods is never as simple as it sounds; local conditions and craft always are part of the process—as science studies had taught me. The problem is even greater when the issues involve human meaning, choices, and actions, which depend on histories of individuals, local conditions under which individuals act (including social groupings relevant to the data collecting event), and people's complexity of orientations, perceptions, and motives in the moment. Further, when the object of study is creative, intentional action of individuals and collectives—as through writing—no two events are the same. In fact, treating two different writing events as the same destroys the very phenomenon you are looking for, because writing involves creating situationally meaningful and often unique communication. Add to these the particularity, position, and purposes of the observing analyst. These issues troubled me throughout my research career, especially as I tried to build theory on the basis of that research. It drove me to think about what robustly might reappear across individuals and circumstances. If there was repetition of texts or actions, that itself was the result of intentional or creative work, which then might mean different things to the different participants. If there was something replicable it would be in underlying processes. Methods became a way of uncovering those underlying processes, which would be confirmed only if many investigators found those same processes in many instances in different circumstances using different methods.

The concept would then be made stronger every time a methodologically careful researcher could locate the phenomenon operative in their data. Additionally, whenever writing and teaching practitioners found a concept useful in leading to greater success in their practice, it would further strengthen the reliability and replicability of the phenomenon. The continuing uptake in practice would suggest that the phenomenon (or something close enough to the phenomenon to be identifiable by the terms proposed) was describing something, and that thing turned out to be a useable idea. Practice has a wisdom, but that wisdom can grow with research-based theory and that research-based theory can be tested in practice. So as I went on my journey of theorizing I kept close attention to both empirical and practical work, as well as to their interplay.

In *Shaping Written Knowledge*, some concepts became important to make sense of the detailed evidence—including that of genre and how it evolved in relation to changing disciplines. Issues of disciplinary regulation embodying ideology became important for the study of the *American Psychological Association Style Manual*. Issues of role and role conflict (as informed by sociological research and theory) held the key to understanding the social structures, norms, and values that arose around scientific publication. Theoretical issues concerning the nature of facticity also haunted me because the search for facts motivated the creation and circulation of knowledge. I struggled to explain how texts were written human productions but yet could accountably report empirical experiences with the world beyond the text. While this epistemological question of knowledge production and its matched question of ontological trust in the world represented may seem philosophically abstract, to me they became very much practical and empirical issues of how to write so as to reliably represent the world. This turned the issue from a philosophic question to an empirical research question of just what was going on in disciplinary and scientific writing.

How can Ideas Travel Across People and Fields?

As I became aware of how different the epistemologies, ontologies, and ideologies of fields were, I realized these hard-won perspectives and practices were the consequence of extensive discussions, practical work, evidence gathering, theory-building, and contention among dedicated scholars in their respective fields. I could hardly expect them to adopt my theoretical perspective wholesale. The best I could do was to make phenomena found through my research robustly visible and practically useful to people of various perspectives. They then could make sense of writing phenomena in their own ways, within their own disciplinary perspectives. Over time, if I could show to people of different ideological and disciplinary orientations things they could recognize and identify in the world around them in their own terms, then readers might accede to these things existing, even if shown through the odd theoretical lenses I offered them. In turn, readers might come to accommodate their ideas about the world to accept the newly recognized phenomena, perhaps causing them to reorganize their understanding to include what they have now seen and could not unsee, without having to directly buy into whatever theoretical frame I was offering. Of course, the recognition of a new phenomenon would bring along some theoretical and methodological baggage. Let me provide an analogy: accepting the reality of something seen through a microscope would entail accepting that a microscope works and that there was a world too small to see with our unaided eyes. It would also challenge the viewer to give accounts of the workings of microscopes and the nature of the microscopically seen objects.

In adopting this rhetorical strategy of showing things that once seen cannot be unseen in *Shaping Written Knowledge*, I was foremost interested in showing that experimental reports evolved, and there was significant variation within and across disciplines and over time. Secondarily, I wanted to show that these changes resulted from active rhetorical choices by writers speaking to the discussions of their times to advance their best views of doing science. Only tertiarily did I have hopes for the more theoretical argument that scientists were concerned with developing credible representations of the world. The penultimate theoretical chapter of *Shaping Written Knowledge* put together a plausible account of how all these might fit together, and the final chapter presented some practical consequences of that account. But it wasn't necessary for readers to accept these two chapters to accept the studies in the more empirical chapters. Presenting theory as a kind of explanatory afterthought was a kind of rhetorical modesty in recognition of the great variation in readers' beliefs. Even though a particular set of evolving and growing understandings helped me see the things I then would be able to show the readers, I would not make accepting those ideas a required entry-ticket to seeing what I found. Rather showing what I found might open the doors for readers to come to new ideas, when they might find my theoretical offerings useful.

In writing the conceptually driven chapters of this book, I was constantly challenged to make the prose as transparent and simple as the subject allowed, without misleading oversimplification. I took as my slogan a version of Occam's razor I had read as a teenager attributed to Einstein: "Everything should be made as simple as possible, but no simpler."[12]

As mentioned earlier, some readers stumbled over preliminary drafts of my early studies, and this sent me on a quest throughout the rest of my career to identify the essence of what I wanted to say and build my sentences around that. I kept constantly revising at the sentence and paragraph level with this in mind.

Learning to simplify sentence style and argument structure never ends, and readers may still find my prose wanting. The search for clarity and simplicity of expression led beyond greater readability to greater precision in my thought, particularly in formulating concepts and eliminating distractions, excessive words, or other wastes of readers' cognitive resources that would leave meaning fuzzy, imprecise, or hard to decode. My goal was to have the edges of concepts and the connections among them to be as tightly constructed and hard edged as a system of plumbing so that the exact size and shape of each component would be specified, as well as how and where it connected to each other part to fit within an entire working system. If I was uncertain about how any piece might or might not fit with others, I sought to be candid and to identify the uncertainty or fuzziness as much as I could.

Although my attitude toward prose revision could be considered quixotic in a field so protean and historically unfolding as writing studies, I felt only in this way could we try to understand the principles behind creativity, invention, and change in writing and other symbolic communications. This stance put me at odds with much of my training in the humanities, which encouraged a kind of brilliance that excited the reader's individual associations and sparks of imagination. While I continue to value creative excitement and abductive leaps, we need to be as clear as possible with each other to create a shared system of ideas grounded in evidence and observed phenomena.

Historical Inspirations

After I finished *Shaping Written Knowledge*, my study of Joseph Priestley led me to appreciate his understanding of the communal practice of science. I incorporated into my own values and practices some of his insights into the communal

---

12. Though Einstein apparently said it in a more technical way https://www.championingscience.com/2019/03/15/everything-should-be-made-as-simple-as-possible-but-no-simpler/

practices still at play within the modern scientific world. His advocacy for transparency of methods, evidence, and reasoning resonated with me—but he also argued for a transparency of theories in relation to other extant theories, so one would not only advocate for one's own ideas but would try to place them fairly in relation to the ideas of others.

Priestley was not the only writer I studied who fundamentally influenced my ideas. From almost all I learned directly what they did as writers, by observing their texts, the genres they wrote in, and the processes by which genres evolved and were deployed in organized situations. From a subset of these writers, I learned practices which informed my teaching and my own writing. From others, I learned strategies and tricks they used in their texts which I could borrow, transform, or steal. Others had insights into writing and their rhetorical situations which helped me think my way into my situations. Some, moreover, were also wise about writing and expanded my vision of what writing could be, how to go about doing it, how it worked in the world, and how it could be a way to engage in the world. I consider these mentors.

A special few of these historical mentors had inspiring visions that engaged and extended my values. They taught me ways of being. These included Joseph Priestley and Adam Smith, both of whom pursued capacious transdisciplinary enlightenment quests to understand the world and how through writing they could contribute to the human experiment. They forged new practices as part of their growing analysis of what it meant to be a writer within a communal conversation. Others, whom I wrote about as scholars rather than subjects, had a similar impact on me—Lev Vygotsky, George Herbert Mead, Harry Stack Sullivan, Alfred Schutz, Robert Merton. Seeing the world through their eyes expanded my own sense of being a writer, and the sense of writing I could share with my students. Many writers I studied were smart and clever people, some even brilliant, but only some illuminated my world. They showed me deeper things about writing and being. They were the ones that held my hand as this mood of theorizing came over on me.

Trying to Explain: Coherence as a Kind of Integrity

As I started to develop a more robust, empirically-grounded view of writing, I found myself endlessly explaining to my colleagues in writing studies and other fields how things appeared to me. This theoretical explanation started with codas to some articles, closing chapters in books, articles devoted to syntheses of literatures and findings, then more elaborate theoretical presentations, culminating in the two volumes of *Literate Action* appearing in 2013. How I learned and developed as a writer as I moved beyond the institutional strictures of schooling became increasingly directed by what I was coming to understand writing to be. This understanding of writing kept opening up planes of considerations that could be attended to and made accountable to conscious choices.

A series of presentations in the late 1980s and early 1990s forced me to start working out my ideas more explicitly and articulating them more clearly—as well as connecting them with other work going on in science studies and writing. Writing book reviews as well led me to grapple more fully with other people's work and to elaborate my own positions in response. Equally, the opportunity to write introductions or prefaces to collections challenged me to find coherent themes within the diverse chapters in each collection and to articulate my emerging ideas in relation to what each volume had to offer.

The attempt to synthesize my emerging ideas coalesced in the project of putting together a volume of my selected essays in 1994 called *Constructing Experience* (Bazerman, 1994b). I wanted the book to be more than a random collection, even though the essays responded to different local exigencies. To me, they seemed to come out of an emerging coherence, which I wanted to make evident in the collection. In eighth grade I was attracted to and quoted Whitman's now-clichéd "containing multitudes" excuse for contradictions but I no longer found that satisfactory. A push for integrity/integralness kept driving me to find ways to articulate how parts fit together and what my vision was. Collecting my articles challenged me to explain how each part of my development and work was heuristic for each other. In *Shaping Written Knowledge*, coherence came out of the view of genre, how a genre arose and changed, how it served to meet the needs of a time, how writers came to make choices, and how genres came to organize the work and social relations of scientific communities. Now in *Constructing Experience*, the task was to show how my work in apparently disparate domains of the profession of writing and its teaching fit together into a coherent project. The essays I had published in writing studies included four different kinds with different seeming motives—1) sharing classroom perspectives and practices; 2) describing and synthesizing areas of inquiry that helped me understand writing; 3) puzzling through problems in understanding writing; and 4) offering empirical and theoretical studies. To explain how they fit together, I first wrote a brief autobiographical introduction (6 pages), along with briefer introductions to each of the four sections (1–2 pages each). These explained how each chapter grew from earlier practices and connected across sections.

But it was one thing to assert continuity and another to give a coherent vision that would connect the various pieces more conceptually. I felt the pressure to articulate that theoretical vision. I remember spending many hours sketching out different fragments of ideas, which seemed to be falling into different perspectives and time scales. Some seemed intimate, concerning my own practices and processes, while others were global, thinking about large social systems. My mind kept evoking an image from a passage I read as an undergraduate in Milton's *Paradise Lost* of the world suspended in space, encased within different spheres yet hanging from a common pendant. This imagery led me to characterize the theory as moving outward from the most located internal personal perspective of the writer (a phenomenology), through the outside view of the intimate observer (a social psychology), to the middle-range observer of literate social systems (a sociology), to the most distant overview (a sociocultural history of rhetoric). Across these differently-scaled perspectives, however, topics recur, viewed at different scales: location, situation, action, resources, typification, genre, produced text, histories of experiences, identity, roles, audiences, interactants, expectations. I also considered the kinds of situations and roles which we are likely to take when we adopt each of these perspectives. I suppose you could also call this a kind of inverse mandala, with the concrete experience at the center and ideas emerging in the outer circles.

This retelling a story from multiple perspectives I came across a number of times in reading literature; *Rashomon* is a classic example, one that I first came across as a teenager. I also was fascinated by informational displays that had transparent overlays of complex systems to display the different layers, as in anatomical graphics. Later in my dissertation I drew on this technique as I described in layers a complex ceremonial event which included a procession through streets of London, decorations, plays, music, and recitation of poems.

The "Introduction II: Sketches towards a Rhetorical Theory of Literacy" in *Constructing Experience* offered a vision from four different points of view. It was dense and long—almost 40 pages, but it had no footnotes or even organized evidence. It had some examples to make the vision concrete, but it hardly offered a warrant or an argument. Nor did it even recognize all the thought of others that I drew on. This sketch left me with a sense of obligation and desire to lay out the full story, with evidence, citations, and reasoning that might persuade. This obligation set off two more decades of finding out how to tell that story. Along the way I gave a promissory note in the form of a 1997 conference presentation and published paper (Bazerman, 2000c), saying that in order to elaborate our knowledge of writing we needed a history of the emerging social purposes and forms of writing and a comprehensive new theory of rhetoric based on the problematics of writing instead of high stakes, platform-spoken performance. During the ensuing fifteen years I engaged in a number of projects that served to build the knowledge necessary to do this—including editing research and reference series, and a handbook which attempted to pull together the knowledge of the field, grounded in historical and social developments. I will discuss these in the next two chapters. I also continued to noodle around with many smaller essays elaborating theory and bringing parts together.

Chapter 24. Elaborating the Theory: Finding a Point to Stand On

Writing the theoretical introduction in *Constructing Experience* was only a first gesture towards a more coherent and elaborated theory. As I was seeing it to press, I continued writing essays and making presentations, working out various theoretical problems. A first question for me was why even write theory. Within that volume I had included a couple of earlier essays that started to formulate an answer. In a 1990 essay for a volume on responding to student writing, I used my emerging theories to understand some practical problems of teaching, such as what happened interactionally when I responded to student writing (Bazerman, 1990d). The following year in a festschrift for James Kinneavy, I discussed how he wanted to develop a framework to guide teaching and improve student writing (Bazerman, 1991d). Elsewhere, I considered how classroom interactions were socially constructed by teachers' and students' moment-by-moment responses within institutional arrangements and interests (Bazerman, 1992f). This reframing of student-teacher interactions was part of my emerging understanding that genres were only one aspect of the typifications that comprised the social arrangements within which activities and texts emerged, not only in the classroom, but throughout society. If we were to teach writing and improve students' choices as writers, we need to develop a deeper understanding of what writing was and did, and how it has emerged, changed, and differentiated within the different spheres of life.

The protean and emergent nature of the typifications at play in writing led me to consider what even constituted a moment and how this was negotiated by participants ("Whose Moment?" delivered as a conference paper around 1991, and published a chapter in *Constructing Experience* in 1994). Structurationist ideas of social organization helped me formulate how texts contributed to emergently quasi-stabilized social arrangements, roles, and available actions, leading to my chapter on Genre Systems (Bazerman, 1994d), and then to explain how genre and genre systems created "Habitats for Social Action" (delivered in 1994, but not published until Bazerman, 2004f). In working on Edison, I considered patents and intellectual ownership as emerging objects (Bazerman, 1993h & 1997h). At about this time I also saw how other regulated and institutionalized documentary systems provided structured places for action; the example of the U.S. income tax system became paradigmatic for me of an emergent and changing documentary system that, nonetheless, at each moment seemed tightly strung through institutionalized structures and regulations (Bazerman, 1999d). A number of other articles elaborated and applied these ideas to writing in disciplines and professions. Over the next few years, I drew on David Russell's formulations of activity systems (Russell, 1994), and I collaborated with him on a couple of collections that encouraged work in a similar vein (Russell & Bazerman, 1997i; Bazerman & Russell, 2003g).

Another confirmation of this socio-historic view of genre and activity systems came when I was asked to contribute to a collection on letters. I had first written about scientific letters as the basis for the scientific article in *Shaping Written Knowledge*, but I kept coming across other instances where letters had a formative role in the emergence of other genres. As I put the cases together and examined them more closely, I saw a repeated pattern. The explicit sociality of letters—identifying author, recipients, date, location of sending, affiliation and cordiality gestures, and specificity of purpose or request—mediated specific interactions. With repetition and time, the sociality became more implicit or stylized within emergent genre conventions. As the genres signaled recognizable social interactions, the texts shed socially-identifying features of letters to foreground the specific information needed within the now typified transaction. Institutional arrangements came to rely on the specialized genres, and the genres became further stylized as their meaning became sedimented within the transactions of the organizations. Decrees of kings became stylized into orders, laws, and communiques. Commercial letters gave rise to memos, reports, and order forms. Financial instructions to banks became checks and paper money, and now digitized electronic transfers. And so on, through many spheres. Of course, some written genres had different origins, such as transcriptions of public speeches, but the stylization of letters has been one of the robust means by which forms of writing became meaningful social documents. This process revealed how genres had recognizable social bases and became infrastructural for institutions that stretch across distances and times (Bazerman, 2000b).

Seeing literate action within mutable but quasi-stable genres and social structures also led me to rethink rhetoric, which had become a standard theoretical frame for much of writing studies in the US I did see writers acting rhetorically as they attempted to carry out their interests and communicative needs strategically within specific situations, but rhetorical theorists had tended to present rhetoric through a limited number of concepts which they applied universally—while my theory was all about changing genres, changing social arrangements, and human invention. Since the 1970s I had resisted seeing everything as an argument, and saw that writers often engaged in strategic, planful text production with no intent to argue. Over time, I saw more clearly how the terms and situations of traditional rhetorical thinking had derived from the field's origins in oratorical performance in the classical agora and then later in the Christian pulpit. I, therefore, had distanced myself from the term rhetoric, seeing rhetoric as only a special set of historically and institutionally limited cases (see the critique in Bazerman & Russell, 1994e). I tried then to formulate an alternative view of rhetoric (Bazerman, 1993c), but got no purchase from rhetorical theorists and scholars, not even a counter-argument or a passing riposte or rejection. While still whistling in the wind, I called for a new theory of rhetoric based on writing and the social situations made possible by writing (Bazerman, 1997e, 1999d, 2000c). I still hoped, optimistically, that more fully articulated theory of rhetoric, grounded in the problematics of writing, might be useful and of interest to some in writing studies and the teaching of writing.

A Plan for Coherence

By the mid 1990s I started taking notes and drawing up outlines towards a theory book, tentatively titled *Becoming*, to indicate the historical sweep of emergent literate social systems, genre options, and communicative resources available to a writer, as well as the way the literate world provides a field for the development of the individual, across the lifespan. I wanted to combine this broad theoretical picture with practical guidance to writers who wanted to understand more deeply what they were doing, so they could act more creatively and effectively. I was trying to juggle a coherent and readable account that would make intuitive sense to writers and teachers with the multi-disciplinary theories and research that would elaborate the reasoning and evidence. That was a lot of different sized and shaped items to juggle, some with sharp edges. At the end of 1997, as I was revising the Edison book, I realized a strategy of separating the theory project into two volumes might resolve the tension between the practical and theoretical goals. The first volume would be a shorter (perhaps 100 pages), practical rhetoric for writers and teachers that would offer direct, though sophisticated, advice with only enough discussion of the work of others to make the concepts intelligible. The second volume would at greater length (perhaps three times the length of the first) elaborate all the concepts in the theory and would discuss the full interdisciplinary resources I would draw on; it would have fuller documentation. A decade and a half later I completed two books following that basic plan, with the first volume being about 165 pages, though the second volume was mercifully much shorter than I had imagined, only about thirty percent longer than the first. The works cited list of the second, however, was about eight times the length of the first volume (Bazerman, 2013c, 2013d).

In 1997, I outlined both volumes and opened up separate computer files for each of the proposed chapters, placing notes in each to identify what topics might be covered and how. I also started to draft a few of the earlier chapters. File names and chapter organization changed as the books evolved, but most of the topics in the original outline found their place in the final books. I had hoped that the tables of contents of the two volumes would be parallel, with each chapter of the rhetoric being explained in a shadow theoretical chapter. I initially started to work on the two books in tandem, working on the matching practical and theoretical chapters at the same time. The logic of explaining and elaborating the theories from different disciplines and perspectives, however, pulled me in different directions in the two books. Consequently, the outlines of the two started to diverge, as did the writing of the chapters. Nonetheless, in the final version the concepts in each are mirrored in the other, though across different chapters. I provide a map of the correspondences in the introduction of the second volume.

The volumes took so long to write in part because I was working on other things, including the *Handbook of Research on Writing*, appearing in 2008, which helped me think through the scope of the field I was drawing on (see chapter 25). I wanted to let the ideas for the theory books cook slowly, examining the relevant literatures carefully, and being precise in my formulations. I was aware that this would be the synthesis and culmination of much of my inquiry over the years, as I was entering my sixties in 2005. The theory volumes appeared just as I was turning 68. I did not expect to have such a long life, as my father died at age 48 in 1965, my mother at age 58 in 1974, and my brother, my only sib, at age 63 in 2004. I had long been self-conscious about mortality and the necessity of getting things done while I could. But I also wanted to get things done right.

I had the formulations, examples, and sequences of reasoning for a number of the early chapters in both volumes well worked out as I had been writing and talking about the ideas in them for years. I also had been discussing in classes and publications a number of the authors and texts that had influenced the development of the ideas. Still, I had to reread the relevant texts and commentaries carefully to identify the aspects of those works important for my presentation. As these resources were interdisciplinary and often not explicitly related to writing, I needed to select how much to tell about them in the most relevant way and to explain exactly how I was using those ideas and why. Meeting these challenges was well within the kinds of writing I had been doing about those materials. I was, nonetheless, surprised by insights that came when I started articulating those ideas and sequencing them to unfold their relationship. Carefulness and constant revision kept the process slow.

Later chapters in the first, practical book, however, required greater problem solving and new ways of formulating topics that had long been part of writing studies. Topics such as motivation, strategics, invention, meaning and representation, organization, style, and processes were obviously of continuing importance to writing, but I had a different perspective and way of talking about them. Traditionally these were seen primarily in relation to the individual writer and the production of individual texts, with some attention to the audience. I needed to place these within larger social systems and more dynamically unfolding sequences of texts and histories of cultural practices. Even psychological elements of writing needed to be reframed within this larger socio-historical perspective.

The second, theory book required me to revisit interdisciplinary domains at greater length and greater detail. The early chapters required a rearticulation of my major influences from cultural psychology, phenomenological sociology, and interdisciplinary pragmatic social sciences. The major prior discussions of these authors had been framed within the projects of other disciplines, but I needed to reframe them from the perspective of writing. In further chapters I needed to discuss other disciplinary traditions which I saw as relevant to writing, but through the framework of the three traditions which lay behind my approach. This meant I needed a double reinterpretation of those traditions—seeing them as sociocultural and then applied to writing.

Other chapters took even longer to work out my perspective. I particularly had a problem with the linguistics chapter, even though (or perhaps because) linguistics seemed so close to writing studies. Writers of course use language and rely on psycholinguistic processes. Even more proximate to writing studies, applied linguistics included the teaching of second language writing in its portfolio, and is in many countries outside the US the main disciplinary home of writing education. Over the years I had become familiar with a number of varieties of linguistics and applied linguistics, and found a number of different approaches useful practically and theoretically. But I had found none of them fully satisfactory or consistent with the views I had been developing about writing. It took me years to puzzle through exactly where the points of connection and difference were, and what points I wanted to make that would clarify my theoretical position without becoming unnecessarily quarrelsome.

One difficulty was that linguistics over the last century has tended to see spoken language as more "natural" and fundamental, with written language as epiphenomenal and filtered through normative systems of schooling, publication, and politically dominant dialects. I understood how the interest in spoken language made sense given that humans spoke long before they began to write, that recording technologies in the twentieth century increased convenient access to spoken data, and that linguistics coordinately moved to description from prescription. Nonetheless writing studies needed an understanding of language applicable to writing. Another core challenge was to distinguish between applied linguistics approaches to writing which placed language forms at the center of writing instruction and writing-centered approaches that saw writing as the socially situated production of meaningful, effective texts to mediate shared social understandings.

A further difficulty was that utterance-based linguistic and semiotic approaches which were most theoretically compatible with my work—associated with Bakhtin and Volosinov, but also implied in the work of their contemporary Vygotsky—had not yet been and might never be brought into the canonical form of a quasi-stable description of language, which still remained a central motivating task for most linguistics systems. To this day, utterance-based linguistics serves mostly to critique the limits of more traditional language systems. Even functional linguistics was more a program than a system, and the most systematized version of functional linguistics—Hallidayan Systemic Functional linguistics I found to be caught between its theoretical recognition of the social fluidity of language and its linguistic motive to produce a language system. I have great respect for SFL and find many of its concepts and concrete linguistic findings of great value for writing, but I still cannot adopt it as a fully adequate system.

Despite my lack of fundamental commitment to any linguistic system, I understand how writing practices and institutions have created the impulse, need, and use for language systems, and I see systematization of language as part of the process, growth, and instruction of writing. Language systems are necessary tools for writers to negotiate alignment between writers and readers, particularly as texts travel across space and time. But I see no grammar or linguistics system as absolute or foundational—though some would want to ground language in psychology and the brain, the nature of the sign, or physiology. While each of these dimensions may contribute to and constrain the languages we use, I do not see any of them as foundationally determinative. Insofar as I see anything as constant, it is the social processes by which people negotiate meaning well enough to carry out their practical purposes.

My problem in writing this chapter was to adopt an appropriate stance that would recognize and respect the value of various branches of linguistics and discuss their important role in writing without requiring me to advocate for any one system. Ultimately, I adopted the stance of examining why writing throughout its history relied on and motivated the systematization of language. This then allowed me to consider how different linguistic systems were of various use to writing. Of all the unorthodox views that I presented in those two volumes, my view of language may be least persuasive, not because I am any less persuaded myself or less committed to it, but because the many committed adherents of different systems will not be happy with my lack of adherence to any of them. My views might have few natural allies within any branch of linguistics.

A Note on Technology and Process

I want to end this chapter with a note on my drafting practices which had developed over the years since I had begun writing on a Kaypro II computer around 1983, but actually grew out of earlier practices from the days of typewriters. Prior to personal computers, but after I started to pay attention to writing processes, I sketched out ideas on notepads to get my thoughts down, but then wrote my first full drafts (either by hand or typed) rarely referring to the notes. Then I would revise from those drafts, typing a final clean copy. When I first began writing on desktop computers with the early cumbersome programs, requiring many formatting codes, such as Wordstar, I continued to free-write and sketch ideas on notepads. But when I switched to Apple computers and I first encountered what was then called WYSIWYG (What you see is what you get) formatting, I started writing my initial notes directly onto the computer. When I was ready to write a full draft, I would start typing at the top of the file, pushing my earlier notes and sketches down to the bottom as my text lengthened. Sometimes when I felt that I had covered topics I erased the related material at the bottom of the file. When I felt I was losing the direction in my draft I would outline what I had done to that point and/or introduce subheadings to structure the argument. Even when doing my interim outlines, I still usually would not refer to my notes now at the end of the file, as they had served just to bring all the thoughts and material I wanted to discuss to mind and helped me order them. At most I would skim those notes and sketches to see whether I had dropped any topic, information, or strong formulations, but I almost always found I had indeed covered everything I had intended and said it better the second time around. Then I would copy the text in a clean file and delete all the excess at the bottom. I would use this new file to revise, rework, and clean up.

The extensive synthesis and thinking through of the implications of the material for these theory books, however, put even more pressure on the idea sketching process. For this pair of books, I in fact often used chapter drafts themselves as discovery documents, getting everything down in them and then abandoning the drafts when I started afresh to put the material together in what I thought a more effective way. It is only when I felt I had close to a satisfactory draft that I would begin intensive revision of existing text.

Figure 24.1. Generations of my writing technologies

Part Five. Participating in a Field and Its Future

Figure 25.1: Institutional me. Photo courtesy of Charles Bazerman.

Chapter 25. Editing as Writing and Developing Writing: Understanding What Others are Doing in Their Writing

As I was developing my own teaching, research, and theory program, I started to become more conscious of how I could contribute to the growth of the field as a whole, beyond my personal publications. Initially I thought simply that my work would only thrive if there were people doing similar work, which I therefore wanted to foster. But as I became more aware and thoughtful about the value of different lines of work, and as I was able to view writing studies through more of a science studies lens, I saw that the field as a whole needed to thrive and become more robust in order for us all to contribute to the advancement of writing practices and writing education. Science studies also made me more aware of some of the intellectual and institutional tools needed to support a thriving discipline. In turn, I found my own work deepening as I was able to gain a more sympathetic understanding of other people's research programs.

These developments were happening as I continued my own work. So the remaining chapters of this book create a bit more complex chronology, with some parts overlapping in time with earlier chapters, and then going forward with multiple streams of engagement happening simultaneously. As I moved into the later parts of my writing career, I also started to look more to the future of the field to support possible lines of work that might endure in the work of others.

An important step in this communal engagement was taking on editorial roles which stretched across several decades and into the present. Elsewhere I have written on my editorial work as part of my contribution to the field and have drawn some lessons as to how to edit most effectively (Bazerman, 2022c). In editing, moreover, I was also developing my own skills of writing. I was learning to work collaboratively with others and help them build the strongest texts they could. By evaluating their texts, seeing how the texts were constructed, and spotting the as yet unrealized potentials in their texts, I was learning to appreciate different ways of going about and representing research. I had to stretch my mind to look down the paths the authors were taking.

A good friend from college, Gabor Brogyanyi, the graduate student who helped introduce me to the mysteries of *explication du texte*, died from AIDS during the early years of that disease when he was a professor at Bowdoin. While we had been roommates when he was a graduate student and I was a first-year undergraduate, he never let on about his being gay or his struggles with it, and I was too naive to pick up on the clues. As part of his memorial, I volunteered to edit a small, privately published collection of his poems, only a few of which had previously been published. In reading through his manuscripts twenty years after we were roommates, I started to feel his struggles, his pain, and the sadness of his early passing. This experience, while not a complicated technical matter, nonetheless, opened me to the way editing brings one closer to the vision, thoughts, and experience of authors.

Developmental Editing of Academic Collections and Series

My first small steps in scholarly editing grew out of some conference panels I organized in the late 1980s that then became special sections in two journals. I had come to see, as many academics do, the value of organizing panels to bring together several scholars with related work to share thoughts. Bringing their papers together for a journal section is a common next step. Negotiating with journal editors, coordinating schedules and drafts, and monitoring length requirements were good training in managing projects. The actual writing of introductions grew directly from my chair's role in the panels, offering some context and synthesis while adopting an editor's voice (Bazerman 1989c, 1989d).

A more extensive volume co-edited with Jim Paradis (Bazerman & Paradis, 1991e) grew out of a chance conference chat about our shared desire to see more careful and systematic use of evidence in historical studies of scientific writing and the need to shift rhetorical attention from canonized texts to actual practices. While rhetorical teaching embodied in canonical texts may influence the actual practices of any period, it was not necessarily a one-way flow from theory to practice as was too often represented.

Both of us as writers had previously attempted to enlist our readers, but we now had to enlist other authors, so that they could see their work fitting within our potential volume. To ground the work in actual historical writing practices we set explicit criteria for proposals on the kind of systematic evidence required; these criteria then influenced our selection of projects to invite for full manuscripts. In dividing up which editor would primarily work with each author (though we both periodically looked at all the developing chapters), we became more explicit about work we felt comfortable mentoring and those that seemed to fit the other's expertise. Jim and I acted as editors on each other's work, which stretched us both in appreciating each other's intellectual world. In working with the chapter authors we also came to identify what we saw as promising in the evidence they offered but had not yet framed well. All of the proposals we chose already had interesting in-depth research materials, so the developmental work was about what the authors could do with this material, how to identify and bring out the main story of each study, and find the bigger meaning within the rich particularities of their data. As I had come to ask, they had evidence of something, but of what? We also guided authors into more explicit and careful representation of their theories, methods, and evidence. This process is no doubt similar to what other editors experience and learn, but for us, of course, it was new. All this inspection and evaluation of the authors' work further raised our awareness of our own methodological standards and practices.

Jim and I turned out to have somewhat different editing goals. While we were both committed to the emergence of social forms and their elaboration, I expected more positioning within prior theory, while Jim was more looking with an historian's eye focusing on actors and their local conditions. This difference impacted the way we worked with authors, as I kept up dialog with my authors to get more systematic with their theories and their analytical methods, while Jim focused on evidence from archival research. At one point he wondered why the chapters I was mentoring kept constructing preliminary reviews of literature, often out of a similar body of articles, but then at some point he said he now understood that there was an interrelated set of studies here, advancing a common vision. All the authors in my side did share that orientation, but it took some dialog to elicit the theories they were working with. At the same time, I had a bit of trouble in understanding where some of Jim's articles were going, which then led me to query him and his authors about making the important themes more explicit. In turn, Jim's influence made my own chapter on Joseph Priestley more historically focused on a single author and how the author's way of thinking and writing emerged out of his social conditions, identities, and projects.

Editing another person's work requires you to read it carefully. Even more, when editing it developmentally, you view the work at several stages, try to see where it is headed, and suggest ways to help the text emerge. You get to know the text as you try to align with the thinking and material of the author. In particular, I looked at the reasoning, sequencing, and elaboration of arguments to see their warrantability and readability, so that readers would follow and assent to the text's reasoning. This task led me to question my own sense of what made a credible argument, what was needed to fulfill the claims, what would distract, and what would make visible and more memorable the meaning and import of the claims. While I had thought about these issues in my own writing, grappling with the work of others forced me to take on problems and paths of reasoning I would be unlikely to have gone down on my own.

In my editing, I tried to reflect back to authors what I was finding in their texts and then ask whether that matched their intentions. Then I asked questions to elicit more about what I saw as needing elaboration and to query whether some parts were essential, and for what purpose. Only then would I make suggestions about how things might be phrased more sharply, what topics might be gone through more swiftly or avoided because they raised distracting questions, or what should just be eliminated as not necessary—though often all these issues would be resolved in the prior questioning. But I found it most enlightening when authors wanted to go in different directions or otherwise pushed back at my suggestions, indicating that I was missing what they were trying to say—perhaps because I was relying on inappropriate assumptions or perhaps because I was just misreading or being dense.

Conversations were particularly intense in the early stages of development of the chapters, as I met with authors at conferences in the middle of noisy coffee shops and hotel lobbies. I kept trying to wrap my mind around what they had and where they were going, and then ask questions and make suggestions in harmony with what I was understanding. I regularly reminded myself and the authors, however, that this was their text and final choices always remained with them. As they made their arguments, assumptions, and methods more explicit, I was also able to align better with where they were headed. This process created a kind of unity in the volume that extended beyond the initial vision, but still realized our original intention to create space for individuals to research the actual social practices of writing in different times and places.

Co-editing with David Russell

I then co-edited several books and special issues with David Russell. Since we had been having a continuing dialog on our research and growing theoretical ideas for several years before collaborating, we started out more closely aligned. When I read a draft of David's volume on the history of Writing Across the Curriculum (Russell, 1991), I was excited by what he had found and our conversations over the manuscript led to a strong collaborative trust. Our first collaborative project to elaborate our shared vision of WAC was a volume of *Landmark Essays in Writing Across the Curriculum* (Bazerman & Russell, 1994e). In our discussions of what texts to include, we set out a vision of the historical trend of the field and its current manifestations. Research about actual disciplinary practices we saw as important to inform the curricular, institutional, and faculty development components of WAC. These impulses as well guided us in preparing the headnotes of the selected landmark essays. The trajectory and implications of our approach contested some of then-current approaches to writing and rhetoric, as in two introductory essays we challenged assumptions of rhetorical theory and approaches to WAC that did not engage sufficiently with the variety of disciplinary writing. As I had discussed earlier in this book, I had mixed experiences in challenging views, but in this case David and I came to the conclusion that it was necessary here to define the space we were marking out in contrast to other approaches that already had claimed a lot of the turf.

David and I then wanted to create a publication space and shared identity for a growing group of scholars interested in following similar lines of investigation. We proposed a co-edited special issue on writing for an interdisciplinary journal *Mind, Culture, and Activity* devoted to activity theory, which we were drawn to as providing a more comprehensive framework within which to locate genre (Russell & Bazerman, 1997i). Our call for proposed papers articulated that theoretical commitment to understanding the relation of activity to writing practices.

The process of developmental editing was similar to that in the earlier volume with Jim Paradis, but since the theoretical orientation was already more tightly focused, we were able to help each other see further down our distinct but closely related paths.

A few years later David and I followed up that special issue of five articles with a longer volume of fourteen new chapters, with an even greater focus on the emergent nature of work, communities, and individuals engaged in writing activities (Bazerman & Russell, 2003g). My own development as an editor and writer continued as I came to know more about the ways the authors' minds and writing practices worked to produce their separate contributions. The more I worked with authors, the more I could make suggestions that would support the paths they were going down. I came to see that they would go farthest by following their own lights; whatever I had to offer needed to fit with where they were heading. The important thing for the volume's coherence was that the chapters would remain in dialog whether they explicitly disagreed on significant points or simply looked at different material and phenomena. This awareness of the distinctiveness of each chapter also increased my own understanding of the capaciousness and inventiveness of writing and the great differences among writers and their paths of development.

Simultaneously with these collections, I became the sole editor of a book series with Erlbaum on the related theme of *Rhetoric, Society, and Knowledge*, explicitly inquiring into how socially organized activities produced, distributed, and applied knowledge within society. Again, the series supported the growth of a body of work and a group of researchers who would keep expanding the general approach and demonstrating its wide reach and implications for society. Each study was particular and detailed in its methods, data, and evidence. Working with authors as their books emerged over time from proposals through drafts and publication, I was able to appreciate more fully the contribution of each, what they were seeing, and the tools that they were to bring to bear. Since many of the authors themselves were writing teachers my editing could draw on common practical knowledge we shared. Often I just needed to remind them about something they regularly did with their students in order to apply it to themselves. Sometimes we do not remember that we ourselves are the same as our students, with the same problems they have. Once I reminded authors to get back to basics we all knew and preached, they would say, "of course" and would do all the rest of the work on their own with no further commentary needed from me. It was delightful to see how familiar principles would ramify in much improved texts. Often enough when we also discussed some new, more subtle issue at a more advanced level that might not come up with their students, the authors would quickly know exactly what to do, pursuing the work in their own way. This certainly heightened my appreciation of how much craft knowledge writing teachers develop, as well as the value of knowing what you wanted to accomplish in revision.

Working with authors in depth over their projects (some of them repeatedly) built friendships and gave me an ongoing interest in where their work was headed. I felt I had become a better reader of their new work, though I was regularly surprised by new steps they were taking.

Editing Reference Works

As writing studies expanded, reference works were needed to make the field's findings more available. Although knowledge in our field had been growing for decades, it was not accessible—too many wheels were being reinvented without awareness of prior work. When a colleague approached me to co-edit a series of reference guides on rhetoric and composition, I accepted quickly. Even after the print publisher stepped back from their commitment and the initiating editor also dropped out, I persisted and sought open access publishing with the WAC Clearinghouse in conjunction with print-on-demand editions from Parlor Press.

The initial plan for the volumes was tightly templated to ensure focused reference coverage distinct from the author's personal research program or argument. The volumes needed to be accessible to teachers of writing working with all ages and levels, as well as other writing practitioners and policy makers. The early volumes, however, revealed authors needed some flexibility, so the sections became functions that needed to be addressed rather than mandated chapters. The reference stance and the broad review of history, theory, research, current directions, and implications for practice, however, remained.

I recruited broadly among experts in the field, often from people with different interests and perspectives than my own because I wanted to ensure that all aspects of the field were being covered. When the series first started, the paucity of reference works meant many topics needed to be covered, though the volumes would appear only gradually. Over the years other books reviewing research and practice appeared, so the need to cover all topics lessened; nonetheless, the series remained open to all areas of the field, especially if they have not yet gotten good synoptic coverage. A few years ago, I invited a couple of younger co-editors (Anis Bawarshi and Mary Jo Reiff) to open the series to more recent developments and allow continuity. Anis and Mary Jo had produced the excellent reference guide on *Genre* with efficiency and professionalism, showing real understanding of the purpose of the series, so I knew they could carry through in editing further volumes. It turns out that they had marvelous insights and expertise which I learned from, and that together as a team we have readily converged on judgments that were more thoughtful than would have come from any one of us as individuals.

While this series started to provide reviews of work in specific areas with an emphasis on the application to practice, in the early years of the twenty-first century writing studies still didn't have a general research handbook or encyclopedia that would bring together in one volume all the different lines of work and could provide the foundation for continuing research and theorizing. I proposed such a volume to Erlbaum and began working with an editor, Naomi Silverman, who continued to work with me even as Erlbaum was purchased by Francis and Taylor, shortly thereafter to be acquired by Routledge. Despite the changes of ownership, I felt no disruption of the kind of personal support and flexibility granted initially by the small publisher. I also was given a slow timeline that allowed gradual building of the contents with lots of consultation and giving the authors adequate time to prepare in-depth chapters, with multiple cycles of revision. As the book was in the latter stages, I found out about another handbook that would be coming out somewhat earlier, edited by MacArthur, Graham, and Harris (2006), with a more limited focus on schooling and educational psychological approaches. I resisted speeding up my timeline, but rather let the book cook slowly as it needed. There was also another reference work on a similar timeline focused on composition and the classroom edited by Peter Smagorinsky (2006). When my book came out (Bazerman, 2008b), I saw the three books as complementary; I built an alliance with the other editors in shared conference presentations and other communications. My relationship and friendship with each of them grew and we were to work together in various ways over the ensuing years.

My proposal was from the beginning based on the multidimensionality and interdisciplinarity of writing studies. I needed to reach out to different fields for chapter ideas and authors. To realize the broadness of this vision I relied on a large board of advisors with recognized expertise in the many domains that needed to be covered. I solicited chapter ideas from members of the board and circulated for comments an evolving table of contents built around five sections: history, society, individual, school, language. As the chapter topics emerged, I also asked the board for suggestions for potential authors. I later would use members of the board to review individual chapters in their areas of expertise. When I then invited authors for particular chapters, I offered an initial list of subtopics to be covered, asking the authors to make a counter proposal that drew on their particular expertise and vision. Of course, their suggestions showed me much more of their fields than I imagined existed. In a few cases I suggested a few additions or adjustments, most often to monitor the boundaries of the chapters and to avoid unproductive overlaps and gaps between chapters. Ultimately, I was able to find admirable and timely coverage for almost all the topics. In the introductions to the section of the published volume, I only had to suggest a few remaining interdisciplinary areas that I thought might be relevant.

Once the parameters of the chapters were established, the authors already had a good idea of the nature of the reference volume and their task, so my continuing editorial work, while detailed, was not unusual and involved, making a few organizational or style suggestions, monitoring chapter lengths, and keeping up deadline pressures, though the authors were quite professional about all these things.

The handbook further expanded my scope of understanding of the breadth, depth, and detail of the field. By the end of the project, I had a sense that I finally had a grasp on the parts of the field as they existed at the time. This then positioned me to carry out my further projects with a much better sense of what the field contained and what I might usefully contribute to the continuing growth of the field; particularly, it gave me the confidence I needed to move forward with the pair of theory books which I described in Chapter 24. Together this handbook and the theory books fulfilled a commitment I made in my 2000 article calling for a fuller history and social accounting of writing to demonstrate its impact on our way of life, our institutions and schooling, as well as our individual ways of thinking (Bazerman, 2000c). With these two projects completed, I felt I had accomplished what I had promised and was secure in the framework I had been developing. I now had the leisure to think what to do next to carry the work forward.

Publication Venues and Open Access

Choosing publication venues for projects is also the work of writers and editors, and requires learning how to navigate gatekeepers to reach appropriate audiences. The publishing landscape as well has changed, with two forces dominating—corporatization and the internet. Together these have led me to rely increasingly on open access publication through academically run organizations, which I now seek whenever possible.

In the early years of my career publishing textbooks and then scholarly books, a number of small academic and corporate publishers held values consistent with academic interests and were culturally close to universities. They sought quality books (by academic standards), were interested in novel approaches, and were willing to invest in projects with only modest returns or high risks. But over time corporate consolidation and public ownership have redirected publishers to assured short-term profits to maintain stock prices. The values of publishers became corporate and prices of books and journals escalated, coming increasingly in conflict with academic values, not only in what they offered but in how available their products were to people with little access to large research libraries.

The corporate hold and predatory behavior were particularly troublesome for the field of writing studies, which arose largely outside of elite research universities and whose knowledge was widely useful outside of such elite institutions. Writing professionals often worked at less well-funded or smaller institutions with teaching missions and little budget for research libraries. Further, many teachers of writing worked in less affluent nations that could not invest heavily in internationally-priced higher education materials. The situation only became worse with the arrival of the internet, which led corporate publishers to find ways to maximize their dwindling hold on the publication process. Much of the production of scholarly labor had always been dependent on the volunteer labor of academics, but now digital tools allowed even more of that work to be distributed to volunteer academic labor, with the corporate publishers focusing on marketing and controlling access rather than editorial support or even the production and distribution of copies. As I became attuned to this increasing cultural divide between corporate publishers and academic authors and editors, I sought answers from the corporate owner of a journal I had been on the board of. The evasive and bad faith answers they gave and their increasingly predatory behavior gave me little choice but to resign from the board. Yet at the same time the internet and digital publication tools made open access publication possible, produced almost entirely by voluntary academic labor, perhaps with a few hired editorial assistants.

Initially I understood these dynamics only from the needs and processes within the United States, where the limited number of journals inhibited the growth of writing studies, and textbooks were the only effective channel for the dissemination of practices. With international experience, however, I came to see this situation inhibiting the needed advancement of writing globally, as writing was so central to citizenship, economy, and personal opportunity everywhere. Writing studies was growing in all regions, but venues were few and distribution was often regionally limited. The flow of knowledge across borders was an important dynamic for our field, allowing for contribution from scholars in all regions and diverse perspectives.

In writing studies in the US, the leader in the academically controlled, low-cost field was the WAC Clearinghouse, which provided free open access publication with creative common licenses, keeping manuscript ownership with the authors. The low per-volume costs they do have are covered by contributions and institutional sponsors, supplemented by arrangements with on-demand print publishers that offer print copies to those who want them. In recent years they have also added more international and multi-lingual titles, even as European and South American scholars have also been developing free open-access publishing venues drawing on the institutional arrangements available to them.

From the earliest entry of the Clearinghouse into open access publishing, I have supported and advocated for them (see Bazerman, Blakesley, Palmquist & Russell, 2008e). In recent years, I have tried to have as many of my publications as possible circulated in open access through the WAC Clearinghouse or like endeavors, though at times the logic of distribution for particular works has meant seeking publication from a more traditional publisher. Even then, whenever I have had influence in the choice of publishers, I have argued for ethical, reasonable pricing along with open access distribution after a short embargo.

Chapter 26. Administrative Writing: Making Genres, Actions, and Topoi Work in Institutions

Throughout my career I have learned to do some kinds of organizational writing, and have come to see its value in moving an organization forward, maintaining its memory, setting agendas, identifying tasks, organizing work, inviting people to engage, supporting people, and keeping people on task. Writing regularly mediates among stakeholders, groups, or levels of organization. Each of these writing tasks requires understanding the social, organizational, and institutional contexts for the communications, identifying the genres to write in, and deploying the argumentative topoi that would fulfill expectations, gain cooperation, or win approval.

These skills are familiar to anyone who has been in any leadership position, which changes one's relationship to the individuals and institutions involved. Cynicism can grow with such knowledge or appreciation can increase of the complexities of organizations and the difficulties of coordinating people of different perspectives and interests. One may even learn both. In my case I learned more to appreciate than to disdain, but that was a function of the opportunities and situations that became available to me, and it certainly changed throughout my career. The most important thing I learned through unfortunate experiences was selecting those leadership and administrative positions where I could have a positive effect, avoiding predictable failures or unneeded pain.

Advocacy for Writing in CUNY and Georgia Tech

Unusually for someone in my generation in the teaching of writing, I have never been a writing program administrator or director of a writing center or any equivalent position, though not for my lack of trying. Early in my career at Baruch College I had been a member, and then the chair (and for a time the sole member) of a departmental composition committee in a department without any administrative structure for the teaching of writing, despite that being the overwhelmingly dominant task for both the full-time and the many part-time instructors. As Composition Committee Chair, I could only advocate for some policies and institutional arrangements and propose curricula for departmental vote. Mostly what I learned was what didn't work in the face of the self-interests, identities, institutional agendas, or perspectives of colleagues and other more powerful actors. I did learn, however, how positions and actions were framed within institutional arrangements—constrained by regulations and procedures. I learned to identify where levers for change lay and, more often, where they did not.

Eventually administrative roles for writing did emerge in composition at Baruch—I would like to think in part as a delayed result of my advocacy, though other factors had little to do with me. By that time, however, my years of advocacy had made me *persona non grata*, so candidates were hired from the outside. At CUNY beyond my campus I had, however, taken on organizational roles as the first secretary of the CUNY Association of Writing Supervisors (CAWS) and founding co-editor of the Newsletter CAUSES. In these roles I learned the value of being able to shape the historical record of the organization and identifying issues requiring attention and action. I organized the minutes of meetings around action items, foregrounding decisions made and projects looking forward, while keeping the deliberations *in camera*. Similarly, I saw the newsletter as a means of keeping the attention of the organization looking forward to resolve problems and build programs. In doing so I was coming to learn how barely visible roles could shape futures—by coordinating energies and attentions of multiple actors. These lessons continued as I was to organize a research reading group and then become co-chair of CAWS and enter the leadership of other professional organizations. These lessons also entered into my growing research and theoretical awareness of how documents formed the knowledge of organizations and became the site of institutional reasoning and planning. I came to see texts and writing as infrastructural to complex forms of social organization that extended beyond immediate co-presence of participants, but which then could also inform, regulate, and direct face-to-face participation.

Given the frustrations I encountered in advancing writing programs at Baruch, after a four-year job search attempting to coordinate spousal positions, I took up a position at Georgia Tech at the same time as my wife moved her position to the University of California Santa Barbara. During my 4 years at Georgia Tech, commuting to Santa Barbara, my role was to help design, get agreement on, and initiate new programs. Using the tools of curriculum design I had previously developed, I was able to facilitate the emergence of a new M.S. in Information Design and Communication, which was in the interest of most department members and leadership at all levels of the institution. I, however, was hired and strongly committed to develop a Ph.D. program in scientific rhetoric and composition, even though I had no formal institutional power beyond being chair of a committee, and was commuting to my family in California. Further, the project was not in the interest of several vocal members of the department, who stood in the way of the project or tried to redirect it for their interests, especially when I was out of town. When the committee started to develop the documents that could realize the proposal, it hit numerous political problems. This reinforced the lessons I had learned earlier that documents and documentary processes could only be successful under the right conditions and at the right moment—when the stars aligned as I often said. Then when the stars did align one needed to move fast to institutionalize the project in ways that would have continuing value. Here the stars were rapidly moving out of alignment. I also learned that being asked to be an agent of change without the institutional roles that would facilitate making those changes was perilous. In the end I again became *persona non grata* for advocating unpopular programs. Nonetheless my years at Georgia Tech had made me more familiar and thoughtful about writing technologies which were becoming ever more important for writing. Also my commuting schedule, while interfering with my ability to move programs forward, gave me more time to focus on my writing and the projects that emerged in the first half of the '90s.

Finding Programmatic Niches at the University of California

After hitting some brick walls at Georgia Tech, I was then happy to take up a position at UCSB in 1994 as a trailing spouse, initially in the English Department. For complicated local political reasons, I was not chosen to direct the writing program in 1991, despite being the leading candidate of the search committee. The previous year the same thing had happened at UCLA. So twice more I had failed to gain the administrative responsibilities of directing a writing program. At UCSB the Writing Program had recently separated from the English Department, which has happy with the divorce, but this left the Writing Program with only contract lecturers and other contingent positions. The English Department had little interest in writing studies or composition so they had little role for me and attempted to reframe my writing studies expertise into teaching literary texts, which was also expected by the English major students in my courses. As a marginal person in the department, again I had plenty of time to devote to my writing which again facilitated my productivity through the remainder of the '90s.

After a few years, however, I was able to arrange a joint appointment with the Education Department, and I started recruiting doctoral students in writing studies. This required no new programmatic approval as the education requirements, to my mind, were ideal for writing studies in a more applied social science mold, with a heavy research methodology requirement supported by a wide range of qualitative and quantitative methods courses, tied to a series of research milestones. The reading lists for qualifying exams were negotiated between advisor, committee, and candidates, in relation to the candidate's projects and career. A number of colleagues also specialized in literacy and language at different ages and levels of schooling and beyond. This facilitated recruiting students and offering courses that located writing studies within literacy teaching and learning across the lifespan, with a focus on empirical research. Since most of the students I recruited had B.A.s (and often M.A.s) in humanities, they already were grounded in literary cultures and were predisposed to reach beyond the typical assumptions and approaches in the humanities. (I present the advantages of such an arrangement in Bazerman et al., 2006f). With time, the Writing Program was also able to hire senate faculty who could collaborate in mentoring doctoral students and offer additional specialized graduate writing studies courses.

Mentoring writing research students for more than twenty years has also helped me as a writer of such research. Helping students focus their research questions has led me to focus my own, while their inquiries have opened my mind to different kinds of questions that could be asked. Working with them on developing their methods has increased my standards of what counts as sufficient evidence, and attuned me to noticing nuance of evidence—while increasing my sense of the various kinds of data that might produce evidence. Working to tighten students' observations and interpretations has also sharpened my own eye for argument structures. Perhaps most, discussing ideas about writing over the years has expanded my theoretical scope and prepared me for writing more synthetic theory exploring activity theory, lifespan development, the connection between social and psychological issues in writing, international comparisons of writing education, and the relationship among various strands of writing studies. All of these have been thematic in my seminars and my more recent publications.

Being a Department Chair as a Writing Challenge

As I was the newest member of the Education Department, but with an advanced rank, I was ripe to be elected as department chair. As several people told me, I had no history with them—and thus was not caught up in departmental politics and divisions. So at the late age of 55 I finally had my first taste of academic administration. This also allowed me to move full-time into the Education Department, which I found a welcoming home for my line of work. Immediately upon my election I sensed a reorientation of my sensibilities and priorities, as I now felt a responsibility for the health and effectiveness of the whole department, which meant taking on causes and supporting members of the department who previously had been outside my scope of interest.

Being chair was for me a practical application of years of studying organizational genres and activity systems. I saw the job of chair largely as producing effective documents to serve the interests of the department and its members within institutional systems. My long practice and reflection on writing prepared me to produce those documents efficiently and without much procrastination or stress. UCSB's well-institutionalized and elaborate system of dual governance meant that the venues and genres for arguing programmatic and personnel issues, as well as department self-reflection and change, were well stabilized. Further, topoi relevant to the different committees and other recipients of institutional texts were readily identifiable, often explicitly set out in regulatory or advisory documents. Much of my writing simply required intertextual attention to the governing documents, including the ubiquitous "red binder" with the system-wide University of California regulations.

I quickly discovered that the most important thing for my sanity was having an efficient and effective staff, which I had fortunately inherited from the previous chair. The next thing I discovered was that the most important thing for maintaining departmental support was successfully presenting personnel cases for tenure, promotion, and other advancement. In our system the chair wrote the letters that reported departmental evaluations to the campus reviewing committees and administrators. To write persuasive letters I had to understand the work of people whose specialties were far from mine and foreground those elements that would most pass muster with the upper reviewing bodies. These letters would always need to make carefully documented, detailed arguments in relation to institutional criteria, explaining weaknesses as well as strengths in each case to maintain credibility. In complex cases the letters could be as long as 6 to 8 single-spaced pages. Since the University of California has many steps within each rank, as well as the standard major promotions, every tenurable or tenured professor was reviewed every two or three years (above scale or distinguished professors were given a bit of breathing space with reviews only every fourth year). Consequently, at least a third of the faculty were up for review every year. Writing these letters was a major part of the job.

Trickiest, though, and where one could lose departmental support (as I did), was holding faculty to regulations and responsibilities, running up against the university's strong traditions of faculty rights and prerogatives, magnified by individual personalities. Course scheduling was particularly sensitive in my department, where faculty over the years had gained expectations of self-scheduling with only limited centralized coordination. The only main point of accountability was the regular promotion considerations. Expectations had become quite flexible with the result that creating some kind of order and equity within course scheduling was fraught with perils. This was a lesson in the intersection between documentary procedures and personal relations, and of recognizing points of leverage and flash points in creating institutional change. Moving the discussion away from sensitive individual cases to departmental approved policies about course expectations and scheduling procedures set in motion a process that eventually created more institutional regularity and rationality over time, years after my chairship.

As chair I was expected to participate in proposals for special projects and programs in response to institutional funding initiatives. The pressures, opportunities, and temptations to respond to institutional initiatives are much greater in education schools than in English departments, not least because of education's role in society and its ties to organizations beyond the university. Education schools are the potential recipients of state and federal government grants, contracts with regional school districts, and private foundation money. Early in my career, however, working within English departments, I had become used to funding being sporadic and relatively small. After going after a few grants early in my career, I had found that they were rarely worth the time for the limited amounts of money, plus restrictions often meant the grants didn't allow you to do what you wanted to do. Further, often enough, the funding wouldn't lead to anything that lasted past the end of the funding, so the project either had to be valuable in the short term or had to clearly lead to some kind of long-term institutionalization. My personal research projects, as well, didn't usually have much of a cost beyond my time, some photocopying, and occasional materials.

Nonetheless, when I became chair of Education, the growth of department programs often depended on state initiative funding, and even maintenance of some of our existing programs required soft money. Consequently, I worked on proposals for a number of programmatic initiatives, even though I was aware that funded programs might vanish when funding ended or personnel changed. As a writing specialist I wound up being at the center of the negotiation and production of the core documents. The actual project narratives were not the challenge, but they depended on the various committees coming to agreement over workable effective plans, that would be sustainable, equitable, and ethical in their procedures and results—as well as being attractive to the sponsors. This required a kind of forecasting of realities that would emerge from planning and proposal documents. I kept trying to imagine what would result from the various provisions we were including in the proposal. I won't go into the details of what happened, but in at least one case the faulty terms of the proposal predicted exactly the fate of one of the programs that did get funded. I was not enamored with this program from the start, but I did my best to try to make it work following the enthusiasms or institutional desires of the other participants, including the Chancellor and Dean. In the planning process I kept pushing on issues of sustainability, long term partner participation, maintaining quality programs, and workability of specific proposed collaborative research groups. I gained some improvements along these lines, but within four or five years this program fell apart on just these issues, leaving the department holding the bag for further expenses and responsibilities. Even the money that came with the initiative was used for purposes that did not add to the department. Other programs, whether funded or unfunded, seemed to me to be similarly futile, as pieces seemed to be pulled together more for the funding than a real vision from those who would carry it out. What vision there was came from the top down—the granters, who had some goals, but from a great distance with little sense of what was concretely to be done nor of the interests of the people who would actually carry out the work. But this may be my sour grapes.

The few projects that were closest to my heart were not funded because higher education writing was not the typical métier of education schools. All this experience reinforced my earlier disposition not to go after funding unless the funding opportunity really matched what I wanted to do.

Organizational Leadership

Immediately following my six years as departmental chair (as I joked in my farewell speech, I had rapidly solved the problem of my lack of prior history with my colleagues), I ran for chair of the Conference on College Composition and Communication. This gave me the opportunity to support my profession while advancing particular themes in the organization—in this case research, internationalization, and the role of writing in documenting realities and fostering social change. The first challenge of writing the candidate's statement was an exercise in topoi and politics which also required some values clarification on my part to articulate what I saw as the importance of our profession and put it in striking terms. Once I was elected, I was introduced to the complexities of the organization I had only seen as a conference goer and journal reader. In the four-year chair cycle, the first-year assistant chair planned and carried out the annual conference, the second-year associate chair supported the chair, the third-year chair took leadership, while the fourth-year past chair tried to look wise and not meddle too much. The organization's permanent professional staff guided us through all the tasks and documents for each year's role: conference planning documents, reports, charges for committees, policy statements, communications with the memberships, and so on. Many of these documents were written collaboratively, but some were the particular responsibility of an individual, such as the platform speeches at the conferences. As an organization leader I had to join with others in evaluating reports from various committees and task forces to come to decisions. The face-to-face political interactions were well-embedded within the documentary procedures of the organization, and fostering documents that successfully inscribed the focus and scope of the organization could have long term impact on the directions the organization would take. Since I wanted to move the organization on specific themes, however, I needed to understand how to plant a few ideas that would sustain after I left the scene. Standard procedures like creating an award or forming a committee with a charge to report on certain issues could redirect the attention of the organization to certain parts of the profession, add knowledge and facts to the organization's deliberations and calculations, or highlight problems that, once visible, might be addressed. Small changes in the documentary systems could gradually modify the portfolio of the organization.

An entirely different leadership opportunity arose from a series of smaller research conferences that graduate students and I initially organized at UCSB. These grew from regional to national and international in scope over the first three iterations in 2002, 2005, and 2008. Other conferences in writing in the US were focused mostly on programs and practices, leaving an unmet need for more research focused meetings, including ones that focused on all ages and levels of writing development. A parallel movement was occurring in Europe with the development of the SIG Writing conference every other year starting in 2004. From early on there was cross-attendance and cross-fertilization between the two groups. Our first conference at UCSB was a simple, one-day regional meeting. It required only standard university room booking and small grant procedures. As the conference grew, space and funding became a bit more difficult, as the application, reviewing, and program planning became more extensive and involved more participants, plus our conference was a lower priority for rooms. Publicity involved only a few messages distributed through standard listservs, and then a website for conference information, proposal submission, registration, program distribution, housing, and other logistic matters. I came to rely on knowledgeable volunteers for the web design, as my skills were and remain basic. As we moved to longer conferences, contracts and guarantees with hotels and caterers also followed well-established paths within those commercial organizations, although we needed to learn about these. In 2011 the conference moved to another U.S. university, George Mason University near Washington, D.C., where Paul Rogers, a former graduate student who had been instrumental in the organization of the first Santa Barbara conferences, had gotten a professorial position. At George Mason he took over the increasingly complex institutional proposals, documentation, and commercial arrangements.

By the 2008 and 2011 conferences, enthusiasm for a regular international conference was manifest, so we decided to create an organization with a constitution and formal leadership structure. At the 2011 meeting the conference scientific committee voted to create the organization and an interim steering committee, with me as interim chair, to write a constitution and by-laws, which included mechanisms and criteria for proposing future venues as well as regular election of leadership. Collaboration skills (both in person and on email) were needed to be able to bring the steering committee into agreement, and some examination of other organizations' documents aided drafting provisions for the constitution, keeping in mind the sustainability of the organization and its processes. With the organization regularized institutionally, the steering committee became focused on the defined functions and agendas set out by the chair, in consultation with vice chair and past chair. Successful meetings were held in Paris in 2014 and Bogota in 2017. The planned conference in Xi'an for 2020 became a virtual event in 2021 because of the pandemic. The next traditional conference was successfully carried out in 2023 in Trondheim, Norway. The organization now is in other hands to direct its course now that I have cycled out of the leadership.

Volumes of selected papers came out after the 2008, 2011, 2014, and 2017 conferences. As Chief editor or co-editor of the first four, I largely followed what I had learned in earlier collections about spotting potentials in proposals, working developmentally with authors, and keeping deadlines urgent. I also learned to support and coordinate contributing editors who may have been doing such work for the first time. Since the volumes were international, challenges appeared in establishing shared international standards, editing chapters in multiple languages, and supporting non-native English speakers who nonetheless wanted to present their chapters in English. As some of these authors were also not as familiar with how to tell their story to an international audience, they needed developmental guidance to realize the potential of their studies.

Most recently, I organized the Lifespan Project which I will discuss in Chapter 30, but some administrative parts are relevant here, particularly in seeking funding to bring the small group of participants together for annual three-day work retreats, with some small incidental expenses. This project, however, fell outside the scope of existing programs of funders, and we had little uptake from formal grant submission processes. When I wrote a brief inquiry email to the Spencer Foundation, however, I immediately got back an invitation to elaborate the plan for special funding outside their regular programs. Following a few short narrative paragraphs, the money was rapidly granted; at the end of the three-year cycle additional funding was granted for the final two years. The money was modest given Spencer's typical programs, but it was more than sufficient for our needs. This consequent administrative component was low key, involving only a few hotel, restaurant, and catering bookings, meeting rooms and technology booking, and contact with journals and publishers.

Administrative writing in its many guises taught me to work in a variety of genres to carry out a range of activities. In each case they required gaining an understanding of the work of these different organizations, the documents by which one carried out actions, the form and timing of submissions, and the interests, roles, and perspectives of the various audiences evaluating documents. Working with these organizations required amalgams of face-to-face interactions with regulatory, procedural, and deliberative documents. In some situations, I was simply moving the gears of stable machines, but in other cases I sought to change the machinery, and in a few cases I tried to create more enduring arrangements by establishing documentary machinery. All these attuned me to what writing can do and how to wield that power.

Chapter 27. The Production and Circulation of Environmental Knowledge: Can Historical Scholarship on Writing Effect Social Change?

My research themes in recent years have roots in long-standing interests about writing. Each has taught me more about the nature of writing, has presented particular challenges in writing about them, and has continued to develop my own writing, as I will elaborate in the remaining chapters.

Writing About Environmental Information

My interest in how environmental concerns could be addressed through writing began in the late 1980s when I was putting together a textbook anthology, *The Informed Reader*, where each unit was devoted to an issue drawing on academic disciplinary scholarship and research (Bazerman, 1989b). At the suggestion of my editor, for the natural sciences issue I focused on the greenhouse effect and climate change. The issue of climate change first came to wide public attention with a *New York Times* story in late 1983 (Shabecoff, 1983). I started the unit with this story because it explained the basic concepts and the consequences for our lives; I continued with a series of articles that progressively went deeper into the science, including some foundational articles from scientific journals, and ended with congressional testimony by a leading scientist. This sequence provided a gradual path for students to enter into a technical understanding and drew a direct connection between technical matters and public policy concerns. Putting this unit together, as well, educated me on the science and on how policy issues could be addressed. This led me to think further about data gathering and the relation to evidence.

For the next decade I didn't do much further on environmental issues. As I was finishing up the Edison book, however, I reflected on how that study showed that complex and multidimensional social projects needed to engage many kinds of writing. Climate change seemed just that sort of problem. By the late nineties, climate change was becoming widely recognized as a pressing issue that would require widespread international cooperation and coordination among many spheres, from the scientific and technical, to the political, financial, and public. As opportunities arose to engage in inquiries, I tried to use them to deepen my engagement with environmentalism and climate change. I vaguely thought that this work might come together as a book, though that has not happened as yet.

Fortuitously, after a presentation at another campus, I got into a discussion with a retired scientist about information and how we have come to use the term. He told me of work he had done in the early 1950s as part of the St. Louis Citizens' Committee for Nuclear Information which had produced a newsletter called *Information*. Through interlibrary loan I obtained copies of the newsletters and dug into the history of the organization as well as the term "information." The term's history went back centuries involving police and spying, but then took on particular meanings in the Second World War concerning scientific military secrets, especially involving the atomic bomb. In the ensuing cold war, the confidentiality of military information was contested both for open scientific use and for the public to make informed policy and citizen choices. In this context the St. Louis Citizens' Committee mobilized the idea of citizen information to advocate for nuclear test bans and to contest the lack of government transparency about nuclear fallout and related dangers. There was a direct line from this campaign to other environmental campaigns, such as for pesticide control, ultimately leading to the creation of the Environmental Protection Agency and the passage of the National Environmental Policy Act. Though the early issues of the newsletter clearly were motivated by an anti-testing political agenda, they attempted to create an "objective" scientific stance for the "information." To do so, the newsletter evoked audience presuppositions and calculations without explicitly invoking them—a technique known in classical rhetoric known as the enthymeme. Unpacking the presuppositions evoked helped me understand a major cluster of meanings we now associate with certain kinds of information (Bazerman, 2001d).

In a consequent project I pursued the governmental response to public pressure for increased information and accountability about environmental issues through examining the Environmental Information Statement (EIS) requirement of the National Environmental Policy Act of 1969 (NEPA) (Bazerman, Little & Chavkin, 2003f). While this project largely relied on the theoretically-shaped archival research and narrative reconstruction of social processes I had become practiced in, identifying the different kinds of documents that would provide evidence of growth of environmental knowledge in the wake of the congressional discussion and passage of NEPA was a puzzle.

How Environmental Knowledge Does and Does not Move Between Domains

Another more complex challenge was presented by an invitation to contribute to a volume of cases exploring Thomas Kuhn's incommensurability hypothesis, that findings in one theoretical frame would lack meaning after a revolutionary shift in paradigms. I had first read Kuhn's *Structure of Scientific Revolutions* shortly after its initial appearance in 1962, as it was circulating among my college friends. I found a personal psychological plausibility in the kinds of uncertainties and confusions that appeared during the moments surrounding revolutionary shifts, though Kuhn himself warned against such personalized psychological readings. Over time, as I began to study the history of scientific writing, however, I came to see his scheme of normal and revolutionary science as oversimplified, creating too strong a distinction between paradigmatic stasis and revolutionary change. I saw shifts of thought and disciplinary alliances occurring in smaller and less disruptive ways. Taking up this invitation was an opportunity to test and elaborate that perception. In seeking a good case to examine the transmission of knowledge across paradigms, I looked for closely related specialties with some boundary disputes, where one field preceded the growth of environmental sciences while the other grew in the wake of new knowledge mandates for environmental information. This described precisely the tensions between the long-standing field of toxicology (a laboratory-based medical study of effects of substances on individuals) and the recent field of ecotoxicology (a field-based statistical study of long-term environmental impacts of pollutants on populations). Once I found this research site, puzzles remained in locating the kinds of documents that would provide evidence of whether and how knowledge flowed between the two specialties. I had constructed specialized corpora of documents previously for study, but this study posed the problem of using intertextual tracing or blockages between two corpora to examine the flow of knowledge. As I immersed myself in the documents of the two fields, including textbooks, research articles, and personal narratives about the development of the fields, these issues sorted themselves out. Synthesizing them into a historical narrative that argued for and illustrated social-literate processes was, again, something I had done before, and it was only a matter of putting these particular facts and materials together into a clear and persuasive story (Bazerman & De los Santos, 2005g).

Another study following shortly thereafter continued pursuing the puzzle of how knowledge moved between domains, but in this case between entirely different social systems: science and the courts. This project was the result of another invitation, in this case to a symposium sponsored by the Project on Scientific Knowledge and Public Policy, an organization devoted to the use of science in the court system. The participants in the organization and the symposium were mostly working scientists or working legal scholars, a number of them quite prestigious in their fields. While I had of course worked on scientific writing and the social organization of science, I had no more than a layperson's knowledge of the courts beyond issues of intellectual property and patents that had come up in studying Edison. I certainly did not have a law degree nor could I consider larger legal reasoning. I again focused on a case, which might help me understand what the processes of transfer were. My first big challenge was to find the right case to look into. Fortunately, the website of the organization (http://defendingscience.org/) had a series of cases which they considered exemplary of the kinds of issues that arose with science in the courts. After spending some time looking at the documents in these cases, I settled on the multiparty case of *In re Phenylpropanolamine* as likely to display the processes I was interested in.

The case documents made evident that the process by which expert witnesses were qualified was crucial to how scientific knowledge entered the courts. It was known as the Daubert hearing, which derives from the case *Daubert v. Merrell Dow Pharmaceuticals, Inc.* I needed to look into the history and precedents of the Daubert hearing and place that in the context of the laws of evidence, with the logic of court witnesses in the production of evidence. As well I needed to look into some of the pharmacological science surrounding the particular drugs involved in the cases. As I looked into these legal and scientific documents, I was able to trace concretely how scientific knowledge came into the judicial proceedings in the form of the testimony of the expert witnesses qualified through the Daubert procedures. My writing task then became to be able to explain these procedures and how scientific knowledge became reformulated and contested as it passed into legal proceedings through expert opinion to become adjudicated in the court judgment. This study highlighted how different institutional purposes and reasoning guided communicative practices, along with informational relevancies and forms of presentation. Further, it revealed how regulations controlled translation of information across institutional boundaries and thus how knowledge from one domain becomes consequential for deliberations in another (Bazerman, 2009d).

How did Congress Resist Environmental Knowledge?

These inquiries into how knowledge migrated or did not migrate across public spheres I thought might prepare me to address the puzzle of why Congress and other political bodies (at least in the US) were so resistant to environmental science. I started from the naive hypothesis that Congress was something like the courts in being a bounded institution with specific procedures for admitting knowledge. Of course, it was foolish to think Congress and similar political bodies acted as rational and clearly bounded institutions. Congress is open to many forces and other organizations; only on occasion does it act anything like a rational deliberative body seeking the best information to identify and solve public policy problems. Of course, I should have known that not just from ordinary political cynicism, but even from the undergraduate papers I had done on pork barrel politics. Even from an activity perspective, Congresspeople needed to be responsive to parties, funders, constituent voters, and news and opinion media, to name just the more obvious. But my theoretic model initially led me to want to treat legislative bodies on the model of scientific communities and the courts—which, faulted and as human as they were, sought something like their institutional ends, relying on the knowledge and regulations inscribed in their documents and professional expectations. After some preliminary work I was reminded of the sad, obvious facts of legislative life, but I still saw that Congress wanted to maintain the appearance of following deliberative procedures in order to maintain legitimacy and to abide by the organizational rules built on the assumption of deliberation. So the question then became how Congressional actors could maintain the trappings of deliberative procedures while still pursuing interests external to the deliberations. Put another way, a rational deliberative body, if it had facts that indicated a social problem, would seek ways to solve those problems by gathering further facts, weighing various concerns, debating alternatives, and then setting out a course of action. But Congress regularly avoided explicitly recognizing the climate change problem, as a way of avoiding action and offering solutions.

I worked with a doctoral student, Josh Kuntzman, on an initial study around 2008. Josh helped me gather and read through the transcripts of the hearings of Congressional committees on climate and environmental issues, which by that time were all accessible on the internet. We repeatedly lost our analytical thread, however, as we found certain members of Congress using readily recognizable tactics to disrupt reasoned deliberation in committee hearings and to transparently protect the interests of a few specific corporate and financial interests. We could make no headway beyond telling each other outraged stories of the pettifoggery of some individuals and their bag of tricks. We were not able to find any underlying mechanisms of knowledge representation, circulation, and use in exposing such rhetorical displays. There wasn't even much political news in showing Congress was dysfunctional or certain actors were carrying out the bidding of particular interests. This exercise, however, did make me familiar with some characters who would keep cropping up in the news, a number of whom became prominent in the Trump administration.

As far as we got was to see the process of agnotology (the systematic production of uncertainty) at work. A couple of books appearing just at that time, *Agnotology* (Proctor et al., 2008) and *Merchants of Doubt* (Oreskes & Conway, 2010) revealed how strategic doubt was first fostered by the tobacco industry and then applied to energy and climate (often by the same individuals). I felt I had little to add to their well-articulated and evidenced studies, so at that time I just synthesized secondary sources to sketch out how different institutions paid attention to climate knowledge and had it enter into its institutional calculations in ways that fit its procedures (Bazerman, 2010g, 2021d). I still felt, however, that some more systematic and extensive study of Congress would be useful, if I only knew how to do it.

I needed strategies for selective search and principles for coding for making sense of the massive piles of documents. Josh, at one point in his general rhetorical reading of actors' strategies, suggested that the *stases* of the hearings (that is, how the questions were framed for deliberation) seemed important in what Congresspeople and witnesses addressed and how they addressed it. This stuck in the back of my mind when an occasion emerged to return to the project. A few years later, while I was immobilized for a couple of months recuperating from a knee injury, I received an invitation to contribute to a volume on genre and climate change. In all my previous projects that required massive corpora, I had relied on visiting archives and endless hours standing over photocopiers or staring into microfilm readers. But now, I could lie in bed, press buttons, and download pdfs of thousands of hearings, of which more than a thousand turned out to be relevant and analyzed in the study. Further they were digitally searchable, so I could use key terms to locate the passages of interest.

Once I focused on *stases*, it became obvious that each hearing was organized around a question or questions, often announced in the title of the hearing, or otherwise specified in the opening remarks of the chair. The committee chair (from the majority party) in fact defined the question and selected the witnesses (though the minority were typically granted one or two courtesy witnesses). This framing of the discussion limited the relevance of the statements and questioning by Congressional members and the strategies they used to get things on the record or keep it off. I kept expanding the corpus to cover Congresses with different configurations of majority party in the two houses along with the presidency, as of course the positions of parties and the potential for legislation would affect how *stases* would be framed and what people would want to get on the record. This global analysis of the structure of hearings led me fairly directly to the selection of hearings and key passages from the 109th and 110th Congresses during the second Bush term through the 111th–114th during the Obama years and the first year of the 115th under Trump. This included all party configurations of the Presidency and the two houses of Congress. I used key terms like "climate change" and "global warming" to identify hearings that would be relevant and then to locate specific relevant discussions within them.

I entered each of the selected hearings and coded them to allow for descriptive statistical aggregation. I recorded the name and other identifiers of each relevant hearing, the committee or subcommittee it came from, the theme of the stasis for the hearing (funding, agency oversight, offshore oil leases, problem finding, military expenditures, etc.), how large a role climate change took in the hearing (based on number of mentions and examination of the discussion, from passing mention through central), and then the particular *stases* and stances adopted by climate change addressers and deniers in the course of the hearings. I also added notes on particularly interesting or striking arguments made by particular individuals. One of the most interesting results was how often climate change deniers did not mention or contest testimony of climate change.

While searching and coding these many hearings was time-consuming and tedious, it gave me something to do while I could not get around. With time, the coding started to turn up some striking patterns with many interesting illustrations. Since I had so much data it would be hard for anyone who was not immersed in it to see those patterns or keep straight what was happening with different changes of control of the houses and presidency, what legislative initiatives were being undertaken at different moments, what the various committees were and their relevance to initiatives, and what the different positions and strategies taken by the various committee chairs were. These provided context for the strategic actions of each member of Congress. I had a hard time in finding the most understandable way to present the story. Aggregating the data too much would wash out the most important patterns of the differentiated strategies of chairs from different parties and the consequent actions of committee members. But as I tried to show the nuances, the detail created struggles for readers to follow. It took a long time, with multiple cycles of feedback from the editors to create the right section summaries and overview charts to help the readers find their way through the material, and to construct intelligible narratives about how committees handled their work in each Congress. I also needed to provide just enough necessary evidence, but no more, no matter how striking the examples I had to cut. The problem of managing the attention and memory of readers so as to have a framework for understanding and sorting details is always a problem in writing, but here it was especially challenging (Bazerman & Kuntzman, 2021f).

The Challenge of Making Rhetorical Analysis Effective for Social Change

These studies together helped me understand and explain some of the complexity of arriving to knowledge about the environment and climate change and how challenging it was to get different systems aligned around the knowledge that eventually was produced. Particularly, the study of Congress revealed how deliberation could be manipulated by position, power, and party. Yet I was left baffled as to what further I could contribute either as a scholar or in a more active role. I never could find a more activist group where my work could be useful. On climate change, many groups are doing good work, and in a practical way are likely familiar with everything I tried to lay out methodically. After all, they are strategically and intentionally carrying out those actions and processes I have been documenting. For others outside these organizations, what I document may be too much an inside game. To rhetoricians and writing studies scholars, these studies are only useful as cases revealing mechanisms that are more widely applicable. As much as I would like, I cannot yet frame an argument in a way that would make a difference in public conversations on the environment as I originally hoped, as the issue is blown by strong crosswinds. Ultimately, it seems that social groups act only when threats become immediate, entering into their most pressing calculations following their typical procedures of reasoning. This is now happening regularly with climate disasters which may finally be changing calculations, choices, and planning in multiple business, financial, political, personal, and other social spheres. As we used to say in the Vietnam War years, sadly, the war only comes home in the body bags. We will see whether the pandemics, droughts, climate disasters, and geopolitical disruptions will mobilize attention and action.

Chapter 28. Data Gathering and Methodology in Writing: Fact Production and Use

My initial study of environmental information, discussed in the previous chapter, continued my interest in the production, representation, and circulation of facts through texts and how inscribed facts are consequential for individuals and societies. Growing up anticipating a career in the sciences, I had come to appreciate evidence and data. Even as my interests turned to the humanities, I maintained commitment to evidence, including texts as evidence in literary studies. My commitment to facts became more self-conscious as a graduate student when my dissertation advisor, J.V. Cunningham, emphasized that a few simple facts about text production, finances of the publishing industry, or historical and cultural conditions could rein in fanciful, speculative literary interpretation.

Nonetheless, as I became more aware of the complexities of fact production and particularly as I engaged with science studies, I needed to grapple with the realization that facts were humanly made and were social constructions. They existed as formulations within human communications. How could facts and even data be humanly produced and yet still provide reliable information about the world? This problem articulated at least as early as David Hume in the eighteenth century was reignited in the theory and science wars of the 1970s and '80s. I soon recognized, however, rather than this paradox being a philosophic puzzle or the dividing line of an ideological battle, it identified sites that could be examined empirically to see how data and evidence were produced and warranted in various different social locations. The social construction of facts offered sites for empirical investigation of how epistemology was managed practically within knowledge producing collectives.

As I turned my attention to academic and disciplinary writing, I saw how the content of disciplinary texts depended on the methods of data collection and analysis viewed as credible in each field. At end of '70s when I started work on "What Written Knowledge Does," while representation of the world was considered one of components of writing (recognized by its place in the rhetorical triangle), I could find no rhetorical study of the role of disciplinary differences of evidence and data, let alone methods, as scientific writing was then largely considered outside the realm of rhetoric. As I examined texts from biosciences, sociology, and literary studies, however, I noticed differences in the kinds of evidence used, where the evidence came from, and how the evidence was made relevant to the argument.

When I came to revise subsequent editions of *The Informed Writer*, I tried to capture some of these disciplinary differences in gathering and representing

237

evidence (see Chapter 18). The sources of the data cut across disparate disciplines in surprising ways. Working with historical artifacts puts geology, evolutionary biology, paleontology, history, archeology, and literary studies into the same pot. Observing contemporary events connects journalism, sociology, anthropology, astronomy, descriptive plant and animal biology, and ecology. Creating experimental events to produce specific kinds of data is of course common in medicine, physics and chemistry, but also in branches of psychology and sociology. Largely theoretic fields, such as philosophy and mathematics, foreground ideas and claims from other texts. Most fields, nonetheless, engage in some abstract reasoning, when evidentiary bases for claims retreat to the background. This approach to where evidence could be found and how it was collected got me thinking about method and epistemology.

The Representation and Analysis of Data

The questions of data, where they come from, and how they are evaluated kept popping up as I studied different instances of scientific writing. In examining Arthur Holly Compton's notebooks (see Chapter 19), I saw how his writing was motivated by the desire to present a new kind of data made possible by a newly invented instrument, the bubble chamber. This method of producing data raised many questions since the visible, recordable data were only photographs of trails condensed by moving particles. From these trails one could infer the kinds of particles, their energies, and their angle of deflection from the initial collision. After calculations based on these assumptions, the photos of these trails were taken as evidence of quantum theory. Some of the photographs were judged by Compton to be defective or to raise other problems, so he excluded them from the final results. His notebooks were careful in recording, evaluating, and interpreting the angles—which then provided the basis of the article (along with a description and rationale of the methods and the theory which was corroborated by this new form of evidence).

Data and method came up again in studying *The Physical Review*, as the kind of data collected and the set of related methods producing them in optical spectroscopy became my constant against which I could identify other kinds of changes in the discourse. Data and method came up again in the history of *The Philosophical Transactions* as evidence became presented more precisely and quantitatively while the conditions producing the data became more specified. Over time, measurement tools improved and experiments became designed more intentionally, based on expanding methodological reasoning. Method was at issue in the way Newton represented the process of his observing and gathering optical phenomena in his various writings. I found Joseph Priestley paying detailed attention to all the previous evidence of electrical phenomena going back millennia, as well as to the evolving machinery that produced and recorded electrical charges. He also recommended that every investigator specify exactly what they did and why, even when experiments failed. Then more recently in the social sciences, I found that the American Psychological Association *Publication Manual* in each revision increased specification in the methods sections in order to restrict what would count as professionally credible data.

The question of credible and relevant data was the central obstacle in knowledge traveling readily between the two apparently close specialties of toxicology and ecotoxicology. Because toxicology was a laboratory experimental medical specialty and ecotoxicology was a field-based statistical study, differences in sources of evidence and methods used to gather and analyze the data were sources of resistance to the credibility and usefulness of knowledge transferring across the fields. These differences of methods reflected underlying ideologies and epistemologies. Ultimately, however, the need for the findings of the other field to deal with problems within each led to greater acceptance across specialties, accompanied by a broadening of the epistemologies and ideologies of both.

In studying how pharmacological findings entered into court proceedings in the US, I found the barriers even higher and the procedures for crossing boundaries even more systematic and complex, due to the differences of the structure and purposes of legal and scientific institutions, creating radically different approaches to evidence. Understanding and representing the differences in the institutions was a necessary part of explaining the logic of the procedures surrounding the translation of scientific knowledge into the evidentiary and judgment procedures of the courts. Later, in studying how scientific knowledge of climate change entered Congressional hearings, I found the process controlled not only by the nature of the institutions, but the complexity of interests and motives of legislators and the strategies used by majority parties to support their political agendas. Another earlier study of educational assessment and policy concerned the oversized attention given to learning outcomes that were easily collected and counted, in contrast to the difficulty of gathering data that recognized and supported the accomplishments of progressive educational practices (Bazerman, 2003e).

More personally I experienced the importance of methods, data, and the difference of collection practices as I attempted to publish interdisciplinary research in venues of different fields. I quickly discovered that journals from different fields would not consider manuscripts credible or even relevant if they did not follow those fields' expectations and methods; I needed to obtain field-specific data with field-specific methods positioned within the relevant theories and reasoning of the field. No matter how well I carried out the theoretical work, if I didn't argue from the right kind of evidence, the work would not be seen as worth attention. So although writing was crucial to the objects of study of many fields, it had to be addressed in each field's terms.

In my own field of writing studies, after a first round of research methods books appeared around 1990, little emerged to update or replace them. This led to Paul Prior and myself editing a collection on text analysis methods (Bazerman

& Prior, 2004i). In order to assure the consistency needed in a textbook, we provided a chapter template and expectations to guide the authors, each of whom were expert in the methods presented in their chapters. Each of the chapters focused on one set of methods, and together they indicated how every act of writing brought together simultaneously multiple dimensions. Although humanities traditions of text analysis had a history of eclectic and implicit interpretive practices, we thought it useful to bring their long-standing analytical methods to greater explicitness and to put them into the context of methods from the social sciences, so that researchers could consider which analytic tools best fit their inquiries. Doing this work made me more sensitive to the analytic tools of my colleagues and expanded my own analytic repertoire. There have been similar benefits from my role as a regular seminar leader at the Dartmouth Summer Seminar in Composition Research from its founding in 2011 until now.

How Undergraduates Learn Methods of Data Production and Analysis

These various experiences heightened my curiosity about the processes by which writers came to learn and use these methods, and what the consequences were for their understanding of the phenomena they were looking at. I remained haunted by a diagram in Latour and Woolgar's *Laboratory Life* (1979, p. 46). This diagram suggested how through continuing processes of inscription, the laboratory was in essence a factory for turning mice (along with other inputs like energy, laboratory equipment, chemicals, and office supplies) into scientific articles to be submitted to journals. Latour and Woolgar saw this process of repeated inscriptions as a process of progressive forgetting, obscuring the material lives of the mice, and by extension the world studied. But I also was interested in what was being remembered, focused on, recorded, calculated and reasoned about—the non-fictionality as I discussed in a review I published when *Laboratory Life* first appeared (Bazerman, 1980a). Having something new, revealing, and evidentially persuasive to share with one's disciplinary colleagues seemed to me to be at the heart of academic writing. And learning the methods to produce and think about such evidentiary data was central to disciplinary training and effective disciplinary writing.

To study the learning of methods, I first considered looking at working scientists, but their mature practices and assumptions were deeply tacit, embedded in their view of doing good science, so it would be hard to excavate. Vygotsky had suggested that the best place to study a process was when it was just being formed and was at the foreground of behavior and attention rather than later when it was sedimented and taken for granted (Vygotsky, 1978). I next thought of studying how graduate students learned methods, but I decided to look earlier at undergraduate students when they were first being explicitly introduced to the practices of disciplinary inquiry. At that moment misunderstandings, missteps, corrections, and guidance from their mentors might be most visible. While much undergraduate writing I suspected (accurately, it turned out) would be dominated by textbook presentations of already established knowledge, perhaps supplemented by cookbook lab experiences, yet, as students specialized in their majors, they might be asked to form their own inquiries and gather fresh data. As I began to speak with colleagues about their disciplinary curricula, I found that the senior thesis was often the first place that students produced their own data. Locating useful sites for study turned out to be as much a matter of prepared serendipity as earlier location of and access to specialized archives. That is, I needed to know the kinds of situations I was looking for, and then be able to spot them when they came into view. In this case I had to develop ways of talking to people to see what opportunities emerged.

The first place I could gain access to a senior project was in the mechanical engineering program at a neighboring university. I had gotten to know the coauthor, the mechanical engineering professor who supervised the project, through his participation in one of my seminars. The year-long senior team project proposed, designed, prototyped, and tested in both a lab and the field a low-cost foot prosthesis to be produced at a rural clinic in Honduras. From the four major reports the students prepared, along with related reflective documents and interviews, we could see how they identified the kinds of data they needed to produce for each report and how they went about producing and collecting the data—drawing on the library, site visits, theoretical calculations, active fabrication processes, and lab and field testing. As the students were designing and then fabricating a device which was then tested, they were bringing new objects into the world based on prior fact-finding; these new objects were then the sources of further data. All of these forms of data provided the substance of their reports, and selected data and findings from earlier reports would get carried forward into later reports as authoritative knowledge and assumptions for the next level of work and production. This showed us how data get built into continuing action, innovation, and production. The largest writing challenge of this project was to create an unfolding narrative of the building of knowledge across the year studied, showing how the exigencies of each report required specific kinds of data collection, which then became sedimented into later stages of the project, guiding the later decisions, data-gathering, and reporting (Bazerman & Self, 2017f).

In the next study I wanted to focus more centrally on students' perceptions of the methodological challenges they faced across the year as they developed their projects. Through speaking with people aware of curricular developments across my campus, I learned which departments were currently engaged in self-study of their undergraduate programs and would appreciate more information about how their students learned to write in their fields. After meeting with representatives of several departments, I found the Political Science department to be particularly welcoming and interested in finding out more about writing throughout their program and in their senior honors seminar. With the permission of the chair and members of the department, I pursued the research on a double track, with a study (based on syllabi and faculty interviews) of writing in all the undergraduate political science courses and a more focused interview and text study of self-selected students in the senior honors seminar. The first study was for an institutional report to meet the department's needs, but it provided useful background for the more focused study. In contrast to the engineering study where the reports were the center of the story, the written projects of the senior political science honors students served only as evidence of the consequences of the work students were doing to meet these perceived challenges, which they described during periodic interviews. It turned out the students with richer practical methodological experience and abstract methodological understanding were able to look more deeply into the material they were studying and were able to write more effective and subtle analyses in their final reports. Their final work was exactly constrained and focused by the methodological knowledge that they had. The resulting article again followed the unfolding narrative, but this time with a more phenomenological focus, developing each student's perspective on what they were doing, what challenges they faced, how they were trying to address them, and what they had accomplished at each point (Bazerman, 2019c).

The last study in this series emerged when I was doing an independent study with upper division undergraduates on the issue of data and evidence. All three undergraduates, by chance, were linguistics majors and we started talking about the linguistics courses where they actually worked with a lot of data. They mentioned one instructor who in several different introductory-level courses gave numerous assignments asking students to analyze and interpret data provided by the instructor. This seemed to me a good opportunity to study the impact of the working with data on students' understanding and perception of language. After confirming the teacher's use of such material with colleagues in the Linguistics Department, I found out more about these assignments from the instructor and identified a course he was willing to have studied. Valentina Fahler, a graduate student I was working with at the time, also had a strong background in linguistics, so I asked her to collaborate on this project. The instructor and two of the four Teaching Assistants in the course volunteered to be interviewed—the instructor about the design and intentions of the course and the assignments, and the TAs on what they were observing about the students' struggles and development across the term. The main data, however, came from the students who volunteered to fill out regular questionnaires and provide their assignments. We found, however, student responses on the questionnaire were constrained by the format of questions asked and did not indicate striking changes across the year. Further, since the assignments throughout the year drew on different kinds of materials and asked different kinds of questions as part of the instructor's well-designed developmental sequence, it was not easy to make simple comparisons across the term. Further, as with any group of students, they brought different knowledge and experiences to the class, so it was not easy to aggregate or compare their work quantitatively. However, in going over the data with Valentina multiple times as we did the coding, we formed individualized pictures of the students. When we combined all the data sources including their assignment submissions, we found that we could get a consistent picture of development of each of them, filtered through their individual situations. We could also see some similarities within clusters of students. We went through multiple iterations of descriptions of the development of each student, cross-checking our perceptions for negotiated inter-reader reliability. Eventually we were able to offer a group phenomenological interpretation relying on both individual and small cluster portraits. As we revised towards publication, we had to tighten these accounts and become more selective in the detail to make the portraits readable and the larger patterns more visible (Fahler & Bazerman, 2019f).

These last three studies all presented challenges of choosing and integrating multiple data sources for contextual, phenomenological, and performance evidence. The analyses and presentations needed differing balances and relations among these forms of data, according to the nature of each inquiry. This inquiry into learning data practices is far from complete, not even getting yet to an interim synthesis and articulation. Nonetheless, I hope these studies indicate that data collection and analysis methods are directly relevant for writing studies and writing education, and that quality of many kinds of writing is in part related to the quality of finding and inscribing primary materials to report on and analyze. Students can write better if they have good stuff to write about, and they can draw on more persuasive evidence if they know how to produce and analyze it according to disciplinary standards.

Chapter 29. Writing and Thinking: Psychiatry, Psychology, and Consciousness

Much of my research has focused on the historical evolution and social location of writing, and each writer's strategic response to their situation in relation to evolving genres; nonetheless, the growth of the writer's thinking has always been a motivating undercurrent for me. We invent ourselves in our responses to our located situations, using communicative forms meaningful to those around us, yet it is our growing selves that we draw on, work with, and reflectively bring into those social and historical spaces.

My last year in high school when I started to collect my papers systematically, I did so to keep track of my intellectual growth. At that time I firmly anticipated becoming a physicist and had no sense that I would become a writing teacher. The experience of writing a research paper on the human impact of thermonuclear war in the Telluride Summer Program after my junior year in high school showed me that my writing could address important human problems where answers had not yet emerged and discoveries still needed to be made. While I had done library research before and I had access to the Columbia University library throughout high school, I had never dealt with such a deeply self-motivated inquiry (living as I did in the shadow of the nuclear arms and testing race my whole life until then.)

As a university student I would regularly reread my growing file of writing to see how my thinking had evolved, particularly as I pondered what I valued and what path I might take. Then when I became an elementary school teacher, I looked at young students' writing to see what they thought and valued. I also watched how their changing literate skills affected their demeanor, attitudes toward schooling, confidence in themselves within schooling, and peer relations. At CUNY working with young adults making their transition into the university, I continued to examine student papers as signs of intellectual growth, along with noting the skills we needed to work on. As I saw students' writing evolve, I used my sense of who they were becoming, the ideas and understandings they were developing, and their ways of seeing the world around them as ways to motivate and direct their next piece of writing. I have continued to do this in all my courses, especially as inquiry projects have become central to my pedagogy, whether working with first year undergraduate students or doctoral candidates working on their dissertations.

Problem Solving in Students Learning to Write

Reading Vygotsky helped me to understand better the interactional sources of growth and to enter into the dialogic space of students' Zones of Proximal

Development. I learned to offer just enough clues and supports to help students move forward and gain the rewards of discovery, but without saying so much as to short-circuit growth-producing work nor to displace their impulses towards meaning-making through writing. Vygotsky also made me aware of creating space for them to connect their spontaneous concepts arising from making sense of their lives and organized academic concepts they encountered in their classes (or scientific concepts, as Vygotsky called them), so that they could come to see the collective knowledge and practices of disciplines as personally useful. This conjunction of spontaneous and academic inquiry released energy in their projects that would become more interesting to them, me, and their classmates. While sometimes my dialogs with individual students would be pursued in private communication, as much as possible I pursued dialogs in class and seminar so each student could see the struggles each other had in bringing their writing into being. No matter how varied their projects might be, they almost always were interested in seeing their peers at work and the writing that resulted. They also could provide each other useful suggestions. This collaborative atmosphere of inquiry kept us all in each other's ZPDs, bootstrapping ourselves into our next place of discovery and writing.

As I came to understand problem-solving during writing as the mechanism of learning and growth, I found ways to have students spend more time on task so that they would think more deeply about the challenges their writing presented, from the earliest framing of tasks, problems, and information seeking through final editing. Because projects became so engaging to students, they often exceeded expectations of the assignments, and I set length requirements as a floor, saying if they needed more space, take it. They often did, usually without puffery, repetition, or verbosity. As a writing teacher I saw my task to midwife the content they were discovering, and then how they might put this together in ways that would be intelligible, credible, and convincing to others.

Researching Writing and the Development of Thinking

For a number of years, I did not follow up informal teacher observations about student thinking with focused research, as I was pursuing social and textual issues—how writers were connecting to what was outside them rather than what was occurring within. As I studied influential writers who changed the social and intertextual spaces of others, such as Newton and Priestley, however, I saw their development as writers connected to their development as thinkers in both their overt intellectual productions and their reflections on what it meant to write. Further, their reflections on writing changed in conjunction with their understanding of society, communication, and ideology.

Because Vygotskian theory provided me a powerful way to connect writers' intellectual growth with the social communicative field they engaged in, I wrote an encyclopedia article on implications of Vygotsky for writing (Bazerman, 1998k).

I also reviewed some books on cognition (Bazerman, 1996a, 1997a, 1998a, 2001b) and kept reading socially oriented psychologists like Jerome Bruner and Michael Cole, but could not find a detailed mechanism that connected disciplinary forms of consciousness and disciplinary forms of writing. An essay I wrote on Jack Goody's work on the consequences of literacy eventually helped clarify my thinking (Bazerman, 2006e). He was best known for his work on the psychological consequences of literacy, but Goody was an anthropologist by trade. His book on *The Logic of Writing and the Organization of Society* (1986) provided ways of seeing how literacy impacted society. I reinterpreted his work to connect the social and psychological sides, using an activity theory lens. I argued that cognitive consequences of writing were the result of specific cognitive practices and reasoning associated with domain-specific genres that carried out socially organized activities. Writing gave us new things to think about and ways to think about them, as the production and use of specialized texts became the object of our cognitive and affective attention.

For a conference on genre, I more explicitly presented my ruminations of writing and consciousness formation, which was then published in the conference volume (Bazerman, 2009c). I proposed that learning genres created a cognitive challenge space, at the same time as structuring and providing tools to address the challenge. Over time the writer can internalize these forms of expression, reorganizing the writer's thought. This formulation provided a way of articulating how people entering into disciplines and professions developed the ways of thinking that were practiced in those fields (though with individual variations of perspectives and resources).

The chapter gave me some focused hypotheses that could be tested about exposure to new genres in a way that might speak to psychological research, using forms of data and argument recognizable to that field, which I had initially become familiar with during my study of the APA Manual. In order to carry out these studies I needed to find a subject population where the cognitive change might be robustly visible and where other factors that might influence indicators of thought could be held stable or controlled for. The full details for the selection of the study population are in Bazerman, Simon, Ewing, and Pieng (2013e), but key was finding a group of students with already demonstrated skill in academic writing who were to be introduced to new genres, new professional literatures, new professional practices, and new professional identities. Further, we needed access to them over an extended period where these professional activities, modes of representation, and thought would be repeatedly practiced and become familiar. Finally, the program they were in would need to have specific cognitive goals that would provide measurable accomplishments. The problem is that students develop rightfully down their own paths, incorporating what makes sense for them, but this makes it difficult to determine what kind of intellectual, cognitive growth they engage in, because each student would, in a sense, need a different measure to make visible their cognitive growth. Some programs, however, have particular forms of thinking they want to foster—in this case it was a particular form of teacher thinking valued within a teaching credential and M.Ed. program. This particular supported form of thinking is what could be measured. Through a preliminary ethnographic study, we identified the goals, curricula, and assignments of the one-year program, which then focused our data gathering for our main study with the next cohort the following year. A further methodological puzzle was to find measures of change in thinking independent of the genre of documents which were hypothesized as the means of development; otherwise, we might only be measuring the learning of genre expectations with no more fundamental changes in thought. For this independent measure we examined informal and more spontaneous comments in the classroom and in online forums. A final challenge was to develop emergent collaborative coding and intersubjective rater agreement, through extensive negotiation. Through all of this work, we were able to confirm some key parts of the hypotheses and indicate the likelihood of some other parts. The last, most speculative hypothesis, about moments of conceptual reorganization, was beyond what our data could tell us.

From analyses of many texts and contexts throughout my career, I had learned the importance of being in immediate touch with the data, which meant carrying out all the analysis personally so I could see what might be there. In this case, however, my graduate collaborator, Kelly Simon, had the most detailed understanding of the corpus. I learned to trust her careful observations, while I could ask her the right questions to make sure I understood what was going on qualitatively beneath the numbers. With her detailed knowledge of the corpus, Kelly started noticing something interesting not captured in our coding and analytical procedures. Namely, she noticed what looked like more sophisticated thinking in the sentences which involved references or discussions of sources in contrast to the other sentences. We added several new kinds of codes to our analysis to test the hypothesis that citation and discussion of the literature were associated with higher level thinking and then, if true, to understand the phenomenon more deeply. These new codes tracked whether sources were referred to, the mode of reference, the way the source was used, the degree of critical perspective and independent voice adopted by the student, and the length of the discussion. These new layers of coding revealed striking and robust findings, even more than our study of the impact of genre, showing strong effects in all the dimensions we measured, far beyond our original expectation (Bazerman, Kelly & Pieng, 2014g).

In both these papers working from the Teacher Education data, I had some anxiety about meeting the standards of fields not my own (particularly involving the inferential statistical methods). Even though a graduate student specializing in statistics, Patrick Pieng, did the technical statistical work, I still had to learn to think with these tools and to be able to represent them and what they revealed in terms appropriate to the data and methods. While people trained in these tools early on would have internalized them by this point in their career, for me it was a learning challenge, expanding my writing repertoire.

Kelly, for her dissertation, followed through on another analysis of the same data set to see the effect of data and experience on the students' thinking. Kelly's study highlighted for me the psychological consequences of students engaging in disciplinary data practices, preparing me for the studies of data in undergraduate writing described in the previous chapter.

Understanding Writing Anxiety as a Social, Relational Issue

The course of my writing on psychological issues cannot be understood without looking back on another strand of work, on anxiety, which I had begun earlier in my career. To write about anxiety took confidence and courage which took me awhile to muster, because it would require me to discuss psychiatry, an area in which I was even more amateur and which at that time was still somewhat stigmatized. Further, I would be relying on an out-of-favor theoretician, and the study would identify me as having undergone psychotherapy, even to the point of revealing personal details. These concerns would, over the years, require me repeatedly to muster my courage as I continued to explore the issues that grew out of this work.

Since my early days of teaching, I had been interested in writing anxiety, which was an obstacle to writing and created resistance to growth and development. Anxiety could restrict the writer's ability to reach out, engage, and participate in literate interactions. In therapy I had become familiar with Harry Stack Sullivan's interpersonal psychiatry, which considered anxiety arising through early social interactions to form a self-system, which would influence one's later interactions, though later interactions and relationships could modify both anxieties and self-systems. I thought about how writing itself created interpersonal and social situations which could arouse long-standing anxieties and be generative of new anxieties.

Since writing always means literally putting yourself on the line—exposing your statements to scrutiny and criticism by others—anxiety is endemic. Even more, writing gains force, presence, and reader engagement by saying new things. Writing tempts us into the unknown, the previously unsaid, or at least the things we personally had not said. This is not a false temptation, but the very name of the game, and inherent in the idea of writing as discovery. Finally, since writing can be held in semi-privacy, at least for a while, the writer can build novel meanings, identify and rework thoughts, and push statements further into difference—unless, of course the writer is frozen into silence by anxieties. While sometimes writing just for ourselves may free us of some fears, often enough the writer will wonder whether to share and with whom. Each writer's sense of the self and its boundaries can either constrain or extend exploration of new areas of meaning. Further, even though new supportive interpersonal relations can help relieve anxiety and expand one's ability to try new things in writing, those supportive relations will be conditioned by one's prior ways of developing relationships.

In my own writing I became aware of how anxieties led to procrastination and slowness. I started to recognize uncertainties that could be considered phantasms, and how I worried over some choices more than they needed to be. Other times I was sluggish without realizing why. To some extent, labeling these moments as anxious helped get me back to work. Having the courage to say what I wanted to say became a habitual stance, which often meant pushing through doubts. When I became more conscious of revision, I told myself I could always change or remove statements that didn't seem right or wise later. In revision, however, I found I was often happy with where I had gone, and even went further, with added courage. My revisions focused on making my arguments more concise, elaborated, particular, evidenced, coherently sequential, and synthesized—that is, pushing the text faster and further to where it was going. I came to trust my impulses as having aggregated my thinking and research. I kept pushing into my anxieties, seeing them as obstacles to going into the new places my writing was taking me. Of course, I did not know where I could not imagine going, what tasks or statements would never occur to me, things that still were beyond my sense of self, or even my transgressive self. But even this last phrase "transgressive self" indicates how much I had taken on the identity of courage in entering the dangerous unknown or disfavored.

Awareness of the sensitive psychosocial dynamics of writing attuned me to the arts of building trust. I learned to be accessible within the other person's way of relating, forming bonds, and gaining information. Ultimately I tried to increase their courage to write. Writing education is filled with obvious anxieties about correctness, perfection of form, and school assessment. Even more powerfully, however, writing can raise specters about what the writer feels comfortable saying, of what readers might think, or of exploring ideas and experiences outside one's family, community, self-formed identity, or personality constructs. But, of course, what the teacher or writing mentor can offer or accept is also conditioned by the mentor's own anxieties and self-system, which can affect the interaction with the student. Yet each new teaching and learning situation, each new reaching out offers expansive possibilities for teacher and student. The writing teacher can aid this process of mutual learning by providing an emotionally less fraught space in which students can explore meanings and different ways of saying different things, expanding their expressive potentials and resources. Teachers as well can expand their own sensibilities, understanding, and empathy, as well as dissolve some of their own bounding anxieties as they are able to hear and experience more of what students have to offer. Our professional roles can open ourselves up to the students' writing and thinking as we ask open-ended questions, listen to student answers, understand their struggles and conditions, and appreciate their unanticipated talents and wisdom. Even something as simple as respecting a student's career ambition or political ideology which we would never choose in our own life can help us grow as teachers and people, expanding our sense of self beyond our margins of discomfort.

This expansive interaction though literacy can extend beyond the classroom or even beyond face-to-face synchronous relations. Writers often grow through reading other writers they know only through their texts. Because those writers' texts speak to the readers, they can build a trust that expands the developing writer's vision and even can encourage the developing writer to entertain ideas, perspectives, or verbal pleasures that would be rejected when offered by less admired or trusted authors. As a student, with the encouragement of teachers, I myself learned the value of identifying what I appreciated in my favorite authors and even of imitating authors I may not at first have appreciated. I have since then tried to foster among my students practices of learning from the authors they value to expand their ways of seeing, being, and communicating.

I was pressed into articulating these ideas from my own writing and teaching practices by a recurring discussion among Vygotskians about the role of emotions in learning, especially on the XMCA listserv associated with Michael Cole's Laboratory of Comparative Human Cognition. I felt I had some insight into anxiety because of the reflective practices I had developed in writing and teaching relying on my experience of interpersonal psychiatry. I found these ideas consistent with what I had been taking from Vygotsky and his followers. Both traditions conceived psychological phenomena as primarily social and interpersonal rather than individual and they also saw their work as interdisciplinary, as all dimensions of people's lives were related to each other. As I returned to the texts by and about both Sullivan and Vygotsky, I was surprised to find specific points of historical contact between the two circles in the first half of the twentieth century, which I document in an article (Bazerman, 2001a). These points of contact include Vygotsky's article on "Thought in Schizophrenia," translated into English by Hanfmann and Kasinin (1934); five years later Hanfmann published the first English translation of the last chapter of Vygotsky's *Thought and Language* in the journal founded and edited by Sullivan. Decades later, in 1965, the same Eugenia Hanfmann was co-translator of the first English edition of the book.

In writing an article about the connections between the two traditions, in order to set up the problem of the article I questioned the then current Vygotskian optimistic picture of cooperative learners growing through their ZPDs. Despite my practice of avoiding critiques of others' work, here I felt that exposing an absence was needed to bring together the growth-oriented Vygotskian world (albeit born in the troubled world following the Russian Revolution) with psychiatry's consideration of the more troubled parts of the human psyche and "difficulties in living" (as Sullivan framed it). After noting the neglect of psychiatric concerns in the Vygotskian world, I pointed out Vygotsky himself had been interested in psychiatric issues, particularly noting the influence of Adler in his work, though this had been little commented on at the time I wrote. Vygotsky's articles on schizophrenia and on cognitive deterioration in psychiatric states initially brought his work to the attention of the psychiatric community in the West. This historical link explicitly connected the ideas of Sullivan and Vygotsky. I followed this with a practical account of my experience with a Sullivan-based psychotherapy focused on noting social interaction in talk, which led me to think about writing as a social interaction.

I have spent some time discussing the issues and organization of this essay because the largest problems I needed to solve were how to explain and integrate Sullivan's thinking into the Vygotskian world, both as a rhetorical matter and to sort out the connections in my own mind. This integration forced me to reveal some of the ideas that had come to form my vision of life and most personal relations with others. I moved cautiously and deliberately from the audience's known world of Vygotsky into the foreign and stigmatized world of psychiatry and psychotherapy, to ultimately land on my own experiences. I felt very unsure about whether readers would follow me down this path and what they would think of me by the end.

Shortly thereafter I had the opportunity to present and write another exposition of some of these ideas, but this time for an audience of writing scholars with a psychodynamic orientation (Bazerman, 2001f). Since this new audience was already disposed to seeing emotional and depth issues in writing, although they were not familiar with the application of Sullivan to writing, and since I had already worked out the connections to Vygotsky, this piece was intellectually and emotionally much easier to write. The biggest challenge, which was not much of a stretch, was to explain writing not only as a social act, but as a social exposure and a potential transformation of a social identity, which would trigger Sullivan's social mechanisms of anxiety.

Integrating Writing and Psychology Within Interdisciplinary Social Science

Making progress on the integration of Vygotskian and Sullivanian thought gave me more confidence to formulate an interdisciplinary understanding of writing. My personal understanding and teaching had been informed by multiple disciplines from college onward, as this book already should have made evident. Then when I started to publish on scientific writing I began to explicitly draw on and conceive of syntheses of multiple disciplines (Bazerman, 1983a, 1985b). Again, with genre theory I kept trying to make connections among disciplines (most explicitly in Bazerman, 2004f). Both Sullivan and Vygotsky sought interdisciplinary syntheses, seeing life as multidimensional, unfolding in a unified way, though dimensions could be isolated for analysis. They both pushed outwards from their psychological professions to open doors to other fields. Vygotsky drew on his own complex educational and social background as a Jew in pre-revolutionary Russia and as a teacher of language and literature, in order to engage in the open intellectual ferment of the early soviet years and to see the relevance to psychology of fields as diverse as history, culture, economics, language, semiology, psychiatry, physiology, and sociology. Yet while his research and theory opened doors to these other fields, he never systematically pursued them. After he died young, his followers split along separate disciplinary paths, though they remained sensitive to the multidimensional complexity of the lives they studied. Sullivan, on the other hand, actively sought to create interdisciplinary syntheses in his own work; a posthumous volume of his essays is in fact called *The Fusion of Psychiatry and the Social Sciences* (Sullivan, 1971). Even more, he brought together interdisciplinary teams on a number of projects, foremost of which was his journal *Psychiatry*. The journal had an interdisciplinary board with many of the leading scholars of their generation and published a remarkable range of articles from fields as diverse as economics, medicine, language, literature, anthropology, sociology, and history. The journal explicitly framed its mission broadly in the first issue:

> Originally a specialization with the medical arts somewhat related to psychology (and thus to philosophy), the psychiatry of today is a growing integration of the biological and the social sciences.... Psychiatry... is enriched by and contributes to social science. Medicine, hygiene, philanthropy, education, criminology, penology, religion as a normative influence in life; all of these turn more and more towards a 'rediscovery of the individual,' in the end the study of interpersonal relations in the psychiatric sense. Psychiatry, which finds something useful in each of these activities, has also something to offer, and fair promise of increasing usefulness. (1938, 1: 1, 141)

The journal recognized that problems of living could arise from anywhere in the complex of human life, and solutions may need to be found in economics, culture, governance, or other domains as much as in the psychotherapeutic consulting room. I searched for other attempts to create interdisciplinary social sciences, but they were few, and none had gone as far as this in attempting to reintegrate the social sciences once they had started splitting off from philosophy and then each other in the nineteenth century.

The wide scope of the journal *Psychiatry* for me raised the question of how far the journal had gotten in developing an integrated synthesis and whether there were lessons for future integrations of social science. I further was interested in where the authors placed language and writing within their synthesis (Bazerman, 2005f). With this inquiry I was back on familiar research grounds, examining a run of journals. This project was in many ways even easier than some of my earlier ones, because it only attempted to synthesize the contents of the articles to see whether a coherent theory or mode of analysis emerged. The challenge was to organize and connect the themes in the articles. What I found was that while a number of articles proposed interesting syntheses, no broadly accepted vision emerged; further, despite a number of articles considering language and literary culture, neither language nor writing was a significant part of any of the syntheses. I concluded that, at least from the perspective of writing, no adequate integration had yet been articulated and the problem was not yet solved. This recognition motivated me even more to pursue that integrative project.

Toward My Own Synthesis

To work on that integration, I wrote a series of chapters explaining what I saw as the intersection of socio-historic-cultural studies of writing and psychological studies. Some of these articles were addressed to psychologists and some were addressed to language and literacy scholars, explaining connections across the large divides. But it was not until I came to the two-volume theoretical work described in Chapter 23 and the collaborative work involved in the lifespan project, described in the next chapter, did I come to a more comprehensive synthetic position that rose above the disciplines to unite them rather than do border work between specific ones.

My first opportunity to explicitly address cognitive psychologists came from an invitation from Virginia Berninger to contribute to a volume on *Past, Present, and Future Contributions of Cognitive Writing Research to Cognitive Psychology* (Bazerman, 2012d). From the beginning I was presented with a dilemma about my credibility on the topic before such an audience. Since I was far from a cognitive psychologist of writing (though that's how the volume title positioned the authors), I was intimidated by the presumed audience of cognitive scientists (again as positioned by the book title). But after a confessional opening admitting my lack of credentials for the area, I decided to go bold: to say bluntly how the field seemed to me as an outsider from writing studies. In for a penny, in for a pound, as the adage goes. That remained my stance in all my articles addressed to psychologists, under the assumption I was asked particularly for my difference of views, which they could choose to pay selective attention to or even ignore. I identified my ethos and authority as a practitioner, teacher, and scholar of writing. Further I located my work as arising from a socio-cultural perspective, which already called into question typical psychological assumptions about the individual subject.

Consequently, my opening positioning statement was a rather long two pages. Next, in order to address scholars who might have a very different view of writing, seeing it as an individual psychological accomplishment, I needed to explain the premises of the sociocultural perspective on writing, the implications for what it showed significant about writing, and the contextual picture it revealed about learning to write in contemporary educational settings. Only at the bottom of the seventh page did I get to the actual business of the article to explain what I saw as writing's psychological complexity, both affective and cognitive. Not until the tenth page did I begin to discuss the problem of identifying researchable psychological regularities that might be located, confirmed, and investigated through research. Despite the long and complex introductory nine pages, I did want to propose a coherent and intelligible agenda for psychological research, arguing that the most useful and productive questions could be integrated with sociocultural studies. I offered five specific directions or questions for psychological research, each elaborated in a paragraph or two. Only in the last few pages did I introduce the psychological researchers that I found most useful, but I presented them only in a very limited way, as examples of what might work well in concert with sociocultural approaches. I wanted to speak more broadly to current psychological research rather than to advocate particular approaches, because my suggestions for research directions were much broader than the ideas my favored authors pursued.

In this article I found it difficult to articulate what I had come to believe in terms that would be intelligible and meaningful to people trained in a field with very different starting assumptions and ways of proceeding. Even trickier was to make suggestions that would be actionable in their research world. It was also tricky how to transparently admit my own preferences for psychologists without having that become a dominating filter for both what I had to say and what readers might perceive me to be advocating. I spent much time coming to a structure of the article that I hoped would realize my desired stance and message.

Shortly thereafter I had another opportunity to explain the implications of sociocultural work in an educational psychological context. While the *Handbook of Research on Writing* that I had edited was organized around sociohistoric principles while bringing in other perspectives, *The Handbook of Writing Research* edited by MacArthur, Graham and Fitzpatrick appearing at about the same time took a more decidedly educational psychology approach. In the first edition (2006) there were two articles presenting socio-cultural work as contrasts, distinct from the educational psychology approach. When I was invited to contribute to the second edition (2015), I felt I was now prepared to present sociocultural work in a way that could be better integrated with traditional educational psychology approaches. Following on the strategy of providing a list of useful takeaways, I itemized a series of lessons from sociocultural work that could inform an understanding of how people learned to write, elaborating each in a paragraph or two, and then directing readers through citations to the research behind the statements. The main challenge here was to identify those lessons, select among them, formulate them succinctly, and finally sequence and organize them in readily understood clusters. Since I was already well familiar with the work in the area, and was not attempting a complex theoretical explanation nor recommending research agendas, the actual elaboration of these lessons was not difficult. Further, since I was only offering findings from an explicitly sociocultural perspective and not posing a research agenda, no preliminary authority or theory building was needed. Since I wanted these lessons to be widely applicable and the research behind them readily understood, however, I revised heavily to make the material accessible with as many familiar examples as could be offered in the limited space, relying on as little theory as possible (Bazerman, 2015c).

In two later pieces for educational psychologists, I was explicitly asked to provide critical comments from an alternative view, so my oppositional perspective was given advance license. Nonetheless, I wanted to offer criticism in a way that would generate serious questioning and thought. The first was to be the final commentary article in a special issue of the *Journal of Literacy Research* devoted to articles on "A Developmental Path to Text Quality." I was given prior access only to the abstracts of the articles and not the substance of the arguments. Since I was not given access to the full articles, I couldn't legitimately comment on them or accurately frame a critique. My problem was how to make my concerns clear without entering into a broadside oppositional diatribe, which besides being in danger of not fitting the actual articles also would likely not have much purchase with the audience for this issue. I hit on the strategy of asking questions about each of the terms in the title of the special issue, suggesting how complex each was, how each relied on assumptions, and how much each required further specification or elaboration. I took my inspiration for this strategy from a passage in a satiric novel about academic life that kept me amused throughout grad school, Kingsley Amis's *Lucky Jim*. As the protagonist was delivering an academic paper, he starts to question what he is reading aloud:

> "In considering this strangely neglected topic," it began. This what neglected topic? This strangely what topic? This strangely neglected what? (Amis, 1954, p. 14–15)

So my comment was impishly entitled "A? Developmental? Path? To? Text? Quality?" (Bazerman, 2019a). After an introduction characterizing the complexity of writing, particularly school writing, I asked a series of questions about each of the terms in the title. The list structure seemed to work well here as in the previous few pieces at the intersection with psychology, since it kept me from entering into complex arguments and theoretical discussions. The format created points that could be taken up separately by the readers, as items struck them as useful or engaging, and allowed them to skip past the items which seemed less interesting. Since I had recently emerged from the experience of the Lifespan Development of Writing working group (described in the next chapter), the questions mostly reflected the kinds of questions that came up in the group.

In another special issue, on conceptual constructions of writing in *The Educational Psychologist*, I was also the non-psychologist outsider (Bazerman, 2018d). Psychologists had tended to frame their concepts of writing within models used as general characterizations of phenomena, rather than imposed by analysts, researchers, assessors, teachers, or writers themselves, each for their separate purposes. I immediately saw a fully structured argument that questioned the universality of models by discussing how they were situationally used by different actors. In "What does a model model, and for whom?" my strategy was to denaturalize the use of models in prior psychological discussion about writing by questioning how school writing and curricular goals came to stand for all writing development. I further argued that individual writers used models idiosyncratically and for very different purposes than analysts, researchers, or curricular designers. I suggested that naturally occurring generalities about writing, if they were to be found, would occur at different levels and in different ways than the models and conceptualizations were looking for them. I devoted the latter half of the article to challenges different writers might face in their different developmental trajectories, including those imposed by the structure of language, curriculum, social interaction, the nature of meaning-making, or human physiology and human neurobiology, among other elements that a writer must work with. A seriatim list of fourteen items (in essence a research agenda) was elaborated within a clearly articulated theoretical vision. Steve Graham, who was editing the issue, was generous enough to grant me the space and license to make this broad critique.

I wrote one final article synthesizing the psychological dimensions of studies throughout my career for a composition and writing studies audience in a volume showing the continuing relevance of psychological studies for writing studies in the US In the eighties and nineties, cognitive studies of writing were the leading edge of empirical research, so much so, that if you mentioned writing research, writing teachers would likely assume that you meant process studies within cognitive models. As socially based studies were to become more dominant in the later nineties in the US, the center of cognitive process research moved to Europe. In the US, however, work continued on such psychological issues as reflection, metathought, dispositions, habits of mind, and transfer. As well, advances in brain science were starting to provide new ways of thinking about writing. This volume was to bring together these lines of work and revalorize explicitly psychological research.

My sociohistoric and cultural work had always had an undercurrent of psychological concern, as I have discussed in this and earlier chapters. This undercurrent had become increasingly explicit but placed within the complexities of socio-historic positioning and development of writers. Wanting to present these psychological themes and implications more coherently for my peers in writing studies, I had little problem organizing the essay. I started with a naturalistic description of writing to indicate how much thinking, imagination, and other internalized work went on in writing, and then offered a narrative of my interests in cognitive and affective elements of writing, indicating how the elaboration of ideas and research questions went hand in hand with my sociohistoric investigations. I ended with an explicit overview of my current understanding and research questions, referring to recent articles and current research questions. The main task in writing was identifying and reviewing my prior publications and pedagogical practices that bore on psychological themes, and articulating what the connection was for each. Once I had a good sense of the pieces I wanted to discuss, I could describe the path I had taken to get to my current understanding. This was a story I had been rehearsing in a number of talks, but this retelling took the synthesis one step further in reconstructing how my thinking had developed (Bazerman, 2017c).

Chapter 30. Writing Across the Lifespan

Articulating the psychological components of my work in relation to other dimensions of writing increased my explicit interest in the lifespan development of writing. Lifespan development focuses attention on how the individual develops as a writer, but the individual lives in a particular time and place, has particular learning experiences, writes for specific challenges, and relies on a limited and often idiosyncratic set of available resources. In short, each individual develops in particular social circumstances to follow a unique trajectory. This is the developmental implication of Marx's famous dictum in The Eighteenth Brumaire of Louis Bonaparte (1852): "Men make their own history, but they do not make it as they please; they do not make it under self-selected circumstances, but under circumstances existing already, given and transmitted from the past."

Reflecting on My Development and Others'

When I started teaching literacy and writing, I began reflecting on my own experiences, as most teachers do. At first, I wanted to share what I had learned in the way I learned it, but becoming aware of the uniqueness of each student's conditions and trajectories challenged me to find how to serve their particular needs rather than quixotically attempting to replicate my own path. Working at a neighborhood elementary school, I could see the conditions of my students' lives as I walked through the neighborhood and they told me of their daily happenings. Knowing more of their lives gave me clues as to how I could reach them, and what I could offer that would help them address their life challenges. When I began teaching at an open admissions university that drew students from across New York City, I came to know them through literacy narratives and class discussions. I also came to see the way students approached writing assignments and the resources they brought to their tasks. Concern for their future needs led me to enquire into what they would need to write if they were to succeed in the university and the careers that might follow. Research into disciplinary and professional writing was a direct consequence.

Formulating Lifespan Development as a Problem and a Project

Only when I joined an education school in 1997, however, did I begin to systematically read and make sense of the literature on writing development across all ages. The good fortune of being able to teach graduate students who had taught in primary and secondary schools created an opportunity and an obligation to understand writing at all levels of schooling. In order to put together a seminar on lifespan development of writing I scoured what research there was on writing development at different ages. I was surprised, though, to find how little there was beyond the robust developmental work on emergent literacy in very young children. I was even more surprised to find out how divided the research was by age or school level, as well as by theoretical approach. Further, for children older than five years, much of the research was tied to curricular interventions rather than development situated within the students' understandings, perceptions, and growth, so it was hard to understand development apart from fulfillment of curriculum.

Let me elaborate a bit on this point. Most writing pedagogies (except the most misguided) are successful in doing what they purport to do, and thus can be demonstrated to be a success in their own terms. Students generally learn what we ask them to, as long as we are explicit enough about it, and they engage with the tasks we offer, built on our assumptions of what is important for writing. So, if we test them on the skills and knowledge we value in the curriculum, they show growth in those dimensions over the instructional period. Since there are so many kinds and aspects of writing, the potential lines of growth are as varied as our curricular creativity allows. In turn teachers, noticing the students' responsiveness to their teaching, become ever more committed to their pedagogy and their vision of what writing is and could be. Skilled teachers can create ever more novel curricula and instructional techniques that bring students further along the instructor's desired trajectory—with of course a continuing feedback loop as students followed the lead of the instruction. In a sense writing instruction is potentially a self-fulfilling, self-creating prophecy. This is not necessarily bad. It is even inevitable and valuable as students learn different aspects of writing from different teachers. I certainly did. But this also creates obstacles to understanding writing development apart from the curriculum we offer. If writing is an art, an artifice, it is only what we make of it, and schooling has made particular things of it. This does not mean, however, that all of writing's potential was being taught; nor what might be of most use to the students beyond the particular class; nor what most fit their social, psychological, institutional, cultural, or personal historical conditions; nor what matched students' goals, energies, capabilities, and motivations; nor how students understood what we asked them to do and how they integrated it with other things they had learned about writing. School assumptions and practices concerning writing have given us the appearance of understanding writing development while only offering paths for successful progress through the curriculum. This is why we need to understand the individual writer's development as distinct from the curriculum the students encounter, although that instruction and curriculum are important parts of students' developmental stories.

The first several iterations of the seminar on lifespan writing development were devoted to make sense of the rather disjunct literature studying different ages and educational settings from different perspectives. During the first dozen years the most coherence I could accomplish was to organize my syllabus and to give a few talks about the importance and puzzles of understanding lifespan development. When I had the opportunity to edit a handbook (Bazerman, 2008b), I made sure it included chapters for every level of schooling along with parallel chapters for each corresponding age, to try to see how development might look distinct from curriculum. But no matter how much I tried to get the chapter authors to talk across the divides among age and school level and make distinctions between schooling and development, little clarity or connection emerged across the levels.

Sharing the Problem and Enlisting Colleagues

An invitation to write an editorial for a Spanish education journal provided an opportunity to stir the lifespan pot (Bazerman, 2013a). The exigency was ripe and I was familiar enough with the literature to comment on its limitations. I started the editorial by pointing out that the same child who struggles to hold a pencil in kindergarten a few years later is organizing a report in middle school, then some years later is writing a critical analysis at the university, and eventually is composing a legal brief or a research study. I then presented the obstacles to understanding this lifespan process as a list with each item elaborated in a few paragraphs each (following a pattern I had been developing for exposition of ideas to audiences that may not be familiar with them): disentangling curriculum and development; research on writing in different life periods; the difficulties of longitudinal developmental research; and separation of research traditions. I ended with, "The challenge of creating an integrated developmental picture." Each of the sections I had already thought through over the previous years, so once I had the mode and organization of the exposition, I could do the familiar work of crafting the elaborations in readily understood and forceful terms, to create a warrant and energy for others to join in this inquiry.

As I was finishing the draft, I was in fact already enlisting others into a collaborative discussion. Simply having experts write separate statements, as had occurred in the handbook, was not sufficient to lead to synthesis or a more comprehensive view. Scholars needed to talk together. By the time the article appeared, I had assembled nine experts of different theoretical and methodological approaches, who researched writing development at different ages. The initial group included leading scholars familiar with emergent literacy; primary, secondary and higher education; disciplinary, adult and workplace writing; classroom practice; policy; assessment; and multi-lingual writing; namely, Arthur Applebee, Virginia Berninger, Deborah Brandt, Steve Graham, Paul Kei Matsuda, Sandra Murphy, Deborah Rowe, Mary Schleppegrell, and myself. The participants brought perspectives from linguistics, psychology, sociocultural theory, curricular design, and practice—working at local, statewide, national and international levels. This group was U.S. based, because the No Child Left Behind legislation created a particular exigency in formulating a Common Core Curriculum. Fortunately, most members of the group also had extensive international experience and we crafted our statements to reach beyond NCLB exigencies.

At our first few virtual meetings in 2013 (using recently introduced video conference technologies) we formulated goals, approaches, and processes, while starting to explore funding. We were able to arrange for a small informal grant from the Spenser Foundation to meet face to face for three days annually for the next three years (we were to get an extension for a couple of additional years), with many virtual meetings, email exchanges, and document sharing in between. People gave freely of their time and energy over the five years without recompense, motivated by the value of the exchange, the conclusions we came to, and the strong bonds of respect we developed for each other. During the period of this grant an important member of the group, Arthur Applebee, was gravely ill, though he did not share his illness with us. He wanted to keep his personal struggles from interfering with our ongoing progress. I was very fortunate for at least this brief period to work closely with him and appreciate his great wisdom and broad perspective on literacy education. With his passing, two of his former students (Jill Jeffery and Kristen Wilcox) joined us to carry forward his part of the work.

Although I convened the group, I wanted to keep the organization as lateral as possible so all would have equal voice. While everyone was hardworking, respectful, and motivated, we did need one person to keep the tasks organized and to moderate the discussions. I reluctantly took on that role, but with the understanding I would also maintain my own voice, handing the gavel over to someone else when I was stepping into my participant role (a common committee practice). Over the first year each of us wrote a series of brief summative papers. This helped us become more familiar with the knowledge and views the others brought to the table. These included statements on what constituted writing development, an overview of the research about the age/school group we specialized in, what we each perceived as the points of convergence that emerged over the first year, and how we each now saw the problem of development.

In our second year, we collaborated on a set of principles to guide future studies of lifespan writing development. This seemed to us a significant accomplishment and we wanted to circulate this as a statement from the group. Elaborating these principles in a draft statement became our central focus of work. We were torn between the need to make the statement readily understood and meaningful to a variety of audiences, and to provide sufficient warrant for our claims from the literature. Given the expertise of each of the participants, the citations and elaborations could be massive and weigh the document down. Yet the reviewers of the journals kept demanding more of this despite the journal's word limitations. We finally were able to get a conditional approval of this as an editorial opinion statement, which put an even more stringent word limit while the demands for more discussion of the literature continued. So this revision process became a challenge even for a group where everyone had such long publication experience (Bazerman et al., 2017e).

The radical cutting needed to meet journal requirements increased the group's desire for a book which would have a more complete version of our statement and other collaboratively written chapters (Bazerman et al., 2018e). We each also contributed an individual chapter allowing us to present in greater depth our own perspectives that were not as fully articulated in the Venn intersection of the collaborative statements. We did, however, mutually critique and edit these individual chapters over the last two years of the project. We sought a publisher that would reach teachers, policy makers, and researchers working with all educational levels. While we saw the value in reaching international audiences, we balanced that against the exigencies within the U.S. educational system and the scope of different publishers along with their distribution and price structures. The NCTE Press, although U.S. based, did reach across research, policy, and practice at all educational levels and maintained a modest price structure. Further, the press agreed to open access distribution through the WAC Clearinghouse after a two-year embargo. But this was not an easy choice, and we spent some time discussing it.

Despite my own impulse to move rapidly to a comprehensive synthetic picture, I had to recognize the wisdom in the group's caution that making any substantive claims at this point would privilege assumptions of particular populations or national school systems and would create normative expectations that would not fit the great variability of people's pathways. In this project I came to recognize things I had normalized from my own experience and I had to recognize deeply held assumptions and self-fulfilling prophecies of my own pedagogy. At this point, at least, there was no end to surfacing assumptions. Being in the role of a discussion facilitator pushed me even further to give up assumptions, as I had to appreciate the views being expressed by everyone in order to frame the productive next question and next task. I had to come to see the problem of writing development through the eyes of each of these very knowledgeable, experienced, and smart interlocutors. To keep the conversations going I repeatedly had to step back from my personally invested response to develop a larger frame in which the separate views could thrive and find points of intersection.

In my own chapter for the collection (Bazerman, 2018b), rather than advance any current work or articulate my own prior views about development, I proposed as a thought experiment a massively unrealistic research project of a hundred-year longitudinal study of diverse peoples in diverse national and economic situations, within different schooling systems, career paths, and access to technologies. Many dimensions of quantitative and qualitative data would be collected by teams located in different regions and focusing on varied populations. Perhaps from this massive data we could start to sort out if there were any common processes in writing development or even just common dimensions or variables that would help describe the differing trajectories. In order to sketch some of the problematics and procedures for such a study, I looked in detail to the examples of lifespan longitudinal studies in other disciplines, from physiology and medicine to human development and psycho-social wellness.

We in the group realized that we could not at this point offer answers. At best we could only mark a beginning to encourage future work and discussions. So we designed our article and book with that in mind, as I did in my chapter. We wanted to look beyond our moment to offer a vision for future work that might lead to a more fundamental understanding for writing education. In the few years since, these publications have gotten a modest but growing number of citations, indicating that the ideas have some resonance. Further, a Writing Through the Lifespan research collaborative has formed, led by some younger scholars who can carry forward the endeavor over many years, Ryan Dippre and Talinn Phillips. They have enlisted a growing number of members, held annual conferences (despite the challenges of the pandemic), produced publications from them (to which I have contributed, Bazerman, 2020b and this volume). Other publications are also emerging with a specific lifespan development focus.

I have continued to provide support in other publications for this growing research theme, which I hope will continue beyond my career. A chapter originating in the Dartmouth Conference on Methods allowed me to recount my methodological evaluation of the currently available forms of data available in writing and related studies that could be used for longitudinal developmental studies. I also restated and elaborated the challenges of gathering data that can tell us about writing development (Bazerman, 2021c). I also edited a special issue of the journal *Writing and Pedagogy* on this topic (Bazerman, 2018c). This autobiography is my next experiment about what can be said, at least about my one idiosyncratic case. While a few of the elements I tell in my story may match some experiences of some readers, the particular way they fall together and interact with emerging motives, goals, and discoveries are likely to match with even fewer, if any. But that, I hope is the point: how individual and idiosyncratic our pathways are in writing. I suspect and hope, at least, that some of the kinds of variables that influenced my development, and some of the dynamics that emerged in addressing those particularities will suggest themes that could be followed in contrasting and aggregating different stories of different writers. But I also suspect their stories will raise themes that I was not able to notice in my writing life.

Chapter 31. Learning to Write Across Borders

Despite family and identity challenges, I grew up in a time, place, and social position that favored my intellectual and social mobility. Cultural, educational, and governmental institutions provided me the resources and spaces to work through my personal situation to form a satisfying and rewarding life. The immigration of my parents' families to melting pot New York in the early twentieth century buffered them from the holocaust. My parent's assimilationist efforts provided me with the social privileges of a largely unmarked white person, experiencing antisemitism only at the margin. Success in education provided a path to avoid the worst economic risks that come with class position in the US The only major personal risk I felt was from the military draft to send me to a war I opposed from the beginning, but again educational success protected me. In this relative bubble of security, I explored the European intellectual and artistic culture that filtered into academic life of the sixties. Through my politics and my experience in teaching elementary school, I did learn in a small way what the lack of those privileges meant to those people within the US that were marginalized and lacked the access and expectations I had. But that still was in the dialectic of U.S. society and its Eurocentric cultural views.

Through my early adult years, I had not traveled beyond North America. A few touristic trips to Canada as a child and a young man allowed me to taste some North Americanized British and French flavors without challenging my ideas of what life was like. When I had taken leave as an undergraduate to be trained for the Peace Corps, I spent a couple of weeks in a remote Mexican town, where I did get a brief glimpse of rural poverty and a society steeped in a hierarchical Spanish Catholic culture, with a largely unacknowledged underlay of indigenous language and cultures. I did not understand much but I could see that life was different, even as I was protected by my role as an expert from the north. When I was on the verge of being drafted in grad school, I traveled to Canada to see whether immigration would be an option, but I was so filled with rage about how the politics of the US seemed to be stealing the country from me, I hardly could pay attention to what I saw—or rather what I was seeing was a marginalization that I could not bear to think of. In retrospect it indicates how privileged my social circumstances had been and how hard it was for me to imagine a life without that security.

Learning about Asia

I only started to get glimpses to the world beyond the US through my partner, whom I met in my final year of grad school. Shirley Geok-lin Lim was a Fulbright-Wien student from Malaysia, also pursuing a doctorate with the same advisor. From her I began to understand the complex politics and history of her home country, along with its different family bonds and life cultures. Race relations and social inequities (as well as language policies) there were as complex and troubled as in the US, but in different ways. And the educational institutions which provided both of us opportunities sat differently within our national histories, economies, and cultures. All this started me on the path to understanding my own social and educational positioning within the context of greater international variation. Starting in the late 1970s I started to visit Asia regularly with Shirley, with frequent extended stays for family and work in the following decades. She was becoming a well-known poet and scholar in the region, and through her I made contacts and did assessment work for the National University of Singapore in 1982. I returned for a full year visiting professorship in 1985 to help establish a new program in Academic English.

Working with colleagues from across Asia and the U.K. that year, I started to see different approaches to language education and analysis, and how U.S. composition and writing studies fit within a broader mix of possibilities. I also came to see something of the complexity of the language situation in multicultural and multilingual Singapore where Chinese dialects, Tamil, and Bahasa were all community languages, but where the dominant language of education remained English, following British standards and colonial assessment practices. During the period I was working there, recognition of the value of the local variety of English was just emerging, although "correct" Oxbridge English remained a class and educational marker. It was easier to see the full import of these tensions as an outsider rather than in my own country. Likewise, from the outside I could see the effect of privileging particular literary histories and ideologies of writing, and their relation to the ascription of power. Further, I could see the advantages first language fluency in English gave me both in practice and prestige, during the period when it had become increasingly dominant globally, particularly at more advanced levels.

Even further, the workings of racial and national privilege became visible as I saw that the respect and collegiality offered me was not given to some colleagues from Asia, despite a policy to increase the number of regional professors and decrease the dominance of Anglo-American expats. I realized, oh, that is how white privilege worked and I was the beneficiary of it. I was regularly given the benefit of the doubt, treated politely, and listened to with respect. I know other forms of even more virulent privilege were granted to some Anglo-Americans, even allowing them to get away with malign behavior. Nonetheless, even absent those overt abuses, privilege is at play, based on people's perceptions of who you are and the power you had access to.

On every trip to Asia we made it a point to visit other countries—sometimes to do academic work and sometimes to sightsee, looking for insights into the ways of life, politics, and society in different countries. As I started to develop an academic network I began working with universities in other countries throughout Asia—developing ongoing relationships with people and institutions in Nepal and Hong Kong, then mainland China (fostered by the visiting scholars I hosted at UCSB once I moved to the education school). Each of these deepened my understanding and appreciation of the varieties of cultures, educational systems, and language educational practices. In working with each I had to freshly evaluate what I could offer and how that would fit with their educational systems and social needs. In the process, my assumptions about writing became more and more decentered, and I had to reframe my understanding to encompass all the variation I was meeting.

In Singapore I worked with a number of people trained in the British applied linguistics tradition and met John Swales on one of his trips to the region. I also co-taught a course on Varieties of Written English with Vijay Bhatia, one of his students, and formed a continuing friendship with both. I made a number of visits to Britain and became familiar with some of the applied linguistics faculty at different universities, gaining an insight into their methods and theories as well as their perceptions of issues surrounding global academic English. Applied linguistics and scientific language led to an invitation to Australia where I became more familiar with Systemic Functional Linguistics. Other connections with Scandinavia and elsewhere in Europe broadened my interdisciplinary perspectives and awareness of different educational systems and approaches to language education.

Engaging with Ibero-America

Two nodes became particularly important to the expansion of my view of writing. The growth of the Santa Barbara research conferences on Writing Research Across Borders—resulting in the formation of the International Society for the Advancement of Writing Research—made me more aware and appreciative of the different research traditions, intellectual influences, practical work conditions of scholars and teachers, and educational practices and institutions in different regions. At the same times as WRAB and ISAWR were growing, I started to make connections with Mexican and South American scholars. Encounters at the 2005 conference in Santa Barbara led to a series of consulting visits at the Benemerita Universidad de Puebla, Mexico, to support the nascent writing centers and emerging national network of writing programs led by Fatima Encinas. At about the same time I hosted a visiting scholar, Angela Dionisio from UFPE (Universidade Federal de Pernambuco) in Recife, Brazil. Her mentor, Antonio Luis Marcuschi, a major force in Brazilian linguistic theory and writing education, suggested she make the contact. This began an ongoing relation with UFPE and the newly formed Simpósio Internacional de Gêneros Textuais (SIGET) in Brazil. Recognizing the benefits of supporting networks and organizations, I volunteered to coordinate international participation and co-edit publications that would help share communications internationally. For over a decade I traveled regularly to Brazil, teaching and lecturing in a number of places, with eventually five books translated into Portuguese (thank you, Angela and her colleague Judith Hoffnagel).

During this period I also heard about how Paula Carlino was developing Writing Across the Curriculum in Argentina, and began communicating with her. Through her I met other scholars in the region, learning more about developments in Chile, Colombia, and other South American countries as I started to extend my trips to the region. Then I had the good fortune of having Fulbright Scholars Natalia Avila from Chile and Elizabeth Narvaez from Colombia join me in the same year for doctoral studies. We began a collaborative research group to map out the growth of writing studies and writing programs in the region and to support regional connections (Iniciativas de Lectura y Escritura en la Educación Superior en América Latina—ILEES). Drawing on our several networks, we enlisted other scholars of the region into varying roles in this project.

This growing network of Latin American scholars also participated in ISAWR to make that an even more global organization and to increase the multi-linguality of writing studies, with special focus on first language writing. The WRAB conference in Bogota in 2017 connected local scholars with the global writing community and the conference volume made selected work more visible alongside other international contributions. Not long thereafter, a Latin American organization (Asociación Latinoamericana de Estudios de la Escritura en Educación Superior y Contextos Profesionales—ALES) was formed and publication venues for writing studies increased. To make work from Latin America more available internationally, we have been working with the WAC Clearinghouse to republish works originally published regionally and to translate influential articles into English. This work started with selected papers from the SIGET conferences, but has expanded into an International Exchanges book series with a subseries on Latin America.

The institutional good fortune of my School of Education seeing international visitors as an important asset to our school and UCSB's supportive campus Office of International Scholars and Students has facilitated bringing visiting scholars to campus. I am sure there are historical reasons for both the GGSE and the campus to have such favorable policies, but this certainly helped expand my experience and vision and the roles I was able to take on as an international editor.

I have here, as elsewhere, benefited from the Matthew Effect (Merton, 1968), where good fortune fosters access to even more resources and opportunities, placing one in a more central role. I am highly appreciative of having been in this position, but I am also somewhat abashed, knowing that such good fortune does not fall to most scholars. I cannot deny, nonetheless, that such good fortune has fostered my learning and growth as a writer, particularly as I have matured in the profession. I have tried to pay it forward by reconfiguring systems as much as I could to better serve the needs of our profession and society, in building international networks, in trying to advance open access, in editing the work of others, and in providing reference resources for the profession.

Chapter 32. Looking Backward and Writing Forward

What Has this Story Told Us?

My development as a writer was influenced by many factors—distant, proximate, and internal. Biological and cultural evolution first of all made possible for me to develop as a writing human. With no major discernible genetic biological anomalies and no major bodily accidents affecting my capacity for learning literacy, the particularities of my trajectory of writing development depended on my interaction with the particular time and place I have lived within cultural, political, social, ethnic, and economic history, with all its distinctions, opportunities, resources, and obstacles.

Each life poses a set of problems to the growing person, influencing how they will address the conditions of their life, how they will understand the relations and communications with others, how they will be motivated, and what opportunities they will pursue. For me, many of my challenges and motives led me to writing as a way to pursue and satisfy my needs. A particularly important set of needs was to understand much of the world and relations in terms I could accept, as I found so much confusing and problematic in the people I grew up among. I felt I had to make my own sense of the world and to learn to evaluate skeptically perspectives offered by others, whether in my immediate family or the writers I was to read later. Writing became a major tool to sort these things out and discover more of the world. In turn, writing itself became one of the puzzling things I felt a need to learn more about, to pursue my own growth and the growth of my students. As I pursued these ends, I came to see that understanding writing was the way I could most contribute to our communal life and the human experiment, thereby finding meaning in my own life.

My reactions to my family, school, community, and institutional life motivated my dispositions, stances, strategies, and meanings expressed through my writing. In the early chapters of this book, I have recounted the formative conditions and my reactions to them, but these social motives and dispositions accompanied me throughout my life. As my life became more focused on schooling and the academy, academic contexts with their histories, practices, and evolving conditions became increasingly defining of the problems and ambitions through which I developed as a writer. As I gained some success in the academic world through my writing, my writing started to reach beyond the classrooms of the educational institutions I enrolled in or was employed by. This then created opportunities to engage more widely, but never that far outside an academic world.

Throughout this process, skills, techniques, and tricks I learned earlier returned, sometimes in expected and other times in surprising ways. Of course, early technical matters of letter formation, spelling, grammar, and syntax were foundational and recurrently used, but so were recognition of the importance of meaning, awareness of communicative effect and responsiveness to audience, even though the kinds of meanings, the communicative effects, and audiences changed and became more distant, requiring more subtle understanding and analysis. Also continuing throughout my writing life was reporting about the world (material, social, textual, personal) I experienced; facts I was engaging with; and reused words, phrasing, and genres, even though the extent and my awareness of them grew. Learning that writing had consequences and could influence others and my own understanding also started early but kept growing and ramifying.

Less expectedly, devices and techniques learned in one place could turn up in very different places. Abductive leaps, for example, practiced on the high school math team that helped me to solve obscure puzzles set the stage for flashes of insight in writing, whether for poems, understanding the shape and force of literary texts, seeing the connection of different theories and pieces of evidence to give rise to a new concept, or having sudden visions of the organization of major projects. Of course, the abductive intuitions needed to be worked through and validated by mathematical or textual reasoning, but the trust in their potential gave me confidence to work out whether they could be validated. In another example, the use of the icon, which I first remember learning explicitly about in an undergraduate course on Chaucer, but rested on earlier experiences noticing significant details in texts, became transformed in papers for other courses into considering dramatic scenes, particular poems and lines, and descriptions of buildings as iconic for analysis of authors' thinking. This use of the iconic later turned up in examining scientific texts and disciplinary cultures. This story is rife with many other examples of this sort, of devices and processes of writing turning up far from their initial site of use, discovery, or invention.

Another thing I notice in reviewing this manuscript is how at different moments I latched onto certain phrases, poetic and literary lines, quotations attributed to scientists, or even geometric models to sum up my current state of mind, to identify a stance toward my work, and to guide my future thinking and writing. Composed phrases stayed with me as cornerstones of my consciousness. These odd examples of how transfer happens indicate the complex and idiosyncratic ways that lessons are learned and are carried forth to new settings and projects.

These details of remembered lines, moments of intuitive insight, techniques and devices that recur in unexpected places are also indicative of a larger theme emerging in this narrative. Once I had learned the basic tools of literacy, composing text and composing my consciousness were intertwined, whether from the early jokes I told myself and stories I wrote in class to my young adult search for meaning and a habitable place in this world; from my reaching out to students in my professional life to my years of research and my late career musing on theory. These motives were enacted through text production. Texts were composed from impulses and meanings arising in consciousness. What texts to compose, how to compose them, and what I could say in them possessed my mind. Phrases, text structures, chains of reasoning floated in my head and stayed with me after texts were complete and submitted to instructors or journals. Writing was a way of growing my mind, just as the growth of my mind was realized in the texts I wrote.

As with the authors I discussed in Chapter 21, as well, I found that my changing view of the social worlds I was engaging with and my experiences in communicating in those worlds informed and changed my evolving ways of writing and framing of writing projects. Part of this was broadening contact with more worlds as I took on different roles (moving, for example, from the role of student to role of teacher) and as I moved through different institutions and social groups (up the levels of schooling, engaging with different disciplines, or developing international experiences). But part of it was a deepening of my understanding of whichever context I engaged in; for example, appreciating disciplinary genres and how those genres fit within disciplinary activity systems opened up the kinds of choices I was able to make using those genres. So in a very real sense the communicative world I wrote to at one time would be substantially different than at some previous date, because my perception and understanding of that world changed in addition to any evolution that would have occurred in that world apart from my perception of it. Practicing, teaching, and studying writing changed the writing goals I set for myself and the ways I attempted to realize them.

I said earlier in this book that I started to save my writing to follow the change of my thinking, but in writing this book I used those texts to examine what I was learning about writing. By learning to write those texts, however, I also was also learning to think the kinds of things they expressed and to reflect more comprehensively about the writing I was doing. In the end, I wound up thinking a lot about writing and came to look at much of the world around me through the analytic lens of what I have come to know about writing. As I said in the introduction, this would make a boring movie, of me sitting at a desk, looking around, thinking, and writing, then sending the resulting missives out into the world of teachers, publishers, colleagues, administrators. I have tried to understand that world and how texts move it well enough so that my missives and the missives of others I might influence as a teacher and a colleague might have some positive impact on it.

The Value of Good Luck and Making Good Bets

Luck has played a central role in my writing development. I grew up in a time and place with rapid economic growth from an already substantially middle-class, affluent society, though not equally shared by everyone. There were large numbers of opportunities, enough educational support, and rewards for those who performed well in the ways in which I was successful without the barriers some faced. Consequently, I could live a life of reasonable comfort, even when my family was economically strained or when I was scraping by in grad school and then anxiously looking for first jobs—giving me the opportunity to pursue my interests, academic success, and writing endeavors. Although my family situation placed some difficulties and challenges in my early life and set up some difficult transitions, yet in the long run these transitions seemed to be productive for my writing development, motivation, and ultimately career success. Whether I would have been set on this pathway without those early challenges, or whether alternatively I might have moved more smoothly on this trajectory had my family situation been otherwise, I do not know. But not everyone who faced similar family difficulties has had such a positive outcome. That match between opportunities of my time and place, the accidents of programs and people I encountered, and my particular dispositions and emerging skills that allowed me to find my way, again has to be accounted to luck. I think the best that can be said for me is that I kept my eye out for opportunities, was realistic in my choices, and pursued them with energy, persistence, and guarded optimism.

My choices of commitments turned out to be remarkably lucky, as I entered the university at a time of growth. My commitment to writing education I initially accepted as being institutionally marginal and having major costs in academic rewards as I started my career, but I saw those costs recompensed by doing what I thought valuable. Over my working lifetime, however, the field has gained a degree of legitimacy and has developed a substantial research component which I could participate in and contribute to. My role in the growth of this emerging field brought me increasing economic comfort and leisure to pursue my research and writing with all the resources I needed. I also had good luck in the mentors I met within sponsoring institutional settings. Writing this account has helped me see more clearly all they did for me far above institutional expectations, and I am overwhelmed with gratitude. Even those whom I experienced negatively taught me the complexity of writing for others, and the consequences of these negative encounters were buffered by the luck of institutional settings. An occasional lowered grade, wounded feeling, or rejection by people whose good opinion I sought did not seriously impede my development. Such costs are miniscule compared to the high costs paid by many who have limited access to school; who suffer punitive, regressive schooling; who end schooling prematurely; who are ostracized from careers; or who are even imprisoned or disappeared for the views they put in writing. Although in my fantasies I may imagine how things might have been even better, I know how terribly things may have turned out if situations had been even slightly different.

Each writer's development is necessarily enacted within the contingencies, accidents, and luck—whether fortunate or unfortunate—in the person's life. As important as teaching any particular skill is, as teachers, our most important role may be creating the conditions within which people can advance their writing. We can form at least a small part of the luck of the developing writers we run into, helping them identify the opportunities before them, provide useful tools, and support them to build the strength and persistence to move forward.

Even more fundamentally, this story has reminded me that people's luck depends on the social and institutional conditions which provide obstacles and opportunities to their development, writing development included. The existence of schools, cold war educational programs, universities, private foundations, and state funded scholarships all created the spaces in which I was able to learn and develop. Even the existence of private charitable summer camps and the establishment of the Head Start program in 1965 allowed me to have my first experiences working with young children as a counsellor and a teacher's assistant, which eventually were to lead a career in writing education, inflecting all my writing development as an adult. Even the horrendous Vietnam War in constraining my choices to avoid participating, also directed me to the opportunities I pursued and to reconfirm political consciousness. At every step, choices, actions, and institutions made by others affected where, what, and how I wrote, and thus how I developed—even computer manufacturers in their product designs, timing of releases, availability, and prices. While this story has been told as a single person's journey, the space in which it happens is historical, social, and economic. Context is not just context, not just the wallpaper on the walls of the room; it is the room itself and what happens within it. If we are concerned with whether people develop to be skillful users of such a pervasively important personal, intellectual, social, civil, and economic tool as writing, we need rightfully to be concerned with all the conditions that make possible their luck and give them places to engage their efforts.

So What did I Learn Along the Way and How did These Things Describe a Trajectory of Development?

At different life epochs I had different uses for writing in response to the tasks others posed for me and the opportunities I came across. The writing tasks and opportunities had to do with the institutions and other activity systems I participated in, mostly educational and academic. Since in later years I was increasingly investigating or supporting the writing life of others, wider worlds fell into my view. While I brought with me all I had come to learn and practice in writing, yet each of these epochs posed new problems, inspiring me to reconceive what I had brought and to use it to new purposes. Each epoch as well brought new experiences and challenges that taught me new things about writing.

The following list summarizes leading activities in different periods in my life, as documented in the previous chapters. During each of these periods I worked on other aspects of writing, and I continued to work on and expand on themes foregrounded earlier. Nonetheless, the most challenging and novel problems changed as I moved through my writing development, as this list suggests.

- Learning tools and uses of written language—early schooling (Chapter 2)
- Developing ideas and knowledge—adolescence, college (Chapters 3, 5–13)

- Exploring my understanding of myself and the world to locate my place, values, and priorities—adolescence, college, graduate school (Chapter 4–13)
- Relating to others; sharing my experience, knowledge, and skills; writing as communication—teaching, therapy, creative exploration (Chapters 10–15)
- Academic writing to advance practice and share mutually useful discoveries—writing about pedagogy, textbooks—early to mid-academic career (Chapters 16–18)
- Advancing knowledge for practice through systematic research: focus on questions, research sites, methods, evidence, argument; telling what I was finding in a compelling way—mid-academic career (Chapters 19–22)
- Explaining, elaborating and creating a coherent a vision of writing; developing theory—late career (Chapters 23–24)
- Addressing and supporting collectivities to advance knowledge, teaching, community—late career (Chapters 25–26, 30–31)
- Elaborating and researching issues to fill out my conceptual vision and open up possible issues for the field—late career (Chapters 27–31)

As the scope of my research and theoretical writing has expanded, I have become more aware of how that work contributes to the advancement of communal knowledge and culture. I have sought to support the development of new generations of writers by providing them additional tools to realize their writing motives and to understand what they can accomplish through writing.

Since I have come to see writing as so infrastructural to modern society, I have come to see writing education as crucial to the success of the human experiment, even as our future as a cooperative species hangs in the balance. How much writing can help create shared knowledge, coordinate cooperative endeavors, and advance mutual understanding is still an open question, perhaps even a quixotic hope, but that is the slim thread upon which I measure the value and accomplishment of my life. If we fail in the endeavor, a lot more will fail than my own self-image.

Where do I Go, We Go from Here?

So much of my life has been associated with the academy, it is hard to know what happens following my retirement in June 2022. I am no longer formally a student or a teacher. Everyone is a school dropout at some point, but some do it earlier, for some it takes completion of a degree to call it quits, and some of us keep hanging around as long as we can function. For me, it looks like it took 77 years to figure out how to drop out.

I don't know how many years are left to me, nor what the diminishing energies and waning capacities of old age will allow. I can accomplish ever fewer hours of productive work daily, and I can no longer work late into the night. During the daily periods when I can work, short term memory weakens and I am less able to hold complex structures in mind. Even reading complex texts requires more energy and I need to take more frequent breaks. All this means that my projects are less likely to rely on extensive fresh research. I have had the good luck of greater scholarly longevity than most, but I can't go on forever, and aging inevitably takes its toll.

I have completed most of my commitments and promissory notes I made to myself and others. I have been shedding projects that require the energies and resources of younger people, as well as long horizons to complete ambitious things. My recent research and writing described in the last few chapters has been more to open up and advance topics for others to follow than for me to make much substantive progress on. Just as I stopped producing textbooks once I no longer taught first-year composition and I lost touch with the needs and interests of newer generations of entering undergraduates, I imagine losing touch with graduate students and attending fewer conferences will limit my imagination of what might be useful to accomplish. Yet still a few new ideas and projects might occur to me and I want to do what I can to support the continuing work of the field.

In the exploratory projects described in the last few chapters I have already identified the directions I see promising around the environment, technology, internationalism, and the use of data. Writing articles and studies is my way of seeing down paths, so I have no unspoken agendas for the field to share here. What others might see and pursue, I have little idea, because what they see will arise out of their experiences and visions. New ideas, perspectives, and materials to study through new methods are likely to emerge over time. I hope as well that growing knowledge in other fields devoted to understanding human life will intersect more fully and richly with writing studies because I see writing depending on a broad range of human capacities. In turn, writing has many consequences for other dimensions of human life, from our most internal self-regulation and consciousness to our largest networks of societal engagement, knowledge-making, coordination, and communal action. But exploring these intersections will depend on the interests and visions of new generations in writing studies and in other fields.

Then there are all the externalities that will direct the field's attentions and possibilities, whether educational policies, programs, and fundings; shifts in cultures, and national and international economies; or crises that reorient priorities. Technologies likely will continue to change rapidly, though it is easy to be entranced by immediate changes and miss the underlying continuities and deeper changes, likely to occur at the level of social organization. Crises of climate change and consequent pressures on food, immigration, national and international politics, and education, will likely put demands on writing and communication, but what those demands and uses of writing are unclear. All these will happen, inevitably, but it is hard to predict what will be most salient and determinative for writing.

What I am reminded of at this moment is Joseph Priestley's 1769 *A Chart of History*, which is a long fold-out timeline since the beginning of recorded time; it is perhaps the first published timeline. He left the last column blank for the reader to fill in as events would occur. Or as I realized standing outside the Democratic Convention in Chicago in 1968, we live in history and we make it by what we do.

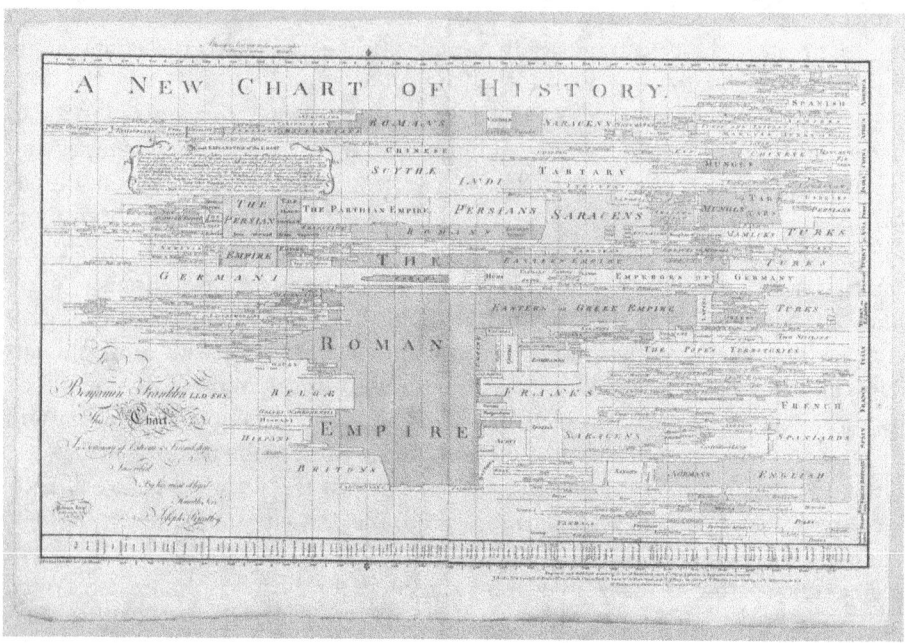

Figure 32.1. Joseph Priestley's large fold-out Chart of History. Notice the blank column on the write right for the reader to fill in. Photo in the public domain.

Figure 32.2. Shirley Geok-lin Lim and myself in retirement. Photos courtesy of Charles Bazerman.

References

Adler, M. (1940). *How to read a book: The art of getting a liberal education.* Simon & Schuster.
Altick, R. (1946). *Preface to critical reading.* H. Holt and Company.
American Psychological Association. (1983). *Publication manual of the American Psychological Association* (3rd ed.).
Amis, K. (1954). *Lucky Jim.* Victor Gollancz.
Beaufort, A. (1999). *Writing in the real world: Making the transition from school to work.* Teachers College Press.
Brandt, D. (2001). *Literacy in American lives.* Cambridge University Press.
Carroll, M. (1968, November 20). Parents bar principal from school in Brooklyn. *New York Times.*
Csikszentmihalyi, M. (1990). *Flow: The psychology of optimal experience.* Harper and Row.
Dear, P. (Ed.) (1991). *The literary structure of scientific argument: Historical studies.* University of Pennsylvania Press.
Elkhana, Y. (1974). *The discovery of the conservation of energy.* Harvard University Press.
Fahnestock, J. & Secor, M. (1991). Rhetoric of literary criticism. In C. Bazerman & J. Paradis (Eds.), *Textual dynamics of the professions* (pp. 74–96). University of Wisconsin Press.
Fleck, L. (1979). *Genesis and development of a scientific fact.* University of Chicago Press.
Flower, L. (1979). Writer-based prose: A cognitive basis for problems in writing. *College English, 41*(1), 19–37.
Geisler, C. (1994). *Academic literacy and the nature of expertise: Reading, writing, and knowing in academic philosophy.* Routledge.
Goldblatt, E. (2012). Writing Home: A literacy autobiography. Southern Illinois University Press.
Goody, J. (1986). *The logic of writing and the organization of society.* Cambridge University Press.
Hammond, P. E. (Ed.). (1964). *Sociologists at work: The craft of social research.* Basic Books.
Herndon, J. (1968). *The way it 'spozed to be.* Simon & Schuster.
Herrington, A. & Curtis, M. (2000). *Persons in process: Four stories of writing and personal development in college.* NCTE.
Kahn, H. (1962). *Thinking about the unthinkable.* Horizon Press.
Kohl, H. (1967). *36 children.* Signet; New American Library.
Kuhn, T. S. (1962). *The structure of scientific revolutions.* University of Chicago Press.
Latour, B. & Woolgar, S. (1979). *Laboratory life: The construction of scientific facts.* SAGE.
MacArthur, C. A., Graham, S. & Fitzgerald, J. (2006, 2015). *Handbook of writing research.* Guilford Press.

Macrorie, K. (1980). *Searching writing*. Hayden.
Marx, K. (1852). *The Eighteenth Brumaire of Louis Bonaparte*. https://www.marxists.org/archive/marx/works/1852/18th-brumaire/ch01.htm.
Merchant, C. (2006). The scientific revolution and the death of nature. *Isis, 97,* 513–533.
Merton, R. K. (1968). The Matthew effect in science. *Science, 159*(3810), 56–63.
Merton, R. K. (1987). Three fragments from a sociologist's notebooks: Establishing the phenomenon, specified ignorance, and strategic research materials. *Annual Review of Sociology, 13,* 1–29.
Meyer, J. H. F. & Land, R. (2003). Threshold concepts and troublesome knowledge: Linkages to ways of thinking and Practising. In C. Rust (Ed.), *Improving Student Learning: Ten Years On*. Oxford Center for Staff and Learning Development.
Miller, C. (1984). Genre as social action. *Quarterly Journal of Speech, 70,* 151–67.
Miller, G. A., Galanter, E. & Pribram, K. H. (1960). *Plans and the structure of behavior.* : Henry Holt and Company.
Mills, C. W. (1959). *The sociological imagination*. Oxford University Press.
Myers, G. (1989). The pragmatics of politeness in scientific articles. *Applied Linguistics, 10*(1), 1–35.
Nabokov, V. (1966). *Speak memory*. McGraw Hill.
Newton, I. (1983). *Certain philosophical questions: Newton's Trinity notebook*, Ed. J. E. McGuire and M. Tamny. Cambridge University Press.
Newton, I. (1984). *Optical papers. Vol 1, The optical lectures* (A. Shapiro, Ed.). Cambridge University Press.
Oreskes, N. & Conway, E. M. (2010). *Merchants of doubt: How a handful of scientists obscured the truth on issues from tobacco smoke to global warming*. Bloomsbury Press.
Pennebaker, J. W. & Chung, C. K. (2007). Expressive writing, emotional upheavals, and health. In H. Friedman & R. Silver (Eds.), *Handbook of health psychology* (pp. 263–284). Oxford University Press.
Pollard, A. W. & Redgrave, G. R. (Eds.). (1946). *A short-title catalogue of books printed in England, Scotland and Ireland, and of English books printed abroad 1475–1640*. Biographical Society.
Popper, K. (1972). *Objective knowledge*. Oxford University Press.
Primeau, R. (1976). *Writing in the margin: From annotation to critical essay*. David McKay Company.
Proctor, R. N. & Schiebinger, L. (Eds.) (2008). *Agnotology: The making and unmaking of ignorance*. Stanford University Press.
Puttenham. G. (1589). *The arte of English poesie*. Richard Field.
Richards, I. A. (1942). *How to read a page*. W. W. Norton.
Rose, M. (1989). *Lives on the boundary*. Free Press.
Rousseau, J.-J. (1964). *The first and second discourses*. St. Martin's Press.
Russell, D. (1991). *Writing in the disciplines 1870–1990: A curricular history*. Southern Illinois University Press.
Russell, D. (1997). Rethinking genre in school and society: An activity theory analysis. *Written Communication, 14*(4), 504–554.
Shabecoff, P. (1983, October 18). E.P.A. report says Earth will heat up beginning in 1990's. *The New York Times*, A1.

Shaughnessy, M. (1977). *Errors and expectations*. Oxford University Press.
Smagorinsky, P. (Ed.) (2006). *Research on composition: Multiple perspectives on two decades of change*. Teachers College Press.
Spivey, N. N. (1984). *Discourse synthesis: Constructing texts in reading and writing*. International Reading Association.
Stetsenko, A. & Arievitch, I. M. (2004). The self in cultural-historical activity theory: Reclaiming the unity of social and individual dimensions of human development. *Theory & Psychology, 14*(4), 475–503.
Sullivan, H. S. (1938). Editorial statement. *Psychiatry, 1*(1).
Sullivan, H. S. (1971). *The fusion of psychiatry and the social sciences*. Norton.
Swales, J. (2013). *Incidents in an educational life*. University of Michigan Press.
Tomasello, M. (2019). *Becoming human: A theory of ontogeny*. Belknap Press.
Villanueva, V. (1993). *Bootstraps: From an American scholar of color*. NCTE Press.
Vygotsky, L. S. (1967). Play and its role in the mental development of the child. *Soviet Psychology, 5*(3), 6–18.
Vygotsky, L. S. (1978). *Mind in society: The development of higher psychological processes*. Harvard University Press.
Vygotsky, L. S. (1986). *Thought and language* (A. Kozulin, Trans.). MIT Press.
Warner, S. A. (1963). *Teacher*. Simon & Schuster.
Zaporozhets, A. V. (1997). Principal problems in the ontogeny of the mind. *Journal of Russian & East European Psychology, 35*(1), 53–94.

Charles Bazerman Publications, Interviews, and Edited Book Series

Publications

1970

C. Bazerman. (1970). Three Poems, *Brooklyn Poets*, Brooklyn Poets' Cooperative, 1972–1975.

C. Bazerman, Book reviews in *The Nation* *Ch 17[13]
- Toward the End, an Effete Snob, September 18, 1972, 215, 7, 215–216.
- Art and the Accidents of Flesh, November 6, 1972, 215, 14, 440–441.
- What They Felt in Place of Joy, November 27, 1972, 215, 17, 53.
- A Fine Scheme for Criticism, February 5, 1973, 216, 6, 184–186.
- Building the New Jerusalem, April 23, 1973, 216, 17, 537–538.
- Victories of Happy Madness, September 10, 1973, 217, 7, 218–219.
- Serving the Larger Design, March 9, 1974, 218, 10, 311–312.
- Danger, Fear, and Self-Revulsion, November 15, 1975, 221, 16, 502–504.

1974

C. Bazerman. (1974). Book review. [Review of *Venetian Phoenix: Paolo Sarpi*, by J. Lievesay] *Seventeenth Century News*, Winter, 82–84.

1975

C. Bazerman. (1975). Book review. [Review of *Grassroots*, by Fawcett and Sandberg] *Causes*, p. 2.

1976

C. Bazerman. (1976). A student guide for messing up your first English paper. *College Composition and Communication*, 27(3), 296–297.

C. Bazerman et al. (1976). Statement on the College Board's Test of Standard Written English (for the CUNY Association of Writing Supervisors). *College Composition and Communication*, 27(3), 287–89. *Ch 17

1977

C. Bazerman. (1977). Help, short story, *New Voices*, 6.

C. Bazerman. (1977). Time in play and film: *Macbeth* and *Throne of Blood*. *Literature/Film Quarterly*, 5(4), 333–38. *Ch 17

---

13. Asterisks and chapter numbers designate discussion in the text.

1978

C. Bazerman. (1978). The grant, the scholar, and the university community. In S. Hook, P. Kurtz & M. Todorovich. *The university and the state* (pp. 221–226). Prometheus.

H. Wiener & C. Bazerman. (1978). *English Skills Handbook*. Houghton Mifflin. *Ch17, 18. Revised and reissued in parts as:

- *Reading Skills Handbook*, 1978, 1982, 1985, 1988, 1991, 1994, 1997, 2000. Longman: 2006.
- *Basic Reading Skills Handbook*, 1988, 1991, 1994, 1997, 2000. Longman: 2006.
- *Writing Skills Handbook*, 1983, 1988, 1993, 1998, 2003.
- *All of Us: Cross-Cultural Reading Skills Handbook*, 1992, 1995, 1999.
- *Reading College Textbooks: A Skills Handbook*, 1997.
- *A Reader's Guide*. 1999.
- *Side by Side: A Multi-Cultural Anthology*. Houghton Mifflin, 1993, 1996.

1980

C. Bazerman. (1980). Book review. [Review of *Laboratory Life*, by B. Latour and S. Woolgar] *Society for the Social Studies of Science*, 5(2) 14–19. *Ch 19, 28

C. Bazerman. (1980). A relationship between reading and writing: The conversational model. *College English*, 41(6), 656–661. Reprinted in *Allyn & Bacon Sourcebook for College Writing Teachers*, Ed. James MacDonald. Allyn & Bacon, 1996. 2nd ed., 2000. *Ch 18

1981

C. Bazerman. (1981). *The informed writer: Using sources in the disciplines*. Houghton Mifflin, 1981; 1985; 1989; 1992; 1995. *Ch 18, 28

C. Bazerman. (1981). What written knowledge does: Three examples of academic discourse. *Philosophy of the Social Sciences*, 11(3), 361–88. Reprinted in *Landmark Essays in Writing Across the Curriculum*, edited by Bazerman and Russell, Hermagoras Press, 1994; in *Norton Book of Composition Studies*, edited by Susan Miller, Norton, 2009; and in *Ethnographic Discourse*, edited by Paul Atkinson and Sara Delamont, SAGE Publications, 2008, *Ch 19

1983

C. Bazerman. (1983). Scientific writing as a social act: A review of the literature of the sociology of science. In J. Anderson, J. Brockmann & C. Miller (Eds.), *New essays in technical writing and communication* (pp. 156–184). Baywood, *Ch 19, 29

1984

C. Bazerman. (1984). Modern evolution of the experimental report: Spectroscopic articles in *Physical Review*, 1893–1980. *Social Studies of Science*, 14, 163–96. *Ch 20

C. Bazerman. (1984). The writing of scientific non-fiction: Contexts, choices and constraints. *Pre/Text*, 5(1), 39–74. Reprinted in V. Vitanza (Ed.), *Ten Years of Pre/Text*. University of Pittsburgh Press. *Ch 20, 28

1985

C. Bazerman. (1985). Physicists reading physics: Schema-laden purposes and purpose-laden schema. *Written Communication*, 2(1), 3–23. *Ch 20

C. Bazerman. (1985). Studies of scientific writing: E pluribus unum. *4S Review*, 3(2), 13–20. *Ch 29

1987

C. Bazerman. (1987). Codifying the social scientific style: The *APA Publication Manual* as a behaviorist rhetoric. In J. Nelson, A. Megill & D. McCloskey (Eds.). *The rhetoric of the human sciences* (pp. 125–144). Madison: University of Wisconsin Press. *Ch 20

C. Bazerman. (1987). Literate acts and the emergent social structure of science. *Social Epistemology*, 1(4), 295–310. *Ch 20

1988

C. Bazerman. (1988). *Shaping written knowledge: The genre and activity of the experimental article in science*. University of Wisconsin Press, 1988. Italian translation: *Le origini della scrittura scientifica*. Il Lavoro Editoriale in the series, History of Mentality, 1991. Chapter 2 reprinted in *Landmark essays in the rhetoric of science*, Ed. R. Harris. Mahwah, NJ: Erlbaum, 1996; Routledge, 2018 (pp. 263–279). *Ch 20, 23, 28

1989

C. Bazerman. (1989). Book review. [Review of *Changing order*, by H. Collins] *Philosophy of the Social Sciences*, 19(1), 115–118.

C. Bazerman. (1989). *The informed reader: Contemporary issues in the disciplines.* Houghton Mifflin, 1989. *Ch 18, 27

C. Bazerman. (1989). Rhetoricians on the rhetoric of science (Symposiu). *Science Technology and Human Values*, 14(1), 3–6.

C. Bazerman. (1989). What are we doing as a research community? (Symposiu). *Rhetoric Review*, 7(2), 223–224.

1990

C. Bazerman. (1990). Book review of T. Becher. *Academic tribes and territories. English for Specific Purposes*, 9(3), 265–266.

C. Bazerman. (1990). Comment and response. *College English*, 52(3), 329–330.

C. Bazerman. (1990). Discourse analysis and social construction. *Annual Review of Applied Linguistics*, 11, 77–83.

C. Bazerman. (1990). Reading student papers: Proteus grabbing Proteus. In B. Lawson, S. Sterr & W. R. Winterowd (Eds.), *Encountering student texts* (pp. 139–146). NCTE. *Ch 24

C. Bazerman. (1990). What's Interesting? *English Basics*, Winter.

1991

C. Bazerman. (1991). The second stage of writing across the curriculum (Multiple review essay). *College English*, 53(2), 209–212.

C. Bazerman. (1991). Book review. [Review of *Writing biology*, by Greg Myers] *Newsletter of the Society for Literature and Science*.

C. Bazerman. (1991). How natural philosophers can cooperate: The rhetorical technology of coordinated research in Joseph Priestley's *History and present state of electricity*. In C. Bazerman & J. Paradis (Eds.), *Textual dynamics of the professions* (pp. 13–44). University of Wisconsin Press. Reprinted in T. Kynell & M. Moran (Eds.), *Three keys to the past*. Ablex, 1999. *Ch 21, 23

C. Bazerman. (1991). Theories that help us read and write better. In S. Witte (Ed.). *A rhetoric of doing: Festschrift for J. Kinneavy* (pp. 103–112). Southern Illinois University Press. *Ch 24

C. Bazerman & J. Paradis (Eds.). (1991). *Textual dynamics of the professions*. University of Wisconsin Press. *Ch 25

1992

C. Bazerman. (1992). Book review. [Review of *Contending rhetorics*, by George Dillon] *Contending rhetorics. Language in Society*, 21(3), 501–503.

C. Bazerman. (1992). Book review. [Review of *Reading to write*, by Linda Flower et al.] *Journal of Advanced Composition*, 12(1), 236–242.

C. Bazerman. (1992). From cultural criticism to disciplinary participation: Living with powerful words. In M. Moran & A. Herrington (Eds.), *Writing, teaching, and learning in the disciplines* (pp. 61–68). Modern Language Association. Reprinted in R. Jones (Ed.), *Harcourt Brace guide to writing in the disciplines*. Harcourt Brace, 1998.

C. Bazerman. (1992). The interpretation of disciplinary writing. In R. H. Brown (Ed.), *Writing the social text* (pp. 31–38). Aldine de Gruyter.

C. Bazerman. (1992). Linguistic and rhetorical studies of writing in disciplines. *Encyclopedia of higher education*. Pergamon.

C. Bazerman. (1992). Where is the classroom? *English Basics*, Winter. Reprinted in A. Freedman & P. Medway (Eds.), *Learning and teaching genre* (pp. 25–30). Portsmouth NH: Boynton-Cook. *Ch 24

1993

C. Bazerman. (1993). Beyond the composition ghetto. *Literacy Across the Curriculum*, 8:3.

C. Bazerman. (1993). Book review. [Review of *Cooperating with written texts*, by Dieter Stein] *Cooperating with written texts. American Anthropologist*, 95(4), 1031.

C. Bazerman. (1993). A contention over the term rhetoric. In T. Enos (Ed.), *Toward defining the new rhetorics* (pp. 3–7). Southern Illinois University Press. *Ch 19, 24

C. Bazerman. (1993). Foreword. In N. Blyler & C. Thralls (Eds.), *Professional communication: The social perspective* (pp. vii–x). Sage.

C. Bazerman. (1993). Forums of validation and forms of knowledge: The magical rhetoric of Otto von Guericke's sulfur globe. *Configurations*, 1(2), 201–228. *Ch 21

C. Bazerman. (1993). Intertextual self-fashioning: Gould and Lewontin's representations of the literature. In R. Selzer (Ed.), *Understanding scientific prose* (pp. 20–41). University of Wisconsin Press. *Ch 21

C. Bazerman. (1993). Money talks: The rhetorical project of Adam Smith's *Wealth of Nations*. In W. Henderson, T. Dudley-Evans & R. Backhouse (Eds.), *Economics and language* (pp. 173-199). Routledge. *Ch 21

C. Bazerman. (1993). Patent realities: Legally stabilized texts and market indeterminacies. In J. Hultberg (Ed.), *The narrative construction of the anxious object* (pp. 5-12). University of Goteborg. *Ch 24

C. Bazerman. (1993). The publicity wizard of Menlo Park. *Electric Perspectives*, 17(6), 30-41 *Ch 22

C. Bazerman. (1993). Response. *Rhetoric Society Quarterly*, 23(2), 54-58.

C. Bazerman. (1993). Royal Society of London. In T. Enos (Ed.), *Encyclopedia of rhetoric* (pp. 645-648). Southern Illinois University Press.

C. Bazerman. (1993). Writing in the disciplines. In A. Purves (Ed.), *Encyclopedia of English studies* (1309-1311). Scholastic Press.

1994

C. Bazerman. (1994). Afterthoughts: Who made nonfiction a negation? In Vitanza (Ed.), *Ten years of Pre/Text* (pp. 214-216). University of Pittsburgh Press.

C. Bazerman. (1994). *Constructing experience*. Southern Illinois University Press. *Ch 19, 23, 24

C. Bazerman. (1994). Electrifying words: Edison's announcement of the incandescent light. *Journal of Business and Technical Communication*, 8(1), 135-147. *Ch 22

C. Bazerman. (1994). Systems of genre and the enactment of social intentions. In A. Freedman & P. Medway (Eds.), *Genre and the new Rhetoric* (pp. 79-101). Taylor & Francis, 1994. Reprinted in C. Miller & A. Devitt (Eds.) *On rhetorical genre studies*. (pp. 113-134). Routledge, 2019. *Ch 24

C. Bazerman & D. Russell (1994). *Landmark essays in writing across the curriculum*. Hermagoras Press. *Ch 24

1995

C. Bazerman. (1995). Influencing and being influenced: Local acts across large distances. *Social Epistemology*, 9(2), 189-199.

C. Bazerman. (1995). Response: Curricular Responsibilities and Professional Definition. In J. Petraglia (Ed.), *Reconceiving writing* (pp. 249-259). Erlbaum,

1996

C. Bazerman. (1996). Book review. [Review of *Cognition in the wild*, by E. Hutchins] *Mind, Culture, and Activity*, 3(1), 51-54. *Ch 29

C. Bazerman. (1996). Editor's introduction. In D. Winsor, *Writing like an engineer: A rhetorical education* (pp. vii-vii). Erlbaum.

C. Bazerman. (1996). Students being disciplined: Getting confused, getting by, getting rewarded, getting smart, getting real. University of Minnesota Interdisciplinary Studies of Writing.

1997

C. Bazerman. (1997). Book review. [Review of *Psychology as metaphor*, by A.J. Soyland] *Theory & Psychology*, 7(1), 141–142. *Ch 29

C. Bazerman. (1997). Concepts in action. *Readerly/Writerly Texts*, 4(2), 9–20.

C. Bazerman. (1997). Discursively structured activities. *Mind, Culture, and Activity*, 4(4), 296–308.

C. Bazerman. (1997). Editor's introduction. In A.D. Van Nostrand. *Fundable Knowledge: The Marketing of Defense Science and Technology* (pp. ix–x). Erlbaum.

C. Bazerman. (1997). Genre and Social Science. In T. Enos (Ed.), *Making and unmaking the prospects for rhetoric* (pp.83–90). Erlbaum. *Ch 24

C. Bazerman. (1997). *Involved: Writing for college, writing for your self*. Houghton Mifflin. *Ch 18

C. Bazerman. (1997). The life of genre, the life in the classroom. In W. Bishop & H. Ostrom (Eds.), *Genre and writing* (pp. 19–26). Boynton/Cook.

C. Bazerman. (1997). Performatives constituting value: The case for patents. In B. Gunnarsson, P. Linell & Nordberg (Eds.), *The construction of professional discourse* (pp. 42–53). Addison Wesley. *Ch 24

D Russell & C. Bazerman. (1997). The Activity of Writing; The Writing of Activity. Special issue of *Mind, Culture, and Activity*, 4(4). *Ch 24, 25

D. Russell & C. Bazerman. (1997). Editors' introduction. *Mind, Culture, and Activity* 4:4, 223.

1998

C. Bazerman. (1998). Book review. [Review of *Cognition and context*, by B. Nardi (Ed.)] *Mind, Culture, and Activity*, 5(1), 73–75 *Ch 29

C. Bazerman. (1998). Book review. [Review of *Future of the book*, by G. Nunberg (Ed.)]. *Written Language and Literacy*, 1(2), 297–300.

C. Bazerman. (1998). Editor's introduction. In J. Swales, *Other floors, other voices: Toward textography and beyond* (pp. ix–x) Erlbaum.

C. Bazerman. (1998). Editor's introduction. In J. Petraglia-Bahri, *Reality by design: The rhetoric and technology of authenticity and education* (pp. ix–x) Erlbaum.

C. Bazerman. (1998). Editor's introduction. In D. Atkinson, *Scientific discourse in sociohistorical context: The Philosophical Transactions of the Royal Society of London, 1675–1975* (pp. vii–ix) Erlbaum.

C. Bazerman. (1998). Editor's introduction. In P. Prior. *Writing/Disciplinarity: A Sociohistoric account of literate activity in the academy* (pp. vii-viii) Erlbaum.

C. Bazerman. (1998). Emerging perspectives on the many dimensions of scientific discourse. In J. Martin & R. Veel (Eds.), *Reading science* (pp. 15–30). Routledge.

C. Bazerman. (1998). Green giving: Engagement, values, activism, and community life. *New Directions for Philanthropic Fundraising*, 22, 7–22.

C. Bazerman. (1998). Looking at writing; Writing what I see. In T. Enos & D. Roen (Eds.), *Living rhetoric and composition* (pp. 15–24). Erlbaum.

C. Bazerman. (1998). The rhetoric of technology. *Journal of Business and Technical Communication*, 12(3), 381–387.

C. Bazerman. (1998). Vygotskian theory. In M. Kennedy (Ed.), *Theorizing composition* (pp. 333–337). Greenwood. *Ch 29

1999

C. Bazerman. (1999). Changing regularities of genre. *IEEE Transactions on Professional Communication.* 42(1), 1–2.
C. Bazerman. (1999). Editor's introduction. In P. Dias, A. Pare, A. Freedman & P. Medway. *Worlds apart: Acting and writing in academic and workplace contexts* (pp. vii-ix) Erlbaum.
C. Bazerman. (1999). *The languages of Edison's light.* MIT Press. *Ch 22
C. Bazerman. (1999). Singular utterances: Realizing local activities through typified forms in typified circumstances. In A. Trosberg (Ed.), *Analysing the discourses of professional genres* (pp. 25–40) John Benjamins. *Ch 24

2000

C. Bazerman. (2000). Editor's introduction. In A. Blakeslee, *Interacting with audiences* (pp. xi–xii). Erlbaum, 2000.
C. Bazerman. (2000). Letters and the social grounding of differentiated genres. In D. Barton & N. Hall (Eds.), *Letter writing as a social practice* (pp. 15–30). John Benjamins. *Ch 24
C. Bazerman. (2000). A rhetoric for literate society: The tension between expanding practices and restricted theories. In M. Goggin (Ed.), *Inventing a discipline* (pp. 5–28) NCTE, 2000. *Ch 23, 24, 25

2001

C. Bazerman. (2001). Anxiety in action: Sullivan's interpersonal psychiatry as a supplement to Vygotskian psychology. *Mind, Culture, and Activity,* 8(2), 174–186. * Ch 13, 14, 29
C. Bazerman. (2001). Book review. [Review of *Evolution of consciousness,* by E. MacPhail] *Mind, Culture, and Activity,* 8(4),315–317. *Ch 29
C. Bazerman. (2001). Editor's introduction. In L. Flower, *Learning to rival* (pp. ix–x) Erlbaum.
C. Bazerman. (2001). Nuclear information: One rhetorical moment in the construction of the information age. *Written Communication,* 18(3), 259–295. *Ch 27
C. Bazerman. (2001). Politically wired: The changing places of political participation in the age of the internet. In J. Yates & J. Van Maanen (Eds.), *IT and organizational transformation* (pp. 137–154) Sage.
C. Bazerman. (2001). Writing as a development in interpersonal relations. *Journal for the Psychoanalysis of Culture and Societ,y* 6(2), 298–302. *Ch 29
C. Geisler, C. Bazerman, Doheny-Farina, L. Gurak, C. Haas, Johnson-Eilola, D. Kaufer, A. Lunsford, C. Miller, D. Winsor & J. Yates. (2001). Itext: Future directions for research on the relationship between information technology and writing. *Journal of Business and Technical Communication,* 15(3), 269–308.

2002

C. Bazerman. (2002). The case for writing studies as a major discipline. In G. Olson (Ed.), *The intellectual work of composition* (pp. 32–38) Southern Illinois University Press.

C. Bazerman. (2002). Distanced and refined selves: Educational tensions in writing with the power of knowledge. In M. Hewings (Ed.), *Academic writing in context* (pp. 23–29) University of Birmingham Press.

C. Bazerman. (2002). Editor's introduction. In P.-J. Salazar. *An African Athens* (pp. xi–xii) Erlbaum.

C. Bazerman. (2002). Editor's introduction. In B. Sauer, *Rhetoric under uncertainty* (pp. xvii–xviii) Erlbaum.

C. Bazerman. (2002). Genre and identity: Citizenship in the age of the internet and the age of global capitalism. In R. Coe (Ed.), *Ideologies of genre* (pp. 13–37) Hampton Press.

2003

C. Bazerman. (2003). Rhetorical research for reflective practice: A multi-layered narrative. In C. N. Candlin (Ed.), *Research & practice in professional discourse* (pp.79–94) City University of Hong Kong Press.

C. Bazerman. (2003). Statement at the progressive caucus. *College Composition and Communication,* 55(2), 351–354.

C. Bazerman. (2003). Textual performance: Where the action at a distance is. *JAC: Journal of Advanced Composition,* 23(2), 379–396.

C. Bazerman. (2003). What activity systems are literary genres part of? *Readerly/ Writerly Texts,* 10, 97–106. *Ch 18

C. Bazerman. (2003). What is not institutionally visible does not count: The problem of making activity assessable, accountable, and plannable. In C. Bazerman and D. Russell (Eds.), *Writing selves, writing societies: Research from activity perspectives* (pp. 428–483). The WAC Clearinghouse; Mind, Culture, and Activity. https://doi.org/10.37514/PER-B.2003.2317.2.13 *Ch 28

C. Bazerman, J. Little & T. Chavkin. (2003). The production of information for genred activity spaces. *Written Communication,* 20(4), 455–477. *Ch 27

C. Bazerman & D. Russell (Eds.). (2003). *Writing selves, writing societies: Research from activity perspectives.* The WAC Clearinghouse; Mind, Culture, and Activity. https://doi.org/10.37514/PER-B.2003.2317 *Ch 24, 25

2004

C. Bazerman. (2004). Book review. [Review of *Communicating science: The scientific article from the seventeenth century to the present,* by A. G. Gross, J. E. Harmon & M. Reidy] *Isis,* 95, 341–342

C. Bazerman. (2004). Editor's introduction. In J. Lauer, *Invention* (p. xv). Parlor Press; The WAC Clearinghouse.

C. Bazerman. (2004). Intertextualities: Volosinov, Bakhtin, literary theory, and literacy studies. In A. Ball & S. W. Freedman (Eds.), *Bakhtinian perspectives* *on languages, literacy, and learning* (pp. 53–65) Cambridge University Press. *Ch 19

C. Bazerman. (2004). Intertextuality: How texts rely on other texts. In C. Bazerman & P. Prior (Eds.) *What writing does and how it does it* (pp. 89–102) Erlbaum, 2004.

C. Bazerman. (2004). A Reflective Moment in the History of Literacy. In B. Huot, B. Stroble & C. Bazerman (Eds.), *Multiple literacies for the twenty-first century* (pp. 435–440) Hampton Press.

C. Bazerman. (2004). Social forms as habitats for action. *Journal of the Interdisciplinary Crossroads*, 1(2), 317–334. Translated in Portuguese as Formas socais como habitats para ação. *Investigações Lingüística e Teoria Literária*, 16(2) (2003), 123–142.

C. Bazerman. (2004). Speech acts, genres, and activity systems: How texts organize activity and people. In C. Bazerman & P. Prior (Eds.), *What writing does and how it does it* (pp. 314–346) Erlbaum.

C. Bazerman. (2004). Student writing and writing education in national contexts: Continuing a dialogue. *Revista de ABRALIN*, 3, 243–259.

C. Bazerman & P. Prior (Eds.). (2004). *What writing does and how it does it.* Erlbaum.

B. Huot, B. Stroble & C. Bazerman (Eds.) (2004). *Multiple literacies for the twenty-first century.* Hampton Press.

2005

C. Bazerman. (2005). Communication in the scientific community. In S. Restivo (Ed.), *Science, technology, and society* (pp. 55–61) Oxford University Press.

C. Bazerman. (2005). The diversity of writing. *Quarterly of the National Writing Project*, 24, 2.

C. Bazerman. (2005). An essay on pedagogy by Mikhail M. Bakhtin and response. Symposium in *Written Communication*, 22(3), 333–374.

C. Bazerman. (2005). *Gêneros textuais, tipificação e interação.* Cortez.

C. Bazerman. (2005). A response to Anton Fleury's "Liberal education and communication against the disciplines": A view from the world of writing. *Communication Education*, 54(1), 86–91.

C. Bazerman. (2005). Practically human: The pragmatist project of the interdisciplinary journal *Psychiatry*. *Linguistics and the Human Sciences*, 1(1), 15–38. *Ch 14, 29

C. Bazerman & R. De los Santos. (2005). Measuring incommensurability: Are toxicology and ecotoxicology blind to what the other sees? In R. Harris (Ed.), *Rhetoric and Incommensurability* (pp. 424–463). Parlor Press. *Ch 27

C. Bazerman & J. Little. (2005). Knowing academic languages. In U. U. Melander and H. Naslund (Eds.), *Text I Arbete/Text at Work* (pp. 261–269) Upsalla University.

C. Bazerman, J. Little, T. Chavkin, D. Fouquette, L. Bethel, and J. Garufis. (2005). *Writing across the curriculum.* Parlor Press; The WAC Clearinghouse. Translated in Spanish as *Escribir a través del Currículum. Una guía de referencia.* Córdoba, Argentina, 2016.

2006

C. Bazerman (2006). Analyzing the multidimensionality of texts in education. In J. Green, G. Camilli & P. Elmore (Eds.), *Complementary methods for research in education*, 2nd ed. (pp. 77–94) American Educational Research Association.

C. Bazerman (2006). Editor's introduction. In A. Horning et al., *Revision* (pp. xi–xii). Parlor Press; The WAC Clearinghouse.

C. Bazerman (2006). Foreword: Persuasive economies. In G. Smart, *Writing the economy: Activity, genre and technology in the world of banking* (pp. 1–5) Equinox.

C. Bazerman (2006). *Gênero, Agencia e Escrita*. São Paolo: Sariava.

C. Bazerman (2006). The writing of social organization and the literate situating of cognition: Extending Goody's social implications of writing. In D. Olson & M. Cole (Eds.), *Technology, literacy and the evolution of society: Implications of the work of Jack Goody* (pp. 215–240) Erlbaum. Translated into French in *Pratiques*, 113(1) (2006), 95–115. and into Spanish. *Revista Signos Estudios de Linguistica*, 41(68) (2008), 355–380. *Ch 29

C. Bazerman, D. Fouquette, C. Johnston, F. Rohrbacher & R. A. De los Santos. (2006f), What schools of education can offer the teaching of writing. In V. Anderson & S. Romano (Eds.), *Culture shock and the practice of profession* (pp. 309–324) Hampton Press. *Ch 26

C. Bazerman & A. Herrington. (2006). Circles of interest: The growth of research communities in WAC and WID/WIP. In S. McLeod (Ed.), *Inventing a profession: WAC history* (pp. 49–56). Parlor Press.

2007

C. Bazerman. (2007). Editor's introduction. In S. Macleod, *Writing program administration* (pp. vii-vi). Parlor Press; The WAC Clearinghouse.

C. Bazerman. (2007). *Gêneros textuais, intertextualidade, e atividade: Teórico consideração* Cortez.

C. Bazerman. (2007). WAC for cyborgs: Discursive thought in information rich environments. In P. Takayoshi & P. Sullivan (Eds.), *Labor, writing technologies, and the shaping of composition in the academy* (pp. 97–110) Hampton Press.

D. Figueiredo, C. Bazerman & A. Bonini (Eds.). (2007). *Genre and Social Identities*. Special issue of *Linguistics and the Human Sciences*, 3:1.

2008

C. Bazerman. (2008). Editor's introduction. In E. Long, *Community literacy and the rhetoric of local publics*. Parlor Press; The WAC Clearinghouse.

C. Bazerman. (ed.) (2008). *Handbook of research on writing: History, society, school, individual, text*. Erlbaum. *Ch 25

C. Bazerman. (2008). Students need language support to write for academic publications. *UC Mexus News*, 44, 15–16.

C. Bazerman. (2008). Theories of the middle range in historical studies of writing practice. *Written Communication*, 25(3), 298–318. *Ch 19

C. Bazerman, D. Blakesley, M. Palmquist & D. Russell. (2008). Open-access book publishing in writing studies: A case study. *First Monday, 13.* http://www.uic.edu/htbin/cgiwrap/bin/ojs/index.php/fm/article/view/2088/1920 *Ch 25

C. Bazerman & P. Prior. (2008). Participating in emergent socio-literate worlds: Genre, disciplinarity, interdisciplinarity. In J. Green & R. Beach (Eds.), *Multidisciplinary perspectives on literacy research* (pp. 133–178) NCTE.

C. Bazerman & P. Rogers. (2008). Writing and secular knowledge apart from modern European institutions. In C. Bazerman (Ed.), *Handbook of research on writing: History, society, school, individual, text* (pp. 143–156) Routledge.

C. Bazerman & P. Rogers. (2008). Writing and secular knowledge within modern European institutions. In C. Bazerman (Ed.), *Handbook of research on writing: History, society, school, individual, text* (pp. 157–176) Routledge.

2009

C. Bazerman. (2009). The diversity we become: Education and agency in writing unique selves within evolving communities / a diversidade que viemos a ser: educação e agir autônomo na inscrição de eus autênticos em comunidades dinâmicas, *Revista Triângulo,* 2(1), 13–29.

C. Bazerman. (2009). Editor's introduction. In J. Ramage, *Reference Guide to Argument.* Parlor Press; The WAC Clearinghouse.

C. Bazerman. (2009). Genre and cognitive development. In C. Bazerman, A. Bonini, D. Figueiredo (Eds.). *Genre in a changing world.* The WAC Clearinghouse; Parlor Press. https://doi.org/10.37514/PER-B.2009.2324.2.14. Reprinted as Écrire pour apprendre: La maîtrise des genres et le développement sociocognitif du scripteur. *Pratiques de décembre 2009, 143/144.* *Ch 15, 29

C. Bazerman. (2009). How does science come to speak in the courts? citations, intertexts, expert witnesses, consequential facts and reasoning. *Law and Contemporary Problems,* 72(1), 91–120. *Ch 27, 28

C. Bazerman. (2009). Prefacio. In Marcos Baltar, *Radio escolar* (pp. 9–11). Editoria da Universidade de Caxias do Sul.

C. Bazerman. (2009). The problem of writing knowledge. In S. Miller (Ed.), *Norton book of composition studies* (pp. 502–514) W. W. Norton.

C. Bazerman, A. Bonini & D. Figueiredo. (Eds.) (2009). *Genre in a changing world.* The WAC Clearinghouse; Parlor Press. https://doi.org/10.37514/PER-B.2009.2324.

A. Bonini, D. Figueiredo & C. Bazerman (Eds.). (2009). *Writing education in Brazil.* Special issue of *L1,* 8(2).

2010

C. Bazerman. (2010a) Chair's letter. *College Composition and Communication,* 61(3), 597–601.

C. Bazerman. (2010). Continuing a dialogue. *China Journal,* 3, 38–39.

C. Bazerman. (2010). Editor's introduction. In A. Bawarshi & J. Reiff, *Genre* (pp. xi–xi). Parlor Press; The WAC Clearinghouse.

Bazerman, C. (2010). Editor's introduction. In G. Otte and R. Mlynarczyk. *Basic Writing* (pp. xi–xii). Parlor Press; The WAC Clearinghouse

C. Bazerman. (2010). Paying the rent: Languaging particularity and novelty. *Revista Brasileira de Lingüística Applicada*, 10(2), 459–469. Translated as "Pagando o aluguel: particularidade e inovação na produção da linguagem," in C. Lemos Vóvio, L. Soares Sito & P. Baracat De Grande (Eds.), *Letramentos: rupturas, deslocamentos e repercussões de pesquisas em linguística aplicada* (pp. 163–178) Editora Mercado de Letras.

C. Bazerman. (2010f) Preface. In Santos, S. (). *EFL writing in Mexican universities: research and experience*. Universidad Autónoma de Nayarit.

C. Bazerman. (2010g) Scientific knowledge, public knowledge, and public policy: Genred formation and disruption of knowledge for acting about global warming. *Linguagem em (Dis)Curso*, 10(3), 445–463. *Ch 27

C. Bazerman. (2010). The wonder of writing. *College Composition and Communication*, 61(3), 571–580.

C. Bazerman & M. Baltar (Eds.). (2010). Special issue on genre. *Revista Brasileira de Linguistica Aplicada*, 10(2).

C. Bazerman, G. J. Kelly, A. Skukauskaite & W. Prothero. (2010). Rhetorical features of student science writing in introductory university oceanography. In C. Bazerman, B. Krut, K. Lunsford, S. McLeod, S. Null, P. Rogers, A. Stansell (Eds.), *Traditions of writing research* (pp. 265–282) Routledge.

C. Bazerman, B. Krut, K. Lunsford, S. McLeod, S. Null, P. Rogers, A. Stansell (Eds.). (2010). *Traditions of writing research*. Routledge.

2011

C. Bazerman. (2011a) Church, state, and the printing press: Conditions for autonomy of scientific publication in early modern Europe. In Britt-Louise Gunnarsson (Ed.), *Scientific Writing in the Age of Linneaus* (pp. 25–44) De Gruyter Mouton Press.

C. Bazerman. (2011b) Electrons are cheap; Society is dear. In D. S. Meyeering (Ed.). *Writing in Knowledge Societies*. The WAC Clearinghouse; Parlor Press. https://doi.org/10.37514/PER-B.2011.2379.2.04.

C. Bazerman. (2011). Genre as social action. In Gee, J. & Handford, M. (Eds.). *The Routledge Handbook of Discourse Analysis* (pp. 226–238) Routledge.

C. Bazerman. (2011). The orders of documents, the orders of activity, and the orders of information. In Danish in H. Nielsen, H. Høyrup & H. Christensen(Eds.), *Systemer for dokumenter, systemer for aktivitet og systemer for information* (pp. 63–78). Nye Vidensmedier: Kultur, Læring, Kommunikation. Reprinted in English. *Archival Science*, 12(4), (2012) 377–388.

C. Bazerman. (2011e) Standpoints: The disciplined interdisciplinarity of writing studies. *Research in the Teaching of English*, 46(1), 8–21.

C. Bazerman. (2011f) The work of a middle-class activist: Stuck in history. In S. Kahn (Ed.), *Activism and Rhetoric: Theories and Contexts for Political Engagement* (pp. 37–46) Routledge. Updated 2nd edition (pp. 190–200), (2020). *Ch 5

2012

C. Bazerman. (2012). Academic writing, genre, and indexicality: Evidence, intertext and theory. *Intercompreensao: Revista de Didactica das Linguas*, 16, 11–22.

C. Bazerman. (2012). *Géneros textuales, tipificación y actividad*. Benemérita Universidad Autónoma de Puebla.

C. Bazerman. (2012). Preface. In J. Early & M. DeCosta-Smith, *Real world writing for secondary students: Teaching the college admission essay and other gate-openers for higher education* (pp. ix–x). Teachers College Press.

C. Bazerman. (2012). Writing, cognition, and affect from the perspective of sociohistorical studies. In V. Berninger (Ed.), *Past, present, and future contributions cognitive writing research to cognitive psychology* (pp. 89–104) Psychology Press. *Ch 29

C. Bazerman. (2012). Writing with concepts: Communal, internalized, and externalized. *Mind, Culture, and Activity, 19*(3), 259–272.

C. Bazerman, C. Dean, J. Early, K. Lunsford, S. Null, P. Rogers & A. Stansell (Eds.). (2012). *International advances in writing research: Cultures, places, measures*. The WAC Clearinghouse; Parlor Press. https://doi.org/10.37514/PER-B.2012.0452.

C. Bazerman, N. Keranen & F. Encinas. (2012). Immersed in the game of science. In Bazerman et al. (Eds.), *International advances in writing research: Cultures, places, measures* (pp. 387–402). The WAC Clearinghouse; Parlor Press. https://doi.org/10.37514/PER-B.2012.0452.2.22.

C. Bazerman, N. Keranen & F. Encinas. (2012). Facilitated immersion at a distance in second language science writing. In M. Castelló Badia & C. Donahue (Eds.), *University writing: Selves and texts in academic societies* (pp. 235–238). Emerald.

2013

C. Bazerman. (2013). Comprendiendo de un viaje que dura toda la vida: la evolución de la escritura. Understanding the lifelong journey of writing development. *Revista Infancia y Aprendizaje/Journal for the Study of Education and Development, 36*(4), 421–441. *Ch 30

C. Bazerman. (2013). Global and local communicative networks. In A. S. Canagarajah (Ed.), *Literacy as translingual practice: Between communities and classrooms* (pp. 13–25) Routledge.

C. Bazerman. (2013). *A rhetoric of literate action. Literate action, volume 1*. The WAC Clearinghouse; Parlor Press. https://doi.org/10.37514/PER-B.2013.0513. Translated into Portuguese: *Retórica da ação letrada*. Parabola, 2015. *Intro, Ch 24

C. Bazerman. (2013). *A Theory of literate action. Literate action, volume 2*. The WAC Clearinghouse; Parlor Press. https://doi.org/10.37514/PER-B.2013.4791. Translated into Portuguese: *Teoria da ação letrada*. Parabola, 2015. *Intro, Ch 24

C. Bazerman, K. Simon, P. Ewing & P. Pieng. (2013). Domain-specific cognitive development through writing tasks in a teacher education program. *Pragmatics & Cognition, 21*(3), 530–551. *Ch 29

2014

C. Bazerman. (2014). La escritura en el mundo del conocimiento, Writing in the world of knowledge. *Verbum 9*, 11–21, 23–35.

C. Bazerman. (2014). Preface. In F. Navarro, *Manual de Escritura para Carreras de Humanidades (Encountering Academic Writing)* (pp. 5–10) Universidad de Buenos Aires.

C. Bazerman. (2014). Sisters and brothers of the struggle: Teachers of writing in their worlds. *College Composition and Communication,* 65(4), 646–654.

C. Bazerman. (2014). Book review. [Review of *Writing instruction that works: Proven methods for middle and high school classrooms,* by A. Applebee & J. Langer] *Pedagogies,* 9(2), 175–178.

J. andersen, C. Bazerman & J. Schneider. (2014). Beyond single genres: Pattern mapping in global communication. In E-M. Jakobs & D. Perrin (Eds.), *Handbook of writing and text production* (pp. 305–322) Mouton De Gruyter.

C. Bazerman & A. Devitt. (2014). Genre perspectives in text production research. In E-M. Jakobs & D. Perrin (Eds.). *Handbook of writing and text production* (pp. 257–262) Mouton De Gruyter.

C. Bazerman, K. Simon & P. Pieng. (2014). Writing about reading to advance thinking: A study in situated cognitive development. In P. Boscolo & P. Klein (Eds.), *Writing as a learning activity* (pp. 249–276) Brill. *Ch 29

A. Bork, C. Bazerman, F. Poliseli-Correa, V. Cristovão. (2014). Mapeamento das iniciativas de leitura e escrita em lingua materna na educacao superior resultados preliminares. *Prolingua* 9(1), 2–14.

2015

C. Bazerman. (2015). Five concepts: 1c - writing expresses and shares meaning to be reconstructed by the reader (pp. 21–23) ; 2 - writing speaks to situations and contexts through recognizable forms associated with those situations (pp. 34–37); 2a - writing represents the world, events, ideas, and feelings (pp. 37–39); 4a - text is an object outside of oneself that can be improved and developed (with H. Tinberg) (pp. 61–62); 5a - writing is an expression of embodied cognition (with H. Tinberg) (pp. 74–75). In L. Adler-Kassner & E. Wardle (Eds.), *Naming what we know.* Utah State University Press.

C. Bazerman. (2015). A genre based theory of literate action. In N. Artemeva & A. Freedman (Eds.), *Genre studies around the globe* (pp. 80–94). Inkshed Press.

C. Bazerman. (2015). What do sociocultural studies of writing tell us about learning to write? In C. MacArthur, S. Graham & J. Fitzgerald (Eds.), *Handbook of writing research,* 2nd Ed. (pp. 11–23). Guilford, 2015. *Ch 29

2016

C. Bazerman. (2016). Creating identities in an intertextual world. In A. Chik, T. Costley & M. C. Pennington (Eds.), *Creativity and discovery in the university writing class* (pp.45–60) Equinox. Translated as Portuguese in Criando Identidades em um mundo textual. In Messias Dieb (Ed.) A aprendizagem e o ensina da escrita (pp. 115–132) Pontes, 2018.

C. Bazerman. (2016b) with chapter commentaries by D. H. Espíndola, M. P. Escudero, R. P. Carrillo, D. Rodríguez-Vergara, A. V. Ahumada. Escritura y desarollo cognitivo en un mundo intertextual: Dialogos con la obra de Charles Bazerman. Benemerita Universidad Autonoma de Puebla.

C. Bazerman. (2016). Preface. MJ Braun and Gae Lyn Henderson (Eds.). *Managing democracy: Propaganda and the rhetorical production of economic and political realities* (pp. 7–10) Southern Illinois University Press.

C. Bazerman. (2016). Social changes in science communication: Rattling the information chain. In J. Buehl & A. Gross (Eds.), *Science and the internet: Communicating knowledge in a digital age* (pp.267–282) Baywood.

C. Bazerman, N. Avila, A. V. Bork, F. Poliseli-Corrêa, V. L. Cristovão, M. Tapia-Ladino, Elizabeth Narváez. (2016). Intellectual orientations of studies of higher education writing in Latin America. In S. Plane, C. Bazerman, P. Carlino, F. Rondelli, C. Boré, C.Donahue, Catherine Boré, M. M.Larruy, P. Rogers, D. Russell (Eds.), *Recherches en écriture : regards pluriels / Writing research from multiple perspectives* (pp. 329–346). University of Metz; The WAC Clearinghouse. https://doi.org/10.37514/INT-B.2017.0919.2.15.

C. Bazerman & M. Moritz. (2016). Special issue on writing in Latin American higher education. *Ilha do Desterro, 69*(3).

F. Navarro, N. Ávila, M. Ladino, V. Cristovão, M.Moritz, E. Narváez & C. Bazerman. (2016). Panorama histórico y contrastivo de los estudios sobre lectura y escritura en educación superior publicados en América Latina. *Revista Signos: Estudios de Lingüística, 49*(1), 78–99.

S. Plane, C. Bazerman, P. Carlino, F. Rondelli, C. Boré, C.Donahue, Catherine Boré, M. M.Larruy, P. Rogers, D. Russell (Eds.). (2016). *Recherches en écriture : regards pluriels / Writing research from multiple perspectives*. University of Metz; The WAC Clearinghouse. https://doi.org/10.37514/INT-B.2017.0919.

M. Tapia-Ladino, N. Avila Reyes, F. Navarro, C. Bazerman. (2016). Milestones, disciplines and the future of initiatives of reading and writing in higher education: An analysis from key scholars in the field in Latin America. *Ilha do Desterro, 69*(3), 209–222.

2017

C. Bazerman. (2017). The Brazilian blend. In Eliane G. Lousada, Anise D'O. Ferreira, Luzia Bueno, Roxane Rojo, Solange Aranha, Lília Abreu-Tardelli (Eds.), *Diálogos Brasileiros no estudo de gêneros textuais/discursivos* (pp. 645–650) Araraquara Letraria.

C. Bazerman. (2017). Equity means having full voice in the conversation. *Revista Lenguas Modernas, 50*(2) 33–46

C. Bazerman. (2017). The psychology of writing situated within social action: An empirical and theoretical program. In P. Portanova, M. Rifenburg & D. Roen (Eds.), *Contemporary perspectives on cognition*. The WAC Clearinghouse; University Press of Colorado. https://doi.org/10.37514/PER-B.2017.0032.2.01 *Ch 29

C. Bazerman. (2017). What do humans do best? Developing communicative humans in the changing socio-cyborgian landscape. In S. Logan & W. Slater (Eds.), *Perspectives on academic and professional writing in an age of accountability*. Southern Illinois University Press.

C. Bazerman, A. Applebee, D. Brandt, V. Berninger, S. Graham, P. Matsuda, S. Murphy, D. Rowe, M. Schleppegrell. (2017). Taking the long view on writing development. *Research in the Teaching of English, 51*(3), 51–60. *Ch 30

C. Bazerman & B. Self. (2017). Writing the world to build the world, iteratively: Inscribing data and projecting new materialities in an engineering design project. In R. Durst, G. Newell & J. Marshall (Eds.), *English language arts research and* *teaching: Revisiting and extending Arthur Applebee's contributions* (pp. 91–106) Routledge. *Ch 28

2018

C. Bazerman. (2018). Commentary. In Ken Hyland, *The essential Hyland* (pp. 100–105) Bloomsbury.

C. Bazerman. (2018). Lifespan longitudinal studies of writing development: A heuristic for an impossible dream. In C. Bazerman, A. Applebee, V. Berninger, D. Brandt, S. Graham, J. V. Jeffery, P. Kei Matsuda, S. Murphy, D. W. Rowe, M. Schleppegrell & K. C. Wilcox, *Lifespan development of writing abilities* (pp. 326–365). NCTE. *Ch 30

C. Bazerman (Ed.). (2018). Lives of writing. Special Issue on writing development across the lifespan. *Writing and Pedagogy*, 10(3), 327–331. *Ch 30

C. Bazerman. (2018). What does a model model? And for whom? *Educational Psychologist*, 53(4), 301–318. *Ch 29

C. Bazerman, A. Applebee, V. Berninger, D. Brandt, S. Graham, J. V. Jeffery, P. Kei Matsuda, S. Murphy, D. W. Rowe, M. Schleppegrell & K. C. Wilcox. (2018). *Lifespan development of writing abilities*. NCTE. *Ch 30

2019

C Bazerman. (2019). A? Developmental? Path? To? Text? Quality? *Journal of Literacy Research*, 51(3), 381–387. *Ch 29

C. Bazerman. (2019). Development makes history, where inside meets outside. In S. A. Daghé, E. B. Bronckart, G. S. Cordeiro, J. Dolz, I. Leopoldoff, A. Monnier, C. Ronveaux, B. Vedrines (Eds.), *La construction de la didactique du français comme discipline scientifique* (pp. 83–92). Presses Universitaires du Septentrion (University of Lille).

C. Bazerman. (2019). Inscribing the world into knowledge: Data and evidence in disciplinary academic writing. In C. Bazerman, B. Gonzalez, et al. (Eds.), *Conocer la escritura: investigación más allá de las fronteras; Knowing writing: Writing research across borders* (pp. 279–294) Universidad Javeriana. *Ch 28

C. Bazerman. (2019). *teaching and studies of writing in English*. Translation of previously published essays into Chinese by Dr. Huijun Chen (陈会军). Beijing Normal University Press.

C. Bazerman, B. Gonzalez, et al. (Eds.). (2019). *Conocer la escritura: investigación más allá de las fronteras; Knowing writing: Writing research across borders*. Universidad Javeriana.

V. Fahler & C. Bazerman. (2019). Data power in writing: Assigning data analysis in a general education linguistics course to change ideologies of language. *Across the Disciplines*, 16(4), 4–25. https://doi.org/10.37514/ATD-J.2019.16.4.18 *Ch 28

2020

C. Bazerman. (2020). Always already in flux: A response to Anne Freadman. *Canadian Journal for Studies in Discourse and Writing/Redactologie*, 30(152). http://journals.sfu.ca/cjsdw

C. Bazerman. (2020). Preface. In R. J. Dippre & T. Phillips (Eds.), *Approaches to Lifespan Writing Research: Generating an Actionable Coherence* (pp. xxi–xxii). The WAC Clearinghouse; University Press of Colorado. https://doi.org/10.37514/PER-B.2020.1053.1.1 *Ch 30

2021

C. Bazerman. (2021). Emergent learning in the emergency/Aprendizagem emergente na pandemia. *Revista Triangulo*, 14(1), https://doi.org/10.18554/rt.v14i1.5469.

C. Bazerman. (2021). The ethical poetry of academic writing. *Educação, Sociedade E Culturas*, (58), 185–188. https://doi.org/10.24840/esc.vi58.152.

C. Bazerman. (2021). The puzzle of conducting research on lifespan development of writing. In K. Blewett, C. Donahue & C. Monroe (Eds.), *The expanding universe of writing studies: higher education writing research* (pp. 403–416). Peter Lang. *Ch 30

C. Bazerman. (2021). Scientific knowledge, public knowledge, and public policy: How genres form and disrupt knowledge for acting about anthropogenic climate change. In S. Auken & C. Sunesen (Eds.), *Genre in the climate debate* (pp. 34–50) De Gruyter Open Poland. https://doi.org/10.1515/9788395720499-004.

C. Bazerman. (2021). The value of empirically researching a practical art. In N. Ávila Reyes (Ed.), *Multilingual contributions to writing research: Toward an Equal Academic Exchange* (pp. 103–124). The WAC Clearinghouse; University Press of Colorado. https://doi.org/10.37514/INT-B.2021.1404.2.04.

C. Bazerman & J. Kuntzman. (2021). How the US Congress knows and evades knowing about anthropogenic climate change: The record created in committee hearings, 2004–2016. In S. Auken & C. Sunesen (Eds.), *Genre in the climate debate* (pp. 51–84) De Gruyter Open Poland. https://doi.org/10.1515/9788395720499-005 *Ch 27

2022

C. Bazerman. (2022). Escolarizando para la vida, todas las vidas: oportunidad, dilema, desafío y pensamiento crítico. In M. Vergara Fregoso, R. García Reynaga & S. Ayala Ramírez (Eds.), Literacidad crítica, formación e inclusion. Editorial Universidad de Guadalajara.

C. Bazerman. (2022). Revisiting the Early Uses of Writing in Society Building: Cuneiform Culture and the Chinese Imperium. Una vuelta a los primeros usos de la escritura en la construcción de la sociedad: la cultura cuneiforme y el imperio chino. Literatura y Linguistica, 46, pp. 61–76. https://doi.org/10.29344/0717621X.46.3156.

C. Bazerman. (2022). Won't you be my neighbor? In G. Giberson, M. Schoen & C. Weisser (Eds.), *Behind the curtain of scholarly publication: Editors in writing studies*. Utah State University Press. *Ch 25

2023

C. Bazerman. (2023). Change, Change, Change—and the processes that abide. In Rogers, Paul M., David R. Russell, Paula Carlino & Jonathan M. Marine (Eds.). (2023). Writing as a human activity: Implications and applications of the work of Charles Bazerman. The WAC Clearinghouse; University Press of Colorado. https://doi.org/10.37514/PER-B.2023.1800.2.17.

C. Bazerman. (2023). What we teach when we teach writing: A big picture in a small frame. In Rogers, Paul M., David R. Russell, Paula Carlino & Jonathan M. Marine (Eds.). (2023). Writing as a human Activity: Implications and applications of the work of Charles Bazerman. The WAC Clearinghouse; University Press of Colorado. https://doi.org/10.37514/PER-B.2023.1800.2.18.

Forthcoming

C. Bazerman. (forthcoming). Longtime writing teacher; Latecomer to ELA. In Avila, J. Leaders in English language arts educational Studies: Intellectual self portraits. Brill.

C. Bazerman. (forthcoming b). Prologo. In Waigandt, D., Castagno, F., Giammarini, G., Lizarriturri, S. & Novo, M. *Inclusión y prácticas letradas en educación superior en Argentina*. Colección *Encrucijadas lectoras* del Centro de Estudios Latinoamericanos de Educación Inclusiva (CELEI), Chile.

C. Bazerman. (forthcoming c). Reproduction, critique, expression, and cooperation: The writer's dance in an intertextual world. *Revista de Educaccion a la distancia*.

Interviews

T. H. Crawford & K. Smout (1995). An Interview with Charles Bazerman. *Composition Studies*, 23(1), 21–36.

'Writing is Motivated Participation': An Interview with Charles Bazerman. (1995). *Writing on the Edge*, 6(2), 7–20. Reprinted in J. Boe, D. Masiel, E. Schroeder, and L. Sperber (eds.), Teachers on the Edge: The WOE Interviews, 1989–2017 (pp 181–193). Routledge, 2017.

Charles Bazerman on John Swales (1998). *English for Special Purposes* 17(1), 105–112.

Working Inside and Outside Composition Studies (with Richard Lloyd Jones, Charles Cooper and Lee O'Dell.) (1999). In M. Rosner, B. Boehm and D. Journet, eds. *History, Reflection, and Narrative: The Professionalization of Composition, 1963–1983* (331–341). Ablex.

An Interview with Professor Bazerman: Interdisciplinary Perspectives on Writing (1999 Marc). *Kairos* 1, 5–8.

50 Years of Research on Writing: What Have We Learned? (2008). Panel with George Hillocks and Peter Elbow. UCTelevision. YouTube. Posted 31 January, 2008. http://www.youtube.com/watch?v=mrcq3dztoUk.

D. Motta-Roth & C. Bazerman. (2015). Literate action, writing and genre studies: Interview with Charles Bazerman. Calidoscópio 13(3), 452–461.

Interview with Charles Bazerman/ Entrevisa com Charles Bazerman. (2016). In Sweder Souza & Adail Sobral(Eds.), *Gêneros, entre o texto e o discurso: Questões Conceituais e Metodológicas*. Mercado de Letras.

M. Mendoza (2016). Charles Bazerman: "Los textos que decidamos leer y escribir van a determinar cómo interpretamos el mundo." https://tinyurl.com/5fhbuuua.

J. Craig, M. Davis, C. Martorana, J. Mehler, K. Mitchell, A. N. Ricks, B. Zawilski, and K. Blake Yancey (2016). Against the rhetoric and composition grain: A microhistorical view. In B. McComiskey (Ed.), *Microhistories of composition* (pp. 284–306). Utah State University Press.

D. Waigandt (2016, November). The inevitability of teaching writing: An interview with Charles Bazerman. Argentinian Journal of Applied Linguistics, 4(2), 23–38.

Interview on podcast Pedagogue (2020) https://www.pedagoguepodcast.com.

El Group Relif. Entrevista de Charles Bazerman. (2020). https://entrevista-de-charles-bazerman-con-el-group-relif-disponible-online.

TC Camp (2022). The Built Symbolic Environment: Words To Live By. Room 42. https://tccamp.org/episodes/the-built-symbolic-environment-words-to-live-by/.

Book Series Editing

Rhetoric, Knowledge and Society (Published by Lawrence Erlbaum Associates)

D. Winsor (1996). *Writing Like an Engineer: A Rhetorical Education.*

A.D. Van Nostrand (1997). *Fundable Knowledge: The Marketing of Defense Science and Technology.*

P. Prior (1998). *Writing/Disciplinarity: A Sociohistoric Account of Literate Activity in the Academy.*

J. Petraglia-Bahri (1998). *Reality by Design: The Rhetoric and Technology of Authenticity and Education.*

J. Swales (1998). *Other Floors, Other Voices: Toward Textography and Beyond.*

D. Atkinson (1998). *Scientific Discourse in Sociohistorical Context: The Philosophical Transactions of the Royal Society of London, 1675–1975.*

P. Dias, A. Paré, A. Freedman & P. Medway (1999). *Worlds Apart: Working and Writing in Academic and Workplace Contexts.*

L. Flower, E. Long, and L. Higgins (2000). *Learning to Rival: A Literate Practice for Intercultural Inquiry.*

A. Blakeslee (2000). *Interacting with Audiences: Social and Rhetorical Practice in Ordinary Science.*

P. Salazar (2002). *An African Athens: Rhetoric and the Shaping of Democracy in South Africa.*

B. Sauer (2002). *Rhetoric Under Uncertainty.*

Reference Guides to Rhetoric and Composition (Published by Parlor Press and The WAC Clearinghouse)

J. Lauer (2004). *Invention.*

C. Bazerman, J. Little, T. Chavkin, D. Fouquette, L. Bethel, and J. Garufis. (2005). *Writing Across the Curriculum.*

A. Horning et al., (2006). *Revision.*

G. Otte and R. Mlynarczyk (2010). *Basic Writing.*

S. McLeod (2007). *Writing Program Administration.*

E. Long (2008). *Community Literacy and the Rhetoric of Local Publics*.
J. Ramage, M. Callaway, J. Clary-Lemon, and Z. Waggoner (2009). *Reference Guide to Argument*.
A. Bawarshi & J. Reiff (2010). *Genre*.
A Horning and E. Kraemer (2012). *Reconnecting Reading and Writing*.
B. Ray (2015). *Style: An Introduction to History, Theory, Research, and Pedagogy*.

www.ingramcontent.com/pod-product-compliance
Lightning Source LLC
Chambersburg PA
CBHW052132070526
44585CB00017B/1797